Lecture Notes in Computer Science 8295

Commenced Publication in 1973
Founding and Former Series Editors:
Gerhard Goos, Juris Hartmanis, and Jan van Leeuwen

T0212841

Quan Z. Sheng   Jesper Kjeldskov (Eds.)

Current Trends
in Web Engineering

ICWE 2013 International Workshops
ComposableWeb, QWE, MDWE, DMSSW,
EMotions, CSE, SSN, and PhD Symposium
Aalborg, Denmark, July 8-12, 2013
Revised Selected Papers

 Springer

Volume Editors

Quan Z. Sheng
The University of Adelaide
School of Computer Science
North Terrace
Adelaide, SA 5005, Australia
E-mail: qsheng@cs.adelaide.edu.au

Jesper Kjeldskov
Aalborg University
Department of Computer Science
Selma Lagerloefs Vej 300
9220 Aalborg East, Denmark
E-mail: jesper@cs.aau.dk

ISSN 0302-9743   e-ISSN 1611-3349
ISBN 978-3-319-04243-5   e-ISBN 978-3-319-04244-2
DOI 10.1007/978-3-319-04244-2
Springer Cham Heidelberg New York Dordrecht London

Library of Congress Control Number: 2013956506

CR Subject Classification (1998): H.3, D.2, H.5, H.4, K.6, C.2

LNCS Sublibrary: SL 3 – Information Systems and Application,
incl. Internet/Web and HCI

Typesetting: Camera-ready by author, data conversion by Scientific Publishing Services, Chennai, India

Printed on acid-free paper

Springer is part of Springer Science+Business Media (www.springer.com)

Preface

ICWE 2013 marked the 13th edition of the International Conference on Web Engineering and was held during July 8–12, 2013, in Aalborg, Denmark. As in previous years, the conference's main program was complemented by a number of co-located workshops, tutorials, and a doctoral consortium. All of these satellite events are designed to give researchers and practitioners an opportunity to interact in a setting that is both more informal and focused at the same time. This volume presents revised contributions to the workshops and the doctoral consortium.

Workshops have always played an important role in the ICWE community as they are a vessel both for exploring new trends and for in-depth discussions on core topics of Web engineering. The workshop chairs reviewed and accepted seven workshop proposals. These workshops cover rich research challenges such as social data management, cloud service engineering, agile Web development, and quality management in Web engineering. Some of these workshops have a long-standing tradition in the Web engineering community. The seven workshops successfully held at ICWE 2013 include:

- ComposableWeb 2013: The 5th International Workshop on Lightweight Composition on the Web
- QWE 2013: The 4th International Workshop on Quality in Web Engineering
- MDWE 2013: The 9th International Workshop on Model-Driven and Agile Engineering for the Web
- DMSSW 2013: The Second International Workshop on Data Management in the Social Semantic Web
- EMotions 2013: The First International Workshop on Engineering Mobile Web Applications
- CSE 2013: The International Workshop on Cloud and Service Engineering
- SSN 2013: The First International Workshop on Semantic Social Networks

The PhD Symposium, which featured eight presentations, complemented the conference and workshop program. The ICWE 2013 PhD Symposium offers a unique opportunity for PhD students to explore and develop their research interests in an interdisciplinary workshop, under the guidance of a panel of senior researchers in the field of Web engineering.

This proceedings volume would not have been possible without the work of the enthusiastic and committed workshop and doctoral consortium organizers. We thank all our colleagues who dedicated their time and skills to making the ICWE 2013 satellite events a success. We also thank the researchers, practitioners, and PhD students who contributed their work to this volume. Finally, we would like to thank the general chair of ICWE 2013, Peter Dolog, and the program chairs, Florian Daniel and Qing Li, for their feedback and constant support.

September 2013   Quan Z. Sheng
                                                     Jesper Kjeldskov

Message from the ComposableWeb 2013 Workshop Chairs

In the context of the Web, the word "mashup" is used to denote Web applications that are materialized by integrating data, services, and/or presentation of other (data) sources or applications. Some applications focus on integrating RSS feeds, others on integrating RESTful services or SOAP services, others on Atom feeds, and there are those that focus on integrating user interfaces. We believe mashups – and especially mashup tools with their models, languages, and instruments for mashup development – do bring *innovation*, in that they tackle integration at the user interface level (most mashups integrate presentation content, not "just" data), they aim at simplicity more than completeness of features (up to the point that advanced Web users, not only programmers, can develop composite applications), and they allow fairly sophisticated development tasks in the Web browser.

Over the last few years, we have seen many efforts invested in research on mashups, in both the industrial and the academic context, yet we are still far from a common understanding of the problems that drive the research, of the approaches that best fit given problems, and even of the benefits of the results achieved so far. In light of these considerations, we organized the fifth edition in the ComposableWeb Workshop series, to stimulate the discussion of key issues, approaches, open problems, innovative applications, and trends in the area of Web mashups and lightweight composition on the Web.

For this year's edition of ComposableWeb, and thanks to the thorough reviewing efforts by our loyal Program Committee, we were able to select four qualitative research papers and one demo paper on a mix of topics, ranging from interactive APIs, semantic-guided composition and multi-device mashups, to tools for social applications and media enrichment on distributed displays. As in previous years, the ComposableWeb Workshop could count on a large audience. This year, on average 40 people attended the workshop, which ensured challenging questions and lively discussions. The research papers were complemented with an interesting keynote talk by Marco Winckler, who enlightened participants on how techniques from HCI and task analysis can be beneficial for mashups and Web composition. Finally, in the good tradition of ComposableWeb, we finished with an exciting demo session (the by now famous "Demo Mania"), where we had several authors and even some workshop participants spontaneously showing their research artifacts and tools.

We thank all authors for their submissions, the Program Committee for their continued reviewing efforts, and the numerous and enthusiastic audience, for making ComposableWeb a success.

September 2013

Sven Casteleyn
Cesare Pautasso
Geert-Jan Houben

Organization

Program Committee

Luciano Baresi	Politecnico di Milano, Italy
Florian Daniel	University of Trento, Italy
Oscar Diaz	University of the Basque Country, Spain
Peter Dolog	Aalborg University, Denmark
Schahram Dustdar	Technical University of Vienna, Austria
Peep Küngas	University of Tartu, Estonia
Maristella Matera	Politecnico di Milano, Italy
Moira Norrie	ETH Zurich, Switzerland
Achille Peternier	University of Lugano, Switzerland
Gustavo Rossi	Universidad Nacional de La Plata, Argentina
Tomas Vitvar	Czech Technical University of Prague, Czech Repuclic & Oracle
Eric Wohlstadter	University of British Columbia, Canada
Christian Zirpins	Karlsruhe Institute of Technology, Germany

Message from the PhD Symposium Chairs

The PhD journey is not easy, specially for the first steps. Doubts about the interest of the area, the appropriate strategy, or the novelty of the approach are repeating worries that overshadow PhD students. The good news is that the community can help. The PhD Symposiums offer a unique opportunity for students, especially in their first years, to share their excitement and thrill but also their doubts and uncertainties. For ICWE 2013, we enjoyed a panel of senior researchers in the field of Web engineering (see below). Thanks are due to them for their guidance and time. But we also promote interaction among the PhD students themselves. Despite coming from a variety of areas, students found in their mates the perfect companions to share their eagerness and doubts. Eight students presented their work. It is our hope that this PhD Symposium helps them on their way to the PhD goal.

September 2013

Oscar Díaz
Marco Winckler

Organization

Program Committee

Sven Casteleyn — Vrije Universiteit Brussel, Belgium
Antonella De Angeli — University of Manchester, UK
Martin Gaedke — Chemnitz University of Technology, Germany
Irene Garrigós — Universidad de Alicante, Spain
Nora Koch — Ludwig-Maximilians-Universität München, Germany
Emilia Mendes — Blekinge Institute of Technology, Sweden
Moira Norrie — ETH Zurich, Switzerland
Gustavo Rossi — Universidad National de La Plata, Argentina

Message from the SSN 2013 Workshop Chairs

Today, Web users and community interaction pose a growing challenge. With the emergence of the collaborative Web, many projects have been developed in this domain for community detection, online community analysis, or communication network. However, few take semantics into account. Adding semantic identification in communities will allow for a better understanding of their underlying topics beyond textual statistical analysis or tag-based methods. It will also enable the interconnection of communities with semantic-based content (e.g., Yago, DBpedia, etc.)

The goal of the SSN workshop is to bring together researchers from three relevant domains: Semantic Web, collaborative Web, and social network analysis. This year we received five submissions from four countries. Each contribution was reviewed by two members of the Program Committee; we selected two papers. The first presents a user interest identification method with the original help of linked data. The second one extends community modelling approaches using Semantic Web technologies.

We would like to thank all authors for their submissions, and all members of the Program Committee for their commitment. We are also grateful to Roberto De Virgilio for his help.

September 2013

Lylia Abrouk
David Gross-Amblard

Organization

Program Committee

Sihem Amer-Yahia	CNRS-LIG, France
Franois Bry	LMU Munich, Germany
Stefano Cerri	LIRMM, France
Fabien Gandon	Inria, France
Thomas Gottron	University of Koblenz, Germany
Markus Krtzsch	University of Oxford, UK
Lina Zhou	University of Maryland, USA

Message from the CSE 2013 Workshop Chairs

Services play an important role in today's ever-growing Web applications. Business organizations are globally focusing on exploiting Web and cloud services to address their needs. Web services and service-oriented architecture are believed to be one of the most important enabling technologies for cloud services. Cloud services promise several benefits, such as reduced expenses, and support simplicity in providing flexible and on-demand infrastructures, platforms, and software as services for consumers. However, due to the highly dynamic, distributed, and non-transparent nature of cloud services, the expected benefits are not fully met. The International Workshop on Cloud and Service Engineering (CSE 2013) aims to provide an international forum for researchers, developers, and practitioners from multiple disciplines to discuss their innovative ideas and share their knowledge of exploring trends in service engineering methodologies, enabling technologies, and the state of the art.

CSE 2013 received several submissions from different countries. Each submission was reviewed by at least three Program Committee members. The submissions were evaluated based on novelty, problem significance, scientific quality, and research contributions. The Program Committee eventually selected two papers. The selected papers focus on developments and innovation in the areas of cloud and service engineering, as well as on security and privacy in social networks.

We would like express our gratitude to all authors for their submissions and their active participation and we would like to thank all the Program Committee members for their excellent work.

September 2013

Talal H. Noor
Lina Yao
Xiaoqiang Qiao

Organization

Program Chairs

Talal H. Noor   The University of Adelaide, Australia
Lina Yao   The University of Adelaide, Australia
Xiaoqiang Qiao   The Institute of Software, Chinese Academy of Sciences

Program Committee

Abdelkarim Erradi	Qatar University, Qatar
Anne H.H. Ngu	Texas State University-San Marcos, USA
Athman Bouguettaya	RMIT University, Australia
Boualem Benatallah	UNSW, Australia
Brahim Medjahed	University of Michigan, USA
Chung Lawrence	The University of Texas at Dallas, USA
Daniele Bonetta	Università della Svizzera Italiana, Switzerland
Florian Daniel	University of Trento, Italy
Guglielmo De Angelis	ISTI-CNR, Italy
Hua Zhong	Chinese Academy of Sciences, China
Jinhui Yao	University of Sydney, Australia
Jun Wei	Chinese Academy of Sciences, China
Malik Zaki	Wayne State University, USA
M. Brian Blake	University of Notre Dame, Australia
Mike Ma	University of Adelaide, Australia
Paolo Giorgini	University of Trento, Italy
Rafael Accorsi	University of Freiburg, Germany
Salima Benbernou	Université Paris Descartes, France
Sherali Zeadally	University of the District of Columbia, USA
Sven Graupner	HP Labs, Palo Alto, USA
Yi Wei	University of Notre Dame, Australia
Jian Yu	Swinburne University of Technology, Australia
Zakaria Maamar	Zayed University, UAE

Message from the EMotions 2013 Workshop Chairs

The sales and the penetration of mobile devices in the market are overtaking those of desktops. Nowadays, new-generation mobile device such as smartphones and tablets are becoming the users' preferred technological companions; they use them as the prime way of accessing the Internet in general and Web content specifically.

The marriage between Web and mobile technology offers many opportunities, but also presents new challenges and constraints. On one hand, the introduction of Web technology into mobile phones has created a new milestone for the development of interactive mobile applications. Currently, most mobile devices are robust enough to run a tiny Web browser that allows users to access Web applications everywhere and at any time, e.g., when on the move, or even to use several devices concurrently. From the developers' point of view, Web technology allows the deployment of a single Web application that is immediately accessible through many mobile platforms, thus reducing the costs of creating and maintaining embedded applications on an increasing number of mobile platforms. On the other hand, mobile and cross-device usage scenarios, and the new capabilities of mobile devices, force Web technology, and corresponding engineering methods and techniques, to evolve to respond to these new requirements and user demands. Web applications have to be tailored to deal with the constraints imposed by mobile technology such as small screens, low (and sometimes expensive) bandwidth, limited browser capabilities, different usage situations, cross-device use, etc. Then again, they might also benefit from the user's mobility, and its associated information (e.g., the user's geo-location, sensor data), to dynamically customize the Web application and its content.

All these constraints and opportunities require appropriate methods and tools for engineering Web applications that are aimed to be accessible through any kind of device. The goal of the First International Workshop on Engineering Mobile Web Applications (EMotions 2013) was thus to bring the attention of the Web engineering community to the opportunities and challenges brought by recent advances on mobile technology allowing ubiquitous access to Web applications through mobile devices. We are interested in theories and practice for the development of mobile Web applications including models, methods, tools, frameworks, and case studies that describe Web applications running on mobile Web browsers.

This first edition of the workshop received a limited amount of submissions. Consequently, and to preserve quality, we decided to organize EMotions 2013 as a compact, one-session workshop. All papers received three reviews, based upon which we accepted three qualitative contributions on a mix of topics relevant for the workshop. In particular, Cecilia Challiol discussed a framework for augmenting existing websites with (personalized) mobile hypermedia features, Elgin Akpinar elaborated on the study, with improvement and evaluation of a page segmentation algorithm, and Louis Olsina discussed ISO 25010-based quality models and frameworks in the context of mobile (Web) Apps. EMotions 2013 received great interest from the conference attendees: while competing with main conference tracks, it still succeeded in attaining an average of 30 participants. To conclude the workshop, there was an interesting, even somewhat controversial open discussion on the future of the mobile Web and the relationship with cross- and multi-device computing.

We thank all authors for their submissions, the Program Committee for their excellent reviewing efforts, and the workshop attendees, for making the first edition of the EMotions workshop a success.

September 2013   Marco Winckler
                                                          Sven Casteleyn

Organization

Program Committee

Luca Chittaro	University of Udine, Italy
Rodrigo de Oliveira	Telefonica Research, Barcelona, Spain
Oscar Diaz	University of the Basque Country, Spain
David Lamas	Tallinn University, Estonia
Panos Markopoulos	Eindhoven University of Technology, The Netherlands
Célia Martinie	Université Paul Sabatier, France
Maristella Matera	Politecnical University of Milan, Italy
Niels Olof Bouvin	Aarhus University, Denmark
Vicente Pelechano	Universidad Politecnica de Valencia, Spain
William Van Woensel	Vrije Universiteit Brussel, Belgium

Message from the DMSSW 2013 Workshop Chairs

This volume collects the papers selected for presentation at the second edition of the Workshop on Data Management in the Social Semantic Web (DMSSW 2013), in conjunction with the 2013 International Conference on Web Engineering (ICWE 2013), held in Aalborg (Denmark) during July 8–12, 2013.

Learning from the experience of the first edition, the DMSSW 2013 International Workshop followed the increasing interest in social networks and the Semantic Web and aimed at bringing together these perspectives with the one focused on data management, fostering the collaboration and cross-fertilization between these two related communities. In fact, the huge amount of social network data available today is pushing the development of data management techniques to enable the study of complex relationships among the members and resources exchanged within the borders of a social network. At the same time, the resource description framework is an ideal and widespread graph-based framework in which to represent the semantic content of documents such as Web pages, blogs, tweets, and posts, and their relationships. We refer to the combination of the two worlds as the social SemanticWeb (SSW). The importance and amount of SSW data are impressively increasing as is the call for new data management models and techniques.

This resulted in a very broad spectrum of topics addressed in the accepted papers of this second edition of DMSSW 2013, ranging from methods, models and techniques, to case studies and practical experiences related to the SSW. We received submissions from international institutions spread over the world. The accepted papers were selected based on their originality, timeliness, significance, relevance, and clarity of presentation. We scheduled a program composed of three accepted papers and a keynote that stimulated discussions on data management issues related to the social networks and the Semantic Web technologies. The keynote talk, by Andrea Calì (University of London, UK) on "Ontological Reasoning in the Web of Data," highlighted future research directions in this setting.

We wish to thank all the authors who submitted papers and all the workshop participants. We are also grateful to the members of the Program Committee for their thorough work in their timely reviewing of the submitted contributions with patience and competence. Finally, we wish to thank the DIMES Department (University of Calabria, http://www.dimes.unical.it/) and ICAR Institute of the National Research Council (http://www.icar.cnr.it/) for their financial contributions to the organization of the workshop.

September 2013

Devis Bianchini
Roberto De Virgilio
Andrea Pugliese

Organization

Workshop Chairs

Devis Bianchini   University of Brescia, Italy
Roberto De Virgilio   Università Roma Tre, Italy
Andrea Pugliese   Università della Calabria, Italy

Program Committee

Matthias Broecheler   University of Maryland, USA
Andrea Calì   University of London, UK
Yu Deng   IBM T.J. Watson Research Center, USA
Thomas Gottron   University of Koblenz-Landau, Germany
Sergio Greco   University of Calabria, Italy
Andrey Gubichev   Technical University of Munich, Germany
Claudio Gutierrez   University of Chile
Norbert Martinez-Bazan   Universitat Politecnica de Catalunya, Spain
Cristian Molinaro   University of Calabria, Italy
Giuseppe Pirrò   Free University of Bolzano, Italy
Achim Rettinger   Karlsruhe Institute of Technology, Germany
V.S. Subrahmanian   University of Maryland, USA
Maria Esther   Vidal University Simon Bolivar, Venezuela

Message from the MDWE 2013 Workshop Chairs

The 9th International Workshop on Model-Driven and Agile Engineering for the Web (MDWE 2013) was held in conjunction with the 13th International Conference on Web Engineering (ICWE 2013) in Aalborg (Denmark) on July 10, 2013. This workshop continued with the successful series of MDWE workshops that have been held jointly with ICWE conferences since 2005, with exception of MDWE 2008 that was held in Toulouse jointly with MoDELS 2008.

MDWE tries to compare two of the most important trends in Web application development. On the one hand, agile development, which promotes an adaptive planning, evolutionary development, and encourages a rapid and flexible response to change. On the other hand, model-driven development, which is mainly focused on the application of innovative technologies and methods principally oriented to automatic generation, maintenance, and modernization of Web systems. This year's call for papers invited the submission of original high-quality papers on both model-driven and agile approaches covering different steps of the software development life cycle.

In response to the call for papers, six submissions were received. Each submitted paper was formally peer reviewed by at least three referees, and five papers were finally accepted for presentation at the workshop and publication in the proceedings. There were lively discussions following the presentations on actual topics in the model-driven and agile Web engineering domain.

The presented papers dealt with the improvement of the MDWE approaches introducing new concerns such as supporting working offline in websites, modeling the access-control for Web content management systems or including a process description for the design of rich Internet applications. On the other hand, the contributions also enhance the MDWE processes by further including existing software engineering techniques such as an approach for extending Web modeling languages with aspect-orientation or a reverse engineering approach for converting a legacy Web application into a REST API. Further details about the presented papers and all the information relevant to the workshop are available at: http://mdwe2013.dlsi.ua.es/.

The most important contribution of MDWE is the open discussion space that provides for solid theory work with practical on-the-field experience with model-driven approaches. The papers in this volume reflect this spirit, and show how different approaches respond to the new challenges in the development of Web applications.

We would like to thank the ICWE 2013 organization for giving us the opportunity to organize this workshop, especially the workshops chairs, Michael Sheng and Jesper Kjeldskov, who were always very helpful and supportive. Many thanks to all those who submitted papers and particularly to the presenters of the accepted papers. Our thanks also go to the Program Committee for their timely and accurate reviews and for their help in selecting the papers.

September 2013   Santiago Meliá
                                                                 Manuel Wimmer

Organization

Steering Committee

Geert-Jan Houben   Delft University of Technology,
     The Netherlands
Nora Koch   Ludwig-Maximilians-Universität München,
     Germany
Gustavo Rossi   Universidad Nacional de La Plata, Argentina
Antonio Vallecillo   Universidad de Málaga, Spain

Program Committee

Luciano Baresi   Politecnico di Milano, Italy
Hubert Baumeister   Technical University of Denmark, Denmark
Alessandro Bozzon   Delft University of Technology,
     The Netherlands
Marco Brambilla   Politecnico di Milano, Italy
Javier Cánovas   INRIA École des Mines de Nantes, France
Sven Casteleyn   Vrije Universiteit Brussel, Belgium
Jorge Cuéllar   Siemens AG, Germany
Olga De Troyer   Vrije Universiteit Brussel, Belgium
Jukka Eckstein   IT Communication, Germany
Marina Egea   ATOS Origin, Spain
Piero Fraternali   Politecnico di Milano, Italy
Geert-Jan Houben   Delft University of Technology,
     The Netherlands
Gerti Kappel   Vienna University of Technology, Austria
Nora Koch   Ludwig-Maximilians-Universität München,
     Germany
Maristella Matera   Politecnico di Milano, Italy
Vicente Pelechano   Universidad Politécnica de Valencia, Spain
Juan Carlos Preciado   Universidad de Extremadura, Spain
Werner Retschitzegger   Johannes Kepler University Linz, Austria
Gustavo Rossi   Universidad Nacional de La Plata, Argentina
Fernando Sánchez   Universidad de Extremadura, Spain
Javier Troya   Universidad de Málaga, Spain
Antonio Vallecillo   Universidad de Málaga, Spain
Marco Winkler   Université Toulouse, France
Agustín Yagüe   Universidad Politécnica de Madrid, Spain
Gefei Zhang   Arvato systems Technologies GmbH, Germany

Message from the QWE 2013 Workshop Chairs

The development and usage of Web applications in different platforms and devices are continuously increasing. Web applications, a combination of information, integrated functionalities, and services, have become the most predominant form of software delivery today, with users and businesses choosing to rent or use software rather than buy it. This has led to increased and focused attention on quality models, processes, and methods that facilitate understanding, evaluating, and especially improving their quality and quality in use.

This was the main motivation that led us to organize the fourth edition of the International Workshop on Quality in Web Engineering (QWE 2013) that was held in conjunction with the 13th International Conference on Web Engineering (ICWE 2013).

The purpose of the workshop was to discuss the most innovative and advanced experiences for guaranteeing the quality of Web applications, and the role that Web engineering methods and tools can play in this endeavor. Special emphasis was placed on quality models, methods, and evaluation strategies, and the way in which their systematic employment can help to understand and improve different software entities, such as, for example products and systems mainly related to the new generation of Web applications.

The accepted papers mainly contributed in this direction. The scientific program of this year's QWE edition consisted of five accepted papers and an open discussion. Paper presentations and discussion were distributed in two sessions taking into account a half-day workshop format. All submissions went through a rigorous blind-review process by our Program Committee, and only submissions with positive comments were selected for publication.

Concluding, we would like to thank all the authors who contributed to QWE with their papers, presentations, and enriching comments. We are also grateful to the members of the Steering Committee for their support and advice. Lastly, we would like to thank all the members of the workshop Program Committee for their efforts in the reviewing process, and the ICWE organizers for their support and assistance in the production of these proceedings.

July 2013

Cinzia Cappiello
Adrián Fernández
Luis Olsina

Organization

Organizers

Cinzia Cappiello	Politecnico di Milano, Italy
Adrián Fernández	Universitat Politécnica de Valencia, Spain
Luis Olsina	Universidad Nacional de La Pampa, Argentina

Steering Committee

Silvia Abrahão	Universitat Politécnica de Valencia, Spain
Cristina Cachero	University of Alicante, Spain
Cinzia Cappiello	Politecnico di Milano, Italy
Maristella Matera	Politecnico di Milano, Italy

Program Committee

Giorgio Brajnik	University of Udine, Italy
Ismael Caballero	University of Castilla-la-Mancha, Spain
Coral Calero	University of Castilla-la-Mancha, Spain
Tiziana Catarci	University of Rome, Italy
Sven Casteleyn	Vrije Universität Brussel, Belgium
Florian Daniel	Politecnico di Milano, Italy
Emilio Insfran	Universidad Politécnica de Valencia, Spain
Gjergji Kasneci	Hasso Plattner Institut, Germany
Sergio Lujan-Mora	University of Alicante, Spain
Geert Poels	Ghent University, Belgium
Gustavo Rossi	LIFIA, UNLP, Argentina
Monica Scannapieco	Italian National Institute of Statistics ISTAT, Italy
Marco Winckler	Paul Sabatier University, France

Table of Contents

9th International Workshop on Model-Driven and Agile Engineering for the Web (MDWE 2013)

2nd International Workshop on Data Management in the Social Semantic Web (DMSSW 2013)

Tasks Model Composition: Beyond Data, Representing User Activities

Marco Winckler

Interactive Critical System (ICS) Team,
Institute of Research in Informatics (IRIT), Université Paul Sabatier
118 route de Narbonne, 31062 Cedex 9 Toulouse, France
winckler@irit.fr

Abstract. The aim of this paper is to illustrate, by way of a few case studies, the value of model-based task analysis in interaction and design specification of Web mashups. Task analysis is recognized as one fundamental way to focus on the specific user needs and to improve the general understanding of how users may interact with a user interface to accomplish a given goal when using an interactive system. It is argued that some of current challenges to the design and development of Web mashups are commonplace when building task models. So that, in some extension, model-based task analysis can help designers of Web mashups to better understand and describe users' tasks for combining data sources. The cases studies presented hereafter focused on tasks carried out by both developers and end-users of Web mahsups. More than simple illustrations, all cases studies are issued from real life applications.

Keywords: model-based task analysis, Web mashups, task composition.

1 Introduction

The development process for building Web mashups focus on the integration of resources and services available online [5]. So far, most of the research on Web mashups has been devoted to mapping mechanisms allowing data integration, data transformation, and/or representation of processes for composing Web services. However, a deeper understanding of users tasks is required if we want to move forward from simple data integration to more interactive and user friendly Web mashups.

In the field of Human-Computer Interaction (HCI) domain, task analysis is a fundamental way to focus on the specific user needs and to improve the general understanding of how users may interact with a user interface to accomplish a given goal when using an interactive system. In order to provide a representation of user tasks, the HCI community has proposed several task modeling notations [1]. Task models do not imply any specific implementation, so that one can focus on dependencies between activities, availability of resources required to perform tasks and steps users should follow to achieve a task. In the last years, we have been using task model to solve a variety of problems related to the development of interactive systems. Hereafter we summary in three case studies some of the lessons learned that are not alien to the development process of Web mashups.

Q.Z. Sheng and J. Kjeldskov (Eds.): ICWE 2013 Workshops, LNCS 8295, pp. 1–2, 2013.

2   Lessons Learned

Task Refactoring for Helping Developers: Task model are structured around two concepts: task decomposition (a hierarchy) and task flow (order of task execution). When adequately combined, these concepts provide an exhaustive representation of large quantity of information in a single model. However, when applied to real-life systems, tasks notations end up in very large, hard-to-manage models thus making task modeling a time-consuming and sometimes painful activity. In [3] we have investigated structuring mechanisms for task models including encapsulation of task, reuse and task patterns. The lessons we learned is that without the proper structuring mechanism, developers can be easily overwhelmed by their models and lose the focus on the end-users, thus creating ineffective compositions.

Flexible Task Composition to Cope with Many End-Users Needs: During the development of an incident reporting systems [4], we have found out that users could equally achieved their goal by performing different tasks and the choice on which task to perform depended on too many factors that could be decided beforehand, so the system should support all alternatives. Thus alternative was built as a task pattern that is used as a plug & play element in the overall task model. By exploring temporal and logical operators available on tasks models notations, it was possible to accommodate all alternative in a single task model without compromising the required flexibility.

User-Defined Procedures from Task Patterns: In [2] have proposed a Domain Specific Language (DSL) a tool support allowing users to specify their own procedures over the Web by combining task patterns. The underlying task model is orchestrated by the DSL but users don't need to know how to model tasks to use the tool. Moreover, the task composition can be done on the fly accordingly to the user's needs. Two lessons can be learned from this work: i) task models feature patterns useful in many compositions; and ii) compositions can be done on-the-fly by users.

3   Conclusions

In this paper we have provided a few examples of problems that we have solved using model-based task analysis. We suggest that of the solutions presented can provide insights to the development of innovative Web mashups.

References

1. Diaper, D., Stanton, N.A. (eds.): The Handbook of Task Analysis for Human-Computer Interaction, 650 pages. Lawrence Erlbaum Associates (2004)
2. Firmenich, S., Rossi, G., Winckler, M.: A Domain Specific Language for Orchestrating User Tasks whilst Navigation Web sites. In: Daniel, F., Dolog, P., Li, Q. (eds.) ICWE 2013. LNCS, vol. 7977, pp. 224–232. Springer, Heidelberg (2013)
3. Martinie, C., Palanque, P., Winckler, M.: Structuring and Composition Mechanisms to Address Scalability Issues in Task Models. In: Campos, P., Graham, N., Jorge, J., Nunes, N., Palanque, P., Winckler, M. (eds.) INTERACT 2011, Part III. LNCS, vol. 6948, pp. 589–609. Springer, Heidelberg (2011)
4. Winckler, M., Bach, C., Bernhaupt, R.: Identifying User Experience Dimensions for Mobile Incident Reporting in Urban Contexts. IEEE Transactions on Professional Communication 56(2) (June 2013)
5. Yu, J., Benatallah, B., Casati, F., Daniel, F.: Understanding Mashup Development. Internet Computing 12(5), 44–52 (2008)

The Interactive API (iAPI)

Florian Daniel and Andrea Furlan

University of Trento, Via Sommarive 5, 38123, Trento, Italy
daniel@disi.unitn.it, andrea.furlan@studenti.unitn.it

Abstract. The claim of this paper is that *reuse on the Web* – if sensibly facilitated – can be achieved in a much more intuitive and efficient fashion than today. The idea is to invert the current perspective on reuse by moving away from programmer-oriented artifacts, such as APIs, web services and data feeds, and focusing on user-oriented artifacts, i.e., graphical user interfaces (UIs). The paper defines a new kind of API, the *interactive API (iAPI)*, which reconciles the intuitiveness of interactive UIs with the power of programmable APIs and enables (i) *programmatic access* to UIs and (ii) *interactive, live programming*. The paper discusses use cases and implementation options and lays the foundation for *UI-oriented computing* as a discipline.

1 Introduction

On the Web, *data* is typically shared via XML dialects like RSS [9] or Atom [8] feeds, plain XML, web services or, more recently, via so-called micro-formats (http://microformats.org), which enable the extraction of structured data from web pages via HTML annotations. If data are not explicitly made accessible, data extraction tools like Dapper (http://open.dapper.net) allow one to extract structured data from websites even without annotations. *Application logic* is mostly accessed via web services (both SOAP services [2] and RESTful services [4]) or code libraries (e.g., in JavaScript). The reuse of *user interfaces* (UIs) is only scarcely supported so far. Web mashups [11] are the most prominent example of integration at the presentation layer. W3C widgets [10] are a standard client-side technology, Java portlets [1] a standard server-side UI technology for simple, stand-alone applications that can be assembled into a composite page. However, mashup tools typically still rely on proprietary UI component technologies [12] and, like portlets and widgets, feature only the reuse of coarse-grained, programmer-oriented components.

The promise of the service composition (e.g., BPEL [5]) and mashup approaches [11] was that they would enable generic people to develop. Yet, if we take a critical look at how composite applications and services are developed today we recognize that development is still a prerogative of programmers. Mastering all the above technologies implies a learning process that is tedious and time-consuming even to **expert programmers**, let alone **non-programmers**. All the attempts to enable non-programmers failed, as they insisted on abstracting APIs or services that were invented for programmers. Non-programmers

Q.Z. Sheng and J. Kjeldskov (Eds.): ICWE 2013 Workshops, LNCS 8295, pp. 3–15, 2013.

simply don't know what services or data formats are [7]. What they know is how to use a user interface.

The observation of this paper is that there is however a variety of applications on the Web, whose development could be significantly *sped up* to programmers and *enabled* to non-programmers, if only we had the right component technology in place. The **types of applications** we have in mind are non-mission-critical applications, such as:

- *Simple application integrations*, which require interoperability among web applications;
- *UI-centric web mashups*, which require sourcing and combing data, application logic and/or UIs from the Web;
- *Website evolutions*, which require restructuring or extending existing websites;
- *Simple web automations*, which require batch processing of repetitive on-line tasks (beyond http://ifttt.com); and
- *Personal web processes*, which require support for long-lasting on-line tasks that also involve user interactions.

The practices underlying these applications are sourcing or extracting *data* from websites, processing data and accessing remote *application logic*, copying and pasting pieces of *UIs* from existing websites, and similar – all tasks that are relatively common on the Web. None of these practices, however, is currently supported by a *single* component technology and in the reach of *non-programmers*.

A simple, but good example of how reuse *could* be is the following **scenario**: Imagine a researcher wants to re-structure her website, reusing the list of publications of her old website and adding citation counts from Google Scholar. She would like to focus only on the design of the new layout of her publications and to be able to simply drag and drop the content of her old table of publications to the new layout. Next, she would like to be able to tell her new website to query Google Scholar for each of the publications in the table, e.g., by recording a set of actions that she exemplarily performs manually and that her website could replay for each publication – ideally, everything without writing any new line of code.

As the scenario shows, the aim of this work is to turn UIs into first-class programming artifacts. To this aim, the paper specifically provides the following **contributions**:

- The design of a new type of API, the *interactive API (iAPI)*, which enables (i) *programmatic access* to UIs and (ii) *interactive programming*;
- The discussion of the core iAPI *uses cases* and *implementation options*;
- The proposal of a simple *iAPI annotation format* and *runtime middleware*;
- The proposal of *UI-oriented computing* as a discipline of component-based development for non-programmers based on iAPIs.

Next, we define the context of this work, i.e., web user interfaces. Then, we introduce iAPIs and describe their use cases and a possible implementation. We then outline the benefits of iAPIs and the challenges of UI-oriented computing.

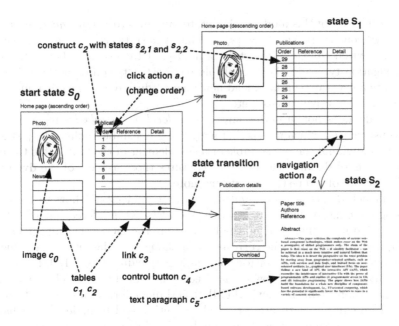

Fig. 1. UI constructs, states, actions and state transitions in web UIs

2 Preliminaries: Web User Interfaces

Figure 1 provides a schematic example of a *graphical web user interface* made of two pages (Home and Publication details) and a set of UI constructs (tables, images, buttons, links, text, etc.). The figure apparently shows three pages, but attention: the Home page is shown twice. From a UI point of view it can be in two different states, depending on the order of the publications (ascending vs. descending). *State* is an important aspect of UIs, as in each instant of time a user can perform only those actions that are supported by the UI constructs available at that time (e.g., if the publications are in ascending order, he can only ask for the descending order).

Adapting traditional human-computer interaction and system models [3] to the Web, a graphical web **user interface** can be seen conceptually as an extended finite state machine of the form $ui = \langle C, S, S_0, A, act \rangle$, where:

- $C = \{c_i\}$ is the set of all *UI constructs* of the UI;
- $S = \{S_j | S_j = \{s_{i,j}\}\}$ is the set of *states* the UI may traverse in response to user interactions, with $s_{i,j}$ being the state of the i-th UI construct in state j (e.g., hidden);
- S_0 is the *start state* of the UI;
- $A = \{click, type, drag, drop, ...\}$ is the set of typical *actions* a user can perform on web UIs; and
- $act : C \times S \times A \rightarrow S$ is the *transition function* that tells how the UI transitions from one state to another in response to an action $a \in A$ on a construct $c \in C$.

The peculiarity of this model is that states are not atomic but *aggregations* of states of UI constructs, i.e., $S_j = \{s_{i,j}\}$. That is, a state change may correspond to the contextual change of the state of multiple UI constructs. For instance, a user navigation typically affects multiple UI constructs contemporarily, e.g., it may create a new table of data, load new images, display new heading and text, expose new interactive controls, etc.

The model does not prescribe any specific *level of granularity* regarding the set of constructs C, which means that a given $c \in C$ can be a full table, just as it can be an individual cell of the table or a sub-element of the text inside the cell. The best level of detail is the one that captures those aspects of the dynamics of a UI that are of interest, and nothing more.

This model of UIs is *conceptual* and aims to understand how to turn UIs into programming artifacts. In practice, Web UIs are rendered out of HTML markup, UI state is managed by the browser via the DOM (Document Object Model), and state transitions correspond to changes to the DOM, e.g., due to programmatic modifications or user navigations (yielding a new DOM) – everything managed by the web browser "for free." The aim of the model is to provide an interpretation of this low-level HTML/DOM model oriented toward the users of the UI, to equip it with user-oriented semantics, and to understand what it actually means to enable users to manipulate UIs instead of syntax elements.

3   The Interactive API (iAPI)

The problem with web UIs is that they do not have enough machine-processable *meaning*, which could be used to enable their interactive manipulation and programming. HTML constructs like `<table>` or `<ul>` are only syntactical markup. Constructs of more advanced UI markup languages, such as XUL   (`https://developer.mozilla.org/en/docs/XUL`)   or   XAML (`http://msdn.microsoft.com/en-us/library/ms752059.aspx`), only format and arrange UI elements.

There are two key ingredients that UIs currently miss: once rendered, they cannot be *programmed* in a principled fashion (of course, it is always possible to hack into the UI markup and inject JavaScript code or extract data, but this is neither good practice nor does it produce good results in general) and it is not possible to use them as *design constructs* while already rendered in the browser.

What is needed is graphically illustrated in Figure 2, which focuses on the table of publications of Figure 1: the table's UI must be complemented with a dedicated *API*, which provides programmatic access to the table, and with a set of *graphical controls*, which allow the user to operate the API interactively and, thereby, to program the table. Depending on the purpose of the specific UI construct or set thereof, the API's capability can be more or less complex. For instance, the API in Figure 2 allows one to emulate user actions on the table (`do`), to extract the visible data, to source the full data underlying the table or to clone the table along with its data. In the case of a form, the API will provide for the *processing of data* in input and produce results in output; the API may

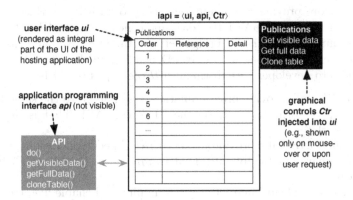

Fig. 2. The model of interactive APIs exemplified with a possible rendering

also communicate user interactions via suitable *events*, and so on. We call the artifact that brings these aspects under one hood an *interactive API*.

3.1 iAPI Model

An *interactive API (iAPI)* is a piece of graphical user interface (a sub-tree of the DOM), e.g., a table, form or sub-area of a web page, that provides both *interactive* and *programmatic* access to its UI constructs, application logic and/or data. That is, to the common user an iAPI is a visual What-You-See-Is-What-You-Get (WYSIWYG) artifact that can be manipulated via dedicated, artifact-specific graphical controls (see Figure 2), which may also mediate between the user and possible back-end logics (e.g., exposed via web services). To the developer, an iAPI in addition also exposes a programmable API, e.g., in JavaScript, which enables programmatic access.

Conceptually, an iAPI can be modeled as a tuple $iapi = \langle ui, api, Ctr \rangle$, where:

- $ui = \langle C, S, S_0, A, act \rangle$ is a *UI* as defined previously, but limited to the UI constructs of interest to the iAPI;
- $api = \langle do, O, E \rangle$ is the *API* of the iAPI, with

  - $do : C \times A \to \bot$ being an operation that allows one to *emulate* user actions $a \in A$ on ui;
  - O being a set of *operations* providing iAPI-specific functionality; operations may act locally only (e.g., `getVisibleData`), or they may invoke remote application logic (e.g., `getFullData`); and
  - E being a set of *events* emitted by the iAPI (e.g., in reaction to a navigation action);

- Ctr is the set of *graphical controls* injected into ui to make the features of api accessible interactively.

iAPIs therefore provide programmatic access to both the Surface Web (the graphical UIs) and the Deep Web (the data and logic behind the UIs). The graphical controls injected into the UI bridge between the Deep Web and the Surface Web and make programming interactive. Depending on the *level of support* an iAPI provides to developers, we distinguish **three types** of iAPIs:

- *Basic iAPIs* only provide programmatic access limited to the same features a user can perform manually on the UI of the iAPI. That is, $iapi^{base} = \langle ui, \langle do, \emptyset, \emptyset \rangle, \emptyset \rangle$.
- *Intermediate iAPIs* also provide advanced, iAPI-specific operations and events, but still programmatically only. That is, $iapi^{int} = \langle ui, \langle do, O, E \rangle, \emptyset \rangle$, with $O, E \neq \emptyset$.
- *Full iAPIs* provide for interactive programming and enable live, UI-oriented reuse. That is, $iapi^{full} = \langle ui, \langle do, O, E \rangle, Ctr \rangle$, with $O, E, Ctr \neq \emptyset$.

Which kind of iAPI suits best a given reusable application feature depends on the interpretation of the iAPI developer as well as its expected target user. For instance, if the target users are developers, there is no need for graphical controls to manipulate the iAPI; however, if the target users are common web users, graphical controls become mandatory.

Like the model of UIs, also the iAPI model does not prescribe any *level of granularity*. An iAPI may cover a full web page, just like it may be defined only for the table of publications as exemplified in Figure 2. A web page may contain multiple independent iAPIs. It is the developer of the website who decides which features of the site to make accessible for UI-oriented reuse and how. A sensible design will focus on conceptually self-contained features, comprising own UI constructs (e.g., a table or form), application logic and/or data.

3.2   iAPI Use Cases

In order to appreciate the power of this UI-centric perspective on reuse, it is important to understand which new, functional features iAPIs are able to provide to developers. Figure 3 distinguishes four core *iAPI use cases*:

(a) **Operating UI**: The basic use case is programmatically interacting with a UI, i.e., *operating* it by emulating user interactions, without further reusing any of its features. The use case leverages on the *do* function, which could be programmed by recording and re-playing user interactions.

(b) **Extracting data**: The second use case is *extracting data* from a UI (e.g., from a table), in order to reuse them inside another piece of software, using own, new UI constructs for the rendering of the data. The use case makes use of data extraction operations in O, whose graphical control could, e.g., simply be dragged/dropped over a new table.

(c) **Extracting logic**: The more advanced use case is *extracting application logic* from an iAPI, e.g., by processing data via a form and extracting the output from the form's response page or by invoking a remote web service. The use case uses the *do* function to automate form processing as well as the operations and events in O and E.

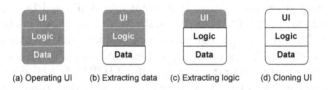

(a) Operating UI (b) Extracting data (c) Extracting logic (d) Cloning UI

Fig. 3. The four core uses cases of iAPIs for UI-oriented computing. White blocks correspond to what is reused, gray blocks are neglected.

(d) **Cloning UI**: The most advanced use case is *cloning* a complete piece of UI, along with its underlying application logic and data. This means reconstructing the UI of the iAPI locally and connecting them to the remote iAPI's logic and data. The use case copies *ui* and makes use of all other features, e.g., by dragging/dropping the piece of UI into a new web page.

These four use cases represent a unified and principled solution to the development practices described in the introduction, which otherwise would require mastering a wide set of different component technologies and protocols.

3.3 Implementation Options

Although iAPIs are apparently complex software artifacts themselves, their implementation can be kept relatively simple. Recalling the structure of iAPIs, i.e., $iapi = \langle ui, api, Ctr \rangle$ with $api = \langle do, O, E \rangle$, it is important to note that the *ui* comes essentially for free, in that it is simply a part of a web application's UI, which would be there anyway, with or without the iAPI. Similarly, the function *do* can be provided once for all via a dedicated UI wrapper that enables emulating user interactions with *ui* (similar to Selenium, http://seleniumhq.org, but with advanced iAPI support). Only the operations O and the events E require an iAPI-specific implementation, while the graphical controls *Ctr* can be automatically generated out of their definitions, given a respective rendering convention. As for the operations and events, we identify three options:

– **Ad hoc implementation**: It is always possible to implement dedicated operations and events via custom JavaScript code included in web pages. Each iAPI would have its own implementation.
– **iAPI annotations**: If we carefully examined how these implementations look like, we would easily identify recurrent patterns for data extraction from HTML markup, fetching data from a remote source, or invoking remote web services. Instead of implementing these functionalities imperatively in JavaScript, it is possible to factor out the repetitive code into an independent code library and to configure it via declarative annotations of the HTML markup of *ui*. For instance, data extraction can be supported via microformats, while logic extraction may require new annotation elements.

– **iAPI-ready markup**: Instead of annotating HTML, iAPIs could become an integral part of the HTML standard itself, with own elements to equip UIs natively with interactive programming capabilities and integrated browser support for the rendering of their graphical controls. The idea is similar to the `<header>` and `<navigation>` elements of HTML 5, whose only purpose is to add semantics to the markup and not to actually format content.

Independently of their implementation, the intriguing aspect from a software engineering point of view is that an iAPI's *api* does not exist as independent software artifact. It cannot live without its UI. Both must be instantiated together, and the API's life cycle is tightly coupled to that of its UI counterpart.

This implies some requirements for the construction of new software artifacts (e.g., a web page) out of a set of iAPIs. Specifically, integrating multiple iAPIs requires (i) instantiating the source web pages, (ii) instantiating their iAPIs and (iii) setting up a communication channel among them. The instantiation of the web pages may occur directly inside the web browser or outside in a GUI-less rendering engine, such as HtmlUnit (`http://htmlunit.sourceforge.net`). The instantiation of the iAPIs requires an extension of current rendering engines (e.g., a JavaScript parser and iAPI runtime container). Communications can be set up via interactions among conventional APIs (browser-internal) or web services/sockets (inter-browser) provided by the extensions.

4   A First Implementation

4.1   iAPI Micro-format

The idea to enable the specification of iAPIs is to follow an approach that is similar to that of micro-formats (`http://microformats.org`), with one key difference: while micro-formats provide ready annotations for data types of individual domains (e.g., *hCard* describes people and organizations, and *hCalendar* describes events), the iAPI annotation format provides a set of instructions (i) for the free description of data types of own domains, (ii) for the reuse of existing micro-formats, and (iii) for the reuse of web services or data feeds.

In line with micro-formats, also the iAPI annotation format uses the `class` attribute of HTML to host its annotations (an example follows). Table 1 summarizes the minimum set of instructions identified so far for the reuse of data.

Table 1. Basic iAPI annotations elements

Instruction	Parameter	Description
iapi	–	Identifies an iAPI inside HTML
datafeed	Feed name	Defines an iAPI for data extraction
dataitem	Item name	Identifies individual data items
dataattribute	Attribute name	Identifies individual attributes of an item
rss	URL	References an equivalent RSS data source
source	URL	References a web resource for iAPI reuse
iapiid	ID	Identifies an iAPI to be reused inside a source

Given these instructions, a web page that wants to make its data available in the form of an iAPI can be annotated as follows (we call this the *source page*):

```
<ul id="1" class="iapi datafeed:Publications rss:RSS_URL">
  <li class="dataitem:Publication">
    <span class="dataattribute:Author">F. Daniel and A. Furlan</span>.
    <span class="dataattribute:Title">The Interactive API (iAPI)</span>.
    <span class="dataattribute:Event">ComposableWeb 2013</span>
  </li>
  ...
</ul>
```

The annotation identifies the unnumbered list as iAPI (`iapi`), enables the extraction of data (`datafeed`) structured into `dataitem`-s and `dataattribute`-s, specifically of publications with authors, titles, and events. The URL of the `rss` instruction provides an alternative resource where to fetch the same data from.

If a **developer** wants to reuse the data exposed by this iAPI (inside a *target page*), he only needs to specify the following line, whose annotation identifies the table as iAPI and tells where to fetch the respective data from (the effect of the interpretation of this annotation format is illustrated in Figure 5):

```
<table class="iapi source:SourceURL iapiid:1"></table>
```

As for now, the annotation format proposes only a set of instructions for the specification of *data extraction* use cases, both from the iAPI's HTML markup as well as from RSS data sources. To limit the annotation effort as much as possible and to foster reuse, inside an `iapi` element it is further possible to use common micro-formats to annotate data, such as the *hCard* and *hCalendar* formats described earlier. The next step will be the design of instructions for the specification of the other iAPI use cases.

4.2   iAPI Middleware

In order to use iAPIs in practice and to enable interactive development, it is necessary to provide for suitable interpreters and runtime environments, i.e., for an *iAPI middleware*. In Figure 4 we illustrate the architecture of an according Chrome browser extension we developed to support the previous annotation example, which acts as middleware. The extension is based on a so-called *background page* for the overall management of the extension and a *content script* for the interaction with the DOM of the page loaded in the browser window. When loading a page, the *iAPI parser* identifies possible iAPIs in the page, and the *HTML augmenter* injects the respective graphical controls. If the identified iAPI reuses data from another source, the HTML augmenter loads (via the *loader* module) the source page, extracts the annotated data, reformats it according to the host HTML element of the target page (e.g., the *Content formatter* turns the unnumbered list into a table), and augments the target page with the newly formatted data. Other parsers support fetching data from different data sources, such as RSS feeds or micro-formats. This is enough to execute the annotations of the source and target pages described above.

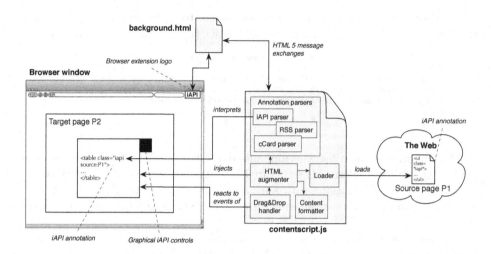

Fig. 4. Architecture of the iAPI middleware Chrome extension

With the help of the *Drag&Drop handler*, the extension is also able to intercept drag-and-drop events among browser windows and to allow generic **web users** without programming knowledge to drag iAPIs (via the injected graphical controls) from one page to another. This enables the extension to automatically generate the annotation of a target iAPI with information of the source iAPI and to realize the interactive, UI-driven development scenario depicted in Figure 5. Ideally (but this is not implemented yet), the extension would then store the so defined reuse logic either locally or remotely, so as to be able to re-run it as soon as the user returns to the same target page.

5   Benefits and Research Challenges

The aim of this paper is to reconcile the twofold requirement of speeding up development to programmers and of enabling non-programmers to develop. The result are interactive APIs (iAPIs). The approach leverages on the front-end of applications, instead of on their back-end, and proposes a visual, interactive reuse paradigm. Incidentally, these design choices come with some unexpected but highly *beneficial side-effects*:

– The *deployment* of iAPIs is contextual to the deployment of their host application. iAPIs are an integral part of an application's UI and do not require separate deployment or maintenance. They are natively aligned and consistent with their applications. This is different from web services, which are deployed independently and easily diverge from their applications.
– The *documentation* of iAPIs comes for free to their developers. There is no need for abstract descriptors, IDLs or textual API descriptions. The UI of the page hosting the iAPIs and the graphical controls injected into it already tell everything about the capabilities of the iAPIs contained in the page.

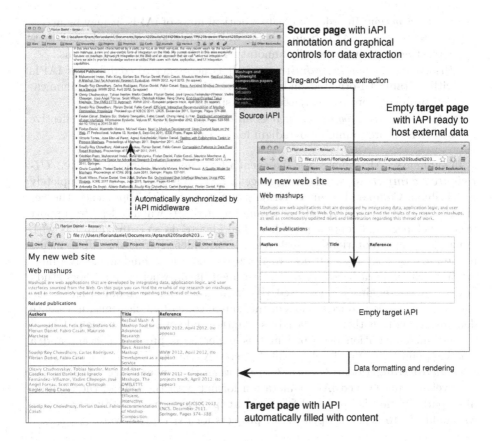

Fig. 5. The concept of interactive, UI-oriented development explained with an example (a video of the flow is available on-line via http://goo.gl/bAzS2)

- The *retrieval* of iAPIs does not ask for new infrastructure or query paradigms. Being iAPIs an integral part of the Surface Web, it is enough to query for a desired functionality via common web search. If a suitable iAPI exists, its web page will pop up under the search results. Again, this is different from web services, whose registry infrastructure (UDDI) is a well-known failure.
- Finally, *understanding* the logic of an iAPI does not require programming skills or computer science knowledge. Common web browsing skills are enough to understand the available features and how to operate them.

These properties make iAPIs a technology that is intrinsically *Web-ready* and that has the potential to *boost reuse* on the Web. Yet, in order for this to happen, a set of ***research and engineering challenges*** ask for suitable answers:

- *iAPI development*: It is crucial to sensibly conceive how iAPIs are developed, in order to keep their development sustainable. An interpretable annotation format (as exemplified in Section 4) or markup language seems promising, but this is not the only option.

- *iAPI extraction*: In order to create a critical mass of iAPIs, it may be necessary to "extract" iAPIs from existing web applications, similar to web data extraction, e.g., by externally annotating third-party web applications.
- *UI-oriented computing infrastructure*: It is necessary to complement iAPIs with suitable UI-oriented middleware, runtime environments, communication protocols, browser extensions, and similar.
- *Interactive, live programming*: It is an HCI challenge to design an effective UI-oriented programming paradigm for non-programmers.

In summary, iAPIs aim to set the agenda for a new line of research, i.e., **UI-oriented computing**, which brings together SE/WE and HCI in a completely new fashion. Compared to micro-formats or Semantic Web approaches, the bet of iAPIs is that turning UIs into programming artifacts will also lead to support from developers and content providers. The idea to do so is to equip UIs with semantics (via annotations), which do not only identify reusable UI elements inside an page, but also tell how to reuse them. This is fundamentally different from the approach, for example, described in [6], where the authors study how to reverse-engineer Java-based UIs from Java code by monitoring UI usage via aspect-oriented extensions of the source code of applications, in essence demonstrating that there is a lack of semantics and support for reuse of UIs.

The implementation described in this paper is as proof of concept and a starting point for future development. Concretely, via the *W3C Interactive APIs Community Group* (`http://www.w3.org/community/interative-apis`) we aim to develop a full-fledged iAPI annotation format with the help of the community (participation is open and free). On `http://www.interactive-apis.org` we would like to host the open-source projects for iAPI middleware.

References

1. Abdelnur, A., Hepper, S.: Java Portlet Specification, Version 1.0. Technical Report JSR 168, Sun Microsystems, Inc. (October 2003),
   `http://download.oracle.com/otndocs/jcp/PORTLET_1.0-FR-SPEC-G-F/`
2. Alonso, G., Casati, F., Kuno, H., Machiraju, V.: Web Services: Concepts, Architectures, and Applications. Springer (2003)
3. Dix, A., Finlay, J., Abowd, G., Beale, R.: Human-Computer Interaction, 3rd edn. Prentice Hall (2004)
4. Fielding, R.: Architectural Styles and the Design of Network-based Software Architectures. Ph.d. dissertation, University of California, Irvine (2007)
5. Jordan, D., Evdemon, J.: Web Services Business Process Execution Language Version 2.0. Oasis standard, OASIS (April 2007),
   `http://docs.oasis-open.org/wsbpel/2.0/OS/wsbpel-v2.0-OS.html`
6. Li, P., Wohlstadter, E.: View-based maintenance of graphical user interfaces. In: AOSD, pp. 156–167 (2008)
7. Namoun, A., Nestler, T., Angeli, A.D.: Service Composition for Non-programmers: Prospects, Problems, and Design Recommendations. In: ECOWS, pp. 123–130 (2010)

8. Nottingham, M., Sayre, R.: The Atom Syndication Format (December 2005),
   http://www.ietf.org/rfc/rfc4287.txt
9. RSS Advisory Board. RSS 2.0 Specification (2009),
   http://www.rssboard.org/rss-specification
10. Web Application Working Group. Widgets Family of Specifications (May 2012)
11. Yu, J., Benatallah, B., Casati, F., Daniel, F.: Understanding Mashup Development. IEEE Internet Computing 12(5), 44–52 (2008)
12. Yu, J., Benatallah, B., Saint-Paul, R., Casati, F., Daniel, F., Matera, M.: A Framework for Rapid Integration of Presentation Components. In: WWW, pp. 923–932. ACM Press (May 2007)

Semantic-Guided Communication and Composition in a Widget/Dashboard Environment

Peter Wehner and Robert Krüger

Fink & Partner Media Services GmbH, 01309 Dresden, Germany
{peter.wehner,robert.krueger}@finkundpartner.de

Abstract. Composite websites based on widget/dashboard environments offer top grade adaptability to theoretically any task requirement or user preference. In productive use, however, the usability of a running dashboard depends on the intelligence that has been incorporated when developing the underlying software framework. This is especially true for widget/dashboard frameworks that allow for an ad hoc inter-widget-communication. The paper shows a press media software company effort to semantically enrich the inter-widget-communication of a widget/dashboard framework called NewsDesk. Employing this enrichment, NewsDesk widgets will be able to share ontology-based data and operate in activities and roles. Preliminary results of the ongoing work will be reported, featuring the enhancement of the inter-widget-communication protocol as well as an approach to offer widget composition proposals based on widget template and instance usage patterns.

Keywords: Composite Websites, Domain Knowledge, Industry Experience, Semantics, Usability, User Interface Integration.

1 Introduction

Despite the exponentially growing amount and complexity of multimedia data, current web-based access to asset collections is still characterized by a static cycle of manual keyword search and list-/chessboard-style result representation, usually showing the details of only one result item at a time. The introduction of rich client widget/dashboard environments did overcome this obstacle of static web page rendering by offering free widget compositions and thus much more task- and user-oriented user interfaces. However, this new flexibility is not for free because an ad hoc inter-widget-communication, if provided at all, has to be designed and implemented in the framework in advance. Such a way, a framework-based approach to inter-widget-communication may start from simple descriptions of the exchange of raw types like strings. However, such simple communication descriptions will not intelligently serve complex application scenarios where a dashboard composition comprises more than one widget of the same type or where the data on exchange has a record- or even a graph-based layout. The evolvement of semantic technologies seems to provide means to grasp complex application scenarios featuring more appropriate description methods. Due to well defined data retrieval endpoints, semantic

Q.Z. Sheng and J. Kjeldskov (Eds.): ICWE 2013 Workshops, LNCS 8295, pp. 16–26, 2013.

technologies also allow for a seamless integration into running widget/dashboard frameworks that aspire to instantly query an ontology-based fact database. Obviously, the support for more sophisticated application scenarios amounts to framework enhancements that include a semantic enrichment of the underlying inter-widget-communication protocol. The enhancements are supposed to enable the widget/dashboard framework to adopt semantic patterns for the composition and communication of widgets. Mostly important to the industry, this will raise the degree of usability and eventually stimulate the productivity of the end user.

The paper continues as follows. The following subsections provide an insight into NewsDesk, the widget/dashboard framework in question, as well as into SENSE, a running research project that features the semantic advancement of NewsDesk. Section 2 introduces related work by reference. Section 3 discusses the semantic enhancements of the NewsDesk-framework in detail, namely the different layers of widget-communication descriptions as well as the widget-composition automation and shows some examples. The paper concludes in section 4 with an outlook to the remaining work regarding NewsDesk and SENSE.

1.1   NewsDesk: A Widget/Dashboard-Framework

NewsDesk is a software framework for widget/dashboard environments that has been developed using pure XHTML and JavaScript over the last couple of years by fink & Partner Media Services GmbH, Germany. It aims at providing a high-flexible user interface runtime to promote usability by adaptability [1]. As a software framework, NewsDesk assists both the developer in advancing and the end user in employing the overall system. The target audience ranges from cross media journalists, browsing any type of electronic content, to newsroom teams, keeping track of the latest news of the world. To support this wide consumer range, NewsDesk scales up to multiple browser windows that may be mapped to monitor walls efficiently.

A widget, being not only the visual but also the conceptual core component of the NewsDesk-framework always adheres to a dedicated lifecycle that comprises the stages of implemented, template, instance (configured instance) and favorite, as being depicted in Fig. 1.

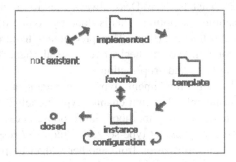

Fig. 1. Widget representation lifecycle

To exemplify, end users will usually instantiate a widget by dragging a representation from the left hand templates area to the dashboard area of NewsDesk. They may then configure the widget according to the requirements and may eventually save the configured widget for later re-instantiation as a favorite by dragging a representation from the dashboard area to another left hand favorite's area of NewsDesk. Note that a dashboard, containing widgets, as well as a workspace, containing dashboards, may also be saved down as favorites. The ongoing dashboard composition process course may in addition benefit from several positioning options such as fixed, absolute, snap-in-column and free-grid layouts. Fig. 2 shows a typical press media scenario where pictures become lined up to accompany textual content.

Fig. 2. A picture gallery for online publication

Besides the composition and organization of widgets, NewsDesk also offers ad hoc inter-widget-communication, which is determined to be independent from the current widget composition on a dashboard. That is, no end user side checks for compatible communication partners have to be performed during widget instantiation. Instead, any compatible communication wire will be established automatically by using some event broker architecture on provider and consumer roles of a widget comparable to Faison's approach [12]. That is, NewsDesk always tries to connect widgets with a compatible communication description. This is done by computing compatible pairs of widgets using a dedicated algorithm. This preeminent feature has so far being evolved to comprise communication checks over several channel, event and object types, including a visual "drag and drop" action.

Communication channels implement typical communication interactions in widget/dashboard environments. The first channel type models a "fire and forget" to allow a widget to just notify its neighborhood, no response is expected, and includes "drag and drop". The second channel type serves a "request / response", such that a widget may request certain information from another widget by providing some data by itself. The third channel type is equal to the second one but operates asynchronously. The fourth channel type eventually enables widgets to exchange system messages with the backend of NewsDesk.

Event types are essentially strings that are required to have a descriptive nature regarding the communication, for example "refreshView" or "publishPicture". They serve the known "publish / subscribe" approach for event-based communication.

Object types, finally, may or may not accompany events on a channel. They have to be registered as identifiers in the scope of NewsDesk's runtime to establish an object type vocabulary over time. The following Fig. 3 and Fig. 4 show some simplified XHTML-based provider and consumer communication descriptions for a widget.

```
...<ndw:communication>
   <ndw:provider>
      <ndw:channel type="sendChannel">
         <ndw:event type="itemSelectedWidgetEvent">
            <ndw:data type="String" />
         </ndw:event>
      </ndw:channel>
   </ndw:provider>
</ndw:communication>...
```

Fig. 3. Provider communication description

```
...<ndw:consumer>
   <ndw:channel type="sendChannel">
      <ndw:event type="itemSelectedWidgetEvent">
         <ndw:data type="String"
            callbackfunction="SendConsumer.onPing"/>
      </ndw:event>
   </ndw:channel>
</ndw:consumer>...
```

Fig. 4. Consumer communication description

1.2   NewsDesk and SENSE

The SENSE research project, where SENSE is an acronym for "Intelligent Storage and Exploration of large Document Sets", is a joint effort of five partners from industry and science [2]. SENSE aspires to set up a continuous flow of semantically enriched data between and within different tiers of modern software architectures, focusing on widget/dashboard environments and hierarchical storage management systems. The basic idea of SENSE differs from common approaches in the semantic community by not only regarding application but also technical domain annotations to actual data. The SENSE consortium shares the opinion that furnishing modern software architectures with additional semantics from the technical domain will particularly promote the scalability of systems running large document collections over time.

SENSE features a semantic repository at the heart of its concept to mediate the different interconnected system tiers through dedicated application and technical domain ontologies. Recalling a widget/dashboard environment as just one of the considered system tiers in the project, this is where NewsDesk comes into play. In fact, SENSE facilitates another opportunity to evolve the NewsDesk-framework. Tackling terms of semantics this time, the evolvement will primarily affect the inter-widget-communication but will eventually also pay off in achieving a smarter guided widget-composition process and therefore promote NewsDesk in terms of usability.

2   Related Work

Widget/dashboard environments have been introduced to allow end users to compose personalized applications, focusing on certain functionalities provided by widgets. Essentially, Sire describes a dashboard as a place in the user interface that offers limited space to compose a set of widgets, probably underpinned by spatial arrangement tools as snap-in-columns [3]. This is in contrast to web service frontends that bundle or integrate a set of data streams by using mostly generic user interfaces [4].

The interactive widget composition did become most popular due to AJAX-based community sites like netvibes [14], script libraries like gwt that powered iGoogle [15] or productive systems like Oracle Metalink [18]. The frontend flexibility and user experience of widget/dashboard environments was such superior to known backend web portal approaches that even newer standards like JSR-286 [16] missed a wider acceptance. However, most widget-based sites or script libraries simply disregard widget-communication aspects. Most probably, this is due to the potential problems of data compatibility or even conversion. Approaches to layout configurable wires upon established widget-compositions seem to turn out into developing and running actual adapter toolkits, see IBM mashup center for example [17].

Approaches to set up a flexible communication scheme range from loosely coupled event broker architectures as introduced by Krüger [6] to complex model oriented descriptions as proposed by Pietschmann [5]. Chudnovskyy takes a more lightweight approach by analyzing and learning the interactions users do perform but does not promote automation [7]. He additionally uses semantic concepts to describe data which has been published alongside the communication channels. Paulheim explicitly employs different ontologies to separate communication aspects from facts of a certain application domain [9]. He thereby integrates whole applications at the desktop level by annotating their communication capabilities and needs. Concerning the general task of mapping facts between ontologies, Kalfogulou and Schorlemmer published a comprehensive overview of the ontology mapping methods available [10].

In parallel to enhancing the communication infrastructure semantically, even user interface interaction starts to capitalize on the benefits of semantically described data. For example, Dachselt limits the amount of data presented to the user by means like FacetZooming [8]. Hyvönen, on the other hand, enhances auto-completion tools by employing semantically different concepts with suggestion components [11].

3   Enhancements of the NewsDesk-Framework

Running NewsDesk-based applications in industry revealed a couple of extension options both at the developers and at the end users side. Concerning the communication description of object types, see section 1.1, a more advanced infrastructure to model common and complex interaction patterns was necessary. The data on exchange needs to be equipped with structure and context information and may even just reference uniform resources from the semantic web. End users, on the other hand, claim to gain a more intelligent framework support when managing the multitude of widget composition possibilities. This may include simple functionalities like temporarily locking a widget out of the dashboard communication. Another sophisticated functionality may adapt the widget selection shown in the templates area of NewsDesk according to the current dashboard composition.

Building on semantic technology, see section 1.2, most of the enhancements of the NewsDesk-framework employ existing or new ontologies, certain inference techniques and a living fact database. They improve the auto wiring algorithm for the widget instantiation process and in turn reapply the auto wiring algorithm against non-occupied communication slots to offer proposals for widget composition. The following sections 3.1 to 3.3 report:

- how domain knowledge has been introduced at the object types layer,
- how the idea of activity roles in widgets compositions has been implemented and
- how domain knowledge as well as widget activity roles become applied to offer composition proposals for an existing dashboard layout.

3.1   Communication Data Description

While using object types, see section 1.1, as filters to compute inter-widget-communication patterns has proved to be a manageable criterion, past NewsDesk installations suffered from an uncontrolled growth in more or less undocumented object type/attribute naming. That is, similar name tokens have been used with no respect to already registered vocabulary. Connecting the NewsDesk-framework to the technology stack of SENSE, the semantic repository in particular, allowed employing RDFS as a modeling platform for the data structures on exchange between widgets. Semantic technology also allowed adopting the concept of domain dependent and independent knowledge.

The design of the developed "pmedia" ontology, that will furthermore furnish the object type layer, represents domain knowledge and abstracts known concepts from existent ontologies or extends them when necessary. For the press media domain, the IPTC rNews standard, which is in parts sourced from the schema.org initiative [20], has been utilized. The XHTML-based communication description of widgets, that actually expresses the available facilities, has been extended to include the semantic descriptions in RDFa format [19]. Such a way, any requirements to provide a mapping from the system-side communication scheme of the widgets and the domain dependent "pmedia" ontology can be accomplished easily [9]. To give an example, a video widget showing a number of videos in a structured manner may describe its capability of publishing a sns:VideoObject by selection as depicted in Fig. 5.

```
…<ndw:communication xmlns:sns="http://sense-projekt.de/">
   <ndw:provider>
      …<ndw:event type="itemSelect">
         <ndw:data type="sns:VideoObject"/>
      </ndw:event>…
   </ndw:provider>
</ndw:communication>…
```

Fig. 5. Publishing an event along with video data

A maps widget then again, which is capable of locating any kind of sns:Place on a map, may define such a communication offer as shown in Fig. 6.

```
…<ndw:data type="sns:Place"
   callbackfunction="ND.MapsWidget.onLocation"/>…
```

Fig. 6. Consuming an event accepting place data

A sns:VideoObject that includes two predicates, namely contentLocation and regionsAllowed of rdfs:domain sns:Place, may therefore be easily connected to a maps widget, that may show all the provided locations and color them differently according to the predicates rdfs:range. That is, computing the data wise communication compatibility of two widgets can be achieved by detecting whether one widget communication description is nothing less than a sub graph of one another. Widget communication descriptions may therefore be specified in a hierarchical, more generic manner without tempting the wiring algorithm to traverse proof-by-case code. It should finally be stressed, that a continuous use of persistent uniform resource identifiers (URI) is mandatory when mapping communication structures that way.

3.2   Communication Intent Description

Providing the object type layer of NewsDesk with graph-based data structures added a lot of expressiveness to the communication descriptions. The next enhancement, which is an intermediate step towards composition modeling, just adapts the communication event layer to these new possibilities. The original descriptive event naming scheme, which served the "publish / subscribe" approach for event-based communication, has been upgraded to a so-called "actrole" ontology to indicate the activity role of widgets to be associated. Amongst others, typical activity roles comprise "locateObject", "displayResultsList" or "displayResultDetail". The "actrole" ontology in fact rather constitutes a tag library than a semantic network. However, it is determined to be independent from the application domain, press media here, and therefore from the "pmedia" ontology. Fig. 7 shows an extended communication description for an activity role of "locateObject".

```
…<ndw:communication xmlns:sns=http://sense-projekt.de/
      xmlns:act="http://sense-projekt.de/activity">
  <ndw:consumer>
    …<ndw:event type="itemSelect">
        <ndw:data type="sns:VideoObject"
          activity="act:locateObject"
          callbackfunction="widget.onVideoRecieved" />
    </ndw:event>…
  </ndw:consumer>
</ndw:communication>…
```

Fig. 7. Consuming an event in a locateObject activity role

The reason for setting up a definition-oriented, domain independent ontology is the introduction of the third and last new model component, the "composition" ontology, which builds upon the before mentioned "pmedia" and "actrole" ontologies on a superior level. That is, the "composition" ontology integrates "pmedia" and "actrole" and renders the accumulated knowledge executable without mixing up domain dependencies in the communication descriptions. Moreover, the "composition" ontology does no longer model communication in a widget-aligned context but from an overall dashboard point of view. It actually strives to improve the auto wiring of widgets by providing a comprehension of the composition and communication structure patterns. Such patterns may denote a search, an exploration or a comparison scenario etc.

For example, imagine the existence of two identically typed widgets, both of them consuming a sns:VideoObject and both of them describing their activity role as "displayResultDetail". This may imply that the end user most certainly tries to compare two detail views of the same object type. Since some aspects or rules of the "composition" ontology may suggest that one video detail view widget is usually sufficient on a dashboard, NewsDesk may deduce a comparison scenario. The detail view widgets may be altered to obtain an additional lock icon to interrupt the widget communication, which essentially provides a still view, see Fig. 8.

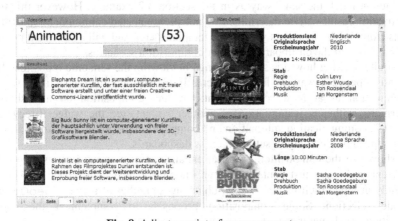

Fig. 8. Adjust user interface components

To continue the example in Fig. 8 and pinpoint another utilization of the "composition" ontology, imagine now that another search and result widgets have been added to the composition. Again keeping to one-to-one cardinalities between the different widget descriptions would rewire the communication to produce two separated chains of search, result and display or two distinct search scenarios, respectively.

The modeling of the "composition" ontology should be carried out by domain experts in dedicated RDFS resources or inference rules upon the "pmedia" and "actrole" ontologies. This also includes the specification of so-called fixed compositions that quite have some relevance in industry. They lower the notable learning curve coming along with free widget/dashboard user interaction and provide a fast time-to-market of new widget families.

3.3   Composition Proposal Generation

Sections 3.1 and 3.2 reported how existing communication skills of the NewsDesk-framework have been extended by modeling and employing different ontologies. This section deals with adding composition guidance features to the NewsDesk-framework that builds upon that knowledge. Composition guidance is an aspect becoming primarily relevant when the number of widgets in the templates area, see section 1.1, arrives at a critical amount. Actually, continuously raising the number of available widget templates will at some point decrease the chances of the end user to complement a dashboard composition efficiently.

A more intelligent approach to cope with larger widget template collections obviously consists of preselecting and proposing widgets that would fit in or supplement a current composition. Hence the NewsDesk-framework interface has been enhanced to provide a dedicated section in the left hand area of the workbench where generated composition proposals will be shown for the current dashboard. The proposal list will be grouped by the activity role, see section 3.2, of the offered widgets. A short guidance text based on the deduced scenario of the current composition will be added as well.

The proposal engine references the "composition" ontology and its inferior ontologies in much the same way as in the section 3.2 example. However this time, the evaluation result will be determined by not yet connected communication skills of widgets from the dashboard as well as the templates area and will also regard possible transformations of the dashboard to further composition scenarios.

It is quite exciting how this simple change in viewing the semantic repository facts apparently opened a way up from the actually aspired automation of inter-widget-communication to at least semi-automatic widget composition on a dashboard. Furthermore, with any instantiation of another widget, see the widget lifecycle in section 1.1, communication automation and composition proposals will stimulate each other and push productivity in setting up new dashboards.

To showcase the composition proposal enhancement in an example, suppose that the current dashboard just contains a venn diagram widget as a typical provider of differently grouped multimedia assets, publishing a number of `sns:VideoObject` on node selection. Some composition proposals to complement the current composition are shown in Fig. 9.

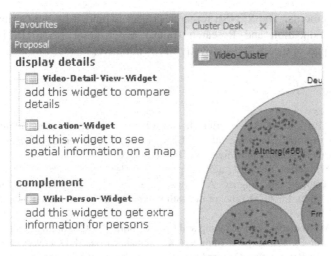

Fig. 9. Widget proposals for a venn widget publishing video

4   Conclusions and Outlook

The reported enhancements of the NewsDesk-framework affected both the object type and the event layer of the inter-widget-communication infrastructure. Several domain dependent and independent ontologies have been modeled to base the enhancements on semantic technologies. The framework has such a way been enabled to improve the ad hoc algorithm-based predictability of NewsDesk's inter-widget-communication due to an extended communication description of widgets as well as fact data from the semantic repository of SENSE. Example applications of the improvements include the evaluation of exchanged data graphs and the mapping of widget activity roles in a composition. The enhancements even allowed for an employment of the ad hoc wiring algorithm to not only bind communications but also visually propose widgets to complement a current composition.

However, the effort necessary to transfer the semantic annotations between the ontologies and the communication descriptions as well as the semantic repository facts and the web-browser was extensive. Consistently using persistent uniform resource identifiers with namespaces all along the way showed up to be imperative to ensure proper disambiguation of concepts.

Current work continues by evaluating the introduced enhancements from an end users point of view at remote sites of associated partners. The use case study comprises interactive exploration scenarios against large multimedia document collections, video yet, as being investigated by the SENSE-project. According to the results of the use case study, future work may take a closer look at ideas to either deduce scenario patterns from the history of user interaction or to implement cascading communication wiring where a widget gets allowed to commute itself from a consumer to a provider and vice versa.

Acknowledgements. The SENSE research project is funded by the German Federal Ministry of Education and Research (bmbf) under grant No. 01IS11025A and constitutes a part of the "KMU-Innovativ: IKT" initiative.

References

1. Wehner, P.: NewsDesk - Ein hochflexibles, Widget-basiertes Framework für Informationsportale. In: Proc. of the GeNeMe 2010 Conference - Gemeinschaften in Neuen Medien, Technische Universität Dresden (2010)
2. The SENSE project, http://sense-projekt.de
3. Sire, S., Paquier, M., Vagner, A., Bogaerts, J.: A Messaging API for Inter-Widgets Communication. In: ACM Proc. of the 18th International Conference on World Wide Web (2009)
4. Cáceres, M.: Widgets 1.0: Packaging and Configuration. W3C Working Draft 22 (2008)
5. Pietschmann, S., Radeck, C., Meißner, K.: Semantics-Based Discovery, Selection and Mediation for Presentation-Oriented Mashups. In: Proc. of the 5th International Workshop on Web APIs and Service Mashups, ACM ICPS (2011)
6. Krüger, R.: Kompositions- und Kommunikationsmodell für Web-Widgets. Master Thesis. Lehrstuhl für Multimediatechnik, Technische Universität Dresden (2009)
7. Chudnovskyy, O., Müller, S., Gaedke, M.: Proc. of the 4th International Workshop on Lightweight Integration on the Web, pp. 93–96 (2012)
8. Dachselt, R., Frisch, M., Weiland, M.: FacetZoom: a continuous multi-scale widget for navigating hierarchical metadata. In: Proc. of the SIGCHI Conference on Human Factors in Computing Systems, pp. 1353–1356 (2008)
9. Paulheim, H.: Ontology-based Modularization of User Interface. In: Proc. of the 1st ACM SIGCHI Symposium on Engineering Interactive Computing Systems. ACM (2009)
10. Kalfogulou, Y., Schorlemmer, M.: Ontology mapping: the state of the art. University of Southampton, The University of Edinburgh (2003)
11. Hyvönen, E., Mäkelä, E.: Semantic autocompletion. In: Mizoguchi, R., Shi, Z.-Z., Giunchiglia, F. (eds.) ASWC 2006. LNCS, vol. 4185, pp. 739–751. Springer, Heidelberg (2006)
12. Faison, T.: Event-based Programming: taking events to the limit. Apress, Berkeley (2006)
13. Hohpe, G., Woolf, B.: Enterprise Integration Patterns: Designing, Buliding and Deploying Messaging Solutions. Pearson Education, Boston (2003)
14. Netvibes/Universal Widget Technology, http://netvibes.com
15. Google Web Toolkit, http://google.com/ig, https://developers.google.com/web-toolkit
16. Hepper, S.: Java specification request JSR-286. Portal2.0 Documentation. SUN Inc. (2008)
17. IBM Mashup Center, http://ibm.com/developerworks/lotus/products/mashups
18. Oracle Metalink, https://supporthtml.oracle.com
19. W3C RDFa Core 1.1 - Syntax and processing rules for embedding RDF through attributes (2012), http://www.w3.org/TR/2012/REC-rdfa-core-20120607
20. International Press Telecommunications Council: The IPTC rNews Standard and the schema.org Initiative (2011), http://dev.iptc.org/rNews/, http://schema.rdfs.org

MultiMasher: A Visual Tool
for Multi-device Mashups

Maria Husmann, Michael Nebeling, and Moira C. Norrie

Institute of Information Systems, ETH Zurich CH-8092 Zurich, Switzerland
{husmann,nebeling,norrie}@inf.ethz.ch

Abstract. The proliferation of a wide range of computing devices from tablets to large displays has created many situations where we no longer use a single device only. Rather, multiple devices are commonly used together to achieve a task. However, there is still little tool support for such scenarios in which different devices need to be combined to control an interface. Our goal is to enable multiple devices to view and interact with multiple web resources in a coordinated manner based on our new idea of multi-device mashups. In this paper, we present a first, visual tool for mashing up devices to access web sites, and discuss how we addressed the challenges as well as interesting issues for further research.

1 Introduction

Nowadays, it is not uncommon for a person to possess multiple computing devices such as a mobile phone, tablet, desktop and laptop computer. At the same time, there are devices that are shared by groups of users such as interactive tabletops or large screens. For example, in a group meeting there could be a mobile phone for each participant, as well as tablets, a laptop computer for the person leading the discussion and a large screen which is used to share information with participants. In order to fully profit from such kinds of ecosystems, it is desirable to use the devices in combination, rather than using each device in isolation. However, this is currently often not possible because most applications are designed for a single device. Moreover, migration between devices requires additional mechanisms and infrastructure as well as modifications to the applications themselves [1].

While recent research in the area of distributed user interfaces has focused on developing frameworks and tools [2,3] to systematically support the distribution and migration of applications across devices, most solutions are usually limited to considering only a single application [4]. On the other hand, there is also a great body of research on web mashups that combine content, presentation and functionality from different web-based sources, with the aim of creating new applications from existing resources. However, research on mashups has so far focused on combining multiple existing web sites and services on a single device [5], whereas our goal is, not only to combine multiple web resources to create a new application, but also to support mashing up multiple devices so that

Q.Z. Sheng and J. Kjeldskov (Eds.): ICWE 2013 Workshops, LNCS 8295, pp. 27–38, 2013.

applications can be distributed between, and accessed from, different devices at the same time. We define a multi-device mashup as a web application that reuses content, presentation, and functionality provided by other web pages and that is distributed among multiple cooperating devices.

Our new idea of such multi-device mashups introduces a number of interesting challenges. Some of these have partly been addressed by the respective research communities in distributed interfaces and mashups, but they need to be combined, adapted and extended to support the design and development of mashup applications that involve multiple devices. For example, while the mashup community has come up with ways to introduce interactions between components that originate from different sources [6], these need to be expanded to support interactions across devices. Instead of each device accessing web content in isolation, in a multi-device mashup, access needs to be coordinated [4]. For example, a selection of a list item on one device may trigger an update both on the current and connected devices. Moreover, mashups traditionally assume a single device and user, but multi-device mashups may involve multiple devices as well as multiple users when devices are shared between users.

To address these challenges and experiment with possible solutions, we developed *MultiMasher*—a visual tool for rapidly designing multi-device mashups. We motivate the need for such a tool by presenting a scenario for a multi-device mashup in Section 2. In Section 3, we then give an overview of MultiMasher, followed by architecture and implementation details in Section 4. Section 5 picks up on some of the issues and discusses them in more detail, while Section 6 gives concluding remarks and an overview of opportunities for further research.

2   Scenario

To illustrate the usage of a multi-device mashup, we consider the following scenario also depicted in Fig. 1: two users, Alex and Bill, are planning a mountain biking trip together at home in their living room. They need to decide on a route and find out how they can get to the starting point by train. Alex has a smartphone, Bill a tablet, and additionally they share their TV for a larger display area. Alex and Bill have split their tasks in the following way: Bill is browsing a route repository such as SwitzerlandMobility[1] and Alex is querying the connections on the web site of the local railway company. When Bill inspects a route, the starting point of the route is sent to Alex' smartphone where she can browse the available railway connections, while Bill checks whether the route suits their criteria for length, difficulty, and scenery. Some starting places may take too long to reach, others may require too many changes of trains, which is a hassle when travelling with bikes. The resulting railway connections of Alex' query are displayed on her smartphone in a list. She can select a connection for which the details are displayed on the large screen, where also Bill's information about the suggested route are visible. If Alex enters a new time on her mobile phone or selects a new connection, the detailed view is updated also on the large screen.

---

[1] http://www.mountainbikeland.ch

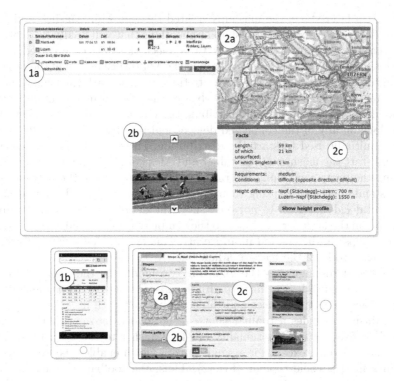

Fig. 1. A scenario using a shared screen, tablet and mobile phone for planning a mountain biking trip. 1a and 1b are elements from the railway website. 1b displays a list of possible railway journeys to a given destination. Selecting a journey updates the detail view in 1a. 2a to 2c are taken from the route repository website. Interaction with one of these elements on the tablet also updates the shared screen and vice versa. The destination for the query in 1b is taken from 2c.

Together they discuss whether the currently visible trip is a good match. During the discussion, they can also interact with the content on the large screen. If they are not happy with the current trip, Bill starts looking for another route.

3 MultiMasher

As a first step, we created MultiMasher, a visual tool that allows mashing up devices for accessing web content of multiple sources. The goal is to build a tool designed to facilitate the quick and easy creation of multi-device mashups, such as the one described in the scenario, through a direct manipulation interface, without the need for modelling or programming. MultiMasher is aimed at both developers and non-technical end-users to assist them in the rapid prototyping of distributed interfaces and development of multi-device mashups. With MultiMasher, users should be able to, not only create multi-device mashups for the devices at hand, but also decide how they should adapt to a different set of devices. At a later stage, the mashups created through MultiMasher could also be used as a basis for complex mashup applications that will finally be deployed.

To create a mashup, a user needs to connect the devices involved to the MultiMasher server. This is done by loading the MultiMasher tool in the browser, which automatically connects the device to the server. More devices can be added at any time. Users can then load the web sites that they want to mashup, select UI elements on that web site, and distribute these to the connected devices. This can be done on any of the connected devices and is not restricted to the device that was initially used to start the distribution. For example, in our scenario, Bill could start the mashup on his tablet and Alex could join on her smartphone designing the parts concerning the railway information. Also, the user can save mashups and continue adapting them at a later point in time. In our scenario, Alex could decide later on to not only show the details of the selected railway connection on the large screen, but also the complete list of available connections. Thus, mashups can be created in an iterative manner in that existing mashups can be reused to form the basis of a new one.

MultiMasher distinguishes the following two modes: In the *design mode*,the users create a multi-device mashup. In the *distribution mode*, a multi-device mashup is active on the devices and the users interact with it.

MultiMasher includes a toolbar that can be loaded into existing web sites. The toolbar exposes the functionality of MultiMasher to the user. By default, the toolbar is hidden except for a small button which enables the design mode and slides in the whole toolbar (Fig. 2). Thus, the toolbar does not take up any screen space, which is rare on some devices, when it is not in use. When in design mode, the user can select UI elements and send them to connected devices, where the elements will be mashed up with the content that has been sent to the device previously.

Fig. 2. The MultiMasher toolbar. The name of the local client is displayed on the right. The clients available for a mashup can be selected from a list (centre). On the left, the distribution mode can be selected.

When a user is creating a mashup, the present client devices are offered for selection (Fig. 2). In a list, each device is a represented visually. For every device, a name is generated automatically, making use of the operating system and browser information. This name can be changed by the user to a name of their own choice. Additionally, there is a visual representation of the available screen space in pixels for each device, which helps the users to map the physical devices to the representations. We imagine that this could also be done in other ways, e.g. by mapping each device to a colour which would be displayed on the actual device and in the representation. Each device can be selected for participation in the mashup. The list of devices is updated as devices join or leave. When a new device joins, it can easily be added to an ongoing mashup. Therefore, it is not required that all devices are present when the user starts the process of creating a mashup. The toolbar also provides an undo functionality that causes the device to leave the current distribution and restores the original web site.

When the design mode is activated through the toolbar, the user can select UI elements by clicking on them or touching them on touch devices. This direct selection method should make it easy also for non-technical users to choose elements, as they do not need to know the underlying structure of the web site. MultiMasher provides visual feedback for selected elements (Fig. 3) by highlighting them. Any number of elements can be selected simultaneously. When at least one element is selected, the user can send it to connected devices, by pressing the distribute button in the toolbar. The selected elements will then be sent to the client devices selected in the device list. MultiMasher supports two modes for distributing UI elements. The first mode, move, sends the element to the target devices without keeping a copy on the source device. In contrast, the second, copy, sends the UI element to the target devices and retains a copy on the source device. In our scenario, the details for a railway journey have been moved from the smartphone to the large screen. They are no longer visible on the smartphone, but only on the large screen. The gallery and the facts for the mountain biking trip have been copied from the tablet to the large screen. They are present on both devices.

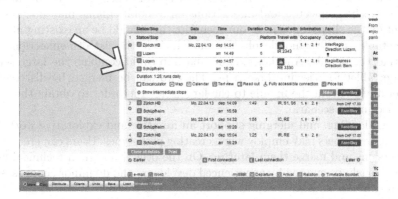

Fig. 3. Selecting UI elements in distribution mode. Coloured outlines provide visual feedback for selected elements.

One of the biggest challenges in MultiMasher was to synchronize interactions of a web site as the UI elements are distributed across devices. MultiMasher provides a first partial solution to synchronizing state by replaying interactions on each device. For example, if a menu allows the selection of content, the menu and the content area can be on two separate devices, thus, leveraging the differing capabilities of each device, such as input modality and display size. Selecting a menu item on the first device will update the content on the second device. In our scenario, selecting a railway connection on the mobile phone, will update the corresponding detail view on the large screen. UI elements that are copied on multiple devices are also synchronized by default. For example in the scenario, a photo gallery is copied on the shared screen as well as on the tablet. As the two are synchronized, when the user navigates through the photos on the tablet, the gallery on the shared screen updates also.

In the future, MultiMasher should also allow users to define interactions across web sites by connecting elements from multiple sources. In our scenario, the starting location of the bike tour is connected to the destination input in the timetable of the railway company. As the user on the tablet navigates among possible bike tours, the user on the mobile phone gets an updated list of connections to the destination and can change query parameters such as the date, which are independent of the bike tour.

MultiMasher allows the user to save created mashups and load them at a later point in time. Once a mashup is loaded, it can be adapted by adding new devices, redistributing elements or adding new web sources. For example, in our scenario, a third user, Chris, could show up with his tablet and would like to search bike tours in parallel to Bill. His device would need to be integrated. Chris may also know another good source for bike tours and would like to show information from this new source on the large screen to Alex and Bill.

Also, multiple mashups can be merged. For example, if two mobile phones are participating in one mashup and a tablet is connected to a shared screen in another mashup, these two mashups can be combined. As a result, all four devices will be connected and interactions on a mobile phone may now update content on the shared screen. In our scenario, there could be an existing mashup of timetables on two mobile phones, one showing the list of connections and the other the details. Another existing mashup could combine the large screen and the tablet for viewing bike trips. The two can be merged by distributing the detail view from the mobile to the large screen in order to obtain the setup described in the scenario.

Saving, loading, and merging support an iterative and explorative work process that developers may employ when creating prototypes. Users can create parallel versions and merge them later on. On the other hand, non-technical users can load mashups created by experienced developers and do minor changes, such as adding a new device.

Saved multi-device mashups can be previewed in MultiMasher before being loaded on the connected devices. The preview tool (Fig. 4) lists all stored mashups that include the given device. When a mashup is selected, a preview of all devices participating is displayed. Each device is presented in a miniature version. Thus, the user can quickly see what devices are involved and how the content is distributed across the devices.

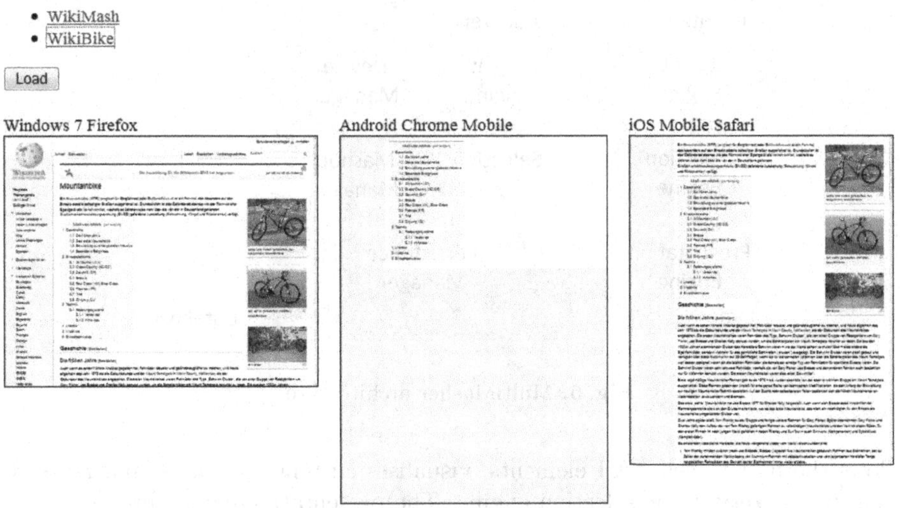

- WikiMash
- WikiBike

Load

Windows 7 Firefox	Android Chrome Mobile	iOS Mobile Safari

Fig. 4. Previewing mashups in MultiMasher. The devices are scaled according to available space in pixels.

4   Architecture and Implementation

In this section, we describe the overall architecture of MultiMasher and then give implementation details. Figure 5 illustrates the client-server architecture of MultiMasher. The server coordinates the communication between client devices and stores created mashups. The device manager informs clients of devices joining or leaving. It extracts operating system and browser information, which are used for device name generation.

The persistence manager stores mashups and device information in a database and retrieves them when an existing mashup is requested for loading. When a mashup is active, the server-side event manager receives events from the client-side event managers and forwards them to all clients involved in the mashup. During the process of creation and adaptation of a mashup, the selection engine in the server receives selections of UI elements from source clients that need to be displayed on target clients in the mashup. The selection engine merges these selections with previous selections for the target clients and notifies the presentation engine in the clients about the updates. The mashup manager handles the creation and adaptation of mashups. It receives changes to mashups from the selection engine and integrates them into the existing mashups. The mashup manager handles the merging of multiple mashups and propagates changes in mashups to the persistence manager. On the client side, an event engine forwards local events to the server and replays remote events locally. With this mechanism, the event engine ensures a consistent state across multiple devices. When a user interacts on source devices, the interaction triggers an event, which will be replayed on all devices in the mashup, thus simulating the interaction and causing the same actions on all devices. The selection engine on the client side

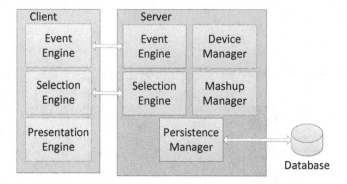

Fig. 5. MultiMasher architecture

allows the user to select UI elements, visualises current selections, and reports them to the server-side selection engine. The presentation engine processes selections from the server and adapts the UI so that only the requested elements are visible. All clients load a full version of the involved web site, but only show the selected elements and their parents. All elements that are not needed are simply hidden. In the future, the presentation engine could be extended with layout information for the visible elements.

The MultiMasher server is implemented in jQuery[2] on top of the Node.js[3] platform. Persistence is achieved with a MySQL database where information about mashups and client devices is stored. As the server needs to propagate events from a source device to all other devices in a mashup, a mechanism for server push is needed. We decided to use the socket.io[4] library which is integrated as a Javascript library on the client side and as a Node.js module on the server side. Socket.io transparently provides a server push mechanism using websockets, if supported by the browser, otherwise it employs fallback mechanisms such as longpolling. Socket.io informs the device manager when a device disconnects and, thus, the device manager is constantly aware of the connected devices.

On the client side, MultiMasher consists of a Javascript library that can be integrated into existing web sites. The integration can be achieved by modifying the HTML file of the web site or via a browser plugin such as Greasemonkey[5].

When the MultiMasher library is loaded into a web site, it injects a toolbar which allows the activation of a design mode in which UI elements can be selected. When in design mode, a transparent overlay is added over the web site. Thus all clicks or touches on the UI are captured by the overlay. This mechanism prevents clicks from activating actions on the web sites, such as following a link. From the click location on the overlay, we calculate the underlying UI element with the elementFromPoint Javascript function on the document node.

---

[2] http://www.jquery.com/
[3] http://www.nodejs.org
[4] http://www.socket.io
[5] http://www.greasespot.net

As we use id attributes for identification, we find the closest parent (including the selected element) in the DOM tree that has an id attribute using jQuery.

When a user designs a mashup, the client sends a list of devices and the selected UI elements to the server. The server notifies the devices of their participation in the mashup and propagates the selection. All elements that are hidden by MultiMasher are marked by a class, so the system can distinguish between elements that have been hidden by the web site itself and those by MultiMasher. Upon activation of a mashup, MultiMasher adds event listeners for DOM events such as click or change. When an event is detected, it is sent to the server, which forwards it to all devices participating in the mashup. When an event is received from the server, it is replayed in all other clients, thus causing the same reaction on all devices. As UI elements are only hidden but not removed from the DOM, events on them can still be triggered. A flag distinguishes local events from remote events. Thus, endless event cycles can be prevented by only sending local events to the server. The approach of replaying events is very simple, but it also has some limitations. In cases where an event triggers an update to the original web server of the source, the update would be executed multiple times. For events that only cause queries, the approach works fine.

5 Discussion and Related Work

Our work on MultiMasher builds on two, so far isolated, research streams on distributed interfaces and web mashups. Existing research in the area of distributed user interfaces has focused on using one existing interface and distributing it across multiple devices. On the other hand, research on mashups has focused on combining multiple existing web sites and services, but on a single device. We aim at the rapid creation of distributed interfaces by reusing parts from existing web sites, thus creating mashups that can span more than one device.

Recently, there has been increased interest in the systematic development of distributed user interfaces [4]. Many of the proposed approaches build from the research on model-based user interfaces that require a specific set of models organised into different abstraction layers [7] and user interface description languages. For example, the work presented in [3] builds on top of the UsiXML langugage and also the MARIA XML language has recently been extended to support distributed user interfaces [1]. When it comes to the implementation, the proposed solutions either require special cross-platform, peer-to-peer toolkits for general graphical user interfaces [8] or use HTML proxy-based techniques in the case of web applications [9]. Our goal was to provide a flexible tool that does not require specific models, languages and protocols and that is compatible with common web interface implementations based on HTML, CSS and JavaScript.

Common to most mashup tools such as Potluck [10], d.mix [11], Firecrow [12] and DashMash [13] is that they have been designed with non-technical end-users in mind. The general goal is to simplify the creation of web mashups based on visual tools for data aggregation and integration, graphical extraction and composition of various web resources and example code. Some of the latest tools can even directly assist end-users in the mashup development process. For example, DashMash [13] can recommend other services that could also be useful in the current design context. However, with most of these approaches, it is not clear who defines and configures available services and how they can scale to supporting the development of complex web applications. An exception is MashArt [5,6] which is a platform designed to support web information system development in the form of mashups. MashArt targets advanced users with the goal of enabling them to create their own applications through the composition of interface, application and data components. The focus is on supporting the integration of existing web services and presentation components using an event-based paradigm so that components can react to events of other components.

While the component-based approach is generally promising, supporting reuse of web components that were originally created for different web sites is a complex issue for which different techniques have been proposed. For example, [14] presents a paradigm they call distributed orchestration which allows integrating web services and interfaces based on workflow and business process modelling techniques. While this approach enables inter-component communication, it is unclear how it supports mashup applications created for multiple users. In contrast, [15] presents an approach that focuses on adding awareness widgets to applications, which could in principle provide a basis for multiuser-aware mashups, but only considers one application and device. We regard our work on Multi-Masher as a combination and extension of these approaches in that we support reuse of different web application components and allow also non-experienced users to distribute them across devices.

In this paper, we have presented a first implementation of MultiMasher that still has some limitations and will be the subject of both technical and user evaluations in the future. For example, we have tested MultiMasher on several existing web sites such as Wikipedia and achieved good results, but there are still open issues when the propagation of interactions generates multiple updates to a database, such as when a comment is posted using one device and the submit button also triggered on all connected devices, or when a web site requires user authentication and the mashup is in fact to be used by more than one user. For example, Twitter and Facebook could not be easily integrated in a mashup with MultiMasher. In contrast, we have achieved good results with web sites which present content without requiring an authenticated user, such as blogs, news, and reviews web sites.

At this stage, MultiMasher only allows users to design mashups for devices that are actually connected to the system at design time. We are currently working on a more flexible solution that allows designing for an unknown set of devices at run-time. For example, a mashup could initially be designed for two tablets. If, at a later stage, a mobile phone is used instead of one of the tablets, the phone could take over that role in the mashup. MultiMasher could analyse the available devices and their characteristics and offer this information to the user. In addition to allowing users to rearrange the mashup elements for the new device, the system could automatically scale the mashup according to the difference in screen size, or otherwise adjust the layout, to facilitate the adaptation to different device capabilities and input modalities.

Moreover, changes may not only occur in the set of devices, but also in the web sites involved in the mashups. Therefore, additional mechanisms are required for MultiMasher to handle changes in the structure of web sites. Similar to other solutions, our selection method is currently restricted to web page elements that have an id attribute. The solution presented in [2] generates id attributes where they are missing. While this technique could be added to our approach, it is insufficient to handle all possible changes, e.g. when an element is moved within the internal DOM structure, or completely removed from the web site. In a related project, we are working on new robust implementation strategies that MultiMasher could build on in the future. In addition, if fully automatic solutions are not possible, the user could be informed and asked for suggestions. As an alternative, we are currently experimenting with a new selection method allowing users to select a region in the rendered web interface by spanning a rectangle with the mouse or finger. This region is then distributed and handled as a new window showing only the selected parts of the web site. However, as some elements may only be visible under certain viewing conditions, this method also needs to take into account that web sites may render differently on different devices, which requires further work.

6 Conclusion and Future Work

Based on a common scenario in which multi-device mashups would be desirable, we have presented our ongoing work on MultiMasher, a visual tool for rapidly developing multi-device mashups. MultiMasher provides an easy selection mechanism for distributing and mashing up UI elements, and is suited for an iterative design process as it implements first mechanisms for saving, loading, and merging multi-device mashups.

MultiMasher already provides much of the required functionality for quick and easy creation of mashups spanning multiple devices. However, at this stage, the resulting applications are not fully suited for a production environment. For example, as the main focus was on rapid prototyping of distributed mashups, we are currently relying on relatively simple mechanisms for the distribution of interfaces and the propagation of interactions. Moreover, privacy and security issues were out of scope. Some of the challenges could be addressed by introducing the notion of users in different roles and providing additional infrastructure. For example, a proxy that acts as the single client to the original web source could be used. However, rather than providing a generic and complex proxy-based solution that can handle all different kinds of scenarios, our goal for future versions of MultiMasher is that tailored proxy clients would be generated as part of the deployment of a multi-device mashup.

Another direction we can see for the future is improving the support for both experienced developers of distributed interfaces and non-technical end-users. This includes building new mechanisms into MultiMasher to support the evaluation of mashups in both static and dynamic multi-device environments.

For example, a user testing mode could be added that logs the interaction of the user with the mashup. As most user interactions are already tracked and sent to the server to keep the distributed interface synchronised, interactions could be recorded and later replayed for further analysis of the users' activities as well as for user performance evaluations in distributed, multi-device scenarios.

References

1. Paternò, F., Santoro, C., Spano, L.D.: Maria: A universal, declarative, multiple abstraction-level language for service-oriented applications in ubiquitous environments. TOCHI 16(4), 19:1–19:30 (2009)
2. Ghiani, G., Paternò, F., Santoro, C.: On-Demand Cross-Device Interface Components Migration. In: Proc. MobileHCI (2010)
3. Melchior, J., Vanderdonckt, J., Roy, P.V.: A Model-Based Approach for Distributed User Interfaces. In: Proc. EICS (2011)
4. Paternò, F., Santoro, C.: A Logical Framework for Multi-Device User Interfaces. In: Proc. EICS (2012)
5. Daniel, F., Casati, F., Benatallah, B., Shan, M.-C.: Hosted Universal Composition: Models, Languages and Infrastructure in mashArt. In: Laender, A.H.F., Castano, S., Dayal, U., Casati, F., de Oliveira, J.P.M. (eds.) ER 2009. LNCS, vol. 5829, pp. 428–443. Springer, Heidelberg (2009)
6. Daniel, F., Matera, M.: Turning Web Applications into Mashup Components: Issues, Models, and Solutions. In: Gaedke, M., Grossniklaus, M., Díaz, O. (eds.) ICWE 2009. LNCS, vol. 5648, pp. 45–60. Springer, Heidelberg (2009)
7. Calvary, G., Coutaz, J., Thevenin, D., Limbourg, Q., Bouillon, L., Vanderdonckt, J.: A Unifying Reference Framework for Multi-Target User Interfaces. IWC 15 (2003)
8. Melchior, J., Grolaux, D., Vanderdonckt, J., Roy, P.V.: A Toolkit for Peer-to-Peer Distributed User Interfaces: Concepts, Implementation, and Applications. In: Proc. EICS (2009)
9. Ghiani, G., Paternò, F., Santoro, C.: Push and Pull of Web User Interfaces in Multi-Device Environments. In: Proc. AVI (2012)
10. Huynh, D.F., Miller, R.C., Karger, D.R.: Potluck: Data Mash-up Tool for Casual Users. In: Aberer, K., et al. (eds.) ISWC/ASWC 2007. LNCS, vol. 4825, pp. 239–252. Springer, Heidelberg (2007)
11. Hartmann, B., Wu, L., Collins, K., Klemmer, S.R.: Programming by a Sample: Rapidly Creating Web Applications with d.mix. In: Proc. UIST (2007)
12. Maras, J., Štula, M., Carlson, J.: Reusing Web Application User-Interface Controls. In: Auer, S., Díaz, O., Papadopoulos, G.A. (eds.) ICWE 2011. LNCS, vol. 6757, pp. 228–242. Springer, Heidelberg (2011)
13. Cappiello, C., Matera, M., Picozzi, M., Sprega, G., Barbagallo, D., Francalanci, C.: DashMash: A Mashup Environment for End User Development. In: Auer, S., Díaz, O., Papadopoulos, G.A. (eds.) ICWE 2011. LNCS, vol. 6757, pp. 152–166. Springer, Heidelberg (2011)
14. Daniel, F., Soi, S., Tranquillini, S., Casati, F., Heng, C., Yan, L.: Distributed Orchestration of User Interfaces. Inf. Syst. 37(6), 539–556 (2012)
15. Heinrich, M., Grüneberger, F.J., Springer, T., Gaedke, M.: Reusable Awareness Widgets for Collaborative Web Applications - A Non-invasive Approach. In: Brambilla, M., Tokuda, T., Tolksdorf, R. (eds.) ICWE 2012. LNCS, vol. 7387, pp. 1–15. Springer, Heidelberg (2012)

From a Simple Flow to Social Applications

Juan Jara, Florian Daniel, Fabio Casati, and Maurizio Marchese

University of Trento, Via Sommarive 5, 38123 Povo (TN), Italy
{juan.jara,daniel,casati,marchese}@disi.unitn.it

Abstract. Currently, there are a lot of people trying to leverage on the success of social networks by implementing social applications. However, implementing social applications is complex, due to the requirements and constraints put by the social networks to protect their data. In this work we present Simple Flow, a tool that simplifies the creation of social applications. Simple Flow proposes a processes-based approach to the design and execution of social applications. Simple Flow targets end-users and programmers with no experience in programming for social networks, giving them the possibility to design processes by concatenating social network actions (like post a message or comment a photo). For the execution of the designed processes Simple Flow interconnects, at runtime, template web pages (one page per action) according to the process design defined previously. These templates abstract the complexities of the interactions with social networks.

Keywords: Social Applications, Design Tools and Techniques, Component-based development.

1 Introduction and Motivation

Social applications are applications that use a social network infrastructure to reach more users and disseminate themselves. These social applications have different goals like meeting new people, sharing experiences, making professional contacts, getting recommendations, advertising products among other activities.

There are a lot of people trying to leverage on the success of social networks by implementing social applications. However, programming social applications has some particular aspects that are different from generic web applications, for example:

- The access to social network resources is usually done through restful APIs (application programming interface), and already learning how to get the desired data from a resource becomes a time consuming task;
- The application authentication, which is the process in which social applications have to authenticate themselves with the social network with which they want to interact; and
- The user permission system. In social networks, usually, only a small portion of the data is public. In order to get the rest of the data, the social applications need to get specific user-permissions, which depend on the data that the applications want to access.

Q.Z. Sheng and J. Kjeldskov (Eds.): ICWE 2013 Workshops, LNCS 8295, pp. 39–50, 2013.
© Springer International Publishing Switzerland 2013

These new aspects increase the complexity required to program social applications and usually discourage the people that approach it.

With our work we aim at reducing the complexity of programming social applications. We propose Simple Flow, a tool that facilitates the way social applications are designed and executed. Simple Flow has a design phase, where users use a process-based approach to design social applications, and an execution phase, in which users can execute the processes from the design phase.

In the design phase, we provide a method that makes it easier to interact with the desired resources in a social network. We abstract the social network API model into **action patterns** (like select user, create a post or upload a photo) that users can combine into processes that model a social application and express its logic.

In the execution phase, we provide a set of **template web pages** (one template per action pattern) that can be linked among each other based on the designed process from the design phase. Each template comes with a set of user interface elements related to the action pattern it represents and also internally handles the authentication process and the user permissions, abstracting from the user the complexity of these procedures.

With Simple Flow we do not only target programmers with no experience in social applications, we want to enable the widest possible set of people to create social applications. For this reason, an additional goal of our work is to grant the ability to create social applications to a set of people that goes beyond professional programmers. It will be part of our future work therefore to identify how far we can go in terms of simplifying this "programming" and in terms of lowering the skill levels required to design social applications.

The remainder of this paper is organized as follows. In the next section we present the context analysis. In Section 3, we explain our social application model. In Section 4, we describe our proposal. In Section 5, we introduce some related work. In Section 6 we present the discussion and the future work.

2   Context Analysis

In this section we explain who needs to create social applications and what types of social applications are the most needed or requested.

2.1   Who Needs to Implement Social Applications?

To learn about the needs of social applications, we searched and analyzed the social applications requests in three application-development outsourcing websites: Freelancer (http://www.freelancer.com/), oDesk (https://www.odesk.com/) and vWorker (http://www.vworker.com/). Most of the requests are related to the creation and management of contests which aim at motivating user participation and brand advertisement. We also found out that there is a constant demand by marketing people for analytic tools that measure the impact of actions in social networks. These tools should be able to compute a wide range of metrics, which are calculated using metrics like the number of posts, comments and likes (or a combination of thereof).

From our own work as researchers we know, for example, that there is a constant need of recruiting people for participating in experiments and user studies. It would be useful to have an application that automatically disseminates information about these experiments and helps recruiting people. There is also the need to create applications for crowdsourcing content creation and content description, all related to a specific topic.

2.2 Classification of Most Required Applications

We can classify the identified needs into the following categories of social applications:

- **Event advertisement:** These applications allow users to define an invitation message and schedule it for periodical dissemination through social networks.
- **Guided content creation:** These applications guide users through the content creation process, e.g., uploading a photo to a specific album to participate in a photo contest, adding information related to the context of a photo, etc.
- **Voting:** These applications present the user with a list of objects and ask him/her to select one or more of them, e.g., asking a user to select from a list of videos the one that he/she thinks is the funniest.
- **Contest drawing generator:** These applications select one or more objects from a list following a specific criterion, e.g., from a list of message posts select the one with most comments.
- **Targeted dissemination:** These applications send, to a selected number of friends, a user defined request, e.g., selecting three friends and asking them to comment a photo.
- **Simple analytics:** These applications get periodically information about specified objects (e.g. albums, photos, posts). This information can be used later for impact analysis, e.g., getting daily the number of likes or number of comments for a photo.

Some of these simple applications can be combined to create more complex ones, e.g., the guided content creation and targeted dissemination can be combined to create an application for crowdsourcing content creation or content annotation among a user's friends.

3 The Social Application Model

The first step for facilitating the programming of social applications is to transform the restful API model to a more familiar model. For this we abstract the typical social networking APIs to action patterns (like select user, create a post or upload a photo). Then we provide a method to combine the action patterns into processes that represent the models of social applications.

3.1 The Action Conceptual Model

We select from social networks the objects that we consider most relevant, e.g., users, posts, photos, comments, etc. Then, for each object, we add their available actions, e.g., upload, comment, like. The result is a set of patterns that represent the actions available to social network users, e.g., select a friend, comment a photo, create a post, etc. From now on, we will refer to action patterns just as actions. The actions can require an input, may produce an output and have some options that slightly modify their standard behavior. All of the previous elements (actions, inputs, outputs, options, etc.) define our action conceptual model. Figure 1 shows the model and the how its elements are related.

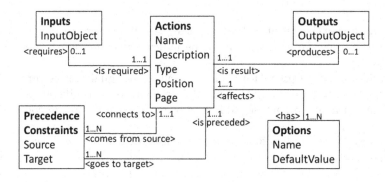

Fig. 1. Simple Flow action conceptual model

We describe the entities in Figure 1 as following:

- **Actions:** are the action patterns that represent a single step in our process model (which is explained in the next section), e.g., *upload photo to wall, like a post, comment an album.* We defined this list by combining the available actions exposed by social networks through their APIs and, by analyzing the interactions in the applications described in the previous section.
- **Precedence Constraints:** represent the relation between actions. The precedence defines what actions can be used in each step of a process during the design of the process.
- **Options:** represent action attributes that are used to modify the standard behavior of its related action. Taking as an example the action *comment an album,* one of the options for this action defines who creates the comment; if it will be the process designer, the user executing the process, or both.
- **Outputs:** represent the data produced by an action after its execution. For example, the *comment an album* action produces a comment object, and the *upload photo to wall* action has a photo object as result.
- **Inputs:** represent the data requirements of an action. For example, the *comment a photo* action requires a photo object that is the target of the

comment. The input object for an action can be chosen from one of the produced outputs by other actions or from objects that already exist in social networks.

The action conceptual model helps us to formally represent and design processes for social networks.

3.2   The Process Model

We combine the actions and the precedence constraints from the conceptual model to produce a directed graph that we call the *action graph*. The actions are connected according to the data navigation structures of social networks (with a major influence from Facebook). The *action graph* is the core of our proposal and is used to guide the user during the design of processes. The *action graph* is our approach to relieve end-users from most of the complexities of designing processes for social networks.

A process is designed by concatenating the nodes from the *action graph*, following the possible paths from one node to another. The first step of a process has to be always the start node of the *action graph* and the last step the end node. Only connected nodes can be executed consecutively in a process.

Figure 2 shows the conceptual representation of the *action graph* during the design of a process. The highlighted node (with a big arrow on top) represents the current selected action. The nodes pointed by the current node represent the actions that can be executed after the selected action. The start node has the "Login" label and the end node has the "End" label.

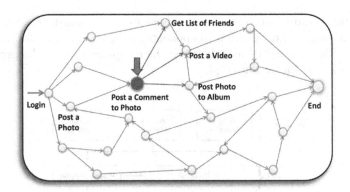

Fig. 2. Conceptual representation of the *action graph*

In the next section we explain how end-users can design and execute processes using the concepts presented in this section.

4   Design and Execution of Social Applications

To test our process model, we propose Simple Flow, a tool for the design and the execution of social applications. Simple Flow uses a process approach to define social applications, that is, social applications are represented as simple processes that run over social networks. Simple Flow has two phases:

- **The design phase:** where users create and define their processes, their logic and what data from social networks it uses and affects.
- **The execution phase:** where users select and run a process; here, Simple Flow runs a process by concatenating predefined template web pages following the process design that was created in the design phase.

We implemented a first version of the design phase and we are working on the implementation of the execution phase. In the following sections we explain in details both phases, for the design phase we show an example of the working UI (user interface) and for the execution phase we sketch an example of how it will work.

4.1   The Design Phase

The design phase is where users define and create the processes that represent the social applications they want to create. The core of the design phase is the action graph, which is our approach to lift from end-users the complexity related to learning how to interact with the social network resources through the social networks APIs.

Design Phase Components. The components of the design phase are classified as data, logic or presentation components as shown in Figure 3. The arrows indicate the dependency relation between the components, e.g., the process designer depends on the action graph.

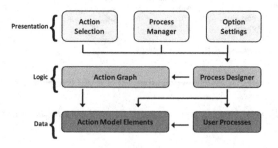

Fig. 3. Components of the design phase

The data layer stores the elements of the action conceptual model and also the user defined processes. The components of this layer are explained as following:

- The *Action Model Elements* contain the instances of the entities of the action conceptual model that was explained in Section 3.1.
- The *User Processes* represent the set of processes already defined by the users by concatenating sequentially actions and that are ready to be executed.

The components of the logic layer are responsible for associating to each action its corresponding elements (inputs, outputs and options) and to also logically relate the actions using the action graph. The components of this layer are explained as following:

- The *Action Graph* represents the navigation structure between actions, it is explained in Section 3.2.
- The *Process Designer* is the component that connects all the elements of an action. When an action is added to a process, it associates to the added action all its corresponding elements like input, output and options. Furthermore, using the action graph, it prepares the actions that could be executed in the next step.

The components of the presentation layer manage how the information is presented to the users. The components of this layer are explained as following:

- The *Process Manager* shows all the steps of the designed process, the input and the output of each action.
- The *Action Selection* shows the list of actions that can be executed after the last selected action.
- The *Option Settings* presents what options the last selected action has available.

Designing a Social Application. Figure 4 shows a view of the UI during the design of a process. Each component of the presentation layer assists the user in the design of a process.

The *Process Manager* shows the process that is being designed and is represented by the table in the "Flow Actions" column. The first column of the table indicates the step of the process associated to the action and the last column indicates the output that will be produced after the execution of the action, this data can later be used as an input for another action. If an action requires an input, its description will contain the following string: "[???]". The step that is currently being designed in Figure 4 is the third one: Comment a Photo.

The *Action Selection* presents to the user a list of actions that can be executed after the current action (the list is contextual to the last action added to the flow). In Figure 4 is represented by the "Available Actions" column. If the user selects an action from the list, that action becomes the current action, which would be the fourth step of the designed process.

The *Option Settings* presents to the user a set of options associated to the current action. In Figure 4 is represented by the "Action Options" column. When

Fig. 4. UI of the design phase during the design of a process

the user selects an action, the options for that action are loaded with default values that express to some degree the intended behavior of the action. The user can change these options to modify the action behavior to meet specific needs.

Figure 5 shows a finished process model. This process represents a social application for crowdsourcing photos that have annotated context information in the form of comments. The goal of this application is to collect photos from several users and to attach to each photo specific data related to the context of the photo. A sketch example of the application during its execution can be seen in Figure 6.

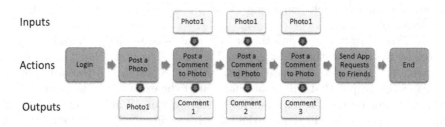

Fig. 5. A process model that represents a social application

The designed processes can be deployed for execution by their owners as a part of Simple Flow. Each process can be disseminated by sharing its link and can be executed by one or more people.

4.2   The Execution Phase

The execution phase is where Simple Flow runs the processes designed in the previous phase. The main element of the execution phase is the action page.

The action page is a template web page that represents an action from the action conceptual model. Each page is prepared to manage all the elements that are associated to the action it refers to (input, output and options). The action page facilitates the creation of social applications by:

- **Implementing a UI for interacting with a social network API:** an action page is related to a specific action, which again is based on one of the social network APIs; therefore, the action page implements a UI for a social network API.
- **Automatically authenticating the application with the social network:** each action page manages internally the authentication process of the Simple Flow application with the social networks and uses these credentials to interact with social networks when users run processes.
- **Managing user permissions:** Simple Flow includes all the required user permissions by the set of actions that it provides; therefore, when users register the Simple Flow application, they will be asked to give the necessary permissions to run any designed process.

The execution phase runs a process by concatenating action pages following the process model. The execution phase starts when a user clicks the link associated to a process. At the beginning of the phase, Simple Flow reads the process information and redirects the user to the first action page and makes this page point to the next action page defined in the process model.

During the rest of the execution phase, for each step of the process, Simple Flow:

- gets the input required by the action,
- prepares the page according to the action options, and
- makes the page point to the next action page.

When the user finishes carrying out the requested action, he/she is redirected to the next page where the cycle starts again. Figure 6 shows a mockup of the action pages for the process model from Figure 5 during the execution phase.

Simple Flow also facilitates the creation of social applications by allowing its users to skip the steps related to registering the social application in the social network and then installing it in a web server (this will be helpful especially for users that only want to implement a few processes).

5   Related Work

In this section we present the works related to end-user development, we group them according to their proposed approach to the creation of applications.

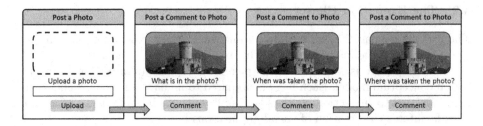

Fig. 6. Execution of the process from Figure 5, steps 2 to 5

5.1 Using Processes

First, we present the IFTTT (If this then that) project [1], which allows users to define simple ECA (Event - Condition - Action) rules over social networks. Users create rules by combining triggers (e.g., an upload of a photo, a post of a message) and actions (e.g., tweeting a message, commenting a photo) with their associated channels (e.g., Twitter, Facebook). The simplicity of IFTTT is what inspired us to build our tool and we think that this is how applications should be designed, specially by end users. IFTTT allows the design of 1-step processes that are executed when their associated trigger is fired. The processes designed with our tool can have more than one step and, generally, are executed directly by users. There is also, Atooma [2], which is an IFTTT like approach for smartphones. The difference with IFTTT is that users can add several triggers for the If this condition and also do several actions for the then that part.

Then we have the BPM4People project [3], which extends BPMN (business process modeling notation) with new task types that represent the unstructured social interactions between the process stakeholders (e.g., social posting, commenting, voting, invitation to activity). Both, the BPM4People project and our tool, propose the design of applications using a process representation. The difference is that the authors in [3] define processes using BPMN, which requires time to learn and make this approach not suitable to end-users.

Then we also have [4], which allows users to define crowdsourcing programs for the crowd computer using a process-based approach. The crowd computer considers humans as part of the hardware of the system and available for the realization of computational tasks. The difference with Simple Flow is that the crowd computer is focused exclusively in the creation of crowdsourcing tasks and the steps of a task can involve or not the interactions with social networks, while Simple flow can define processes that aim or not to define a crowdsourced task but all the steps of a task involve an interaction with a social network.

5.2 Using Mashups

In [5], the authors point to the fact that most of the proposals for general purpose web-service composition (mashups) aimed at end-users failed. On the basis of these failures, the authors propose to use a domain specific approach to mashups. The proposed approach indeed improved the results of the general purpose mashups by lowering the entry barrier for end-users to mashup composition. We can consider Simple Flow as a domain specific mashup, the difference between [5] and Simple Flow is that we also guide end-users during the web-service composition with the action graph, preventing end-users from selecting actions (web-services) that cannot be combined.

Then we have [6], where the authors propose to support the development of mashups by integrating in existing mashup tools two techniques: automatic composition, which automatically creates mashups according to the goals of the end-user and; interactive pattern recommendation, which uses mashup composition patterns to recommend components to the end-user based on the current mashup design. The difference with Simple Flow is that the proposal of [6] depends on the existence and correctness of user-created patterns while in our proposal the recommendation is based on the action graph. However, the proposal of [6] could be integrated in general purpose mashup tools while Simple Flow is constrained to a specific domain.

5.3 Other Approaches

WeFlow [7], a tool for creating simple collaborative applications. The authors propose the use of a specification language (similar to natural language) for defining web applications. WeFlow has a generator engine that takes as input a script written in this language and generates a web application. Although WeFlow has similar goals than Simple Flow, the applications produced by WeFlow do not interact with social networks.

The Jabberwocky programming environment [8], which is composed of three components: a resource management system for human and computer workers, a framework for programming sequential and parallel tasks, and a high-level programming language for abstracting the low-level concepts of their framework. The main difference with our tool is that they define applications using a programming language similar to a structured query language and we use a process model approach.

In [9], the authors propose to use a spreadsheet environment for the construction of mashups. The authors define custom functions that call web services and pass the cell value as input of the service. Then, end-users can compose mashups by linking functions using the cell reference property of spreadsheets. The authors in [9] offer a developing environment that is well-known to end-users, however, they have the same drawbacks as the general purpose mashups.

6 Discussion and Future Work

When designing Simple Flow, we decided to make it as simple as possible to lower the learning curve required to use it. To achieve this, we minimized the number of inputs, outputs and options that each action had, which in turn increased the total number of actions. To explain this better, we take as an example the action of uploading a photo. With this action we have the option to upload a photo to the user stream or to a user album. In the implementation of Simple Flow we could have made this an action with two input parameters, one for specifying the destination of the photo (stream or album) and the other for specifying the identifier of the album in case that the selected destination was an album. Instead, we decided to minimize the number of input parameters, which resulted into two actions to upload a photo: one that uploads a photo to the user's stream (without parameters) and one that uploads a photo to a user album (with one parameter for the album identifier). We think that the overhead of having many actions instead of one can be overcome by giving meaningful descriptions to each action, while still maximizing the simplicity of the interface.

For the users that want more independence from Simple Flow we plan to add the option to export the implemented applications as an installable package. Then, to run the exported applications, they require a new web server to install it and to register the application to the desired social network.

Finally, we plan to carry out user studies to evaluate the design time and the correctness of the applications created using Simple Flow, and the usability of the UI of the page templates during the execution of the designed applications.

References

1. IFTTT: Put the internet to work for you, https://ifttt.com/
2. Atooma, http://www.atooma.com/welcome
3. Brambilla, M., Fraternali, P., Vaca, C.: BPMN and design patterns for engineering social BPM solutions. In: Daniel, F., Barkaoui, K., Dustdar, S. (eds.) BPM 2011 Workshops, Part I. LNBIP, vol. 99, pp. 219–230. Springer, Heidelberg (2012)
4. Kucherbaev, P., Tranquillini, S., Daniel, F., Casati, F., Marchese, M., Brambilla, M., Fraternali, P.: Business Processes for the Crowd Computer. In: La Rosa, M., Soffer, P. (eds.) BPM 2012 Workshops. LNBIP, vol. 132, pp. 256–267. Springer, Heidelberg (2013)
5. Casati, F., Daniel, F., Angeli, A.D., Imran, M., Soi, S., Wilkinson, C.R., Marchese, M.: Developing Mashup Tools for End-Users: On the Importance of the Application Domain. International Journal of Next-Generation Computing 3(2) (2012)
6. Chowdhury, S.R., Chudnovskyy, O., Niederhausen, M., Pietschmann, S., Sharples, P., Daniel, F., Gaedke, M.: Complementary Assistance Mechanisms for End User Mashup Composition. In: WWW 2013, pp. 269–272 (2013)
7. Kokciyan, N., Uskudarli, S., Dinesh, T.B.: User Generated Human Computation Applications. In: 2012 International Conference on Privacy, Security, Risk and Trust (PASSAT) and 2012 International Confernece on Social Computing (SocialCom), pp. 593–598. IEEE (2012)
8. Ahmad, S., Battle, A., Malkani, Z., Kamvar, S.: The jabberwocky programming environment for structured social computing. In: Proceedings of the 24th Annual ACM Symposium on User Interface Software and Technology, pp. 53–68 (2011)
9. Hoang, D.D., Paik, H.Y., Benatallah, B.: An analysis of spreadsheet-based services mashup. In: Proceedings of the Twenty-First Australasian Conference on Database Technologies, ADC 2010, vol. 104, pp. 141–150. Australian Computer Society, Inc., Darlinghurst (2010)

Media Enrichment on Distributed Displays by Selective Information Presentation: A First Prototype

Michael Krug, Fabian Wiedemann, Martin Gaedke

Chemnitz University of Technology, Germany
{firstname.lastname}@informatik.tu-chemnitz.de

Abstract. The Internet offers a wide range of information and media content. Currently, users who are watching a video and look for related information have to search for it by themselves. In our recent work we focused on how to enrich video content with additional related information. This paper presents an approach to extend media enrichment to support the presentation of additional content on multiple distributed displays. Our approach focuses on real time synchronization between a video on one display and the presentation of related information on the same or any other display with a web browser.

Keywords: Media enrichment, mashups, mobile web applications, HTML5.

1 Introduction

While consuming media, the users' need for additional content is becoming increasingly important. Users often inform themselves about the currently watched show on television using the Internet on their mobile devices [1]. For example, the discovered information about the currently watched program can be a list of actors or statistics related to a sportscast. This inspires us to provide the viewers directly with related information instead of having them search for it on their phone or tablet.

The purpose of this paper is to demonstrate our approach for enriching videos with additional related content, while not limiting the presentation of this content to the display that is showing the video. We extend the second screen approach [2] to present information on distributed displays, such as TV, tablet, smartphone or PC. This offers users who are watching a video the opportunity to interact with the additional information. As an example, a map, showing coordinates related to the video content, is displayed on a tablet, thus the users can interact with the map much better compared to displaying it on the screen playing the video.

The rest of this paper is structured as follows: We give an overview of our approach for media enrichment in Section 2. In Section 3, we describe our planned demonstration. Finally we conclude the paper and provide an outlook to further developments.

Demonstration: The prototype presented in this paper is available for testing at: **http://vsr.informatik.tu-chemnitz.de/demo/chrooma/icwe13/**

Q.Z. Sheng and J. Kjeldskov (Eds.): ICWE 2013 Workshops, LNCS 8295, pp. 51–53, 2013.
© Springer International Publishing Switzerland 2013

2   Approach for Media Enrichment on Distributed Displays

Our approach for media enrichment on distributed displays uses three components implemented as JavaScript classes: *SmartScreen*, *MessageCenter* and *SmartTile*.

A *SmartScreen* is an abstract representation of a web browser window. It is the host for multiple *SmartTiles* and contains a *MessageCenter* for communication purposes. The *SmartScreen* provides a mashup environment for *SmartTiles* and is responsible for adding, removing and arranging them in a device-specific grid. Fig. 1 illustrates the process of media enrichment on two displays using our components.

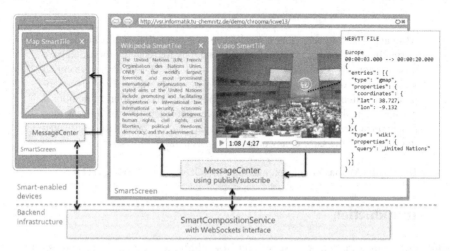

Fig. 1. Media enrichment using SmartTiles

SmartTiles are widgets that can process and display a certain kind of information. They have a unique name, which describes their type, a method for initialization and one for processing an event. *SmartTiles* can be created and removed on runtime. Users can rearrange them using drag-and-drop. New types of *SmartTiles* are derived from a basic *SmartTile* class using prototype-based inheritance and can be added like plug-ins. When a *SmartTile* is added to the *SmartScreen* it can subscribe to one or more topics, which can be changed at any time. A special type of *SmartTile* is the video *SmartTile*. Using metadata attached to the video, the tile is publishing events on various topics synchronized to the current time of the playing video. The metadata modeling and processing is described in our recent work [3]. We implemented other *SmartTiles* that can display a map, Tweets containing a word, tagged images or an extract from Wikipedia. There are also *SmartTiles* that process the information and publish it in a converted form, like translation or geocoding.

The *MessageCenter* manages the information exchange using a publish/subscribe mechanism. This offers loosely coupled, asynchronous communication. Information is encapsulated within an event as structured or unstructured data. To support publication to other *SmartScreens*, a synchronization mechanism is necessary. Thus, we implemented a WebSockets server as a part of the *SmartCompositionService*, which distributes all events it receives to all connected clients except the sender. Therefore, we extended the publish/subscribe mechanism as follows: on every publication the event is sent to the server. If an event from the server is received, the *publish* method is called without sending it back to the server to prevent a loop. This approach assures that each client behaves equally regardless of where the event was published.

An event has a lifetime defined by the metadata of the video. Thus, an "information is not relevant anymore" event is published, which admits the *SmartTiles* to remove their content. A *SmartTile* that is currently displaying information will not get a new event to assure that the content is displayed as long as it is valid. To prevent redundant display of the same information in the same kind of way, an event is not published to multiple *SmartTiles* of the same type on the same *SmartScreen*.

3   Demonstration of Media Enrichment

In the demo session we are presenting our first prototype for media enrichment on distributed displays. We are using a video clip of the German newscast "tagesschau", which is annotated with metadata. The video will be displayed on a large display like a PC and related additional content on the same display and on a smaller one like a tablet. This will demonstrate the real time synchronization between both displays. Further on, the demo illustrates the selective information presentation by showing additional content only on the display where the corresponding *SmartTile* is present.

4   Lessons Learned and Outlook

With this first prototype we built the basis for achieving media enrichment on distributed displays by selective information presentation. We provide several widgets, called *SmartTiles*, which form a mashup to enrich media on multiple displays. The prototype supports distributing information to multiple *SmartTiles* using a publish/subscribe mechanism and across multiple *SmartScreens* using WebSockets in real time. This works on desktop as well as on recent mobile browsers using standardized Web technologies. Our future work will focus on extending the prototype to support widget exchange between multiple *SmartScreens*. Additionally, we will conduct user studies to examine human information perception while using multimedia mashups.

Acknowledgement. This work was supported by the Sächsische Aufbaubank within the European Social Fund in the Free State of Saxony, Germany (Project Chrooma+).

References

1. Smith, A., Boyles, J.: The Rise of the "Connected Viewer" (2012)
2. Cruickshank, L., Tsekleves, E., Whitham, R., Hill, A., Kondo, K.: Making Interactive TV Easier to Use: Interface Design for a Second Screen Approach (2012)
3. Oehme, P., Krug, M., Wiedemann, F., Gaedke, M.: The Chrooma+ Approach to Enrich Video Content using HTML5. In: Proceedings of the 22nd International Conference on World Wide Web Companion (WWW 2013 Companion), pp. 479–480 (2013)

Modeling and Utilizing Quality Properties in the Development of Composite Web Mashups

Andreas Rümpel, Vincent Tietz, Anika Wagner, and Klaus Meißner

Faculty of Computer Science
Technische Universität Dresden
01062 Dresden, Germany
{andreas.ruempel,vincent.tietz,anika.wagner,
klaus.meissner}@tu-dresden.de

Abstract Ubiquitous Web resources and their manifold combinability are causing app development with current Web mashup platforms to be a challenging task, especially for low-skilled Web users. Hence, mashup composition demands for expressing quality requirements to facilitate selection and customization processes. Existing quality metamodels only provide guidelines or abstract categories, but neglect mashup-specific measuring directives and machine-readable representations. Therefore, we present a tailored quality property metamodel for composite Web mashups. We show, how it supports different settings of mashup development and execution. Finally, we demonstrate the metamodel's deployment in a mashup infrastructure and its utilization in different use cases.

1 Introduction

Modern mashup platforms, providing easy-to-couple mashup components, invite Web users with no programming skills to build their own applications with few time effort. Unlike in traditional software engineering, the mashup paradigm does not involve distinguished test departments with considerably high human and time resource costs to ensure quality requirements. Instead, mashup applications are created very situationally, since the paradigm strives for rapid development. Thus, to support instantly available and usable mashups, enforcement and monitoring of quality requirements has to be ensured by the development and execution platform. At least, beyond basic model-based application composition, cf. [1], quality assurance on an interface level of mashup components can be handled by employing semantic interface descriptions. Yet, only basic data type compatibility can be verified during application development.

Quality requirements may cover a variety of scenarios, such as user-driven filtering of candidate mashup components, device-specific requirements or resources availability at runtime. As a foundation, they have quality properties in common, which apply to mashup components or applications in question. Thus, a mashup-tailored *quality property metamodel* has to specify eligible properties, which can be provided or assigned by measuring. Without loss of generality, Figure 1 illustrates three example use cases for different kinds of quality requirements specification in a mashup development platform.

Q.Z. Sheng and J. Kjeldskov (Eds.): ICWE 2013 Workshops, LNCS 8295, pp. 54–65, 2013.

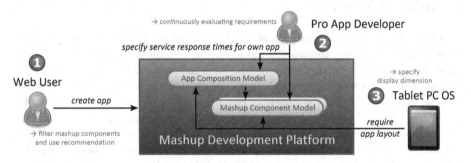

Fig. 1. Quality requirements use cases with unified mashup platform and models

In use case ①, a Web user without advanced skills or experience in developing applications with programming languages wants to find appropriate mashup components for a certain task. He uses an EUD (end user development) platform such as [2], which provides a browser for available mashup components. Assuming a huge number of mashup components, the user desires to get a recommendation involving custom quality requirements, pointing at component quality properties with the help of frontend. Use case ② is initiated by a professional app author, being familiar with modeling mashups. He wants to specify application-wide and component-specific quality requirements, which should hold at runtime. Therefore, a requirements evaluation module triggers context monitors to observe different measurable quality properties like response times of service components. Quality property values will have to be evaluated continuously at runtime. Since quality requirements are not limited to originate from human stakeholders, use case ③ involves a mobile device as a requirements source. On the application level, the device requires a certain application layout and different display size parameters. As a consequence, the mashup has to arrange its mashup components, which themselves should adapt their internal presentation, at least at deployment time. Additionally, the mashup platform could exchange components with regard to those device-specific requirements.

To support all outlined use cases by one holistic approach, we propose a quality property metamodel as a basis for customized requirements specification and evaluation in composite Web mashups. Our model, see Section 3, is able to describe quality properties for different quality requirements stakeholders, i. e., mashup components and mashup applications and it can be easily extended to consider the runtime platform, the device which the application is running on and the user profile. Therefore, we introduce mashup-specific quality properties completing non-functional properties known from Web services models, cf. related work in Section 2. Hence, quality properties may be used during development, at deployment time and at runtime. Section 4 shows their deployment in a requirements-aware Web mashup infrastructure. The presented use cases are serving as example scenarios to demonstrate model instantiation and management of its contents within an established platform for composite Web mashups, see Section 5. Finally, Section 6 concludes this paper.

2   Related Work

According to [3], quality requirements engineering effort and tooling support decreases when regarding application paradigms in the following order: traditional software systems, Web applications and Web mashups. Thus, there is a huge overall demand on solutions providing requirements specification and evaluation support particularly for the mashup paradigm of application engineering. In general, *quality properties*, ideally accompanied by a defining *metamodel*, might be assigned to each artifact or stakeholder of a software system. In traditional software engineering, a number of quality models have been proposed by the Consortium for IT Software Quality (CISQ), ISO and IEC, e. g., ISO/IEC 9126-1 and the subsequent ISO/IEC 25010 [4]. They are complemented by academic approaches, such as from McCall [5] and Grady [6]. Some properties provide *metrics* such as *customizability* from ISO 9126, which is calculated by the division of the number of functions which can be customized during operation by the number of functions that require the customization capability. However, for the majority of properties, implementation is hard to accomplish in a real system, since they are lacking metrics and scales for automated processing. Further, they are very general and need to be tailored for each specific class of software.

Especially in Web services description, cf. WSMO [7], and matching [8], models for non-functional properties have been proposed several years ago. Although their models are quite extensive, comprehensive implementations are missing. Since they describe Web services, crucial application-specific properties like UI concerns are neglected. Thus, they are not suitable for mashup applications out of the box. An example for a specific quality model for Web applications is provided by [9] and [10]. Based on ISO/IEC 9126, it comprises new properties such as information quality, loyalty and actuality. Since they focus on Web-based applications in general, quality properties are not discussed at a level of granularity typical for mashup components. [11] focuses on *new generation WebApps* and standard completeness of their quality model. However, customized requirements suitability of the described properties is only discussed to little extent. A dedicated quality model for mashup components has been introduced by [12], which focuses on interface quality, data quality and presentation quality. An extension for whole applications was proposed in [13]. Following the previously mentioned ISO standard, provision of quality properties was narrowed down to scaling values within integer values depending on the presence of particular features such as API keys, SSL support or user accounts.

Although quality property modeling approaches, especially for Web services, contain many useful elements, they are often limited to be used as a supporting feature to facilitate service matching. Moreover, they do not contain UI-specific properties, which are essential for mashup applications. First dedicated mashup quality property models compensate that issue to a limited extent. On the downside, their properties are recruited from ISO 9126 and lack concrete scales and measuring facilities to integrate them in a quality-aware mashup platform being helpful in the presented use cases. Thus, a quality property modeling approach with special regard to support customized quality requirements is still missing.

3   Web Mashup Quality Property Metamodel

Since existing quality models are either less formal or lack mashup-suitable properties, we now introduce a tailored quality property metamodel[1] for composite Web mashups. In this regard, we assume the following design principles and requirements. According to the application paradigm of presentation-oriented Web mashups, we include end-users, who are able to conceive and to specify quality requirements, into our target group. In addition, mashup component developers may need to utilize the quality model to describe their components accordingly. Therefore, its characteristics respectively its serialization and presentation need to be understandable by both mashup composers and component developers. With use case ③ from Section 1 in mind, fully automated processing without any human interaction should be possible as well. Furthermore, machine-readable representation is crucial to enable context monitoring and adaptation, e. g., by exchanging composition fragments triggered and invoked by the runtime environment. As mentioned previously, the quality model also needs to consider certain elements and concerns, that are missing in prevalent approaches.

To design the metamodel, we reviewed properties described in existing quality models, see Section 2, regarding the characteristics of mashup applications and the suitability of the metrics to be interpreted by a runtime environment and component recommendation facilities. Thereby, we disregard those with less relevance for the mashup application type. For example, *analysability* [4] cannot be provided by black-box mashup components. Following mashup component models, each component should be easy to install. Therefore, we consider *portability* [5] also as less relevant. However, we also adopted existing properties such as *interoperability, learnability* and *timeliness* from [12] and *actuality, security* from [10]. We added *access mode, data storage, style, bandwidth, source* and *data traffic* to address UI and Web characteristics appropriately. Their representation in our model is described in more detail in the following section as well as the metamodel's structure and noteworthy modeling features.

3.1   Structure of the Quality Metamodel

Quality properties may be carried by different stakeholders in a Web mashup infrastructure. We now focus on the mashup application as well as its constituent components as property carrying entities. Therefore, we treat them in a modularized fashion, as illustrated in the metamodel overview in Fig. 2. Therein, we define the following three model parts, i. e. ontologies:

Basic Property Ontology. defines the concept of a property carrying entity from which all other properties are derived. It comprises about 50 properties, which can be used for describing components and applications, e. g., *actuality, response time, usability, learnability* and *traffic*.

---

[1] Metamodel OWL files: `http://mmt.inf.tu-dresden.de/models/qpm.xhtml`

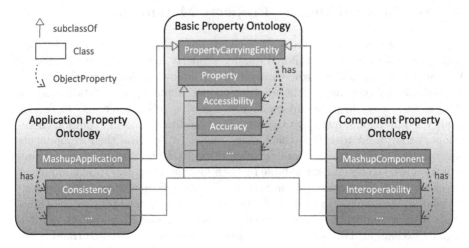

Fig. 2. Quality property metamodel structure overview

Application Property Ontology. defines properties of the mashup application such as *consistency* and *component appropriateness*. In addition, this sub-model contains three properties, that are special for applications: *component suitability, consistency* and *component number.*

Component Property Ontology. defines properties of mashup components. Additionally, it contains seven attributes, that are special for components, e. g., *access mode, interoperability* and *isUI.*

3.2   Metamodel Elements Nature and Features

Our metamodel provides relations between its properties such as the sub-class relationship, e. g., *interoperability* incorporates *data exchange formats, programming language* and *protocols.* Further, each property is associated with formal metrics and information on how the data is acquired. We distinguish provided, collectible and measurable properties. Provided properties are statically defined either by the application composer or the component developer, such as the supported types of *security* mechanisms like *authentication.* Collectible properties are accumulated over time, e. g., with the help of user ratings or by the runtime environment. Values are calculated by a function such as average, minimum or maximum, e. g., *usability* by $\emptyset$(UserRatings). Measurable properties can be acquired instantly and fully automated using context monitors. For certain properties, *concerns* such as API, UI data, backend data, functionality, service or UI are eligible to be assigned. *API* represents the interface providing access to the functionality of a specific mashup building part. Component-internal application logic is represented by *backend data.* In contrast, *UI data* refers to visible data on the user interface of the component or the application, while *UI* targets the presentation of UI elements itself. Of course, those concerns can only be assigned if a UI mashup component is in consideration. *Functionality* represents the general competences, the component or application can execute. Properties, which refer to third-party Web service calls of mashup components, are assigned to *service*. With the help of those concern assignments, very similar quality properties can be semantically separated at a conceptual and implementation level.

Finally, the metamodel provides a descriptive text definition, a data type, a default value as well as value ranges and a unit for each property. As an example, *data traffic*, which is accrued over time and assessed by the metric ($\sum_{i=1}^{N}$ DataTrafficPerSecond$_i$) $\div$ N (N being the whole usage time in seconds) has the unit KB/s and a default value of infinite, since this is the worst value. Additionally, we defined linguistic variables like *low*, *middle* and *high*, that are assigned to concrete values using a membership function, to facilitate configuration of fuzzy specification of quality requirements for our properties.

3.3 Metamodel Content

Table 1 outlines the metamodel's subset of concern-aware properties. We distinguish properties collected from existing quality models, properties adopted to the mashup domain and newly added ones. The semantics of *actuality* was e. g. extended to track the frequency of refreshes from a background service. The added property *source* provides means to describe the origin, i. e., an organization or URI of the used Web services. Usually, this information is not explicitly available for users, whereas it is difficult to put trust in the described artifact. In this context, *security* is also an important aspect, that is explicitly considered in our model by the six sub-properties *authentication*, *authorization*, *data storage*, *data encryption*, *traceability* and *confidentiality*. The security property itself indicates with an integer how secure a component or application is. It can be measured as |usedSecurityMechanism|. To provide means for adaptation, we introduce *bandwidth* and *data traffic* that both belong to the concern of backend data. The former describes the data transfer rate, which the component or application needs to run optimally, whereupon the application bandwidth is assessed by max(Bandwidth$_{Components}$). The latter describes how much data traffic the component or application consumes while running. This also can be utilized to avoid data traffic limits, being of relevance especially on mobile devices.

In existing quality models, the meaning of *consistency* refers to the UI or the backend data. However, in mashups this distinction is not relevant for the user. This is why we decided to consider both equally under this property. Further, we extend *completeness* to the API, UI and background data. For each concern, user ratings can be collected, while the average of this ratings forms the property value. Also, the *availablity* is extended to backend services. The metric for this concern for components is $(1 -$ ConnectionErrors $\div$ |AccessesToService|$) \cdot 100$. *Robustness* does not only handle exceptions after user input, but all exceptions. It can be calculated as follows: $(1 -$ |Exceptions| $\div$ TotalUseTime$) \cdot 100$. Finally, *timeliness* describes, if tasks are fulfilled within a certain time, that is the *deadline* defined by users or developers. For components it is assigned by |ResponsesInTime| $\div$ |Measurements| $\cdot 100$ and for applications by $\emptyset$(Timeliness$_{Components}$). Beside these concern-related properties, we also

Table 1. Quality properties with special concerns

	API	UI data	Backend data	Functionality	Service	UI	App./Comp.
Provided							
Interoperability [12]	●		●				*
Data exchange formats [12]			●				*
Programming language [12]	●						*
Protocols [12]	●						*
◆ Actuality (Currency) [10]			●	○			⊞ *
▽ Access mode			●				*
Credibility [10,9]			●	○		○	⊞ *
◆ Security [14,4,15,5,10,9,16,17]			●	●			⊞ *
Authentication [17,14]				●			⊞ *
Authorization [17,14]				●			⊞ *
▽ Data storage			●				⊞ *
Data encryption [17,14]			●				⊞ *
Traceability [17,14]				●			⊞ *
Confidentiality [17,14]				●			⊞ *
▽ Style						●	⊞ *
▽ Bandwidth			●				⊞ *
Familiarity [9]						●	⊞ *
▽ Source					●		⊞ *
Collectible							
Component suitability [13]	●	●	●	●	●	●	⊞
◆ Consistency [5,9,6,13]		●		●		●	⊞
Adaptability [4,15,5,9,6]			●	●		●	⊞ *
Usability [9,5,6,4,15,13,12]	◗					●	⊞ *
Learnability [9,4,15,12]	◗					●	⊞ *
Accuracy [10,9]		●					⊞ *
◆ Completeness [17,5,10,4]	◗	●	●	●		●	⊞ *
Satisfaction [9]	◗	●	●	●	●	●	⊞ *
Accessibility [10,9]	○					●	⊞ *
Measurable							
▽ Data traffic			●				⊞ *
◆ Reliability [4,15,5,9,16,17,14,6]		○	○	●	●	○	⊞ *
◆ Availability [4,15,9,16,17,14,10]				●			⊞ *
◆ Robustness [17,14]		○	○	●	●	○	⊞ *
Response time [4,15,9,16,17,14,6]				○	●	●	⊞ *
Stability [15]				●			⊞ *
◆ Timeliness [12,13]				○	●	●	⊞ *
▽ Deadline				○	●	●	*

Legend

	from pre-existing models	●	concern is affected directly
	◆ meaning slightly changed	○	concern is affected indirectly
	▽ new property	◗	concern is affected only for components
	⊞ relevant for applications	*	relevant for components

incorporated metadata of components and applications, which can be treated in the same way during model evaluation. Examples are *name, author, certificate, development date* and *keywords*, whose values are provided by the author.

4 Requirements-Based Quality Evaluation

Many regarded metamodels for quality properties lack either implementation and real-world use cases or they are not field-tested to work within an application development or runtime infrastructure. Thus, this section shows the metamodel's integration into a quality-aware platform for composite Web mashups and therefore demonstrates its suitability in a variety of use cases. To this end, we identify essential integration points of the modeled quality properties referring to certain parts of the mashup infrastructure, which are dedicated to perform quality requirements capture and evaluation.

4.1 Quality-Aware Web Mashup Platform

Fig. 3 provides an overview of the quality-aware Web mashup infrastructure, which comprises the following major parts: the device, which allows for user interaction with executed mashup applications, the mashup runtime environment (MRE), the mashup component repository (CoRe) and Web-based resources and services, serving as content providers for mashup components. A mashup application is represented by a composition model specifying layout, screen flow, contained mashup components and their communication. This application model is interpreted by the MRE, which integrates demanded mashup components. According to [18], the described infrastructure is founded on the well-established architecture of CRUISe and EDYRA[2], where each mashup component provides a declarative interface descriptor using the Semantic Mashup Component Description Language (SMCDL). Each mashup component may instantiate the quality property metamodel to reproduce its component-specific quality property values. Thus, quality properties belonging to components may be maintained using the CoRe. Property values are persisted as an extension of SMCDL. Thus, a comprehensive representation of a component including mutable quality properties is achieved. Integration and querying of the application quality properties into the mashup composition model are performed in the same manner.

Mashup components and applications are in the main scope of the presented metamodel. Since user profiles, devices and runtime platforms are also eligible for carrying quality properties, the access methods and modeling conventions hold for them as well. A quality metamodel for mobile device environments is developed in parallel, cf. [19]. It is subject to be integrated in this mashup platform, resulting in extra red bubbles connected to the device and the user in Fig. 3. To add security for model modification, conceptually separated submodels can be merged on demand, depending on the kind of access. If, e.g., the

---

[2] http://mmt.inf.tu-dresden.de/cruise, http://mmt.inf.tu-dresden.de/edyra

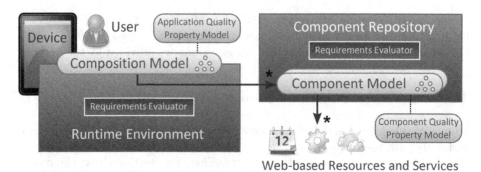

Fig. 3. Quality model integration into the mashup infrastructure

runtime environment or a component browser should display mashup component properties, it can be given access to the whole model. If instead a client is about to modify a quality property, such as adding a rating to the component or setting recently calculated statistical usage data, only the mutable part of the property model is provided through the Web service interface. In this case, the property classification helps to identify runtime-mutable properties.

4.2 Property Capturing and Requirements Evaluation Process

Knowledge of the instantiation location of each metamodel element is not sufficient to run a quality-aware mashup infrastructure. Additionally, we need to distinguish, how and when certain property values are set and updated. There are three kinds of delivering quality property values. First, a component's or an application's author might provide property values, cf. Table 1, which can be edited directly in the corresponding component or composition model or by using a repository frontend. Second, the runtime environment may read context sensors, which are adaptively queried according to the specification in corresponding quality requirements. Context data, such as memory consumption as a measurable quality property, is stored as a value via the repository's Web service and thus persisted into the SMCDL. Third, collectible quality property values such as average user ratings have to be tracked. The repository, CoRe in case of mashup components, is responsible for maintaining this kind of properties.

A major goal of quality property modeling is to evaluate quality requirements, preferably in an automated way. The basic concepts of requirements-driven quality engineering for Web mashups were introduced in [20]. To this end, *requirements evaluators* are designated to perform checks against quality property model instances. In this context, a quality requirement specifies, when or in which temporal intervals it shall be evaluated. Both evaluation at development time, cf. use case ②, and at runtime, cf. use case ③, have to be possible. Thus, requirements evaluators are located at the MRE and at the repository, see Fig. 3, but still the same models can be used. This feature fosters the use of so called end-user development (EUD) tools for user-driven development of applications, which benefit from joint development time and runtime.

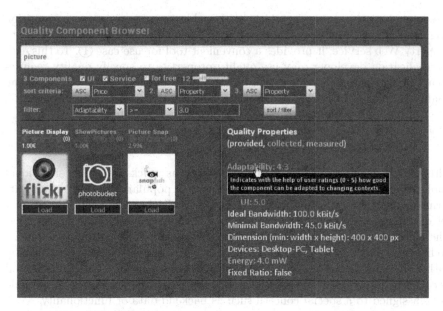

Fig. 4. Browsing mashup components using quality properties

5   Implementation

Beyond the implementation of the quality property metamodel itself, we implemented access and modification interfaces for model instances. Furthermore, a prototypical frontend integration for use case reproduction was built. As indicated in Section 3, the proposed quality property metamodel is implemented using OWL. This brings several advantages like easy modularization or RDF-based querying. In fact, separation of sub-models for components and applications is achieved through model imports. OWL class inheritance is used to distinguish property types. The metamodel implementation integrates well into the existing RDF-based and SMCDL-based mashup modeling infrastructure, including tooling support by means of ontology editors or frameworks. RDF-based quality modeling facilitates SPARQL querying on RDF models, provided by a CoRe Web service. *SPARQL Update* enables model instance modification besides read access. Thus, clients such as a CoRe browser, the MRE or a mashup builder may use this endpoint to manage quality properties. For example, access to the provided properties of a component can be handled with a SPARQL request to the component's OWL representation held in the CoRe, facilitating advanced sorting and filtering by property values. OWL and SMCDL representations are kept synchronized by the repository, making model export continuously available.

For testing quality model instances and the previously outlined property management Web service, we implemented several clients, which are tooling frontends for building Web mashup applications. Beside a CoRe frontend, which is rather an administration tool for browsing and editing quality properties, we integrated a quality component browser into our EUD mashup platform. Fig. 4 shows a screen shot of this browser, which is also able to process larger composition fragments represented by a composition model. As a client for the CoRe quality property Web service, it provides a convenient tool for use case ①. To this end, an application developer may use quality properties to specify quality requirements in a frontend. Sorting based on multiple criteria, filtering and browsing quality properties of alternative mashup building parts as well as displaying a description of all properties is possible.

6   Conclusion

Although Web mashups started their existence as quick-to-develop situational applications for skilled programmers, their current popularity and advanced platforms demand for regarding a huge spread of quality requirements. Based on a set of use cases, we elucidated the need for mashup-tailored quality properties. Therefore, we proposed a quality property metamodel incorporating well-known Web service NFPs and UI-specific properties. Each property is either provided by author, measured or collectible and has concrete measuring instructions as well as concrete data types, ranges and default values. Specific properties are suitable to be assigned to a special concern such as backend data or functionality.

Introducing a Web mashup infrastructure, we outlined, which architectural components are integration points for quality property model instances. Especially mashup components and application compositions were in the focus of use cases as quality property carrying entities. However, the modular metamodel and its OWL-based implementation allow for easy integration of further sub-models such as platform ontologies or user contexts. Prototypical implementation comprises also a Web service for model instantiation, querying and modification as well as frontends including a quality-aware mashup component browser.

Future work concentrates on integrating platform quality models, which are developed in separate research projects. Moreover, current research includes requirements specification, evaluation and automated invocation of adaptivity actions in different scenarios. To expand the target user group in the field of end-user-driven development of Web mashups, fuzzy specification and configuration of quality requirements is another hot topic on our schedule.

Acknowledgements. The work of Andreas Rümpel is funded by the European Union and by the Free State of Saxony. The work of Vincent Tietz is granted by the European Social Fund (ESF), Free State of Saxony and Saxonia Systems AG (Germany, Dresden) within the project eScience (contract no. 080951807).

References

1. Pietschmann, S., Nestler, T., Daniel, F.: Application Composition at the Presentation Layer: Alternatives and Open Issues. In: Proc. of the 12th Intl. Conf. on Information Integration and Web-based Applications & Services. ACM (2010)
2. Rümpel, A., Radeck, C., Blichmann, G., Lorz, A., Meißner, K.: Towards Do-It-Yourself Development of Composite Web Applications. In: Proc. of the Intl. Conf. on Internet Technologies & Society 2011, pp. 231–235. IADIS Press (2011)

3. Tietz, V., Rümpel, A., Liebing, C., Meißner, K.: Towards Requirements Engineering for Mashups: State of the Art and Research Challenges. In: Proc. of the 7th Intl. Conf. on Internet and Web Applications and Services. XPS (2012)
4. International Organization for Standardization, ISO/IEC IS 25010:2011: Systems and software engineering – Systems and software Quality Requirements and Evaluation (SQuaRE) – System and software quality models (2011)
5. McCall, J.A., Richards, P.K., Walters, G.F.: Factors in Software Quality. Concept and Definitions of Software Quality, vol. I (1977)
6. Grady, R.B., Caswell, D.L.: Software Metrics: Establishing a Company-Wide Program. Prentice Hall (1987)
7. Roman, D., Keller, U., Lausen, H., de Bruijn, J., Lara, R., Stollberg, M., Polleres, A., Feier, C., Bussler, C., Fensel, D.: Web Service Modeling Ontology. Applied Ontology 1, 77–106 (2005)
8. O'Sullivan, J., Edmond, D., ter Hofstede, A.H.M.: Formal description of non-functional service properties. Queensland University of Technology (2005), http://www.wsmo.org/papers/OSullivanTR2005.pdf
9. Orehovacki, T.: Proposal for a set of quality attributes relevant for Web 2.0 application success. In: 2010 32nd International Conference on Information Technology Interfaces (ITI), pp. 319–326 (2010)
10. Olsina, L., Mich, L., Sassano, R.: Specifying quality requirements for the Web 2.0 applications. In: ICWE 2008: International Conference on Web Engineering: Workshop Proceedings, pp. 56–62. Slovak University of Technology, Bratislava (2008) ISBN: 9788022728997; Proceedings of: 7th International Workshop on Web-oriented Software Technology, New York, July 14-15 (2008), http://ceur-ws.org/Vol-445
11. Olsina, L., Lew, P., Dieser, A., Rivera, B.: Updating Quality Models for Evaluating New Generation Web Applications. Jnl. of Web Engineering 11(3), 209–246 (2012)
12. Cappiello, C., Daniel, F., Matera, M.: A Quality Model for Mashup Components. In: Gaedke, M., Grossniklaus, M., Díaz, O. (eds.) ICWE 2009. LNCS, vol. 5648, pp. 236–250. Springer, Heidelberg (2009)
13. Cappiello, C., Daniel, F., Koschmider, A., Matera, M., Picozzi, M.: A Quality Model for Mashups. In: Auer, S., Díaz, O., Papadopoulos, G.A. (eds.) ICWE 2011. LNCS, vol. 6757, pp. 137–151. Springer, Heidelberg (2011)
14. Lee, K., Jeon, J., Lee, W., Jeong, S.-H., Park, S.-W.: QoS for Web Services: Requirements and Possible Approaches (2003), http://www.w3c.or.kr/kr-office/TR/2003/ws-qos/
15. International Organization for Standardization, ISO/IEC IS 9126:2001: Software engineering - Product quality (2001)
16. Papaioannou, I., Tsesmetzis, D., Roussaki, I., Anagnostou, M.: A QoS ontology language for Web-services. In: 20th Intl. Conf. on Advanced Information Networking and Applications (AINA 2006), vol. 1, pp. 101–106. IEEE (2006)
17. Ran, S.: A model for web services discovery with QoS. ACM SIGecom Exchanges 4(1), 1–10 (2003)
18. Pietschmann, S., Radeck, C., Meißner, K.: Semantics-Based Discovery, Selection and Mediation for Presentation-Oriented Mashups. In: Proceedings of the 5th International Workshop on Web APIs and Service Mashups, ACM ICPS. ACM (2011)
19. Tietz, V., Mroß, O., Rümpel, A., Radeck, C., Meißner, K.: A Requirements Model for Composite and Distributed Web Mashups. In: Proc. of the 8th Intl. Conf. on Internet and Web Applications and Services (ICIW 2013). XPS (2013)
20. Rümpel, A., Meißner, K.: Requirements-Driven Quality Modeling and Evaluation in Web Mashups. In: Proc. of the 8th Intl. Conf. on the Quality of Information and Communications Technology (QUATIC 2012), pp. 319–322. IEEE (2012)

Quality of Web Mashups: A Systematic Mapping Study

Priscila Cedillo, Adrian Fernandez, Emilio Insfran, and Silvia Abrahão

ISSI Group, Department of Information Systems and Computation
Universitat Politècnica de València
Camino de Vera, s/n, 46022, Valencia, Spain
{icedillo,afernandez,einsfran,sabrahao}@dsic.upv.es

Abstract. Web mashups are a new generation of applications based on the composition of ready-to-use, heterogeneous components. They are gaining momentum thanks to their lightweight composition approach, which represents a new opportunity for companies to leverage on past investments in SOA, Web services, and public APIs. Although several studies are emerging in order to address mashup development, no systematic mapping studies have been reported on how quality issues are being addressed. This paper reports a systematic mapping study on *which* and *how* the quality of Web mashups has been addressed and how the product quality-aware approaches have been defined and validated. The aim of this study is to provide a background in which to appropriately develop future research activities. A total of 38 research papers have been included from an initial set of 187 papers. Our results provided some findings regarding how the most relevant product quality characteristics have been addressed in different artifacts and stages of the development process. They have also been useful to detect some research gaps, such as the need of more controlled experiments and more quality-aware mashup development proposals for other characteristics which being important for the Web domain have been neglected such as *Usability* and *Reliability*.

Keywords: Web Mashups, Product Quality, Systematic Mapping Study.

1 Introduction

Mashups are a new generation of Web applications that combine disparate Web services, RSS, ATOM feeds and other data sources, to produce new applications. Emerging technologies (e.g., Web services, User Interface widget libraries) and specific composition tools (e.g., Yahoo Pipes, Microsoft Popfly) have significantly simplified the access and reuse of such building blocks, leading to a component-oriented paradigm which represents a new opportunity for companies to leverage on past investments in SOA, Web services, and public APIs [4].

The challenge of developing Web mashups has motivated the appearance of a variety of techniques, methods and tools to address their composition process. However, some issues are still largely unexplored such as specific quality issues for this type of Web applications [5]. Although being mashups a type of Web

Q.Z. Sheng and J. Kjeldskov (Eds.): ICWE 2013 Workshops, LNCS 8295, pp. 66–78, 2013.

applications, methods so far proposed for traditional Web applications need to be repurposed to capture the salient characteristics.

As far as we know, no evidence-based studies (e.g., systematic mapping studies, systematic literature reviews) have been reported on how product quality issues are being addressed for mashups. In this paper, we present a systematic mapping study for summarizing *which* and *how* product quality issues of Web mashups have been addressed by existing literature. A systematic mapping study is a means of categorizing and summarizing the existing information about a research question in an unbiased manner [12]. The goal of our study is, therefore, to address *which/how product quality issues are being addressed in Web mashup development* and *how the product quality-aware approaches have been defined and validated*.

This paper is organized as follows. Section 2 discusses related work. Section 3 presents the protocol we defined, employed and validated to conduct the systematic mapping study. Section 4 describes the results obtained. Section 5 discusses the threats to the validity of the results. Finally, section 6 presents our conclusions and suggests areas for further investigation.

2   Related Work

A number of surveys and reviews aimed at analyzing current mashup development approaches and tools have been reported in recent years (e.g., [2, 9, 10, 14]).

Hoyer and Fischer [10] presented a market overview of the different mashup composition tools by classifying and evaluating them according to several perspectives such as general information, functionality and usability. They classified more than 30 tools in their proposed classification model in order to draw market trends in context of Enterprise mashups. However, the evaluated quality aspects were related to the process development rather than the product quality of the generated mashups.

Beemer and Green [2] presented a comprehensive review based on 60 publications that helps researchers to classify the general research topics on mashups. A generic taxonomy was defined according to six categories: access control, integration, agents, frameworks, end-user programming and Enterprise mashups. Although a review methodology was establish and conducted, quality issues of mashups were not identified as a specific research topic.

Grammel and Storey [9] presented an overview of End-User development support in a selected set of mashup development environments. They explored, summarized and compared their features across six different issues: levels of abstraction, learning support, community support, discoverability, user interface design and software engineering techniques. Results showed there is still much room for further improvement. Again, the authors did not discuss the quality of mashups from the product perspective.

Orange Labs [14] presented a survey aimed at evaluating existing composer tools for mashups as well as at refining the design requirements for developing these tools. This work points explicitly the need of quality evaluation approaches, since as it was pointed out in [1] in 2009, 62% of CIOs were seeing mashups as not as reliable as traditional Web solutions and not adapted to enterprises.

Although several related surveys and reviews have been reported, they present two main limitations:

a) There is a need of a more systematic way in order to summarize the existing knowledge in this area, since the majority of these studies are informal literature surveys with no defined research questions, no search process, no defined data extraction or data analysis process.

b) There is a need of surveys or reviews specifically focused on the product quality of Web mashups. We are aware about several studies that address quality issues on Web mashups such as [3, 16, 17]. However, as far as we know, no empirical evidence-based studies have been reported in order to categorizing and summarize these studies.

3   Research Method

A systematic mapping study is a means of categorizing and summarizing all available research that is relevant to a particular research question, topic area, or phenomenon of interest [12]. It aims at presenting a fair evaluation of a research topic by using a trustworthy, rigorous, and auditable methodology. This research method has gained popularity in last years and it has been adopted in several other studies within the Web Engineering field [7, 8, 18].

A systematic mapping study involves several stages and activities. In the *planning* stage, the need for the mapping is identified, the research questions are specified, and the mapping protocol is defined. In the *conducting* stage, the primary studies are selected, the quality assessment used to discover representative studies is defined, the data extraction and monitoring is performed, and the obtained data is synthesized. Finally, in the *reporting* stage, the dissemination mechanisms are specified, and the mapping results are presented. The activities concerning the *planning* and the *conducting* of our systematic mapping are described in the following subsections. The *reporting* stage is presented in Section 4.

3.1   Research Question

We have carried out a systematic mapping study by considering the guidelines suggested in [12, 15]. The goal of our study is to examine which and how product quality aspects of mashups have been addressed from the point of view of the following research questions: a) RQ1: *Which/how product quality issues are being addressed in Web mashup development? and* b) RQ2: *How have the product quality-aware approaches been defined and validated?.* We focused on these research questions since they are tailored to identify which quality characteristics have been the most studied, how these characteristics are related to mashup development dimensions (i.e., stages and artifacts), and how quality-aware techniques by using these characteristics have been defined and validated. In addition, these research questions will allow us to summarize the current knowledge about product quality of Web mashups and to identify gaps in current research in order to suggest areas for further investigation.

3.2   Identifying and Selecting Primary Studies

The main sources we used to search for primary studies were IEEE Xplore and ACM digital libraries. In addition, we have manually searched in the proceedings of the following journals, books and conferences:

- Journal of Web Engineering (JWE).
- ACM Transactions on the Web (ACMTWEB).
- Foundations of Popfly: Rapid Mashup Development (Book).
- World Wide Web conference (WWW).
- International Conference on Web Engineering (ICWE).
- International Conference on Information Integration and Web-Based Applications & Services (iiWAS).
- International Conference on Service Oriented Computing (ICSOC).
- International Workshop on Web APIs and Service Mashups (MASHUPS).

The search string defined for retrieving studies is as follows: *"(web* OR *internet* OR *www)* AND *(mash*) AND quality"*. The asterisk symbol '*' signifies any character whose purpose it is to include any word variation of each search term (e.g., the search term 'mash*' includes the following words: *mashup* OR *mashing* OR *mash-Up* OR *mash* OR . . .)

We experimented with several search strings and this one retrieved the greatest amount of relevant papers. This search string was used in the IEEE Xplore and the ACM digital libraries as well as used in the screening of the other sources that were inspected manually. The period covered was the last 7 years, i.e., studies published from 2006 to 2012. This starting date was selected because, after following up the references of the preliminary retrieved studies, we realized that 2006 was the year in which the term "mashup" has started to appear in the Web Engineering field.

3.3   Inclusion and Exclusion Criteria

Each identified study was evaluated by the researchers conducting the systematic mapping study to decide whether or not it should be included. The discrepancies were solved by consensus. The studies that met the both following conditions were included:

- Studies presenting a method and/or technique to assist designers in the quality evaluation of Web mashups from the product perspective.
- Full papers.

The studies that met at least one of the following conditions were excluded:

- Introductory papers for special issues, books and workshops.
- Duplicate reports of the same study in different sources.
- Short papers with less than five pages.
- Papers not written in English.

3.4   Quality Assessment

In addition to general inclusion/exclusion criteria, it is considered critical to assess the "quality" of the primary studies. A three point Likert-scale questionnaire was used to provide a quality assessment of the selected studies. The questionnaire contained the following questions: a) *Does the study present a method and/or technique for assessing the quality of mashups from the product quality perspective? (agree, disagree);* b) *Has the study been published in a relevant journal or conference? (e.g. CORE ranking, JCR list); and* c) *Has the study been cited by other authors? (Google Scholar).*

The score for each closed-question will be the arithmetic mean of all the individual scores from each reviewer. The sum of the three closed-question score of each study provides a final score which was not used to exclude papers from the systematic mapping study but was rather used to detect representative studies.

3.5   Data Extraction Strategy

The data extraction strategy was defined by breaking down each research question into more specific criterion in which a set of possible options was established. Table 1 shows this breaking down which is intended to make easier the data extraction and paper categorization. In addition, the rationale for each criterion is explained below.

Table 1. Data extraction strategy

Research questions	Criteria	Options
RQ1: Which/how the quality of Web mashups has been addressed?	C1: Product quality characteristics addressed in the studies	a) Functional suitability b) Performance efficiency c) Compatibility d) Usability e) Reliability f) Security g) Maintainability h) Portability
	C2: Stages based on the mashup development process	a) Component Selection b) Mashup composition c) Mashup usage
	C3: Artifacts involved	a) Conceptual models b) Source code c) Final user interfaces d) Components
RQ2: How have the product quality-aware approaches been defined and validated?	C4: Type of approach	a) New b) Extension
	C5: Type of validation	a) Survey b) Case Study c) Experiment d) No validation
	C6: Approach usage	a) Industry b) Academy

With regard to the criterion C1, a paper can be classified in one or more quality characteristics from the ISO/IEC 25010 standard SQuaRE [11]. We employed this standard since it proposes an updated product quality model which has been defined by consensus among experts.

With regard to the criterion C2, a paper can be classified in one or more stages based on the mashup development process proposed in [3]: *Component selection*, if the quality of the mashup is evaluated when components are being selected to create the mashup; *Mashup composition*, if the quality of the mashup is evaluated during the composition stage; and *Mashup usage*, if the quality of the mashup is evaluated once it has been completely defined.

With regard to the criterion C3, a paper can be classified in one or more artifacts: *conceptual models*, if the quality of mashups is evaluated on the intermediate artifacts that are created during the mashup development process (internal quality); *Source code*, if the quality of the mashup are assessed by inspecting the final implementation (external quality), *Final user interfaces*, if the quality of the mashup is assessed by inspecting the user interfaces, and *Components*, if the quality of selected components is evaluated/considered before mashing them.

With regard to the criterion C4, a paper can be classified in one of the following answers: *New*, if it presents an approach from scratch (i.e., an evaluation or technique specifically defined for assessing the quality of mashups); or *Existing*, if it presents an extension of a previous approach (e.g., a technique defined for assessing the quality of Web services that has been applied to evaluate mashups).

With regard to the criterion C5, a paper can be classified in one of the following types of strategies that can be carried out depending on the purpose of the validation and the conditions for empirical investigation [6]: *Survey*, if it provides an investigation performed in retrospect; *Case study*, if it provides an observational study in which data is collected during real/simulated environments; *Controlled experiment*, if it provides a formal, rigorous, and controlled investigation that is based on verifying hypotheses; and *No validation*, if it does not provide any empirical study related to the product quality for mashups.

Finally, with regard to the criterion C6, a paper can be classified according to the context/environment in which the quality evaluation method/technique has been defined or are being used currently (industrial context and/or academic context).

3.6   Synthesis Methods

We applied both quantitative and qualitative synthesis methods. The quantitative synthesis was based on:

- Counting the primary studies that are classified in each answer from our criteria.
- Defining bubble plots in order to report the frequencies of combining the results from different research sub-questions. A bubble plot is basically two x–y scatter plots with bubbles in category intersections. This is useful to provide a map and giving a quick overview of a research field [15].
- Counting the number of papers found in each bibliographic source per year.

The qualitative synthesis is based on including several representative studies for each criterion by considering the results from the quality assessment.

3.7   Conducting the Review

The search to identify primary studies in the IEEE Xplore and ACM digital libraries was conducted on the 29th of December 2012. The application of the review protocol yielded the following results:

- The bibliographic database search identified 80 potentially relevant publications (46 from the IEEE Xplore and 34 from the ACM digital library). After applying the inclusion and exclusion criteria documented in Section 3.3, 29 publications were finally selected (13 from IEEE Xplore and 16 from ACM digital library).
- The manual bibliographic review of the other sources identified another 107 potentially relevant publications. After applying the inclusion and exclusion criteria, the following publications were finally selected: 9 papers (2 from WWW, 0 from ICWE, 1 from WISE, 1 from iiWAS, 1 from SOSE, 2 from ICSOC, and 2 from MASHUPS).

Therefore, a total of 38 research papers were selected by our inclusion/exclusion criteria. Some studies had been published in more than one journal/conference. In this case, we selected only the most complete version of the study.

4   Results

A summary of the results of our study is presented in Table 2. The included papers which are cited in this section as [SXX] are referred to Annex A. The full list of papers included in our systematic mapping study is available at http://www.dsic. upv.es/~afernandez/resources/qwe13.

With regard to the criterion C1 "Product quality characteristics addressed in the studies", results indicate that the most addressed quality attributes were *Performance efficiency* (63%) and *Security* (47%). The rationale is because of the data-intensive nature of mashups where quick and secure access is typically required. The less considered attributes were *Portability* (10%), *Maintainability* (21%), and *Compatibility* (10%). This is in line with some claims stated by other researchers such as *"Quality aspects such as maintainability or scalability play a minor role because the final Mashup is needed only for a short time"* [S04]. Although *Functional suitability* (42%) and *Reliability* (42%) received less consideration than we expected, we were surprised that *Usability* just account the of the 23% studies since this quality characteristic has usually been claimed as one of the most relevant in the Web domain.

With regard to the criterion C2 "*Stages based on the mashup development process*", results indicate that the majority of the studies agree to address quality issues when the mashup is being composed (55%). These studies are aimed at improving the composition process in order to obtain a mashup with better quality. For instance, in [S01] is presented a composition technique based on pipelines in order to improve the *Functional suitability* and *Performance* of the mashup obtained.

Table 2. Results of the systematic mapping

Criteria	Possible answers	# Studies	% Percentage
C1: Product quality characteristics addressed in the studies	Functional suitability	16	42.11
	Performance efficiency	24	63.16
	Compatibility	4	10.53
	Usability	9	23.68
	Reliability	16	42.11
	Security	18	47.37
	Maintainability	8	21.05
	Portability	4	10.53
C2: Stages based on the mashup development process	Component selection	14	36.84
	Mashup composition	21	55.26
	Mashup usage	16	42.11
C3: Artifacts involved	Conceptual models	8	21.05
	Source code	13	34.21
	Final user interfaces	9	23.68
	Components	15	39.47
C4: Type of approach	New	29	76.32
	Extension	9	23.68
C5: Type of validation	Survey	1	2.63
	Case Study	18	47.37
	Experiment	9	23.68
	No validation	11	28.95
C6: Approach usage	Industry	15	39.47
	Academy	33	86.84

The 42% of the papers focused on how to improve the quality when the mashup is completed. Some of these studies such as [S08], are aimed at offering recommendations to previous stages of the development process; whereas others studies such as [S05] are aimed at evaluating the quality in use to report problems. Finally, fewer studies considered the component selection stage to address quality issues (37%). We argue that more papers such as [S03] are needed in order to provide methods or guidelines to select the proper components which lead to a better mashup.

With regard to the criterion C3 "*Artifacts involved*", results indicate that the majority of the studies addressed quality issues at components selected to be mashed (40%). An example can be found in [S03] where components are previously rated in order to assist the evaluation of the obtained mashup. The 34% of the studies showed quality issues at source code of the mashup. An example can be found in [S10], where an algorithm analyses the source code in order to improve efficiency issues. Fewer studies considered the conceptual models (10%) that define the component composition in order to improve quality issues. We found an example of this kind of studies in [S02], where orchestration and business models are analyzed to improve the mashup acceptance. Finally, the 23% of the studies analyzed the interaction of the mashup in order to discover deficiencies, such as for example in [S06], where areas for defining metrics were explored.

With regard to the criterion C4 "*Type of approach*", results indicate that the majority of the papers (76%) presented new approaches to deal with quality issues on Web mashups. Some of these studies such as [S07], proposed ideas from scratch or inspired in other domains. We argue that this finding shows an agreement among authors in the importance of considering Web mashups not only as simple Web applications.

With regard to the criterion C5 "*Type of Validation*", results indicate that the majority of the studies have presented *Case studies* in order to validate their approaches (47%). This is an encouraged result since it improves the situation described in a systematic review presented in [13] which stated a lack of rigorous empirical studies for Web Engineering research. An example of case study can be found in [S12]. However, fewer *Experiments* have been conducted (23%). Experiments should be more employed since they provide a high level of control and are useful for evaluating approaches in a more rigorous way. An example of experiment can be found in [S09]. Finally, surveys are the less preferred study for other researchers (3%) and the rest of the papers (29%) did not provide any kind of validation or they just described proof of concepts.

With regard to the criterion C6 "*Approach usage*", results indicate that the majority of the studies (87%) have been performed from the academic research viewpoint, for instance in [S08]. However, it is also important to note that a worthy 39% of the studies were performed from the industry research viewpoint. These studies, such as [S11], were especially interested at addressing security issues, which have been detected as relevant for practitioners.

It is worthy to mention that the analysis of the number of research studies on quality issues for mashups showed that there has been a growth of interest on this topic since 2007. Figure 1 shows the number of selected publications by year and source. We believe that this growing interest supports the relevance of conducting evidence-based studies in this area.

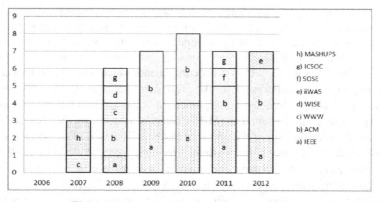

Fig. 1. Number of publications by year and source

The criteria were combined to establish a mapping with the aim of providing an overview of quality issues for mashups. This mapping allows us to obtain more information about how the results from each criterion are related to the others, and what the possible research gaps are. Due to space reasons, Figure 2 only shows one of the bubble plots which is related to compared the criterion C1 *"quality characteristics addressed"* against the C2 *"phases"* and C5 *"type of validation"*. Other bubble plots are available at http://www.dsic.upv.es/~afernandez/resources/qwe13.

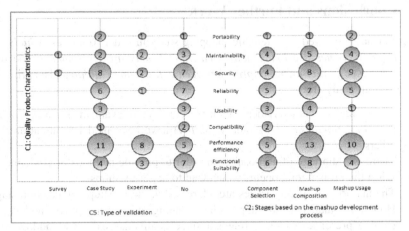

Fig. 2. Mapping results obtained from the combination of C1 against C2 and C5

The mapping results confirm that most important stage for all the quality characteristics is the Mashup Composition. However, it shows research gaps such as relevant quality characteristic have not been validated through controlled experiments (e.g., *Security, Usability, Reliability*) and other characteristics which are important for the Web domain have been neglected (e.g. *Usability, Reliability*).

5   Threats to Validity

The main limitations of this study are the scope of our research questions, publication and selection bias, inaccuracy in data extraction, and misclassification.

The scope of our research question was limited to the product quality of the mashups. However, we realized during the conduction of this mapping that quality of the development process is an interesting extension which will be explored as further work.

Publication bias refers to the problem that positive results are more likely to be published than negative results [12]. We are aware about this inherent limitation to our bibliographic sources. With regard to publication selection bias, we chose the sources where papers about mashup development are normally published, and we compared the retrieved papers against a small sample which was previously identified as relevant papers to appear. However, we did not consider some other bibliographic sources such as SpringerLink or ScienceDirect that may have affected the completeness of our systematic mapping. Moreover, since our bibliographical search was conducted at the end of 2012, some papers not yet indexed in this last period were not considered.

Finally, we attempted to alleviate the threats of inaccuracy in data extraction and misclassification by conducting the classifications of the papers with three reviewers and solving the appeared discrepancies by consensus.

6   Conclusions and Further Work

This paper has presented a systematic mapping study in order to address *which/how product quality issues are being addressed in Web mashup development*, and *how have the product quality-aware approaches been defined and validated*. The principal findings of our study are:

- Some quality characteristics which we consider relevant in the Web domain (i.e., *Functional suitability* and *Usability*) have been paid less attention than others.
- There is a shortage of approaches in order to provide methods or guidelines to select the proper components which lead to better mashups.
- The majority of quality issues are addressed at the mashup composition stage. However, quality-aware approaches dealing with conceptual models are gaining presence, which is relevant since quality issues can be addressed at earlier stages of the mashup development process.
- There is a shortage of controlled experiments provide evidence, in a more rigorous way, about the existing quality evaluation methods/techniques for mashups.

Our results also confirmed some claims stated by other researchers according to the most relevant quality characteristics such as *Performance efficiency* and *Security*. In addition, they have been useful to detect some research gaps, such as the need of more empirical studies, especially controlled experiments involving quality characteristics such as *Security, Usability, Reliability*; and the need of more quality-aware mashup development proposals for other characteristics which being important for the Web domain have been neglected in the mashup development (e.g. *Usability, Reliability*).

Although our findings may be indicative of the field, further work is needed to confirm the results obtained. This further work will include the extension of this systematic mapping by a) including other sources (e.g., SpringerLink, Science Direct), b) identify and including quality issues for the mashup development process itself, c) including compositionality issues, and d) analyzing the rigor of the empirical studies proposed through a systematic review addressing more specific research questions. We are also intended to address some of the research gaps discovered. For instance, addressing usability definition and evaluation of mashups through a usability model tailored to the salient and specific characteristics of them.

Acknowledgements. This work is funded by the MULTIPLE project (TIN2009-13838), the Senescyt program (scholarships 2011), and the Erasmus Mundus Programme of the European Commission under the Transatlantic Partnership for Excellence in Engineering - TEE Project.

References

1. Alkhalifa, E.: The Future of Enterprise Mashups. Business Insights. E-Strategies for Resource Management Systems, (2009).
2. Beemer, B., Gregg, D.: Mashups: A Literature Review and Classification Framework. Future Internet. 1, pp. 59–87 (2009).
3. Cappiello, C., Daniel, F., Matera, M.: A Quality Model for Mashup Components, 9th International Conference (ICWE 2009), pp. 236–250 (2009).
4. Cappiello, C., Daniel, F., Matera, M., Pautasso, C.: Information Quality in Mashups. IEEE Internet Computing 14(4), pp. 32–40 (2010).
5. Cappiello, C., Matera, M., Picozzi, M., Daniel, F., Fernandez, A.: Quality-Aware Mashup Composition: Issues, Techniques and Tools, 8th International Conference on the Quality of Information and Communications Technology (QUATIC 2012), pp. 10–19 (2012).
6. Fenton, N.E., Pfleeger, S.L.: Software Metrics: A Rigorous and Practical Approach (2nd ed.), International Thompson 1996, ISBN 978-1-85032-275-7, pp. I-XII, 1-638 (1996).
7. Fernandez, A., Insfran, E., Abrahão, S.: Usability evaluation methods for the web: A systematic mapping study. Information and Software Technology 53(8): 789-817 (2011).
8. Garousi, V., Mesbah, A., Betin-Can, A., Mirshokraie, S.: A systematic mapping study of web application testing. Information and Software Technology 55(8): 1374-1396 (2013).
9. Grammel, L., Storey, M.-A.: A survey of Mashup development environments. The Smart Internet. 137-151 (2010).
10. Hoyer, V., Fischer, M.: Market Overview of Enterprise Mashup Tools, 6th International Conference on Service-Oriented Computing (ICSOC 2008), pp. 708–721 (2008).
11. ISO/IEC: ISO/IEC 25010 Systems and software engineering. Systems and software Quality Requirements and Evaluation (SQuaRE). System and software quality models, (2011)
12. Kitchenham, B., Charters, S.: Guidelines for performing Systematic Literature Reviews in Software Engineering. Version 2.3, ESBE Technical Report, Keele University, UK (2007).
13. Mendes, E.: A systematic review on the Web engineering research, International Symposium on Empirical Software Engineering (ISESE 2005), pp. 498–507 (2005).
14. OrangeLabs: State of the Art in Mashup tools, SocEDA project, pp. 1-59 (2011).
15. Petersen, K., Feldt, R., Mujtaba, S., Mattsson, M.: Systematic mapping studies in software engineering, 12th International Conference on Evaluation and Assessment in Software Engineering (EASE), pp. 68–77 (2008).
16. Raza, M., Hussain, F. Khadeer, Chang, E.: A methodology for quality-based mashup of data sources, 10th International Conference on Information Integration and Web-based Applications & Services (iiWAS 2008). pp. 528–533 (2008).
17. Saeed, A.: A Quality-based Framework for Leveraging the Process of Mashup Component Selection, https://gupea.ub.gu.se/handle/2077/21953, (2009).
18. Sharma, A., Hellmann, T.D., Maurer, F.: Testing of Web Services - A Systematic Mapping, 8th World Congress on Services (SERVICES 2012), pp. 346–352 (2012).

Annex A: Excerpt of the Papers Selected

Complete list available at: http://www.dsic.upv.es/~afernandez/resources/qwe13

S01. Biörnstad, B., Pautasso, C.: Let It Flow: Building Mashups with Data Processing Pipelines, International Conference on Service-Oriented Computing (ICSOC 2007), pp. 15–28 (2009).

S02. Bozzon, A., Brambilla, M., Facca, F., Carughu, G.: A Conceptual Modeling Approach to Business Service Mashup Development. 7th International Conference on Web Services, (ICWS 2009), pp. 751–758 (2009).

S03. Cappiello, C., Daniel, F., Matera, M.: A Quality Model for Mashup Components, 9th International Conference on Web Engineering (ICWE 2009), pp. 236-250 (2009).

S04. Cappiello, C., Daniel, F., Matera, M., Pautasso, C.: Information Quality in Mashups. IEEE Computer Society. 30–38 (2010).

S05. Jackson, C., Wang, H.: Subspace: secure cross-domain communication for web mashups. 16th International World Wide Web Conference (WWW 2007). pp. 611–620 (2007).

S06. Koschmider, A., Hoyer, V., Giessmann, A.: Quality metrics for mashups. Annual Research Conference of the South African Institute of Computer Scientists and Information Technologists. pp. 376–380 (2010).

S07. López, J., Bellas, F., Pan, A., Montoto, P.: A Component-Based Approach for Engineering Enterprise Mashups. International Conference on Web Engineering (ICWE 2009). pp. 30–44 (2009).

S08. Olsina, L., Lew, P., Dieser, A., Rivera, B.: Updating quality models for evaluating new generation web applications. J. Web Eng. 11, 3, 209–246 (2012).

S09. Riabov, A. V, Boillet, E., Feblowitz, M.D., Liu, Z., Ranganathan, A.: Wishful search: interactive composition of data mashups, 17th International World Wide Web Conference (WWW 2008), pp. 775–784 (2008).

S10. Roy Chowdhury, S., Daniel, F., Casati, F.: Efficient, Interactive Recommendation of Mashup Composition Knowledge. 11th International Conference Service-Oriented Computing (ICSOC 2011), pp. 374–388 (2011).

S11. Dos Santos, C.R.P., Bezerra, R.S., Granville, L.Z., Bertholdo, L.M., Cheng, W., Anerousis, N.: A data confidentiality architecture for developing management mashups. International Symposium on Integrated Network Management, pp. 49–56 (2011).

S12. Wohlstadter, E., Li, P., Cannon, B.: Web Service Mashup Middleware with Partitioning of XML Pipelines. Web Services, 2009. ICWS 2009. IEEE International Conference on. pp. 91–98 (2009).

Toward an Integrated Quality Evaluation of Web Applications with DEVS

Verónica Bogado, Silvio Gonnet, and Horacio Leone

INGAR, Universidad Tecnológica Nacional, CONICET
Avellaneda 3657, 3000 Santa Fe, Argentina
{vbogado,sgonnet,hleone}@santafe-conicet.gov.ar

Abstract. The increasing dynamic and complexity of Web systems turns quality evaluation at any stage of the development into a key issue for the project success in software development areas or organizations. This paper presents a novel approach to evaluate Web applications (WebApps) from their architectures, also considering their functionalities. Discrete EVents System Specification (DEVS) is proposed for behavior and structure analysis based on a set of quality criteria that serve as guidelines for development and evolution of these Web systems. Three quality attributes are considered in this version of the approach: performance, reliability, and availability, but the main advantages are potential scalability and adaptability that respond to the features of these systems.

Keywords: WebApp Quality Evaluation, Software Architecture, DEVS.

1 Introduction

Nowadays, Web has become an indispensable instrument to the most organizations. Thus, developing Web applications (WebApps) becomes a challenge for the software companies. WebApps are software systems with inherent multifaceted functionality and they exhibit sophisticated behavior and structure, which must answer to the demands of high quality and must have the ability to grow and evolve over the time [1]. Visible features at runtime, i.e. during the operation of these systems, such as performance, availability, or security are quality attributes that must to be considered and analyzed during the development and improvement of WebApps. However, software companies still develop this kind of software in an ad-hoc way, increasing problems related to quality. With the aim to assist developers in the design of WebApps, systematic and quantifiable approaches towards high-quality systems are required [2].

Despite the magnitude and impact of WebApps, there are no yet standard quality assessment tools that give support to the software architects/developers during the development of WebApps. However, Software Architecture (SA) is a mean to predict the success or failure of a project providing different views of the system to analysis quality aspects and there are some advances in this issue not only for Web system but for software in general ([3], [4]).

Q.Z. Sheng and J. Kjeldskov (Eds.): ICWE 2013 Workshops, LNCS 8295, pp. 79–91, 2013.
© Springer International Publishing Switzerland 2013

In this work, we integrate structural, functional, and quality aspects in the same analysis to improve quality of Web systems. We propose the construction of an executable model based on Discrete EVent System Specification (DEVS, [5]), where its execution will provide useful information to analyze behavior and quality of complex and sophisticated Web systems applied to several domains. This model is obtained from a Use Case Map (UCM, [6]) model that represents the architecture of the WebApp to be evaluated and the main scenarios. UCMs help architects to understand emergent behavior of complex and dynamic systems. DEVS formalism and its underlying framework for modeling and simulation (M&S) allow us to build an adaptable simulation environment, being an executable model of the WebApp under evaluation. The simulation elements are specified following the principles of modularity and hierarchy. This high level of abstraction enables us to represent suitably the concepts of the SA of WebApps and complex paths to represent complex dynamic scenarios (functionality) under common operation conditions on the Web. Therefore, DEVS allows developers to study potential scenarios and operational profiles of the system by mean of simulation, being a cheap way to prevent problems.

Parallel DEVS is particularly used for the specification of the simulation elements due to it provides a set of features commonly found in WebApps. An Atomic Parallel DEVS has a bag of ports to receive values at the same time with the possible multiple occurrences of its element. It allows all imminent components to be activated simultaneously and to send their outputs to other components having a confluent transition function to solve collisions between internal and external events. Coupled Parallel DEVS specifies components and how they are connected [5].

The rest of paper is organized as follows. Section 2 discusses related work providing an overview. Section 3 summarizes the approach based on DEVS to evaluate quality of Web systems. Section 4 describes a concrete WebApp, simulation outputs, and simple examples of how to use the information to improve the software designs after the evaluation. Section 5 presents conclusions and future work.

2   Related Work: An Overview

Quality evaluation employing architectural designs is becoming a key step in the software development, but it is a growing trend to focus on WebApps because of the demand of this kind of systems. In this context, there are general approaches based on scenarios and qualitative analysis [3]. More formal proposals employ Markov Decision Process with analytical resolution for a quantitative analysis of reliability, performance, or security ([7], [8]). Queueing Theory is useful to measure performance [9], while Petri Nets have been applied to evaluate different quality attributes in an analytical form [10]. These formal techniques have some critical limitations related to the modeling even more in WebApps development [11]. For example, complex systems or software components are reduced to simple states losing important information of the software elements.

Recently, empirical techniques have acquired importance in view that simulation and prototyping provide abstraction level to model real software system. In this way, prototyping has been successfully applied to evaluate SA but with high cost of implementing the prototype [12]. Palladio Component Model (PCM) is a metamodel to predict quality attributes. It has been focused on performance and reliability prediction transforming the concrete SAs into dynamic models ([13], [14]). Nevertheless, it is still necessary dynamic tools that can be as adaptable as the metamodel in terms of expressiveness of the target model, which results in a Queueing Network or Markov Chain losing features in the transformation. Finally, approaches based on the visual notation UCM allow architects to model complex and dynamic system, where scenarios and structures may change at runtime to study performance using Layered Queueing Network [15].

Although there are several approaches for SA evaluation, there is still need of a formal evaluation model that considers not only SA (structure) and isolated quality attributes but includes functionality in the same analysis. Furthermore, the elements of the evaluation model must represent the software elements and their sophistication. In this way, UCM provides elements to represent graphically system structures (simple and complex SA elements) and scenarios (functionality). On the other hand, DEVS is a formalism to specify complex and dynamic systems with the purpose of simulating them under possible scenarios and conditions. DEVS was successfully applied in other domains ([16], [17]). DEVS provides two basic types of models, atomic and coupled, and extensions like Parallel DEVS, which is used in this work. Parallel DEVS has some advantages to simulate Web background allowing concurrence and distributed components.

3 Quality Evaluation with DEVS

In this section, we summarize the elements considering for the simulation environment with DEVS formalism. Due to the need of considering functional requirements in the SA to have a complete view of the system, we propose UCM models as inputs to evaluate the system quality (Fig. 1(a)). UCM is an informal notation that captures functional requirements in terms of causal scenarios representing behavioral aspects at high level design [6]. UCM does not replace Unified Modeling Language (UML), but complements it being a bridge between requirements and design. Due to it is a graphical notation, it is useful to understand emergent behavior of complex and dynamic systems ([18], [19]). In the last few years, UCM has gained an important place to describe WebApps because it provides tools to treat sophisticated components and complex scenarios and operational uses.

UCM notation provides basic and architectural elements (Fig. 1 (a)): responsibilities, paths and components. A path represents a scenario of the system and it is executed after an external stimulus has happened. A responsibility point is a place where the state of a system is affected or interrogated. Stimulus is a start point in an execution where a pointer starts in this place and then is moved along the path. Thus, the pointer enters and leaves components touching responsibility points inside. Finally, end position is reached and the execution is finished by emitting a response. UCM does not prescribe the number of threads associated with a path. So, concurrency can be modeled with AND-Fork/Join elements generating several concurrent subscenarios. Alternative subscenarios can be represented using OR-Fork/Join ([6],[18],[20]).

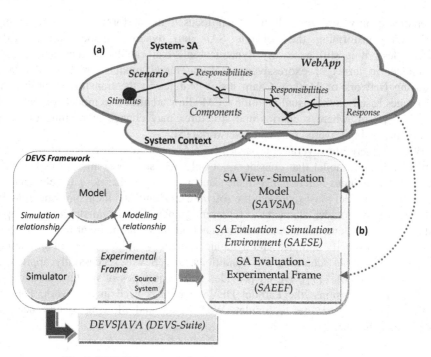

Fig. 1. DEVS Framework for the quality evaluation of WebApps

To complement this flexible but informal notation, we have proposed a DEVS-based simulation environment with the purpose of evaluating software quality. This approach adds semantic to the simulation elements that represent software elements building dynamic models. DEVS formalism specifies the architecture and behavior of Web systems without losing important features of the responsibilities, simple and composite components (hierarchical structures), among others. Furthermore, it integrates several perspectives and quality attributes in the same analysis.

A conceptual framework for modeling and simulation (*DEVS Framework*, Fig. 1(b)) gives support to the formalism. It is composed by three entities [5]: i) *Model*: system specification that defines the structure and behavior to generate data comparable to data from the real world, ii) *Simulator*: computation system that executes the instruction of the model giving life to it, iii) *Experimental Frame*: conditions under which the system is observed for the experimentation and validation of the model. *Modeling* and *Simulation* relationships link these parts. Therefore, the proposed simulation environment (*SAESE*, Fig. 1(b)) has two main conceptual parts: simulation model for SA evaluation (*SAVSM*, Fig. 1(b)) and experimental frame for SA evaluation (*SAEEF*, Fig. 1(b)). *Simulator* is taken from *DEVSJAVA (DEVS-Suite* 2.0[1], Fig. 1(b)) implementation encapsulating this part from the other two. Keeping separate theses entities gives some benefits such as the same model can be executed by different simulators or several experiments can be changed for studying different situations.

---

[1] http://www.acims.arizona.edu/SOFTWARE/software.shtml

DEVS is an adaptable and scalable approach to tackle the SA evaluation problem in the context of Web systems. It provides elements to build simple and complex dynamic systems keeping the semantic of the Web software elements. Elements of the core of UCM notation are specified as models of DEVS formalism.

Fig. 2 summarizes DEVS-based evaluation process, which has four main stages: specify UCM for the WebApp, generate the DEVS-based simulation environment, configure and execute the simulation, and analyses the results to make decisions, where each one involves a set of activities detailed in the diagram. First, architects (or developers) have to specify the SA using UCM notation (*SA UCM*), which can be obtained from the user requirements, if it is an early evaluation, or from the implementation, if it is a late evaluation (activity 1). So functional requirements define the scenarios of the Web system and non-functional aspects provide information to build the SA. This input model is translated into a DEVS hierarchy (activity 2), where each element is translated into simulation elements specified in DEVS, major details can be found in a previous work [21]. So, simple elements of UCM such as OR-Fork/Join, AND-Fork/Join, stimulus (start point) are specified as Atomic Parallel models, being the basis to build more complex structures. In this way, responsibility, simple/composite components, system (SA view), and the whole UCM are specified as Coupled Parallel models.

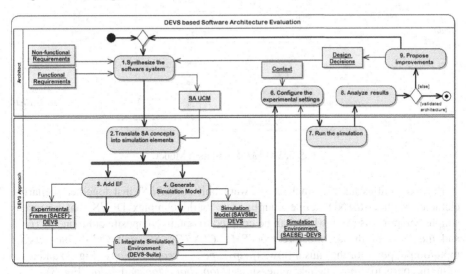

Fig. 2. DEVS-based quality evaluation process

Simulation elements generate the simulation model while configure the EF (activities 3 and 4, Fig. 2). Simulation model represents the WebApp and it is a Coupled Parallel DEVS called *SAVSM*. The background under the Web system operates is represented by the EF, which is also a coupled model (*SAEEF*). These two parts build the whole simulation environment for the WebApp by implementing them in *DEVS-Suite* (activity 5, Fig. 2). Architect/developer has to configure the parameters to run the simulation (evaluation) using information to adjust the probability distributions (activity 6). After the evaluation (activity 7, Fig. 2), a set of measures and quality indicators (explained in the next subsection) are obtained. This information allows architects/developers to analyze the system (activity 8) and can make design decisions if the quality requirements were not achieved (activity 9).

As we have mentioned, simulation elements build a hierarchical structure of DEVS models that represents the whole simulation environment for the UCM of the WebApp. It has two main parts that work together to simulate the dynamic of the system. In this way, the simulation model (*SAVSM*, Fig. 3) represents the WebApp architecture and the main scenarios. An input port is defined (*erip*) to receive requests from external sources (*SAEG* from *SAEEF*, Fig. 3) and a set of output ports to emit the responses, processed requests (*esop*, Fig. 3), and measures (described in Table 1 in the following section) taken from internal components (*rtaop*, *rdtop*, *rrtop*, and *rfailop*, Fig. 3) that are sent to the EF (*SAEEF*, Fig. 3).

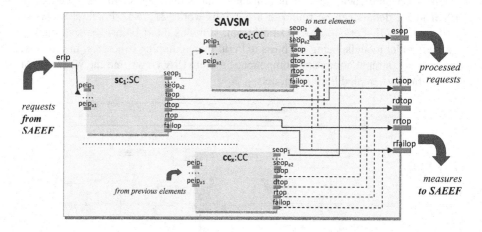

Fig. 3. *SAVSM:* Simulation Model

Responsibilities are the smallest software unit (*CPXRES*) that together scenarios elements such OR/AND define couplings to build complex DEVS that represent simple components (*SC*), which can be coupled to obtain composite components (*CC*) and the view of the architecture (*SAVSM*). *CPXRES, SC,* and *CC* define sets of input/output ports for the causal flows ($peip_1...peip_{a1}$, $seop_1... seop_{a2}$, Fig. 3) and a set of output ports to propagate taken measures (*taop, dtop, rtop,* and *failop*, Fig. 3).

The experimental frame, *SAEEF*, has a simulation element that represents the stimulus of the system (*SAEG*, Fig. 4), which "gives life" to the WebApp. It emits a request as output using the port *rop*. Other component defines the start and end of the quality evaluation (*SAEA*, Fig. 4) sending signals using the port *ssop*. Finally, there is a set of elements called "stat" that are responsible for the calculation of quality indicators, one per quality attribute considered in the evaluation. So, we have defined a DEVS model for the followings quality attributes visible at run time (Fig. 4): performance (*SAEPS*), availability (*SAEAS*), and reliability (*SAERS*). These elements have a set of input ports that receive measures or messages from other simulation elements, which are used to compute quality indicators (described in the next section). The input ports allow *SAEEF* to propagate the measures sent from the *SAVSM* (*rtaip*, *procreqip*, *rfailip*, *rdowntimeip*, and *rrecovtimeip*, Fig. 4) and the signal to start the evaluation (*sip*, Fig. 4). The output interface emits the system indicators (explained in Table 2, next section) for being used in future simulation of more complex environment in the Web context.

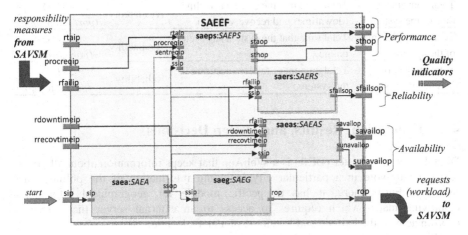

Fig. 4. *SAEEF:* Experimental Frame

3.1   Software Quality Attributes and Related Measures

In this work, metrics related to performance, availability, and reliability are considered to take direct and indirect measures [22]. Responsibilities are the main providers of quantitative information so a set of basic metrics are defined (Table 1).

Table 1. Measures taken from each responsibility

ID	Metric	Description
rta	Turnaround time per request	Time that a responsibility requires to answer to a request.
fdt	Downtime per failure	Time that responsibility is "failed" due to a failure.
frt	Recovery time per failure	Time that a responsibility needs to return to a normal operation after a failure has occurred.
fn	Number of Failures	Failures that have happened in a responsibility.

Measures are propagated through the hierarchy from simple components to the top, *SAVSM* (e.g. *taop*, *dtop*, *rtop*, and *failop* respectively, Fig. 3), sending theses values to the *SAEEF*. Specific simulation elements have a set of specific domain operations that return a more complex value (Table 2). These measures can be quality indicators of the system, being outputs of the simulation environment (Table 2), or responsibilities (e.g. turnaround time or downtime per responsibility, omitted here).

Table 2. Quality Indicators: Simulation Outputs

Metric	Description	Attribute	Sim. Element
Average turnaround time of the system	Average time that the system requires to answer to a request.	Performance	*SAEPS* *(port staop)*
Average throughput of the system	Average number of request served per time unit in the system.	Performance	*SAEPS* *(port sthop)*
Total unavailable time of the system	Total time that the system is offline (downtimes and recovery times).	Availability	*SAEAS* *(port sunavailop)*
Total available time of the system	Total time that the system has been online.	Availability	*SAEAS* *(port savailop)*
Total number of failures of the system	Total amount of failures occurred in the system.	Reliability	*SAERS* *(port sfailsop)*

4 Evaluation, Results, and Design Decisions

Digital electoral register (DER) is a WebApp that keeps information about all people registered to vote in a particular city including information of the polling place locations. Furthermore, it has a specific module for geographical information employing maps, which requires to access to an external server that returns a coordinate with the latitude and longitude of a given location.

This WebApp has two kinds of users: elector and admin. They imply different scenarios and operational uses of the system. The first one is a role defined for anonymous people that ask for the polling locations. Each query generates a request to the system and this workload grows in the last month before the Election Day. This WebApp manages information about 60000 persons in condition to vote. On the other hand, admin users are related to other scenario that implies the refinement of the electoral register and the update of the information (electors and schools). In this process of refinement, the coordinates of each elector address and polling place is updated by submitting a query to the external server *Gmaps*. In the last scenario, a higher load is generated 45 days before the closure of the electoral register (a month before the Election Day).

Following the process presented in Section 3, we first specifies the Web system using UCM notation considering the SA and the main scenarios, then we translate this models into DEVS models, adjust parameters and run the simulation obtaining indicators to analyze the system behavior and validate the quality requirements.

SA was rebuilt from the current implementation applying reverse engineering. We have looked at the structure, functions, and operation of the WebApp to obtain a technology independent architecture to study several scenarios and validate the simulation environment. In this paper, we analyze the server and its behavior under several conditions of uses due to it is the main part of this system and it must to be evolved to manage not only information of people in a city but in a province or state. Consequently, a traditional SA for WebApps is obtained, Client-Server pattern structured in three levels with three main parts related to: presentation, business, and data. The view of the server (*DERSystem-Server*) in particular has a composite component (*WebServer*) and a simple component (*DBServer*), where the composite component has two simple components inside, *BusinessProcessor* and *GMapsLocator*. The first one executes the functionality related to the domain and the other one interacts with *GMaps*. All these components embody fundamental units at runtime for this WebApp. In conclusion, this architecture involves three levels of complexity, where a client requires services to the server specified in Fig. 4, and this server becomes a client to another external server (*GMaps*).

Each element of the architecture takes part according to the scenario. The first scenario is focused on the elector query involving user requests (electors) as stimuli and a set of responsibilities (Fig. 5). So, the scenario starts when a client connects to the server (*r1*), enters the required data and an alphanumeric key that appears as an image (*r2*). User data is validated (*r3*) while Captcha test is executed (*r4*) producing concurrent subscenarios. Finally, the information required in the query is retrieved from the DB, emitting a response with the information or an error message. Here the performance is a critical issue due to the big workload generated by the potential voters near to the Election Day (previous month to this crucial day).

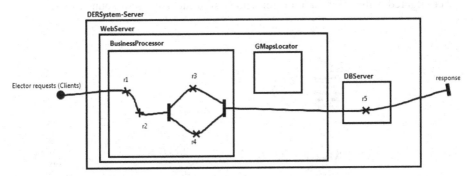

Fig. 5. UCM of the Server: Scenario 1- Elector Query

The second scenario defines a more complex path involving several alternatives in the causal flow (Fig. 6). The stimuli are given by the user requests (admin profile) through the client, which connects to the server (*r1*). Once it is connected, the user can chose between three options that produce three possible subscenarios: elector registration (*r2*), schools registration -polling places- (*r3*), and geographical coordinates updating of registered electors (*r4*). The first two options cause retrieving the neighborhood associated to the given address (*r5*). The alternative paths are joined to require the calculation of the coordinate (*r6*), where this responsibility involves a query to *GMaps*. Lastly, once the coordinates are available, the information is updated in the DB (*r7*) finishing the causal flow.

Regarding operation, this scenario has minor load due to the number of administrators even so during the critical period. Here availability takes an important place.

We describe two quality attribute scenarios as examples. The first requirement is related to system performance specifying that the turnaround time has to be less than 2000 ms under normal operation of *DERSystem-Server* to respond to the user requests (electors). An availability scenario specifies that the unavailable time has to be less than 60 min per month under normal operation of *DERSystem-Server*.

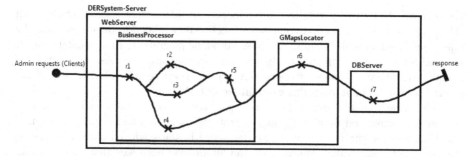

Fig. 6. UCM of the Server: Scenario 2- Elector Register Refinement (admin)

Fig. 7 illustrates the simulation environment for the second scenario and SA of the WebApp in *DEVS-Suite*. Atomic models (grey nodes) compose coupled models that represent responsibilities, simple and composite components, and view. Parameters are configured using information from reports of failures and turnaround times.

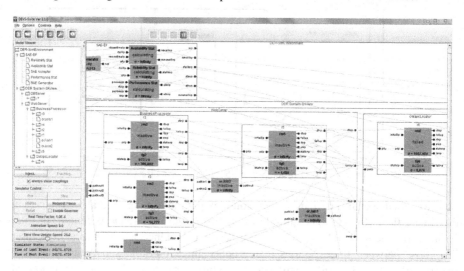

Fig. 7. DEVS Simulation Environment: Scenario 2- Elector Register Refinement (admin)

A late SA evaluation takes place to understand the WebApp (DER System) in an improvement process. In both scenarios, the simulation was run under conditions of each critical period, where the request arrivals are defined by Poisson distribution. Table 3 summarizes these conditions in columns two (period under evaluation) and three (workload). The following columns present the system results (average for ten simulations runs): number of requests sent to WebApp, turnaround time, unavailable time, and number of failures. The real time employed by the simulator to execute each scenario under the defined conditions is detailed in the last column.

Table 3. Summary of results after simulations runs

	Operation time	Requests	Turnaround time	Unavailable time	Failures	Simulation time
Scenario 1	30 days	11514	**1029.63 ms**	**42.96 min**	25.6	21 min
Scenario 2	45 days	3033	**2643.11 ms**	**106.69 min**	47.8	13.5 min

a. PC: Intel Core i7 860 2.80Ghz, RAM 4GB

Highlighted data can be directly used to validate the quality requirements specified previously. The performance requirement is achieved by the first scenario but not by the second one. Regarding availability requirement, the unavailable time has to be less than 60 min per month, so the first scenario is fulfilled but the second one not (should be less than 90 min in 45 days). These examples and other information that describes each responsibility (omitted here, [21]) can be used to make design decisions. It could help architects to find strengths and weaknesses in the complex structure and behavior of WebApps.

Additional information taken from the implementation was used to validate the outputs of the simulation environment detailed in Table 3. Now the simulation environment can be used to evaluate the WebApp under new operational conditions.

5   Conclusions and Future Work

The main contribution of this work consists in evaluating Web systems employing DEVS. A behavioral and structural analysis driven by quality attributes can be done using a high level design specified with UCM notation. This integrated analysis considers the main perspectives of the system: SA (structure), functionality (scenarios), and quality (measures). A DEVS environment is briefly described: simulation model represents the Web system and the experimental frame implements quality goals and the environment that interacts with the system. Despite of this work presented general designs, DEVS approach can be adjusted to specific Web technologies (Web services, presentation design, frameworks as .Net, JAVA EE).

This approach provides several advantages to evaluate quality of WebApps that could improve this kind of complex and dynamic systems. Firstly, high level abstraction, a modular and hierarchical way to build domain-specific simulation elements. Secondly, model decoupled from the simulator. Thirdly, the experimental frame decoupled from the other two parts specifies the conditions under which the system is observed, and the operational formulation of quality goals including one element for each attribute that will be analyzed. Finally, homogenous representation of the simulation elements allows the interchange of them building a simulation environment based on interface and encapsulation of the internal mechanisms.

Regarding the case study, we have implemented the proposed simulation environment for a WebApp, which has a traditional Web architecture client-server. Two relevant scenarios were validated, analyzing quality requirements and obtaining information to make design decisions that improve the current design or to make changes that address new requirements.

Several issues remain open. Other quality attributes that are visible at runtime will be studied, adding components to the experimental frame. In this way, new quality aspects could be considered in the analysis to make design decisions that improve the quality of WebApps. Moreover, it is interesting to include particularities of Web systems in the model, behavioral or structural patterns, which are domain-specific to resolve the inherent complexity of these systems for better results after the simulation.

Acknowledgements. Authors thank the financial support from Universidad Tecnológica Nacional, CONICET, and Agencia Nacional de Promoción Científica y Tecnológica (PAE-PICT 02315).

References

1. Pressman, R.: What a Tangled Web We Weave. IEEE Software 18(1), 18–21 (2001)
2. Casteleyn, S., Florian, D., Dolog, P., Matera, M.: Engineering Web Applications. Springer (2009)
3. Clements, P., Kazman, R., Klein, M.: Evaluating Software Architectures: Methods and Case Studies. Addison-Wesley (2002)
4. Bass, L., Clements, P., Kazman, R.: Software Architecture in Practice. Addison-Wesley (2012)
5. Zeigler, B., Praehofer, H., Kim, T.: Theory of Modeling and Simulation–Integrating Discrete Event and Continuous Complex Dynamic Systems. Academic Press (2000)
6. Amyot, D.: Introduction to the User Requirement Notation: Learning by Example. Computer Networks 42(3), 285–301 (2003)
7. Wang, W., Pan, D., Chen, M.H.: Architecture-based Software Reliability Modeling. Journal of Systems and Software 79(1), 132–146 (2006)
8. Sharma, V., Trivedi, K.: Quantifying Software Performance, Reliability and Security: An architecture-based Approach. Journal of Systems and Software 80(4), 493–509 (2007)
9. Spitznagel, B., Garlan, D.: Architecture-based Performance Analysis. In: Proc. 1998 Conference on Software Engineering and Knowledge Engineering, pp. 146–151 (1998)
10. Fukuzawa, K., Saeki, M.: Evaluating Software Architecture by Coloured Petri Nets. In: Proc. 14th International Conference on Software Engineering and Knowledge Engineering, pp. 263–270 (2002)
11. Singh, L.K., Tripathi, A.K., Vinod, G.: Software Reliability Early Prediction in Architectural Design Phase: Overview and Limitations. Journal of Software Engineering and Applications 4(3), 181–186 (2011)
12. Christensen, H., Hansen, K.: An Empirical Investigation of Architectural Prototyping. Journal of Systems and Software 83(1), 133–142 (2010)
13. Becker, S., Koziolek, H., Reussner, R.: The Palladio Component Model for Model-driven Performance Prediction. Journal of Systems and Software 82(1), 3–22 (2009)
14. Brosch, F., Koziolek, H., Buhnova, B., Reussner, R.: Architecture-based reliability prediction with the Palladio Component Model. IEEE Transactions on Software Engineering (2011)
15. Petriu, D.B., Woodside, M.: Software Performance Models from System Scenarios in Use Case Maps. In: Field, T., Harrison, P.G., Bradley, J., Harder, U. (eds.) TOOLS 2002. LNCS, vol. 2324, pp. 141–158. Springer, Heidelberg (2002)
16. Byon, E., Pérez, E., Ding, Y., Ntaimo, L.: Simulation of Wind Farm Maintenance Operations using DEVS. Simulation 87(12), 1091–1115 (2011)

17. Ferayorni, A.E., Sarjoughian, H.S.: Domain driven Simulation Modeling for Software Design. In: Proc. of the 2007 Summer Computer Simulation Conference (SCSC 2007), pp. 297–304 (2007)
18. Buhr, R.: Use Case Maps as Architectural Entities for Complex Systems. IEEE Transactions on Software Engineering 24(12), 1131–1155 (1998)
19. Amyot, D., Mussbacher, G.: User Requirements Notation: The First Ten Years The Next Ten Years. Journal of Software 6(5), 747–768 (2011)
20. de Bruin, H., van Vliet, H.: Quality-driven Software Architecture Composition. The Journal of Systems and Software 66(3), 269–284 (2003)
21. Bogado, V., Gonnet, S., Leone, H.: A Discrete Event Simulation Model for the Analysis of Software Quality Attributes. CLEI Electronic Journal 14(3), Paper 3 (2011)
22. ISO/IEC 9126-1: Software Engineering – Product Quality – Part 1: Quality Model, Number 1 (2001)

Assessing Corporate Web Sites:
Quality Model and Methodology

Daniela Fogli and Giovanni Guida

Dipartimento di Ingegneria dell'Informazione
Università degli Studi di Brescia
Via Branze 38, 25123 Brescia, Italy
{fogli,guida}@ing.unibs.it

Abstract. The paper presents a new quality model for corporate web sites based on three fundamental concepts: ultimate quality, external quality, and internal quality. External quality is defined in detail through a suitable set of characteristics and sub-characteristics and covers a comprehensive spectrum of the properties a good web site should show. A practical assessment methodology for external quality is finally proposed, which employs expert evaluators instead of actual users, in order to make the evaluation less costly and faster.

Keywords: quality model, ultimate quality, external quality, quality assessment.

1   Introduction

Corporate web sites are more and more pervasive in today economic world and play a crucial role for success in the marketplace. Notwithstanding the variety of good methodologies that have been proposed over the years for the design of web sites, it often happens that users' needs are not satisfied and site owners do not obtain adequate return on their investment. Failure and low effectiveness of many corporate web sites can be related to their poor quality [20].

Quality is a fundamental indicator of the expected success of a web site and therefore its assessment is an important activity all during its life cycle. Assessment can be carried out during the design and development phases in order to identify and correct emerging problems as soon as possible; but quality should also be monitored during the overall operation phase of a web site, in order to guarantee its continuous improvement. Several quality models for web sites have been proposed in literature. Inspired to ISO/IEC 9126 [8] and to the more recent ISO/IEC 25010 [10], such quality models identify sets of characteristics and sub-characteristics that are specific for assessing the quality of web sites (see for example: [3], [15-18], [21-27]). However, some important limitations affect existing quality models:

- The goals of the site owner are not sufficiently considered, if not neglected at all. Indeed, the success of a corporate web site depends not only on the satisfaction of users' needs, but also on the achievement of company goals.

Q.Z. Sheng and J. Kjeldskov (Eds.): ICWE 2013 Workshops, LNCS 8295, pp. 92–103, 2013.
© Springer International Publishing Switzerland 2013

- The usability dimension is overestimated. For example, while all models include usability as a basic quality characteristic, less or no emphasis is given to aesthetics and how it influences user perception of usability, as demonstrated in [2], [11], [13]. Also the usefulness of the contents offered by a website is often neglected.
- The user point of view is prevailing. Usability, aesthetics and usefulness all contribute to the satisfaction of final users, who are, however, only an intermediate target for a web site, whose ultimate goal is a positive impact on the company and its performance.
- There are overlappings among characteristics and sub-characteristics. This happens both in the models inspired to software quality standards (e.g., [22], [26]) and in those based on the web site development model [23] or on the stakeholder organization [24].
- Several models are not scalable. Most models are too complex to be applied to the typical web sites of small and medium enterprises; the possibility to focus only on some quality characteristics, neglecting the others, is generally not considered.
- Applying a quality model is always a complex and time-consuming activity. Quality models are generally not supported by a specific application methodology that allows keeping the evaluation process within precise time and budget limits; their implementation is left to the evaluators who must make all relevant decisions.

The work described in this paper emerges from a long practical experience in the evaluation of corporate web sites, aimed at identifying the causes that led to failures, poor performance or unsatisfactory results [1]. The paper thus analyzes the concept of quality for corporate web sites and proposes a new quality model, which aims at overcoming some of the limitations mentioned above and which can be easily tailored to a variety of cases of practical interest. The model focuses in particular on external quality and proposes a methodology for assessing corporate web sites. The model and the methodology are being tested in a set of real case studies that will be discussed in a future work.

The paper is organized as follows: Section 2 proposes a concept of quality that evolves the definitions provided in quality standards and literature work; Section 3 illustrates the proposed quality model, focusing on external quality characteristics; Section 4 describes the main features of the relevant assessment methodology; Section 5 provides some comparisons with literature work and hints for future work.

2   Defining Quality

According to ISO-8402 [5] *quality* is defined as "the set of characteristics of an entity that give that entity the ability to satisfy expressed and implicit needs". A similar concept is later assumed also in ISO-9000 [9] that defines quality as "the ability of a set of intrinsic characteristics to satisfy requirements".

In the specific case of software products, ISO/IEC 25010 [10] introduces a *product quality* model that encompasses both *internal qualities* and *external qualities* of the system and a distinct *quality in use* model that refers to "the impact that the product has on stakeholders".

As pointed out in [3], [22], [24], there are good reasons that support the need for a different quality model for web sites. In fact, web sites feature a set of peculiarities that make them different from ordinary software products and call for a specific approach to quality and quality assessment. In the following we present a definition of quality partially coherent with most literature approaches, but better specified according to a large practical experience in web site assessment.

First of all, the concept of quality of a web site refers to the goals of its *owner*, namely the company that pays for its construction and expects to obtain concrete benefits from its use, for example, increasing online sales, improving customer care, exploiting brand reputation, disseminating product knowledge. We call this type of quality **ultimate quality**, since it refers to the final objectives that the web site should satisfy or, in other words, to its effectiveness in the target context.

Apparently, this concept of quality shares several aspects with the notion of *quality in use* recalled above, since both generically refer to the impact of the system on the target environment when it is actually used in a specific context. However, differently from quality in use, ultimate quality focuses just on the owner of a web site, and not on all possible stakeholders, who encompass a large variety of actors including, among others, the users. Moreover, our concept of ultimate quality is based on a set of characteristics that strictly depend on the specific company considered and on its goals, and that cannot be of general validity; while a company might focus on increasing sales, another might aim at collecting user feedback to improve product design, and still another might be interested in promoting relationships with the stakeholders. Quality in use, instead, assumes a fixed set of characteristics (namely, effectiveness, efficiency, satisfaction, safety, and usability) [10] of general validity and mostly company independent.

Ultimate quality, while being in a sense the most important aspect of quality, does not allow, however, identification of weak and strong points of a web site, thus failing to provide useful hints about where and in what directions it could be improved. Moreover, it can be noted that a web site is a very particular type of software product, which, in order to be effective, requires the collaboration of users, who exploit the contents it offers and, this way, contribute to the achievement of the goals of the owner. As a further step, we can then define a second type of quality, called – as widely accepted in literature [24] – **external quality**. External quality captures the properties of a web site, which make it attractive, useful and rewarding, thus ensuring a large set of satisfied visitors and then supporting its effectiveness. External quality can be articulated through a suitable set of characteristics (and sub-characteristics) that are of general validity but of course can be more or less important for a specific web site. External quality is clearly a necessary condition for success and therefore we can assume it as a reasonable gauge of ultimate quality.

Turning now to the methods for assessing external quality, it is important to distinguish between two approaches. From a strict theoretical perspective, assessing external quality requires experimentation with suitable samples of users in a suitable test setting. We call external quality measured through user experiments **actual quality** since it represents the quality actually experimented by web site users in a real interaction context. Measuring actual quality is however a complex, time consuming and costly task. Even a single experiment about an aspect of usability – say for example, learnability – can require tens of users, a wide collection of test cases, a number of experimental sessions, and a complex framework for collecting and processing data. Therefore, we introduce a second approach to assessing external quality based on experimentation and analysis of a web site by an evaluator or a panel of evaluators. We call this type of quality **expected quality**, since it represents an estimate of actual quality, possibly less reliable but definitely much simpler and less costly to assess. This difference between actual and expected quality introduces a distinction generally not considered in literature and often neglected in practice, thus introducing imprecision and sometimes even misunderstanding in the assessment. However, expected quality cannot be assimilated to – or confused with – actual quality: they are different concepts and must be considered differently. Asserting that a given web site features a low usability is poorly meaningful if one does not specify whether it has been assessed by users or by web site evaluators.

Finally, if the assessment of external quality reveals weak points or even critical aspects in a web site, it is then important to identify how it might be improved. To this purpose, we must assume the point of view of the designer and assess quality under this new perspective. This brings to the definition of a third type of quality, usually called **internal quality**, which accounts for the reasons behind the external behavior of the web site and points out what is right and what is wrong in its internal structure and operation. Internal quality depends on a variety of design choices – from information architecture to graphics, from page layout to the use of colors – and can be considered as the end-point of a progressive refinement of the concept of quality, from the goals of the owner to the deep technical reasons that can make them satisfied to a certain degree. Clearly, a set of general characteristics for internal quality might be defined, but this issue is outside the scope of the present research.

The concept of quality illustrated above is summarized in Figure 1.

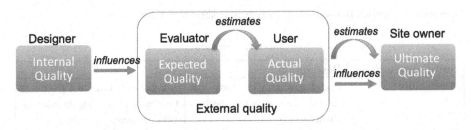

Fig. 1. The concept of quality

In this paper we focus on the quality model behind external quality (Section 3) and we propose a methodology for assessing expected quality (Section 4).

3   The Quality Model

3.1   The Requirements

In the essence, a quality model is made up of a structured system of **quality characteristics** and **sub-characteristics** that a web site is expected to satisfy to a certain degree. The quality model for external quality proposed in this paper is based on three main requirements:

- The model should provide a credible estimate of ultimate quality, that is of the effectiveness of a web site for the purposes of the owner. A quality model that cannot account for this aspect is practically useless and would not be applied outside the research laboratory.
- The model should be simple, both to understand and to apply. Too generic and abstract models cannot be directly applied; whilst, highly refined but complex models are not suitable for mass application, as it is required in the present situation, where almost all companies might largely benefit from an assessment of their web site that can be used as a concrete basis for improvement.
- The model should be tailorable to a variety of different contexts and assessment objectives, and especially to a wide range of companies, from large enterprises to small-medium ones. In particular, one must be free to focus on the characteristics (or sub-characteristics) that are considered more important discarding the others.

Our model for external quality comprises five characteristics, namely **operation, accessibility, usability, impact** and **usefulness**. These characteristics and their sub-characteristics have been derived from literature and practical experience gathered in the assessment of corporate web sites. They are defined in detail in the following, along with example tests that may be carried out to assess each sub-characteristic, which include heuristics, metrics, and checklists, depending on the relevant type.

3.2   Operation

Operation comprises five sub-characteristics as shown in Table 1.

Table 1. Operation

Sub-characteristic	Description	Test
Availability	Does the web site regularly respond to requests from web clients?	Number of failures in a given time interval, average duration of failures, mean time between failures, total time of unavailability
Reachability	Can a search engine easily find the web site?	Page rank with a variety of search terms and search engines
Compatibility	Does the web site operate correctly with a variety of devices?	Correct operation with a variety of web browsers, user agents, assistive devices
Functionality	Does the web site perform correctly?	Corrupted pages, broken or wrong links, navigation errors, correctness of application services, response time
Security	Is the web site able to protect the privacy of the user?	Web site certificates, reputation of site owner

Operation is intended to capture a set of basic properties of a web site whose satisfaction – at least to a minimal degree – is a prerequisite for external quality. It would be pointless analyzing the quality of a system that is frequently not available, not easily reachable in the web, or that might cause damages to the user. Operation is therefore the first and fundamental characteristic of external quality and should be assessed first. It is largely user independent and concerns the behavior of hardware and software infrastructure where the web site is hosted and of some of the technical features of the web site structure.

3.3   Accessibility

Accessibility concerns the possibility for a generic user – independently of his/her personal abilities – to easily and naturally access the web site and its contents.

The sub-characteristics of accessibility (Table 2) are derived from those defined by W3C Web Content Accessibility Guidelines (WCAG) [28]. However, in this context they do not specifically refer to possible user disabilities, but we assume a wider point of view where accessibility is understood as a necessary property for all users, without any exception. The sub-characteristics of accessibility belong to the perceptual ("perceivability"), cognitive ("understandability") and pragmatic ("operability") spheres of an individual. Accordingly, "robustness", which is mentioned in [28], is not present here since it is a technical, user-independent property; it pertains to the concept of "operation" and therefore it has been included in its definition under the name "compatibility".

Table 2. Accessibility

Sub-characteristic	Description	Test
Perceivability	Can users easily perceive the contents displayed?	Text font and point size, size of icons and pictures, use of colors, page layout, use of audio channel
Understandability	Can users easily understand the contents presented?	Foreign language versions, use of appropriate language, context, explanations
Operability	Does the web site support easy operation by the users?	Ease of navigation, search engine performance (precision, recall), interaction with links and other web controls, use of site map, personalization tools

3.4   Usability

Usability is one of the pervading concepts of user-centered design and it is traditionally defined as the property of a web site to be easy to use according to a specified set of criteria [6-7], [19]. The sub-characteristics of usability (Table 3) are derived from the original work of J. Nielsen [19] with minor adjustments. All of them belong to the cognitive and pragmatic sphere of an individual. Coherently, "satisfaction", which is present in Nielsen's proposal, is not included here since it pertains to the emotional sphere and therefore it is classified as a sub-characteristic of "impact", as defined in Table 4.

Table 3. Usability

Sub-characteristic	Description	Test
Learnability	Can users easily accomplish basic tasks the first time they approach the web site?	Time to accomplish a set of sample tasks the first time users approach the web site
Efficiency	Can users proficiently accomplish their tasks after having learned the system?	Time to accomplish a set of sample tasks after suitable training
Memorability	Can users easily re-establish proficiency when they return to system after a period of not using it?	Time to accomplish a set of sample tasks after a period of not using the web site
Robustness	Does the web site support users in avoiding errors or in recovering from the errors occurred?	Number of errors incurred in a given time period, ratio of successes to failures, time spent on recovering from errors

3.5   Impact

Impact is aimed at capturing into a single, coherent concept the main aspects of a web site that pertain to the emotional sphere of an individual (Table 4). These largely depend on cultural and psychological elements and have a primary role for acceptance and loyalty of a web site. These aspects also exert an important effect on user persuasion and decisions [29].

Table 4. Impact

Sub-characteristic	Description	Test
Simplicity	Do users perceive the web site as simple?	Organization of layout, essentiality of information, minimalism of presentation
Aesthetics	Do users consider the web site beautiful?	Just ask the user their subjective opinion
Affectivity	Does the web site generate a positive sentiment in the users?	Classify and count emotions, analyse the relationships between emotions and web site objects, check the evolution of emotions into a stable sentiment
Satisfaction	Do users feel the web site as pleasant and rewarding?	Just ask the user their subjective opinion

The sub-characteristic "simplicity" is inspired to the work of J. Maeda [14], who has shown with clear and convincing arguments the importance of being simple and has proposed a concept of simplicity that perfectly applies to web sites. Simplicity is different from any other property and is perceived in an immediate and natural way by any user, independently of his/her background, culture, and personal profile. "Aesthetics" of web sites has been deeply studied in [11]; this work considers aesthetics as consisting of two main dimensions, namely "classical aesthetics" and "expressive aesthetics", the former emphasizing orderly and clear design, the latter related to designers' creativity and originality. "Affectivity" is a characteristics related to the system's efficacy in stimulating emotions in a user [4]. "Satisfaction" is derived from [19] and shares several traits with the concept of "user experience" [12].

3.6   Usefulness

Usefulness (Table 5) is the characteristic of a web site that accounts for the quality of its content (both information and application services). It belongs to the practical sphere, since content is specifically aimed at satisfying users' needs and at meeting their expectations. Usefulness deeply influences the relationships between the user and the web site in a problem solving perspective.

Table 5. Usefulness

Sub-characteristic	Description	Test
Correctness	Are the contents offered by the web site correct?	Correctness and accuracy of information, correctness of application services, time correctness
Pertinence	Are all the contents offered by the web site relevant to its purpose?	Any immaterial or misleading information or application service present?
Completeness	Does the web site offer to the users all contents relevant to its purpose?	Any key or important information or application service missing?
Reliability	Can users rely on the contents offered by the web site?	Authority of the web site owner, reputation of authors and designers, presence of time marks

4   Assessing Expected Quality: A Methodology

4.1   When and Why to Assess a Web Site

The assessment of expected quality is an important tool to support iterative development of a web site. After each iteration, an evaluation session can greatly help down-stream analysis, both to diagnose design errors and to keep the evolution of the web site strictly focused on the stated quality requirements. Formal evaluation sessions with quality experts must be preferred to informal sessions with users, since the assessment of actual quality is long and costly and cannot be repeated several times during development. The evaluation of expected quality can thus be regarded as a predictive method, playing the same role that heuristic evaluation and cognitive walkthrough play in usability engineering [19]. The evaluation of actual quality with real users may instead be very useful towards the end of the development cycle, when the web site has already been extensively tested and its expected quality is satisfactory. In this case, actual quality can provide further hints for final refinements and also serve as a last field test before go-live. In addition, expected quality should be assessed periodically during the operational life of a web site, especially in case of unsatisfactory ultimate quality. It can reveal strong and weak points of the web site and suggest the priority directions for improvement.

4.2   A Practical Approach

The basic issue in approching the assessment of the quality of a web site concerns whether to assume an absolute or relative point of view. For example, if the assessment of the sub-characteristic *robustness* is *excellent*, does it mean that robustness is achieved to the highest possible degree (absolute judgment) or that it fully meets the stated requirements for the specific web site at hand (relative judgment)? In order to implement an approach that allows clearly distinguishing between absolute and relative assessment, two scales of values must be introduced:

- A first scale is necessary to express absolute evaluations about each one of the sub-characteristics of external quality. We assume here a qualitative scale, made of a finite, total ordered set of labels that we call the **absolute scale** or **a-scale**. For example, a1={*insufficient, poor, fair, good, excellent*} or a2={*seriously insufficient, insufficient, very poor, poor, acceptable, sufficient, fair, moderately good, good, very good, excellent*}, where each value has an intuitive meaning. Of course finer or coarser a-scales may be adopted, according to the precision desired.
- A second scale is then needed to represent the degree to which each sub-characteristic meets stated requirements. We assume again a qualitative scale, called the **relative scale** or **r-scale**. For example, r1={*seriously failed, failed, met, largely met*}.

It is reasonable to assume that the lenght of the r-scale is less or equal than the lenght of the a-scale; in fact, the former has only to represent the degree to which a requirement is satisfied, while the latter must be fine enough to allow an assessment as far as possibile precise and detailed according to the features of the specific case at hand. Of course, before assessment starts, the requirements for each sub-characteristic must be stated. These should be defined according to the goals of the web site owner and to the specific features of the web site. We assume that **requirements** are stated using only the positive values of the a-scale, that is the values above sufficiency; for example, considering the a-scale a1 introduced above, the positive values are {*fair, good, excellent*}. The notation $req(x) = a$, where a belongs to a given a-scale, means that the requirement of the sub-characteristic x is a. Note that it would be inappropriate in general to assume for each sub-characteristic a target value corresponding to the maximum of the a-scale: depending on the case at hand, some characteristics are definitely less important than others and this should be reflected in the requirements.

Moreover, it is necessary to define a suitable mapping between the value $a\text{-}val(x)$ assigned on the a-scale to a given sub-characteristic x, the requirement $req(x)$, and the value $r\text{-}val(x)$ that should be assigned to x on the r-scale. That is, considering again the above example, if the evaluation of *robustness* yields $a\text{-}val(robustness) = poor$ and $req(robustness) = good$, how should this be mapped onto the r-scale? Intuitively, one might expect that being *poor* a far worst value than *good*, the final relative assessment of *robustness* should be *r-val(robustness)= seriously failed*. We call this relation **AR mapping** and clearly we have: AR: a-scale × a-scale →r-scale. The definition of the AR mapping must of course comply with the goal of representing the degree at which a stated requirement about a quality sub-characterstic is met. For example, considering the a-scale a1 and the r-scale r1 introduced above, we might assume the following definition of AR:

IF *a-val(x) - req(x)= y* THEN *r-val(x)=met + y*

where (a) the difference operator "-" denotes the positional distance between a pair of elements of a-scale, and (b) in case the sum *met + y* exceeds the limits of the r-scale, the left- or right-most value is assumed respectively.

So, resuming the example introduced above, we have

$$y = a\text{-}val(robustness) - req(robustness) = (poor - good) = -2$$
$$r\text{-}val(roustness) = met + y = met - 2 = seriously\ failed$$

Based on the above concepts, the **assessment procedure** we propose is then organized in two steps:

1. **Step-1:** for each sub-characteristic *x*, evaluate the degree to which it is satisfied in absolute terms and assign to it a value *a-val(x)* on the a-scale.
2. **Step-2:** for each sub-characteristic *x*, compute its final relative assessment *r-val(x)* on the basis of *a-val(x)*, the stated requirement *req(x)* and the assigned AR mapping.

Now a last point has to be faced, which concerns the eventual aggregation of the evaluations assigned to each individual sub-characteristic into an overall evaluation of the relevant characteristic and, then, the eventual aggregation of the evaluations assigned to each characteristic into a global evaluation of external quality. This aggregation process is clearly possibile through the application of a suitable mean-value operation defined on the a-scale or on the r-scale. However, we stress that if on one side aggregating values into global scores can provide a useful one-shot representation of the quality of a web site, on the other hand it hides much of the details that are necessary to deepen the analysis and to identify concrete actions for quality improvement.

5   Discussion and Conclusion

In this paper, we have presented a new quality model for corporate web sites, which takes explicitly into consideration the goals and expectations of the site owner. The concept that we have called here "ultimate quality" is not encompassed in existing literature and standards, which prefer either defining general models including characteristics for internal quality, external quality and quality in use [17], [24], [27], or focusing on quality in use only [3], [22]. General models are usually very articulated and thus difficult to apply, whilst models focused on quality in use do not consider important characteristics that affect ultimate quality.

In addition, we have proposed a pragmatic approach to quality assessment, based on the concept of expected (external) quality. Condidering quality from the perspective of expert evaluators – instead of that of the users – allows adapting the assessment to the specific development phase of a web site, to the available time and budget, and to the accuracy one desires to achieve. As proposed in [8] and [10], problems identified through the assessment of external quality can then be recognized as dependent from problems in the internal quality, and thus require the intervention of designers.

Furthermore, our quality model is not based on the web site development phases and on the actors involved in such phases as proposed for example in [24], but considers quality itself as having different meanings for the different stakeholders, namely site owner, evaluators, users, and designers. In our opinion, this makes the model and assessment methodology more natural and easier to understand and apply.

Finally, we stress that while some literature works are more oriented towards a specific type of web sites – such as e-commerce sites [25], [26] or web 2.0 sites [24] – the model proposed in this paper, and the relevant assessment methodology, can be tailored to the type of web site at hand, to the needs of the site owner, and to the preferences of the evaluators.

The prototype of an interactive tool for supporting the evaluator in assessing expected quality has been developed and is presently being tested. Moreover, an extended experimentation of the proposed quality model and methodology in concrete cases and the assessment of its adequacy, effectiveness, and ease to use are ongoing; the results of this experimentation will be the subject of a forthcoming paper.

References

1. Guida, G.: La Qualità dei Siti Web per il successo dell'Impresa. Franco Angeli, Milano (2011)
2. Hartmann, J., Sutcliffe, A., De Angeli, A.: Toward a Theory of User Judgment of Aesthetics and User Interface Quality. ACM Trans. on Computer-Human Interaction 15(4), 15:1–15:30 (2008)
3. Herrera, M., Moraga, M.Á., Caballero, I., Calero, C.: Quality in Use Model for Web Portals (QiUWeP). In: Daniel, F., Facca, F.M. (eds.) ICWE 2010. LNCS, vol. 6385, pp. 91–101. Springer, Heidelberg (2010)
4. Isbister, K., Hook, K.: Evaluating affective interactions (Editorial). Int. J. Human-Computer Studies 65, 273–274 (2007)
5. International Organization for Standardization: ISO 8402 – Quality management and quality assurance – Vocabulary (1994)
6. International Organization for Standardization: ISO/IEC 9241-14:1998 – Ergonomic Requirements for Office Work with Visual Display Terminals (VDT)s - Part 14: Menu Dialogues (1998)
7. International Organization for Standardization: ISO/IEC 13407:1999 - Human-Centred Design Processes for Interactive Systems (1999)
8. International Organization for Standardization: ISO/IEC 9126-1:2001 – Software Engineering – Product Quality – Part 1: Quality Model (2001)
9. International Organization for Standardization: ISO 9000 – Quality management systems – Fundamentals and vocabulary (2005)

10. International Organization for Standardization: ISO/IEC 25010:2011 – System and Software Engineering – Systems and Software Quality Requirements and Evaluation (SQuaRE) – System and Software Quality Models (2011)
11. Lavie, T., Tractinsky, N.: Assessing dimensions of perceived visual aesthetics of web sites. Int. J. Human-Computer Studies 60, 269–298 (2003)
12. Law, E., Roto, V., Hassenzahl, M., Vermeeren, A., Kort, J.: Understanding, Scoping and Defining User Experience: A Survey Approach. In: Proceedings of Human Factors in Computing Systems Conference (CHI 2009), Boston, MA, USA, pp. 719–728 (2009)
13. Lindgaard, G., Dudek, C., Sen, D., Sumegi, L., Noonan, P.: An Exploration of Relations Between Visual Appeal, Trustworthiness and Perceived Usability of Homepages. ACM Transactions on Computer-Human Interaction 18(1), 1:1–1:30 (2011)
14. Maeda, J.: The Laws of Simplicity. The MIT Press, Cambridge (2006)
15. Malak, G., Sahraoui, H.: Modeling Web Quality Using a Probabilistic Approach: An Empirical Evaluation. ACM Transactions on the Web 4(3), 9:1–9:31 (2010)
16. Mich, L., Franch, M.: 2QCV2Q: A Model for Web Sites Design and Evaluation. In: Proc. of the 2000 IRMA International Conference on Challenges of Information Technology Management in the 21st Century, Anchorage, Alaska, USA, May 21-24, pp. 586–589 (2000)
17. Moraga, M.A., Calero, C., Piattini, M.: A first proposal of a portal quality model. In: Proc. IADIS International Conference, E-society 2004, Avila, Spain, vol. 1(2), pp. 630–638 (2004)
18. Moraga, M.A., Calero, C., Piattini, M.: Comparing different quality models for portals. Online Information Review 30(5), 555–568 (2006)
19. Nielsen, J.: Usability Engineering, Academic Press Inc. (1994)
20. Offutt, J.: Quality Attributes of Web Software Applications. IEEE Software, 25–32 (March-April 2002)
21. Olsina, L., Papa, F., Molina, H.: How to Measure and Evaluate Web Applications in a Consistent Way. In: Rossi, G., Pastor, O., Schwabe, D., Olsina, L. (eds.) Web Engineering: Modeling and Implementing Web Applications, pp. 385–420. Springer (2008)
22. Orehovački, T., Granić, A., Kermek, D.: Exploring the Quality in Use of Web 2.0 Applications: The Case of Mind Mapping Services. In: Harth, A., Koch, N. (eds.) ICWE 2011. LNCS, vol. 7059, pp. 266–277. Springer, Heidelberg (2012)
23. Polillo, R.: Il check-up dei Siti Web – Valutare la Qualità per Migliorarla. Apogeo, Milano (2004)
24. Polillo, R.: Quality Models for Web [2.0] Sites: A Methodological Approach and a Proposal. In: Harth, A., Koch, N. (eds.) ICWE 2011. LNCS, vol. 7059, pp. 251–265. Springer, Heidelberg (2012)
25. Polites, G.L., Williams, C.K., Karahanna, E., Seligman, L.: A Theoretical Framework for Consumer E-Satisfaction and Site Stickiness: An Evaluation in the Context of Online Hotel Reservation. J. of Organizational Computing and Electronic Commerce 22(1), 1–37 (2012)
26. Stefani, A., Xenos, M.: E-commerce system quality assessment using a model based on ISO 9126 and Belief Networks. Software Quality Journal 16, 107–129 (2008)
27. Yang, Z., Cai, S., Zhou, Z., Zhou, N.: Development and validation of an instrument to measure user perceived service quality of information presenting Web portals. Information and Management 42(4), 575–589 (2004)
28. Web Content Accessibility Guidelines 2.0, http://www.w3.org/TR/WCAG/
29. Weinschenk, S.M.: Neuro web design: What makes them click? New Riders Press, Berkeley (2009)

Enhancing the Conceptual Framework Capability for a Measurement and Evaluation Strategy

Pablo Becker, Fernanda Papa, and Luis Olsina

GIDIS_Web, Engineering School, UNLPam
Calle 9 y 110, (6360) Gral. Pico, La Pampa, Argentina
{beckerp,pmfer,olsinal}@ing.unlpam.edu.ar

Abstract. To provide consistency and repeatability for measurement and evaluation (M&E) projects and programs a well-established M&E strategy is needed. In a previous work, we have discussed the benefits of having an integrated M&E strategy that relies on three capabilities such as an M&E conceptual framework, process and method specifications. Besides, we have developed GOCAME (*Goal-Oriented Context-Aware Measurement and Evaluation*) as an integrated M&E strategy which supports these capabilities. In the present work, we enhance its former conceptual framework with the recently built process ontology, enriching also the M&E terms with stereotypes stemming from the process conceptual base. The augmented conceptual framework has also a positive impact on the other strategy capabilities since ensures terminological uniformity and testability to process and method specifications. For illustration purposes, excerpts of process specifications regarding the new situation are highlighted.

Keywords: Process Ontology, Quality, Measurement, Evaluation, GOCAME, C-INCAMI.

1   Introduction

Besides to establish a set of activities and procedures for specifying, collecting, storing, and using metrics (for a measurement task) and indicators (for an evaluation task) in a systematic way, we argue that more robust analysis and decision-making processes can be achieved if the following three capabilities of an M&E strategy are considered at once: i) a *M&E process specification*; ii) a *M&E conceptual framework*; and, iii) *method specifications*.

Firstly, to assure repeatability and reproducibility for M&E activities and also consistency of results, it is necessary to provide specifications of process (model) views, which prescribes or informs a set of activities, their inputs and outputs, roles, interdependencies, and so forth. The specification of these views can consider different process perspectives such as functional, informational, organizational, amongst others [1]. Secondly, a well-established M&E conceptual framework should be built upon a robust conceptual base, which explicitly and formally specifies the main agreed concepts, properties, relationships, and constraints. Lastly, clear specifications of methods (and tools) are necessary in order to the tasks can be

Q.Z. Sheng and J. Kjeldskov (Eds.): ICWE 2013 Workshops, LNCS 8295, pp. 104–116, 2013.

allotted and performed systematically. Furthermore, a M&E strategy that includes these three capabilities simultaneously is called an integrated strategy. The rationale for this is given in [2].

In this direction, we have built an integrated M&E strategy, named GOCAME (*Goal-Oriented Context-Aware Measurement and Evaluation*). This strategy supports the above three capabilities, namely: the C-INCAMI (*Contextual-Information Need, Concept model, Attribute, Metric* and *Indicator*) conceptual framework [3]; the M&E process specifications for the different views i.e. functional, organizational, behavioral and informational perspectives [4]; and the WebQEM (*Web Quality Evaluation*) methodology and its associated tool.

However, the M&E terms included in C-INCAMI do not allow identifying explicitly if, for example, a measurement is a task, a metric is a method or a measure an outcome, amongst other aspects. So there exists an opportunity to enrich semantically the GOCAME M&E conceptual framework with process terms, which represents an improvement from the conceptual framework capability standpoint.

The contributions of this work are: i) to develop a process conceptual base; ii) to enhance the former M&E (C-INCAMI) conceptual framework adding more semantic to its terms by linking them with the process conceptual base; iii) to improve the M&E process and method specifications giving them a greater semantic consistency. Additionally, we illustrate how the process concepts linked to the M&E concepts help to build better specifications for the process views and their testability.

The rest of this paper is organized as follows. Section 2 summarizes the GOCAME strategy and its three capabilities. Section 3 discusses the process ontology, the enhanced M&E conceptual framework and the impact of this improvement on the other capabilities. Section 4 analyzes state-of-the-art researches on M&E conceptual frameworks, particularly, those which are enhanced by a process conceptual base. Finally, Section 5 outlines the conclusions and future work.

2   GOCAME Overview

GOCAME is a multi-purpose M&E strategy which follows a goal-oriented and context-sensitive approach in defining M&E projects. It is based on the three capabilities mentioned above, which are summarized below.

GOCAME has its M&E terminological base defined as an ontology [5], from which the C-INCAMI conceptual framework emerges. The metric and indicator ontology provides a domain model that defines all the concepts, properties and relationships which in turn helps to design the M&E activities. This way, a common understanding of data and metadata is shared among the organization's projects lending to more consistent results and analysis across projects.

C-INCAMI is structured in six components, namely: i) <u>M&E project component</u>, which allows specifying the management data for *M&E projects*; ii) <u>Nonfunctional requirements component</u>, which allows specifying the *Information Need* for a given *purpose* and the *user viewpoint* related to an *Entity* and quality *focus*. The focus is represented by a *Concept Model* (e.g. a quality model) which includes *Calculable Concepts* (i.e. characteristics), *sub-concepts* (i.e. sub-characteristics) and associated

Attributes. Attributes are measurable properties of an entity under analysis; iii) <u>Context component,</u> which describes the relevant *Context* through *Context properties* which are attributes; iv) <u>Measurement component,</u> which allows specifying *Direct* and *Indirect Metrics* used by *Direct* and *Indirect Measurement* tasks which produce *Base* and *Derived Measures* respectively; v) <u>Evaluation component,</u> which allows specifying the evaluation task through *Indicators,* which interpret attributes and calculable concepts for a non-functional requirements tree. Two types of indicators are distinguished: *Elementary Indicators* which evaluate lower-level requirements (attributes), and, *Derived Indicators,* which evaluate higher-level requirements, i.e. sub-characteristics and characteristics; and vi) <u>Analysis and Recommendation component,</u> which supports data and information analysis in order to provide recommendations for improvement.

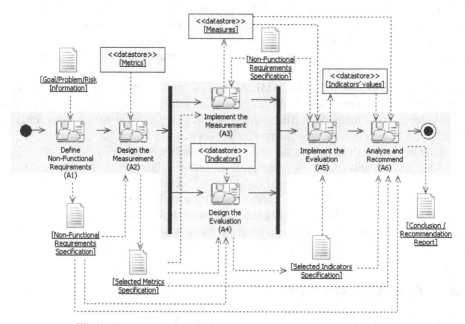

Fig. 1. The functional and behavioral process views of GOCAME

GOCAME has a well-defined M&E process specification [4], which is composed of six main activities as shown in Figure 1. These activities are: (A1) *Define Non-functional Requirements;* (A2) *Design the Measurement;* (A3) *Implement the Measurement;* (A4) *Design the Evaluation;* (A5) *Implement the Evaluation;* and (A6) *Analyze and Recommend.* The M&E process is specified in SPEM language [6]. Additionally, activities can be specified with a template that describes the activity name, objective, pre-conditions, post-conditions, inputs and output, roles, etc. We also observe in Figure 1 that concepts defined in the M&E terminological base are reused such as Metric, Measure and Indicator, amongst others.

Lastly, GOCAME is supported by the WebQEM methodology. This provides the 'how' to implement the requirements, measurement, evaluation, analysis and recommendation activities. It comprises a set of methods, techniques and tools to carry out the description of activities.

3   Updating GOCAME

Aimed at enhancing the GOCAME strategy, we recently developed a process ontology for enriching the terms of C-INCAMI conceptual framework. The terms from the process ontology are used as stereotypes in the C-INCAMI framework with the purpose of adding more semantic to the M&E domain concepts. The augmented conceptual framework has also a positive impact on the other strategy capabilities since ensures terminological uniformity to process and method specifications in addition to testability. Next, we summarize the process ontology and the enhanced M&E conceptual framework. Also, for illustration purposes, we show excerpts of process specifications regarding the new situation.

3.1   A Process Conceptual Base

In the process domain a lack of consensus regarding its terms and meaning is still an issue. For example, in some recent works [6, 7, 8] the *process*, *activity* and *task* terms, even though sharing the same syntax they do not share totally the same semantic. It happens the same with the *process element* term used both in [6] and [7]. On the other hand, there are documents which use other terminology such as in [9], where activities are called *complex activities*, and tasks *atomic activities*. Ultimately, in our process ontology the process/activity/task concepts are used, which are compliant with the meaning given in ISO 12207 [10]. Specifically, a process groups a set of activities and an activity groups a set of tasks, being a task an atomic element.

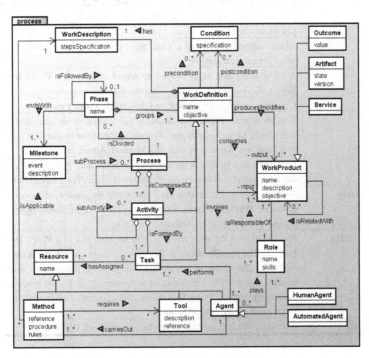

Fig. 2. Terms and relationships for the Process component

Table 1. Definition of Process terms, which are included in Figure 2

Process Term	Definition
Activity	It is a **Work Definition** that is formed by an interrelated set of sub-activities and **Tasks**. Note 1: A sub-activity is an **Activity** at a lower granularity level. Note 2: In engineering projects, while **Activities** are planned, **Tasks** are scheduled and enacted.
Agent	Performer assigned to a **Task** in compliance with a **Role**.
Artifact	It is a tangible or intangible, versionable **Work Product**, which can be delivered.
Automated Agent	It is an automated type agent.
Condition	Situation that must be achieved at the beginning (pre-condition) or ending (post-condition) of a **Work Definition** realization.
Human Agent	It is a human type agent.
Method	Specific and particular way to perform the specified steps in the description of a **Work Definition**. Note 1: The specific and particular way of a **Method** –i.e. *how* the described steps in a work definition should be made- is represented by a procedure and rules.
Milestone	A meaningful event. Note 1: A **Milestone** represents for instance a **Phase** finalization.
Outcome	It is an intangible, storable and processable **Work Product**.
Phase	A group of strongly-related **Work Definitions** defined in a given order. Note 1: A **Phase** ends with a **Milestone**. Note 2: In a phase the **Work Definitions** are **Processes** and/or **Activities**.
Process	It is a **Work Definition** that is composed of an interrelated set of sub-processes and activities. Note 1: A sub-process is a **Process** at a lower granularity level.
Resource	Asset assigned to perform a **Task**. Note 1: An asset is an entity with added value for an organization.
Role	A set of skills that ought to own an **Agent** to perform a **Work Definition**. Note 1: Skills include abilities, competencies and responsibilities.
Service	It is an intangible, non storable and deliverable **Work Product**.
Task	It is an atomic **Work Definition**, which cannot be decomposed. Note 1: Conversely to an **Activity** and **Process**, a **Resource** is assigned (scheduled) to a **Task**, e.g. **Resources** such as a **Method, Agent**, etc.
Tool	Instrument that facilitates the execution of a **Method**. Note 1: An instrument can be physical (hardware), computerized (software) or a mix of both types.
Work Definition	Abstract entity which describes the work by means of consumed and produced **Work Products, Conditions** and involved **Roles**. Note 1: Work represents a **Process**, an **Activity** or a **Task**.
Work Description	Specification of the steps for achieving the objective of a **Work Definition**. Note 1: The specification of the steps is a set of general actions –both **Activities** and **Tasks**- or a transformation function. It represents *what* should be done instead of *how* it should be performed. Note 2: The specification of the description of a **Work Definition** can be formal, semi-formal or informal as for example the natural language.
Work Product	A product that is consumed or produced by a **Work Definition**.

Due to the above mentioned issues, among others, we have built the process conceptual base as shown in Figure 2. It is important to remark that in 1997, we specified a process conceptual base [11], which had been based on seminal works such as [12] and [13], amongst others. The current process conceptual base is built on [11] considering also more recent contributions such as SPEM, CMMI and ISO 12207.

Figure 2 depicts the terms, relationships and main attributes included in our process component. Also in Table 1, the process ontology terms are defined. The definition of attributes and relations will be documented in a follow-up manuscript.

In our ontology, *Process*, *Activity* and *Task* are, at different abstraction levels specializations of *Work Definition*. For instance, a process is composed of sub-processes or activities, which in turn are formed by sub-activities or tasks. In Table 1, the task term is defined as "*an atomic Work Definition, which cannot be decomposed*". Additionally, a process can be divided into *Phases*.

A work definition *consumes* and *produces* one or more *Work Products*. Note that an *Outcome*, *Artifact* or *Service* are kinds of work products. In Table 1, the outcome term is defined as "*an intangible, storable and processable Work Product*", while artifact "*is a tangible or intangible, versionable Work Product, which can be delivered*". On the other hand, a work definition has a *Work Description*, which specifies the steps for achieving its *objective*. It represents 'what' should be done instead of 'how' it should be performed. The semantic of 'how' is represented by the *Method* term, i.e. the specific and particular way to perform the specified steps e.g. in a task. Note that a method concept has the *procedure* and *rules* attributes in Figure 2.

Lastly, taking into account that a task -unlike a process and activity- is scheduled and enacted it has therefore allocated *Resources* such as *Method*, *Tool* as well as an *Agent* that plays a *Role*. In Table 1, the resource term is defined as "*asset assigned to perform a Task*".

So, the above conceptual base is one of the contributions listed in the Introduction Section. This conceptual base contains the key concepts necessary to model and specify different process (model) views, while enriches semantically many M&E terms as we show below.

3.2   Enhancing the GOCAME Conceptual Framework Capability

The second contribution listed in the Introduction Section is to enhance the former M&E (C-INCAMI) conceptual framework adding more semantic to many of its terms. This is done by linking M&E terms with process terms by using UML stereotypes. A stereotype is an UML model element, which is an extensibility mechanism [14]. It is represented syntactically by means of small labels between « and » signs. Moreover stereotypes are applied to a diagram elements or relationships indicating additional meaning.

In our case, we have employed the process terms (Table 1) as stereotype labels for enriching many M&E terms. Figure 3 shows four out of six C-INCAMI components introduced in Section 2. So far, the *measurement* and *evaluation* components are augmented with process terms and relationships. An example of an enriched term is *Metric*, which is stereotyped with «Method» from the process component.

Looking at Table 2, a metric is *"the defined measurement or calculation procedure and the scale"*. Now, with the «Method» stereotype a metric also includes the semantic of a method, which is defined as the *"specific and particular way to perform the specified steps in the description of a Work Definition"*. So a metric specifies *how* should be made the described steps (*what*) of a measurement task. Moreover, if we look at the *procedure* and *rule* attributes of the *Method* term (Figure 2), hence the *Direct/Indirect Metric* has accordingly a *Measurement/Calculation Procedure* and a *Scale* as a *rule*. This new situation is specified in Figure 3.

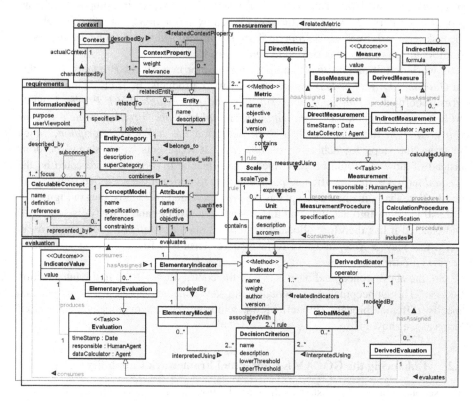

Fig. 3. Main concepts and relationships for C-INCAMI enriched with process stereotypes

It is important to remark that the abovementioned link between components has introduced minor changes in the definition of some *measurement* and *evaluation* terms with regard to previous definitions [3]. In addition, new terms have emerged such as for example *Direct Measurement/Base Measure* and *Indirect Measurement/ Derived Measure* in order to have a more terminological completeness and detail. All these adapted definitions and/or new terms in addition to the link with process terms are shown in Table 2.

Another enhancement has been made on relations among terms in Figure 3, which is aimed at increasing the consistency between M&E and process components. For instance, we added the *consumes* relationship between *Measurement* and *Attribute* terms. Thus a Measurement task *consumes* an Attribute (as input) and *produces* a Measure (as output). Note that the added and renamed relations are highlighted in gray.

3.3   Impact of the Enhanced Conceptual Framework on the Other Capabilities

As introduced in Section 1, besides the *conceptual framework capability*, there exists in GOCAME other two integrated capabilities, namely: the *M&E process specification capability*, and the *method specifications capability*.

Table 2. Definition of M&E terms, which are semantically enriched with process terms

M&E Term	Definition	Process Term
	Measurement Term	
Base Measure	A measure that does not depend upon other measure.	Outcome
Calculation Procedure	Set of established and ordered instructions of an indirect metric or indicator that indicates how the described steps in an indirect measurement or evaluation task should be carried out.	procedure in Method
Derived Measure	A measure that is derived from other measures.	Outcome
Direct Measurement	Measurement that produces a base measure.	Task
Direct Metric	A metric of an attribute that does not depend upon a metric of any other attribute	Method
Indirect Measurement	Measurement that produces a derived measure.	Task
Indirect Metric	A metric of an attribute that depends of metrics of other attributes.	Method
Measure	The number or category assigned to an attribute of an entity by making a measurement. Note 1: It is the measurement output that represents an outcome as work product.	Outcome
Measurement	A task that uses a metric in order to produce a measure's value. Note 1: This task quantifies an attribute by producing a measure as outcome.	Task
Measurement Procedure	Set of established and ordered instructions of a direct metric that indicates how the described steps in a direct measurement task should be carried out.	procedure in Method
Metric	The defined measurement or calculation procedure and the scale. Note 1: A metric is a method which is applicable to the description of a measurement task.	Method

Table 2. (*Continued.*)

Evaluation Term		
Derived Evaluation	Evaluation that produces an indicator's value by assessing a calculable concept.	Task
Derived Indicator	An indicator that is derived from other indicators to evaluate a calculable concept.	Method
Elementary Evaluation	Evaluation that produces an indicator's value by assessing an attribute. Note 1: An attribute is a non-functional elementary requirement from the evaluation standpoint.	Task
Elementary Indicator	An indicator that does not depend upon other indicators to evaluate an attribute.	Method
Evaluation	A task that uses an indicator in order to produce an indicator's value.	Task
Indicator	The defined calculation procedure and scale in addition to the indicator model and decision criteria in order to provide an evaluation of a calculable concept or attribute with respect to a defined information need. Note 1: An indicator is a method which is applicable to the description of an evaluation task.	Method
Indicator Value	The number or category assigned to a calculable concept or attribute by making an evaluation. Note 1: It is the evaluation output that represents an outcome as work product.	Outcome

The process specification capability embraces different process views such as functional, behavioral, informational and organizational. Figure 1 depicts the high-level process specification diagram for the GOCAME strategy stressing the functional and behavioral perspectives. Particularly, the functional view represents what activities/tasks should be performed in the M&E process as well as the inputs and outputs (work products) that will be consumed and produced, respectively. On the other hand, the behavioral view represents the dynamics of the process i.e., sequences, parallelisms, iterations, feedback loops, among other aspects. Note that, in Figure 1 the names of activities as well as work products make use of the M&E terminology like *Measurement, Evaluation, Metric, Measure,* etc. As a consequence, the use of the C-INCAMI conceptual base benefits the terminological uniformity in the specifications of process views. Moreover, the augmented C-INCAMI conceptual base with process terms as shown above has a positive impact on the M&E process and method specifications due to they provide a greater semantic consistency.

In order to demonstrate how the process terms linked to M&E terms allow building more consistent and testable process view specifications, an A3 sub-activity is described. This sub-activity is named *Quantify Attributes* and is depicted in Figure 4. It implies executing, iteratively, the Measurement task for each attribute from the requirements tree. (Recall that a requirements tree is made up of (sub-)characteristics and attributes instantiated from a quality model).

Looking at Figure 4 we can see that each Measurement task execution consumes an attribute and produces a measure, which is stored in the measures datastore. In order to perform the measurement for a given entity attribute the Data Collector must follow the (measurement or calculation) procedure and rules described in the (direct or indirect) Metric respectively. Each metric that quantifies each attribute was previously selected in the A2 activity (recall Figure 1), and added to the Selected Metrics Specification artifact.

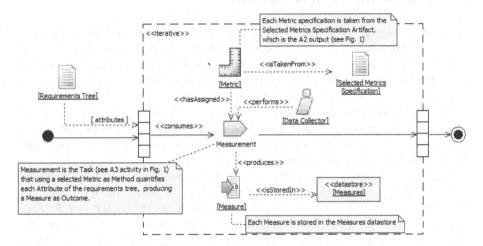

Fig. 4. SPEM diagram for the *Quantify Attributes* activity

Following with the terminological consistency analysis between the process specification and the augmented C-INCAMI conceptual base, we observe in Figure 4 that the task named Measurement consumes an attribute and produces a measure. This process specification is semantically consistent when tested against the C-INCAMI measurement component, since the *Measurement* term (enriched with the «Task» stereotype in Figure 3) is associated to the *Attribute* term with the *consumes* relationship, and to the *Measure* term with the *produces* relationship. Also in Figure 4 the produced measure which is modeled as an outcome is consistent with the *Measure* term in Figure 3, which in turn is enriched with the «Outcome» stereotype from the process conceptual base.

Also, we observe in Figure 4 that the Measurement task *has assigned* a metric as a resource. This is consistent with the augmented M&E conceptual base since the *Measurement* term (i.e. its specialization, either direct or indirect measurement) is related to the *Metric* term (i.e. its specialization, either direct or indirect metric) by the *hasAssigned* relationship. Lastly, the *Metric* term has also the semantic of the Method term in Figure 3, and a *Method* is a *Resource* for the task, regarding the process conceptual base in Fig. 2. In the end, the *hasAssigned* relationship of Fig. 4 is semantically consistent with that in figures 2 and 3.

Finally, the augmented C-INCAMI capability impacts positively on the terminological consistency and testability for the method specification capability. For instance, a metric has the semantic of a method as discussed above, so we can check that a metric template contains all the metadata such as the (measurement or calculation) procedure and its associated rules such as scale. Likewise for indicator specifications. Ultimately, a metric/indicator specifies *how* should be carried out the *what*, i.e. the described steps of a measurement/evaluation task.

4   Related Work and Discussion

An M&E strategy is considered in [2] as integrated if the definitions of process and method specifications make use of a common M&E conceptual base. Particularly in the GOCAME strategy, the process and method specifications use the terms defined in the M&E conceptual framework so-called C-INCAMI. However, by looking at the C-INCAMI terms we cannot clearly identify which process concepts are represented in the M&E domain. Hence, we observed an opportunity for improvement by adding semantic to the former M&E conceptual base using our presented process conceptual base. One impact of this enhancement is that process and method specifications can now be tested for additional semantic consistency.

Regarding the above issue, a related work that focuses on specifying a software quality ontology is in [15]. This quality ontology is based on UFO (*Unified Foundational Ontology*) [16]. Additionally, they developed SPO (*Software Process Ontology*) [9], which is also based on UFO and related with the quality ontology. The quality ontology is divided into three sub-ontologies, namely: quality models, measurement, and evaluation. The quality ontology based on UFO can provide, as indicated by authors, robustness but also can generate some semantic inconsistencies. A clear example of this inconsistency can be seen in the following situation: in the SPO version documented in [16], authors show that *hardware resource*, *software resource* and *human resource* inherit from *resource*; however, in [9] a *human resource* is not a *resource*. This happened since a *resource* represented in SPO is in UFO an *object*, and given that a *human resource* cannot be an *object* from the semantic standpoint, then they decided to remove such a link.

On the other hand, SPO uses terminology which to some extent differs from recognized standards in the process area such as SPEM [6], CMMI [7] and ISO [10]. For example, instead of using the *work product* term authors use *artefact*, not doing distinction with *outcome* and *service* terms. Also they do not use the *task* term but rather the *atomic activity* term, as commented in sub-section 3.1.

Regarding the measurement sub-ontology [15], we observe an ambiguity in using the *measure* term, since sometimes it refers to the value produced by a measurement, while sometimes to the instrument (procedure) for obtaining such a value. This duality of the *measure* term is also observed in [7, 17, 18]. Instead, we make a clear distinction between *measure* and *metric* terms, linking them also to our process ontology -as discussed in sub-section 3.3. Besides to refer to properties of an entity authors use the *measurable element* concept [15]; however, the widely used concept in the M&E literature is *attribute* [17, 18, 19]. Lastly, they do not include context terms as we did in the context component [20].

Finally, SPEM focuses on defining a generic framework for process modeling. Although SPEM was not intended to model concepts for the M&E domain it was a valuable consultation source for developing our process ontology and process view specifications. Another related work is FMESP (*Framework for the Modeling and Evaluation of Software Processes*) [21]. This framework has two ontologies, vis. the software process modeling ontology, and the software measurement ontology. However, so far we have not found any public paper of FMESP, which explicitly relate both ontologies as we did.

5   Conclusion and Future Work

In a previous research, we have developed an integrated M&E strategy so-called GOCAME which relies on three capabilities: C-INCAMI conceptual framework, M&E process view specifications, and method specifications.

In the present work, we have discussed the semantic enhancement of the C-INCAMI conceptual framework capability, by relating it with the process ontology terms. The building of the process conceptual base is one of the stated contributions in the Introduction Section. Moreover, we have enriched the M&E terms with process terms by means of UML stereotypes. Finally, we have illustrated how the augmented C-INCAMI capability impacts positively on the terminological consistency and testability for the method and process view specification capabilities.

As a future line of research we plan to enhance the M&E conceptual framework by adding terms for the Analysis and Recommendations component. Likewise we made in [2], after all these changes be performed the GOCAME improvement gain will be re-evaluated.

Acknowledgments. Thanks to the support given from the Science and Technology Agency, Argentina, in the PAE-PICT 2188 project, and in the 09-F047 project at UNLPam, Argentina.

References

1. Curtis, B., Kellner, M., Over, J.: Process Modelling. Com. of ACM 35(9), 75–90 (1992)
2. Papa, F.: Toward the Improvement of a Measurement and Evaluation Strategy from a Comparative Study. In: Grossniklaus, M., Wimmer, M. (eds.) ICWE 2012 Workshops. LNCS, vol. 7703, pp. 189–203. Springer, Heidelberg (2012)
3. Olsina, L., Papa, F., Molina, H.: How to Measure and Evaluate Web Applications in a Consistent Way. In: Rossi, Pastor, Schwabe, Olsina (eds.) Springer HCIS Book Web Engineering: Modeling and Implementing Web Applications, pp. 385–420 (2008)
4. Becker, P., Lew, P., Olsina, L.: Specifying Process Views for a Measurement, Evaluation and Improvement Strategy. Advances in Software Engineering, Software Quality Assurance Methodologies and Techniques 2012, 1–27 (2012)
5. Olsina, L., Martin, M.: Ontology for Software Metrics and Indicators. Journal of Web Engineering 2(4), 262–281 (2004)

6. OMG-SPEM: Software & Systems Process Engineering Meta-Model Specification V2.0 (2008)
7. CMMI Product Team: CMMI for Development, Ver. 1.3 (CMU/SEI-2010-TR-033). The Software Engineering Institute, Carnegie Mellon University website (2010), http://www.sei.cmu.edu/library/abstracts/reports/10tr033.cfm (retrieved February 06, 2013)
8. ISO/IEC 15504-5: Information technology - Process assessment - Part 5: An exemplar software life cycle process assessment model (2012)
9. Bringuente, A., Falbo, R., Guizzardi, G.: Using a Foundational Ontology for Reengineering a Software Process Ontology. Journal of Information and Data Management 2, 511–526 (2011)
10. ISO/IEC 12207: Systems and software engineering - Software life cycle processes (2008)
11. Olsina, L.: Functional View of the Hypermedia Process Model. In: The Fifth International Workshop on Engineering Hypertext Functionality at International Conference on Software Engineering (ICSE 1998), Kyoto, Japan, pp. 1–10 (1998)
12. Feiler, P.H., Humphrey, W.S.: Software Process Development and Enactment: Concepts and Definitions. In: International Conference of Software Process (ICSP), pp. 28–40. IEEE Computer Society, Berlin (1993)
13. Lonchamp, J.: A Structured Conceptual and Terminological Framework for Software Process Engineering. In: International Conference on the Software Process (ICSP), pp. 41–53. IEEE Computer Society Press, Berlin (1993)
14. OMG-UML: Unified Modeling Language, Superstructure, v2.3 (2010)
15. Barcellos, M.P., Falbo, R., Dal Moro, R.: A Well-Founded Software Measurement Ontology. In: Galton, A., Mizoguchi, R. (eds.) Proceedings of the Sixth International Conference FOIS 2010, pp. 213–226. IOS Press, Amsterdam (2010)
16. Guizzardi, G., Falbo, R., Guizzardi, R.: Grounding Software Domain Ontologies in the Unified Foundational Ontology (UFO): The case of the ODE Software Process Ontology. In: Proceedings de la XI Conferencia Iberoamericana de Software Engineering (CIbSE 2008), pp. 127–140 (2008)
17. ISO/IEC 15939: Software Engineering - Software Measurement Process (2002)
18. ISO/IEC 25000: Software Engineering - Software product Quality Requirements and Evaluation (SQuaRE) - Guide to SQuaRE (2005)
19. ISO/IEC 14598-5: IT - Software product evaluation - Part 5: Process for evaluators (1998)
20. Molina, H., Olsina, L.: Assessing Web Applications Consistently: A Context Information Approach. In: 8th Int'l Congress on Web Engineering, NY, US, pp. 224–230. IEEE CS (2008)
21. García, F., Piattini, M., Ruiz, F., Canfora, G., Visaggio, C.A.: FMESP: Framework for the modeling and evaluation of software processes. Journal of Systems Architecture 52(11), 627–639 (2006)

Weaving Aspect-Orientation
into Web Modeling Languages

Irene Garrigós[1], Manuel Wimmer[2], and Jose-Norberto Mazón[1]

[1] WaKe Research, University of Alicante, Spain
{igarrigos,jnmazon}@dlsi.ua.es
[2] Business Informatics Group, Vienna University of Technology, Austria
wimmer@big.tuwien.ac.at

Abstract. While building Web application models from scratch is well-supported, reuse in Web application modeling is still in its infancy. A promising approach in this respect is aspect-oriented modeling to separate certain concerns from the base application, typically cross-cutting ones, and reuse them in various applications. A few Web modeling languages targeting the design phase have been already equipped with aspect-orientation. However, languages for the early phases of Web modeling lack such support, but especially these phases would tremendously benefit from aspect-orientation. Moreover, all the existing solutions are tailored to a specific modeling language. To improve this situation, we consider aspect-orientation itself as an aspect. This allows us to weave aspect-oriented language features into already existing Web modeling languages. We introduce a generic metamodel module comprising the main concepts of aspect-orientation as well as a tool-supported process to weave it into existing base languages. By having this systematic metamodel weaving process, dedicated modeling as well as design-time weaving support is provided for aspects out-of-the-box. We demonstrate our approach by aspectifying a Web requirements modeling language based on i* and applying the aspectified version of it to a case study.

Keywords: Model-driven Web Engineering, Web Requirements, Aspect-oriented Modeling, Language Engineering.

1 Introduction

Web modeling approaches are becoming mature and tailored to supporting different phases of the Web application development process. Several modeling languages exist for specifying requirements, designs, and architectures of Web applications [3, 7, 16]. While building new Web application models from scratch is well-supported by existing approaches, reuse in Web application modeling is still in its infancy. Reuse in software engineering is generally accepted and promoted to improve productiveness [11, 13]. Although a few Web modeling languages provide dedicated reuse mechanisms, e.g., cf. [15], the majority of languages often miss dedicated abstraction, specialization, and integration techniques for reusing Web models.

A promising approach in this respect is aspect-oriented modeling to separate certain aspects from the base application, typically cross-cutting concerns, and reuse them

Q.Z. Sheng and J. Kjeldskov (Eds.): ICWE 2013 Workshops, LNCS 8295, pp. 117–132, 2013.
© Springer International Publishing Switzerland 2013

in different places of different base applications. In the context of software engineering, the principle of separation of concerns helps us to manage the complexity of the software systems that we develop by identifying and separating the different concerns involved in a given problem. The concerns that cut across other concerns (i.e. crosscutting concerns) are responsible for producing tangled representations which are difficult to understand and maintain.

Aspect-Oriented Software Development (AOSD) aims to identify and specify such crosscutting concerns in separate modules, known as aspects, in order to improve modularity and hence comprehensibility, maintainability and reusability. Some Web modeling languages targeting design modeling have been already upgraded to support some aspect-oriented language features [3, 16]. However, these solutions are language specific and furthermore, they do not consider the possibility of defining aspects at the requirements analysis phase. Reasoning in the early phases of Web application development about cross-cutting concerns as well as reuse possibilities enables a more efficient design of the Web applications which results in improved development and maintenance.

In order to solve these drawbacks, we present an approach that allows to extend a Web modeling language with aspect-oriented features in a non-intrusive and automated way. This approach also allows the definition of early aspects (i.e., at the requirements level). For this purpose, we have defined a generic metamodel where the main concepts of aspect-orientation are represented, and we have implemented a process in order to weave it into existing modeling languages' metamodels.

We demonstrate our approach by using a Web requirements modeling language based on i* (called Web Requirements Modeling Language (WRML)) and applying the aspectified version of it to a case study.

The remainder of this paper is as follows: Section 2 briefly introduces WRML that is later used to illustrate our approach. Section 3 explains our proposal by describing the aspect metamodel and detailing the composition processes. For a better understanding of the approach, a case study is presented in Section 4. Section 5 studies related work, and finally, Section 6 concludes and sketches future work.

2   Running Example: Modeling Web Requirements

In this section we briefly introduce the Web requirements modeling language (WRML) that we will use as a running example in order to illustrate our approach. It is a goal-oriented proposal to specify requirements in the context of a Web modeling method by using i* models [6].

The i* framework [20] consists of two models: the strategic dependency (SD) model to describe the dependency relationships (represented as ─D─) among various actors in an organizational context, and the strategic rationale (SR) model, used to describe actor interests and concerns and how they might be addressed.

The SR model (represented as ◌) provides a detailed way of modeling internal intentional elements and relationships of each actor (◯). Intentional elements are goals (◯), tasks (◇), resources (▭) and softgoals (◯). Intentional relationships are means-end links (─▷) representing alternative ways for fulfilling goals; task-decomposition links

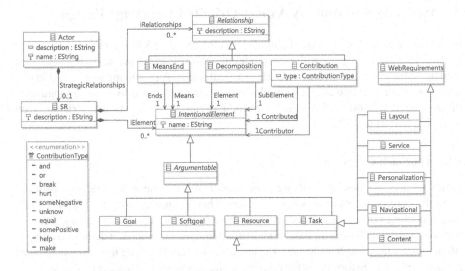

Fig. 1. Overview of our metamodel for *i** modeling in the Web domain

(───┼──) representing the necessary elements for a task to be performed; or contribution links (⇒) in order to model how an intentional element contributes to the satisfaction or fulfillment of a softgoal.

Although i* provides good mechanisms to model actors, their intentions and relationships between them, it needs to be adapted to the Web engineering domain to reflect special Web requirements that are not taken into account in traditional requirement analysis approaches, thus being able to assure the traceability to Web design. To adapt the i* framework to the Web engineering domain we used the taxonomy of Web requirements presented in [5]. As such, the i*'s "task" element, which is used to model functional requirements (FRs), was further specialized in the following Web specific requirements: service, navigational, layout, and personalization requirements. With the aim of considering Web requirements, we defined an i* metamodel extended with each of these requirements. Therefore, the core metamodel specifies metaclasses that represent the i* elements and their relationships, as well as new metaclasses according to the different kinds of Web requirements. Some requirements extend the *Task* metaclass: the *Navigational* (represented by an *N* inside the task symbol), *Service* (represented by an *S*), *Personalization* (represented by a *P*), and *Layout* (represented by an *L*). The *Content* requirement extends the *Resource* metaclass and it is represented as a *C* inside the resource symbol.

It is worth noting that non-functional requirements can be modeled by directly using the *Softgoal* metaclass. Figure 1 shows an excerpt of our metamodel for Web requirements specification. For a further explanation, we refer the reader to [1, 6]. A sample application of the i* modeling framework for the Web domain is shown in Section 4.

3 Aspect-Orientation by Aspect-Oriented Language Design

Nowadays we are facing a pantheon of (domain-specific) Web modeling languages. Extending these languages with new modeling features seems the next necessary step to make them more mature and to tackle practical needs. A promising way to tackle this need is to have reusable language modules that can be attached to existing languages. In this paper, we follow this idea for introducing aspect-orientation to existing Web modeling languages.

3.1 Approach Overview

In this section, we describe how we developed a composable metamodel module covering the core concepts of aspect-orientation. This metamodel module is composable with modeling languages defined as Ecore-based metamodels. For composing the aspect metamodel module with base modeling languages, we propose a dedicated composition process that attaches the aspect-oriented concepts to existing modeling languages and an in-place transformation for relaxing some modeling constraints of the base language to allow for language-specific modeling of aspects with respect to a given base language. By this, we can reuse existing modeling editors to specify aspects as well as validation frameworks to check them before they are composed with base models. Based on the aspect-orientation metamodel module and the systematic process for importing this module to base metamodels, we also present a generic composition process for the model level, namely composing aspects and base models. We demonstrate the approach by using WRML introduced in the previous section as a running example, but we have to stress that the approach is reusable for any other modeling language defined as an Ecore-based metamodel.

3.2 Aspect-Orientation Metamodel Module

In Figure 2, we illustrate the core concepts of aspect-orientation based on our previous work on establishing a reference model for aspect-oriented modeling languages [19]. In this paper, we solely focus on the asymmetric approach to aspect-orientation, namely aspects that are not independent but that have to be composed with base models based on explicit and well-defined join points. The symmetric case, i.e., aspects representing independent models that are composed by merging them based on, e.g., name similarity, we leave as subject to future work.

In the metamodel module shown in Figure 2, we have two kinds of concerns represented (this reflects the asymmetric approach): (i) *aspects* are defining *adaptations* described by a set of model elements and (ii) the *base* concern represents the base model that is, of course, made up of a set of model elements (cf. the top of Figure 2).

To connect aspects with base models, *weavings* (cf. the middle of Figure 2) are used that compose a set of *adaptation rules* describing the *effect* (i.e., an enhancement, a replacement, or a deletion in the base model) of an adaptation as well as the *place* where the adaptation actually takes place by using so-called *pointcuts*. A pointcut selects possible *join points* of an aspect by either statically linking directly to some model elements in the base model by using extensions of the *JoinPoint* meta-class or using an

OCL expressions (cf. meta-attribute *Pointcut.expression*) to dynamically calculate the join points in the base model by selecting elements based on certain conditions.

As join points in the context of this work we consider the container elements that will contain the elements of the assigned aspect. The main reason for this decision is the fact that EMF-based models have to comprise a valid tree with respect to the containment hierarchy, i.e., there is only one root element allowed and all other elements have to be inside a unique container.

In addition to the join points, an aspect may interact with the base model by having further cross-references. This means to substitute some aspect elements with specific model element when introducing the aspects to the base models. For modeling such replacements, we allow for template signatures for aspects (cf. Figure 3). Template signatures contain template parameters that may be bound to concrete model elements or String values. This is defined in the context of join points contained by the weaving models. In particular, join points can have template bindings that again contain a set of template parameter substitutions giving for each formal parameter a concrete value. More details on the template support is presented based on concrete modeling examples in Section 4, Figures 7-8.

Important to note is that the aspect-orientation metamodel module (shown in Figure 2) has two root classes with respect to the containment relationships. First, aspect models may be defined that describe reusable aspects in a first step, and second, weaving models may be created for introducing the aspects to several base models. By this separation, aspects are completely independent of particular base model examples and not specific to one weaving model.

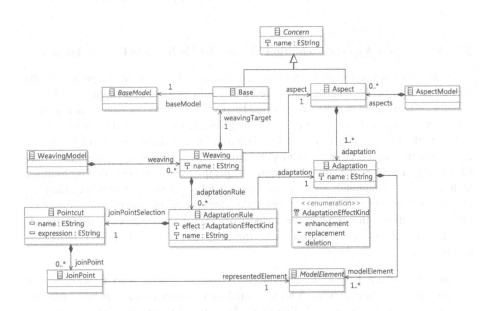

Fig. 2. Aspect-orientation metamodel module in Ecore

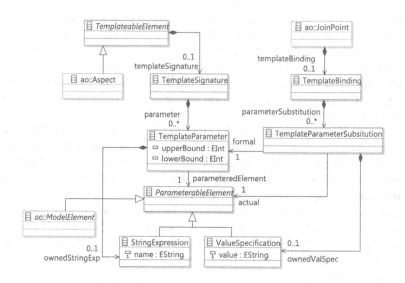

Fig. 3. Templateable aspects (elements from Figure 2 are referred by the prefix *ao*)

Having these concepts defined in the aspect-orientation metamodel module allows to represent aspects and their introduction to base models on a generic level, i.e., agnostic to any metamodel. In the following, we present how this generic aspect metamodel module can be attached to specific metamodels. As one may have already noticed, the abstract meta-classes *BaseModel* and *ModelElement* play an important role in this process.

3.3   Weaving the Aspect-Orientation Metamodel Module into Base Metamodels

To make efficient use of the aspect-oriented concepts described in the previous subsection for a particular language, we foresee a specific process to compute a dedicated metamodel that allows to define well-formed aspect models. As one can see in Figure 2, aspects are composed of a set of different model elements. Thus, also the aspects have to follow the rules of the host modeling language in an eventually relaxed form (because aspects may only represent model fragments, not all language constraints may be meaningful). Thus, we aim for a language-specific aspect language that is equipped with a specific metamodel. This specific metamodel is formed by composing the base language metamodel with the aspect-orientation metamodel module by using some specific join points. By this, we introduce aspect-orientation to languages by using aspect-orientation itself. In particular, the following two steps are necessary to achieve this composition:

– **Step 1:** Aspects have to be introduced to base models by weaving models. For this, the base models have to be identified by the weaving models by setting the *weavingTarget* reference (cf. Figure 2). Thus, it has to be specified on the meta-model level, which model element actually represents the base model in the base metamodel. Normally a root model element containing all other model elements directly or indirectly is used for this purpose in EMF, because the containment relationships span up a tree. Therefore, the language designer has to link the root meta-class of the base language metamodel with the *BaseModel* meta-class of the aspect-orientation metamodel module by using an inheritance relationship.

- **Step 2:** Model elements of the base language are used to specify the adaptation rules, i.e., what has to be introduced, updated, or deleted in the base model. In order to ensure that the elements contained in adaptation rules represent valid model fragments, every meta-class in the base metamodel has to directly or indirectly inherit from the *ModelElement* meta-class of the aspect-orientation metamodel module. By this, the adaptation rules can be populated by ordinary model elements of the base language.

Both steps may be completely automated. While for the first step, a manual selection of root meta-class candidates may be necessary if there is more than one candidate, the second point is completely automatic. All top meta-classes in the inheritance taxonomy of the base metamodel have to be calculated and then these classes get an additional super class, namely, the *ModelElement* class of the aspect-orientation metamodel module. To avoid name clashes, the classes of the aspect-orientation metamodel module are introduced in the base metamodel by using their own package that is integrated as a subpackage in the root package of the base metamodel (normally EMF metamodels have exactly one root package as they exhibit a tree-based package structure). We have implemented support for these two steps by using a parameterizable model transformation, whereas the parameter to be set is the root meta-class of the base metamodel.

Having the classes of the aspect-orientation metamodel module integrated in the base metamodel may be not enough to end up with an appropriate aspect modeling language. Some modeling constraints may be too strict for defining aspects, because aspects represent model fragments and not necessarily complete models that have to fulfill all language constraints. Here similar issues arise as defining a domain-specific transformation language that is tailored for a given modeling language [10]. Thus, we apply a relaxation process to the base metamodel before the composition with aspect-orientation metamodel module takes place to end up with a language that allows to model aspects that may be completed by weaving them into the base models in a flexible way. In particular, this relaxation process requires to reset the lower multiplicities of the references and attributes in the base metamodel to zero in order to make them all optional properties. By this, aspects can be defined as model fragments that are completed by the subsequent weaving step. Again, the relaxation process is automated by a model transformation.

Example. In Figure 4, a small excerpt of the aspectification of the WRML is shown. On the top of this figure, an excerpt of the WRML metamodel and an excerpt of the aspect-oriented metamodel module are illustrated by the two packages as well as the *Actor* meta-class representing the root element of the base metamodel. The two metamodels are merged into one metamodel whereas the *AO* package is now nested into the base language root package. Furthermore, the inheritance relationships are specified as described above and the relaxation takes place. When running this composition process

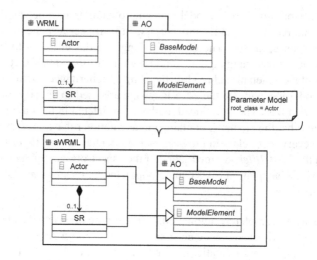

Fig. 4. Aspectification of WRML (excerpt)

on a tuple consisting of a base metamodel and the aspect metamodel, we finally end up with a metamodel that allows us to model aspects that can be checked against the newly created *aspectified* metamodel as well as it allows to define weaving links between a base model (that is an instance of the base metamodel) and aspects. In the next subsection, we show how aspect models and weaving models are specified.

3.4 Modeling Aspects and Weavings with Aspectified Metamodels

Based on the available metamodeling capabilities and out-of-the-box tool support in EMF, we can instantiate the automatically produced aspectified metamodels by standard EMF modeling editors. The particular usage of the metamodel is to model aspect models that define independently from base models certain model fragments that are later integrated with specific base models by using a weaving model. We decided to go for a separation of aspect models and weaving models to allow for aspect repositories from which a modeler may select certain aspects and integrate them to her base model using additional weaving models.

Example. To demonstrate how to use the aspectified metamodels, we present a small instance of the afore enhanced metamodel in Figure 5. On the right-hand side of the figure, a small aspect model is shown that is conform to the aspectified metamodel. The aspect only describes a small adaptation, namely to add a task to an actor by adding it to the SR element. In order to actually use this aspect, a weaving model is residing between the base model and the aspect model. In the upper half of Figure 5, the weaving model uses an explicit joinpoint defined by the modeler that points to the particular SR element that should be enhanced by the aspect, i.e., who should get the task assigned, while in the lower half of Figure 5, no extensional joinpoint is used. Instead, it is described intensionally by a OCL query that is defined by the *Pointcut* object. The OCL query

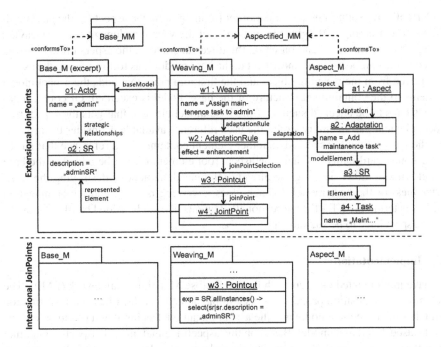

Fig. 5. Aspects and Weaving Models by Example

is evaluated by an OCL engine and all the selected elements are extended by the given aspect. One may think about the OCL query as a mechanism to compute automatically a set of joinpoints. In our example, the evaluation of the OCL query results in the same weaving semantics as has before been extensionally defined. Only the SR element with the description "adminSR" gets the aspect attached when we assume that only one SR element with such a value exists in the model.

3.5 Model Composition Process

Having the weaving models defined between the aspect models and the base models, a composition process is activated to actually introduce the aspects to the base models by producing an enhanced model that is solely conform to the base metamodel. In order to compose models with aspects, several composition strategies are possible:

- *Arbitrary order*: Weavings are contained in one single set and are executed based on their implicit order, i.e., the order in which they are contained in the weaving model.
- *Priorities*: If aspects are building on each other, priorities have to be supported for weavings, i.e., to split the single set of weavings into a sequence of different subsets.
- *Orchestration*: For more complex weaving plans, control structures such as conditionals may be applied to orchestrate the execution of the composition.

Currently, we support no particular order for integrating the aspects to the base models. The order is implicitly given by the order of the weaving elements in the weaving model which is traversed and based on the traversal strategy, the aspect order is given. The concrete composition of one aspect to the base model is as follows: First, the aspect is retrieved from the weaving object and the first join point that adds the aspect model elements to the containment structure of the base model is executed. Of course, constraints have to be checked such as if the base model element that gets the aspect root model element has an empty slot in the used reference available. Consider for instance that the base element has already another element contained by a reference that has as upper bound cardinality 1. Then, the aspect root element cannot be added to the base model without either deleting the already referenced element or destroying the wellformedness of the base model. In such cases a warning is given and the composition process is terminated. Furthermore, not all elements have to be added but the templates of the aspect have to be substituted.

3.6   Implementation

We have implemented our approach for the Eclipse Modeling Framework (EMF). The metamodel composition process has been implemented as a Java-based transformation that takes the base metamodel and the aspect metamodel as input and produces as output the aspectified metamodel. Based on this aspectified metamodel, aspects containing adaptations as well as weavings containing adaptation rules are defined. In particular, we exploit the capabilities of EMF to load several resources within one modeling editor that allows basic inter-model reference support out-of-the-box. The model composition process takes as input the model triple (i.e., base model, aspect model, weaving model) and produces the composed model. Again this process is implemented as a model transformation.

4   Case Study

In this section, we consider the example shown in Figure 6. The figure shows the SR model of a book store. The main goal of the system actor is to manage the book sales. In order to fulfill this goal we have two different alternatives: books can be sold online or books can be sold at the store. We are going to focus on the first task *"books be sold online"*. In order to complete this task, two subtasks should be completed: *"provide book info"* (which is a navigational requirement) and *"provide recommended books"* (which is a personalization requirement).

The data is specified by means of the content requirement *"books"*. Each of the leave tasks is related with this content requirement.

In the following, we show how to model two new concerns in an application independent way by defining aspects using the aspectified metamodel of WRML. Furthermore we show how the aspects can be introduced in the base model by using weaving models. To allow for a more concise representation, we switch from the abstract syntax to a concrete syntax to visualize the models in the rest of this section. For didactic reasons, we present the base model and weave both concerns independent from each other to it. The woven model is illustrated in Figure 9.

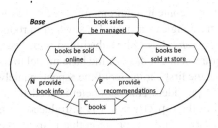

Fig. 6. Base model

4.1 The Shopping Cart Aspect

Concern Description. The first concern we want to model is a shopping cart. The tasks needed are adding a product to the cart and viewing the shopping cart content.

Aspect Model. The shopping cart aspect is shown in the right hand side of Figure 7. This concern includes a general task *"provide a shopping cart"*. It is decomposed into two subtasks to be completed, which are of different type: *"$add <x> to cart$"* (service requirement) and *"view cart content"* (navigational requirement) which are related to the content requirement *"cart"*.

The aspect has a template signature consisting of two template parameters, one is a String expression while the other is a content requirement element. Please note that the name of the first subtask is dynamically computed by including the first parameter, since we can weave this aspect with a base model of any kind of e-commerce application (i.e., not necessarily a book store). The tasks are also related with a content requirement named *"item"* which is a generic element, that will depend again on the type of application of the base model we weave the concern in.

Weaving Model. As we can see in Figure 7, the shopping cart concern is a subtree of tasks with cross-links to content requirements that is introduced in the base model by using a weaving model. The join point (jp) for the aspect is the general task *"books be sold online"* in the base model that acts as container element for the general task *"provide a shopping cart"*. Furthermore, we need for this example additional cross-links from the aspect model elements to the base model elements by binding the template

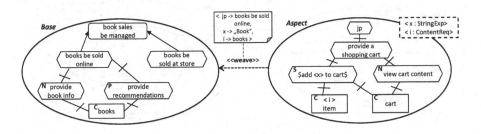

Fig. 7. Shopping cart aspect

parameters. In particular, the content requirement *"books"* has to play the role of the template *"item"* of the shopping cart aspect. Thus, when introducing the aspect to the base model, the template *"item"* has to be substituted with *"books"*. This is done by mapping the content requirement *"books"* of the base model to the template parameter *i* of the aspect. Finally, for the first parameter of the aspect, namely parameter *x*, a primitive String value has to be provided. This parameter is needed for calculating the name of an element contained in the aspect when it is introduced to the base model. Thus, the parameter is also occurring in the expression that is used to calculate the name of a navigation concern (cf. expression *"$add <x> to cart$"*). The rest of the elements contained in the aspect are just "simple" model elements that are woven into the base model by just copying them.

4.2   The Search Engine Aspect

Concern Description. This concern refers to a search engine that we want to reuse. In this case we have defined the search by keyword or by category. We can also refine the search by expanding our keyword list with semantic-related keywords or by listing all the possible items.

Aspect Model. The aspect model of this concern can be seen on the right hand side of Figure 8. It has a goal named *"$<i.name> be searched$"* . Again this concern is modeled in a generic way (i.e., independent of the target base model). This goal is decomposed into two tasks, we can *"search by keywords"* or *"search by category"*. In order to fulfill the first one, a goal *"search to be refined"* and a task *"$search by <x> keyword$"* (service requirement) need to be completed. The search can be refined in two ways: *"by listing all'* or *"by keyword expansion"*. Again in this case, the leave tasks are related with the needed content requirements.

For this aspect, the template signature consists of three parameters. First, a String expression is needed for computing the name of the keyword search task. Second, the content requirement playing the role of the item has to be introduced. Finally, an additional content requirement presenting the categories of the items is considered. Please note that the latter is optional, i.e., the multiplicity of this template parameter is zero-to-one. This has as consequence, that if it is bound to a specific element then the parameterized element

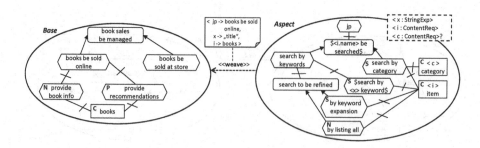

Fig. 8. Search engine aspect

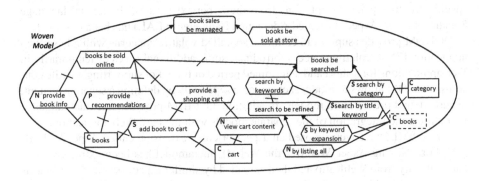

Fig. 9. Resulting model after aspect composition

is substituted by the specific element. Otherwise the content requirement "category" is introduced in the base model.

Weaving Model. As for the shopping cart concern, the join point for the aspect is the general task *"books be sold online"* in the base model. In contrast to the previous example, only one of the two content requirement parameters is mandatory to be bound in the weaving between the base and the aspect model. More specifically, the content requirement *"item"* has to be bound (that is bound to content requirement *"books"* again by using the parameter *i*), but not the content requirement *"category"* (thus it is introduced to the base model in our example, because no binding has been specified for the parameter *c*). Besides the content requirement parameters, we have again a simply typed parameter that is used in the expression ("$search by <x> keyword$") to calculate the name for a task similar as it has been done for the shopping cart aspect. In addition, the content requirement parameter *i* is used also in an expression for calculating the name of another task (cf. "$<i.name> be searched$"). Here the parameter is in the expression for accessing the name of the content requirement that is bound to the content requirement parameter by using an OCL expression.

5   Related Work

With respect to the contribution of this paper, we elaborate on aspect-oriented modeling support in the field of Model-Driven Web Engineering (MDWE).

Baumeister et al. [2] presented one of the early works in MDWE that proposed the use of aspect-orientation for modeling customization in hypertext models. In the UWE metamodel, the Aspect concept has been introduced as a sub-class of the UML meta-class Package. Furthermore an Aspect is defined to have one Pointcut and one Advice each likewise specialized from the UML meta-class Package. The approach distinguishes between static aspects woven at design time and dynamical aspects woven at runtime.

In [3], Casteleyn et al. presented the extension of the Hera-S approach with aspect-oriented concepts for modeling customization concerns in Web applications. More specifically, to separate adaptations from the hypertext models, the textual language Semantics-based Aspect-Oriented Adaptation Language (SEAL) has been designed.

OOHDM provides support to compose so-called volatile concerns with a base Web application [7]. A volatile concern introduces some additional services temporarily in Web applications for a short and determined period of time. For supporting volatile concerns, OOHDM allows to model each concern separately by defining a separate content, hypertext, and presentation models. In addition, OOHDM provides a textual language for defining the integration of the separate models with the base Web application.

For WebML, we have proposed an aspect-oriented extension called AspectWebML [16]. For realizing AspectWebML, the WebML metamodel has been extracted semi-automatically from WebRatio and then extended by similar aspect-oriented concepts as we have used in this paper for the generic aspect-orientation module. However, in [16] the aspect-oriented extension of the language has been manually achieved.

Cicchetti et al. [4] present a weaving model based approach to model Web applications using different viewpoints. While we are separating model fragments from one modeling view, they are concerned with consistency between different viewpoints. This is especially needed for Web models, because several viewpoints are used such as content, navigation, and presentation. To validate consistency between viewpoints, constraints are introduced for weaving links that allow to reason if weaving models are complete and consistent. Thus, they do not use weaving as in aspect-oriented modeling, but as a general form of correspondence links between viewpoints.

To the best of our knowledge, none of the existing Web modeling languages support aspects at early stages of the development. The only exception is the recent work presented by Urbieta et al. [18], which defines an approach for tackling crosscutting workflow behaviour in the requirements phase in the context of the WebSpec requirements modeling language [1,12]. Outside the MDWE field, there exist some approaches that consider specifying crosscutting concerns in the requirements level of a software application [8,14,17]. They mainly propose extensions for UML, i.e., in particular for use cases, to define aspects.

Furthermore, we are not aware of an approach that considers aspect-orientation as a generic concern that can be introduced into existing modeling languages. All the mentioned approaches have been particularly designed for a specific language. In this paper we take a different angle by semi-automatically enhancing existing languages with aspect-oriented modeling features. This has been exemplified in the paper for WRML. However, the application of our approach for re-building the aforementioned languages already providing aspect-orientation support is left as subject to future work.

6   Conclusions and Future Work

In this paper we have presented an approach to equip already existing languages with aspect-oriented modeling concepts by using aspect-orientation itself on the metamodel level. By having aspectified metamodels, aspects and weavings can be systematically modelled and validated by reusing out-of-the-box EMF support as well as a generic design-time model weaver is provided for actually introducing the aspects to the base models. We have demonstrated the approach by using WRML as an example language and showed how Web requirements can be expressed as aspects.

For future work we aim to rebuild already aspect-oriented modeling languages to see wether this is possible in a generic manner or specific adaptations are necessary. Another important point for future work is if different execution orders of given weavings may result in different woven models, i.e., if the aspects are confluent or not. For this we plan to investigate the notion of critical pairs defined for graph transformations [9]. In particular, we plan to provide a mapping to graph transformations in order to reuse the reasoning techniques currently available for determining if a set of graph transformation rules, representing the aspects and weavings, is confluent or not.

References

1. Aguilar, J.A., Garrigós, I., Mazón, J.-N., Trujillo, J.: An MDA Approach for Goal-oriented Requirement Analysis in Web Engineering. J. UCS 16(17), 2475–2494 (2010)
2. Baumeister, H., Knapp, A., Koch, N., Zhang, G.: Modelling Adaptivity with Aspects. In: Lowe, D.G., Gaedke, M. (eds.) ICWE 2005. LNCS, vol. 3579, pp. 406–416. Springer, Heidelberg (2005)
3. Casteleyn, S., Woensel, W.V., Houben, G.-J.: A semantics-based aspect-oriented approach to adaptation in web engineering. In: Hypertext, pp. 189–198 (2007)
4. Cicchetti, A., Di Ruscio, D.: Decoupling web application concerns through weaving operations. Sci. Comput. Program. 70(1), 62–86 (2008)
5. Cuaresma, M.J.E., Koch, N.: Requirements engineering for web applications - a comparative study. J. Web Eng. 2(3), 193–212 (2004)
6. Garrigós, I., Mazón, J.-N., Trujillo, J.: A Requirement Analysis Approach for Using i* in Web Engineering. In: Gaedke, M., Grossniklaus, M., Díaz, O. (eds.) ICWE 2009. LNCS, vol. 5648, pp. 151–165. Springer, Heidelberg (2009)
7. Ginzburg, J., Rossi, G., Urbieta, M., Distante, D.: Transparent Interface Composition in Web Applications. In: Baresi, L., Fraternali, P., Houben, G.-J. (eds.) ICWE 2007. LNCS, vol. 4607, pp. 152–166. Springer, Heidelberg (2007)
8. Grundy, J.C.: Aspect-Oriented Requirements Engineering for Component-Based Software Systems. In: RE, pp. 84–91 (1999)
9. Heckel, R., Küster, J.M., Taentzer, G.: Confluence of Typed Attributed Graph Transformation Systems. In: Corradini, A., Ehrig, H., Kreowski, H.-J., Rozenberg, G. (eds.) ICGT 2002. LNCS, vol. 2505, pp. 161–176. Springer, Heidelberg (2002)
10. Kühne, T., Mezei, G., Syriani, E., Vangheluwe, H., Wimmer, M.: Explicit transformation modeling. In: Ghosh, S. (ed.) MODELS 2009 Workshops. LNCS, vol. 6002, pp. 240–255. Springer, Heidelberg (2010)
11. Li, J., Gupta, A., Arvid, J., Borretzen, B., Conradi, R.: The empirical studies on quality benefits of reusing software components. In: COMPSAC, pp. 399–402 (2007)
12. Luna, E.R., Rossi, G., Garrigós, I.: WebSpec: a visual language for specifying interaction and navigation requirements in web applications. Requir. Eng. 16(4), 297–321 (2011)
13. McClure, C.: Software Reuse: A Standards-Based Guide. Wiley (2001)
14. Rashid, A., Sawyer, P., Moreira, A.M.D., Araújo, J.: Early Aspects: A Model for Aspect-Oriented Requirements Engineering. In: RE, pp. 199–202 (2002)
15. Rossi, G., Schwabe, D., Lyardet, F.: Abstraction and Reuse Mechanisms in Web Application Models. In: Mayr, H.C., Liddle, S.W., Thalheim, B. (eds.) ER Workshops 2000. LNCS, vol. 1921, pp. 76–88. Springer, Heidelberg (2000)
16. Schauerhuber, A., Wimmer, M., Schwinger, W., Kapsammer, E., Retschitzegger, W.: Aspect-Oriented Modeling of Ubiquitous Web Applications: The aspectWebML Approach. In: ECBS, pp. 569–576 (2007)

17. Suzuki, J., Yamamoto, Y.: Extending UML with Aspects: Aspect Support in the Design Phase. In: ECOOP Workshops, pp. 299–300 (1999)
18. Urbieta, M.M., Rossi, G., Gordillo, S., Schwinger, W., Retschitzegger, W., Escalona, M.J.: Identifying and Modelling Complex Workflow Requirements in Web Applications. In: Grossniklaus, M., Wimmer, M. (eds.) ICWE Workshops 2012. LNCS, vol. 7703, pp. 146–157. Springer, Heidelberg (2012)
19. Wimmer, M., Schauerhuber, A., Kappel, G., Retschitzegger, W., Schwinger, W., Kapsammer, E.: A survey on UML-based aspect-oriented design modeling. ACM Comput. Surv. 43(4), 28 (2011)
20. Yu, E.S.K.: Towards Modeling and Reasoning Support for Early-Phase Requirements Engineering. In: RE, pp. 226–235 (1997)

Model-Driven Generation of a REST API from a Legacy Web Application*

Roberto Rodríguez-Echeverría, Fernando Macías, Víctor M. Pavón,
José M. Conejero, and Fernando Sánchez-Figueroa

University of Extremadura (Spain),
Quercus Software Engineering Group
{rre,fernandomacias,victorpavon,chemacm,fernando}@unex.es
http://quercusseg.unex.es

Abstract. Web 2.0 phenomenon, REST APIs and growing mobile service consumption, among other factors, are leading the development of web applications to a new paradigm, named cross-device web application. Those web sites let organizations of all sizes provide a pervasive and contextual access to their information and services, to customers, employees and partners via potentially any kind of device. Most organizations often possess legacy systems which should face an ongoing evolution process to enhance its accessibility and interoperability. Yesterday they had to evolve to provide the user with a Web layer, and now they should evolve again to adapt to the new ways of data and services consumption on the Web. In such scenario, a REST API plays a key role, defining the interaction layer between the legacy system and all its heterogeneous front ends. This work presents a model-driven approach to derive a REST API from a legacy web application within the frame defined by a modernization process. This approach departs from a conceptual model of the legacy application generated by reverse engineering techniques. In this work we detail the API generation process and provide a sample implementation instrumenting one of the studied web development frameworks to evaluate the suitability of the approach.

Keywords: Software Modernization, Software Reengineering, Rich Internet Applications, REST.

1 Introduction

Since the publication of the REST architectural style [4], the design and development of RESTful web services has become the *de facto* standard to define the interaction between Web 2.0 frontends and their backends. Actually, REST APIs may be currently conceived as one of the key factors in the success of a web (cloud) application, so a great effort is dedicated to its development and

* Work funded by Spanish Contract MIGRARIA - TIN2011-27340 at Ministerio de Ciencia e Innovación and Gobierno de Extremadura (GR-10129) and European Regional Development Fund (ERDF).

Q.Z. Sheng and J. Kjeldskov (Eds.): ICWE 2013 Workshops, LNCS 8295, pp. 133–147, 2013.

evolution. REST APIs define, on the one hand, a way of lean integration among a service provider and other applications (consumers), and on the other hand, a mean to get a cross-device web application, spreading the original scope of the web application.

Legacy systems have always considered web service technology as a proper mean to gain interoperability and to decrease their evolution related costs. Since RESTful services became mainstream fueled, first, by the Web 2.0 adoption and, then, by ongoing mobile service consumption raise, legacy applications have searched for alternatives to evolve their interaction layers (web or RPC services) to this new standard and become cross-device web applications.[1]describe how web service ecosystems have risen to become the predominant model in software solutions. Traditionally centralized domains, such as business solutions, electronic shops and electronic auctions are now publishing pieces of their functionality to create web service ecosystems.

The main goal of this work is to present an approach for the automatic generation of a REST API that provides an alternative interface to a legacy Web system. In this work we present, on the one hand, the architecture of a REST support layer defined as an extension of the Struts v1.3 Web development framework and, on the other hand, the model-driven process to adapt such layer to obtain a REST API conformed to the legacy subsystem to be modernized.

The rest of the paper is structured as follows. Section 2 briefly presents an overview of the MIGRARIA project and its MVC metamodel. In Section 3 an illustrative example is depicted. Section 4 introduces our approach to generate a REST API from a legacy web application. The related work is discussed in Section 5. Finally, main conclusions and future work are outlined in Section 6.

2   MIGRARIA Project

The process defined herein is framed within a whole modernization strategy: MIGRARIA project [9]. This project defines a systematic and semi-automatic process to modernize legacy non-model-based data-driven Web applications into RIAs. The process starts with the generation of a conceptual representation of the legacy system by using reverse engineering techniques. According to that project, this conceptual representation is based on the MIGRARIA MVC metamodel that allows the specification of legacy web applications developed by means of MVC-based web frameworks. Once the conceptual representation is obtained, the modernization engineer must decide the legacy system functionalities that should be part of the target system, i.e. the new RIA client. In other words, she must specify the set of components or subsystem to modernize. This decision is carried out in our approach by the selection of the different views included in the subsystem within the generated conceptual model of the legacy application. Note that the modernization process defined by MIGRARIA does not aim at sustituying the current system by a new one. Indeed, its main purpose is to complement the system by the generation of new ways of access and interaction such as a RIA client [8] and its corresponding server connection layer, a REST API in this work.

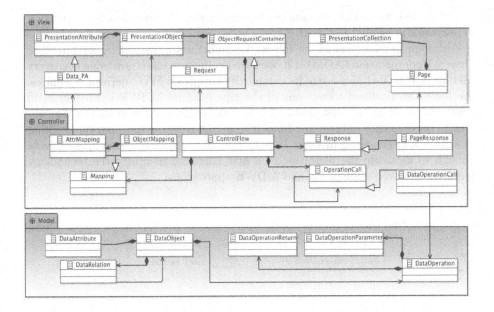

Fig. 1. MIGRARIA MVC metamodel overview

2.1   MIGRARIA MVC Metamodel

Within the MIGRARIA project, a specific language has been defined to generate a conceptual representation of a legacy MVC-based web application: the MIGRARIA MVC metamodel. This metamodel has been designed based on the Model-View-Controller pattern that has become the conceptual foundation of a great number of web development frameworks. In that sense, this metamodel specifies the main concepts of the development of a web application arranged in the three main components of the MVC pattern. Figure 1 presents an excerpt of the MIGRARIA MVC metamodel focusing on the main elements of each component. Such elements and their relations are used throughout this work to develop an illustrative example of the approach. The Model package provide elements to represent data objects, their attributes, their relationships and the operations defined over them. The View package provide elements to represent pages, as main containers, and presentation objects and requests, as main containments. Presentation objects, basically, have a set of attributes, can indicate data input or data output and can be presented individually or inside a collection. Meanwhile, requests are characterized by their parameters and path and define connection points with controller elements by means of the request-handler association. The Controller package provides elements to represent request handlers (ControlFlow), their mappings defined between presentation and data objects, their response defining a relationship with the target page element, and the sequence of operation calls performed to execute the requested action or to fetch the requested data. This metamodel is a comprehensive revision and extension of our work presented last year [8].

Although our intention is to follow the guidelines proposed by Architecture Driven Modernization (ADM) [12], we have declined to use Knowledge Discovery Metamodel (KDM) because of its complexity to specify MVC-derived semantics. We have also declined to use one of the ripe existing MDWE approaches [10] cause most of them are designed within forward engineering approaches. The abstract concepts they defined are difficult to match with the information resulting of a reverse engineering process. In our opinion, the semantic gap may be wide enough to motivate the definition of a new language to bridge the technology platform of a web application and MDWE approaches.

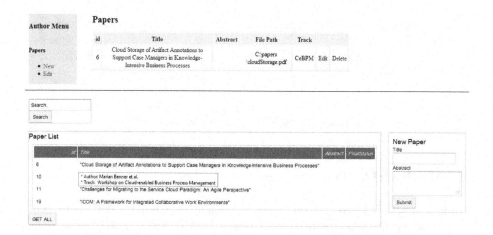

Fig. 2. Legacy Web Application and RIA snapshots

3   Illustrative Example

Figure 2 illustrates a modernization scenario extracted from the main case study of the MIGRARIA project, named the Conference Review System[1]. The data model proposed by [2] has been respected during system development. In this case, the paper submission subsystem has been selected to be modernized. In Figure 2, the top half presents a legacy view listing the papers submitted by a concrete author, and the bottom half shows a possible RIA client as the result of the modernization process. This new client is a composite formed by the legacy views: paperList (in the image), paperCreate, paperEdit and paperDetails. So the generated RIA client follows the single-page paradigm providing all the CRUD operations from a single view [7]. Basically this page is composed of an interactive list of papers, popping up additional information on mouse

---

[1] http://www.eweb.unex.es/eweb/migraria

over event, a search box, and a web form to submit a new paper or to edit an existing one. All the requests performed by that client are AJAX-based and REST-compliant, and used JSON as data exchange format. So the server side needs to provide a convenient connection layer for such client.

Having introduced that modernization scenario, in the next sections we will tackle the generation of a REST API to connect that new RIA client with the legacy application of our case study.

4 The Approach

The main goal of this work is to present an approach for the automatic generation of a REST API that provides an alternative access to a legacy Web system. This process is framed within the modernization framework defined by the MIGRARIA project [9].

Based on the selected subsystem to modernize, the process must generate, on the one hand, a RIA client and, on the other hand, a REST API that allows the communication between the new RIA client and the legacy Web application. In this paper, we focus on the approach defined to generate the REST API in the context of the modernization scenario defined. The REST layer must then fulfill the next requirements:

1. Adapting its behavior based on a configuration file.
2. Adding support for HTTP PUT and DELETE methods, if needed.
3. Adding parse and conversion support for common data formats (JSON, XML).
4. Delegating to a legacy controller the action of handling a REST request (REST-controller mapping).
   (a) Generating the context for the proper execution of the legacy controller (JSON-objects conversion).
   (b) Generating the response according to a particular format (previously decided).

In the specification of the REST API we may identify two different parts clearly separated: (1) a part of the system depending on the Web framework used to develop the legacy application; (2) a part specific for the legacy system being modernized. The former includes all the extensions and adaptations performed in the framework to add it the REST capabilities aforementioned. The latter mainly concerns to the specification of the behavior of the API for a particular Web application, namely: (i) the mappings among REST requests and legacy controllers; (ii) the input (request) and output (response) data conversion among the formats expected by, on the one hand, the RIA client and, on the other hand, the controller. Obviously, while the first part remains unchanged for different legacy Web applications, the second one depends on the concrete legacy system being modernized. The process followed to specify the Web application dependent part is illustrated by Figure 3. As it can be observed, the work presented herein takes the MVC model of the legacy application as input and generates its REST API. This process is defined by the next activity sequence:

1. Identification of the resources related to the subsystem to be modernized.
2. REST URI[2] generation for the identified resources.
3. Identification of the available operations over the resources based on the selected views, their requests and the controllers that manage these requests.
4. Generation of request mappings for the operations available for each resource and for a particular data format.
5. Delegation of the REST request handling to the controllers available in the legacy application and providing the correspondingly data conversions.

A detailed description of both parts of this REST API generation process is provided in the next sections.

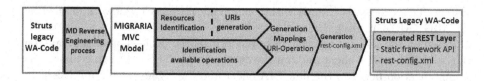

Fig. 3. Process outline

4.1 Framework-dependant REST API Specification

In order to generate a REST API from the legacy application, the framework used to develop the legacy system must be extended conveniently to enable the handling of REST requests. From a modernization point of view, we may rely on two different approaches to obtain this REST API:

1. To generate the REST API from its conceptual description by using model-to-code transformations.
2. To manually implement the REST API and, later, automatically generate its configuration based on the information extracted from the legacy application and the functionality to be included into the target RIA client.
   The main disadvantage of the first alternative concerns to the need of adapting (or redefining) the transformations once and again for each Web framework considered in the approach even, in many cases, for its different versions. Moreover, based on the structural properties of this REST API which clearly contains a static part, it does not seem to make sense to completely generate it from scratch by means of transformations. Thus, the second alternative seems more suitable although it implies implementing and maintaining different versions of the REST API according to the different frameworks and versions. In other words, this second approach requires different implementations for the framework-dependent part for different frameworks and versions whilst the variable part is automatically generated by means of model-to-text transformations. This variable part represents, in our case, the REST API configuration and, thus, it will be automatically generated by model transformations.

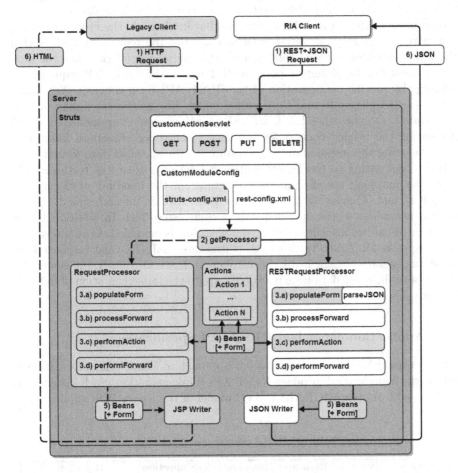

Fig. 4. REST layer for Struts v1.3.X

In order to illustrate how a particular Web framework is instrumented to provide REST API support according to our approach, an implementation for the Struts v1.3 Web framework has been developed. This implementation is graphically described in the process shown in Figure 4. This figure is organized according to the lifecycle of a request in the Struts framework extended with the REST API support. Note that each step in the lifecycle has been enumerated in the figure. The figure shows, on the one hand, the request-response lifecycle for a request generated by the legacy Web application (dashed line) and, on the other hand, the request-response cycle for a REST request generated by the target RIA client (solid line). This comparative illustration allows appreciating the modifications performed to the Web framework in order to incorporate the

---

[2] Uniform Resource Identifier.

REST API support. Notice that the white boxes indicate modified or generated elements. It may be easily observed that the extension has basically required the modification of the classes: *ActionServlet* (that implements the Front Controller [3] in Struts) and *RequestProcessor* (which handles the request lifecycle within the framework). on the one hand, the *CustomActionServlet* class has the next responsibilities: (1) adding support for PUT and DELETE HTTP requests; (2) loading the specific configuration of the REST API for a concrete Web application (rest-config.xml); and (3) deciding which *RequestProcessor* must handle the request. On the other hand, *RESTRequestProcesssor* is responsible of: (1) generating the needed context for the legacy controller invocation (step 3-a); (2) generating the response object according to the specified data format (step 3-b); (3) delegating to the legacy controller (*Action*), according to the REST-controller mapping specified in the configuration, the handling of the request (step 3-c); and (4) delegating the response generation in the corresponding component according to the specified data format (step 3-d). In addition to the commented extensions, the *JSONWriter* class has been added, as an alternative new response composer. In this case, it generates a JSON-valid response from the data generated by the invoked controller (*Action*). Obviously, the generation of responses in other data formats would require the implementation of different Writer classes.

4.2   Application-dependant REST API Specification

Next, we describe the main steps of our approach to extract the information to set up the framework-dependant REST API implementation. Such information is obtained from the MIGRARIA MVC model of the legacy Web application.

Table 1. REST resources and relations

Views	Potential Resources	Resources	I/O	Collection	Relations
paperCreate	paperForm	Paper	I	NO	1 Track : N Paper
	track	Track	O	YES	1 Paper : N Coauthor
paperEdit	paperForm	Paper	I	NO	1 Paper : N Review
	track	Track	O	YES	1 Author : N Paper
	coauthorForm	Coauthor	I	NO	1 Author : N Review
	coauthor	Coauthor	O	YES	N Author : M Track
paperDetails	paper	Paper	O	NO	
	coauthor	Coauthor	O	YES	
	review	Review	O	YES	
paperList	paper	Paper	O	YES	
	author	Author	O	NO	

---

[3] http://struts.apache.org/development/1.x/apidocs/org/apache/
struts/action/ActionServlet.html

Identifying Resources. The specification of a REST API implies to redesign the interaction between client and server from a resource-centric point of view. In that sense, the adequate identification of the involved resources and their relations becomes a fundamental step in the REST API generation process. In order to carry out this activity, the modernization engineer must analyze and query the MIGRARIA MVC model to find out the resources related with those views that compose the subsystem to be modernized. Each view container (page) is composed by one or more presentation objects that define a concrete data view over the corresponding data objects defined at the model component, e.g. presenting some of their attributes. These presentation objects may represent input or output data and they may be either presented individually or organized into collections. In order to identify the model objects, an analysis of the controller component is required to identify the actual mappings defined among presentation and model objects within a concrete view.

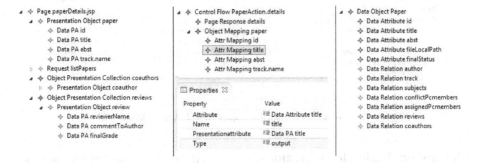

Fig. 5. Resource identification on a MIGRARIA-MVC Model

Figure 5 presents the presentation object *paper*, included in the view *paperDetails*, and its mapping with the data object *Paper*, defined in the controller *paperAction.details*. As the final result of the analysis of the MIGRARIA MVC model, the engineer must obtain: i) the data objects involved in the subsystem to be modernized; ii) their relationships; and, moreover, iii) the different ways of being presented by views and consumed by controllers. All this information is gathered in the potential resources column of the table 1 which shows the results for the paper submission subsystem in our running example. This table contains also the relations established among the collected resources.

Generating REST URIs. Taking as input the information regarding the resources and their relations obtained in the previous step, all the feasible REST URI combinations for each obtained resource are generated by means of the next process. The URIs column of table 2 shows a brief sample of the collection generated for our running example which illustrates the main construction blocks of our process.

The steps of the process are described as follows:

1. Generate base URI pair for each resource:
   (a) /resources
   (b) /resources/{id}
2. Generate base URI pair for each one-to-many relationship:
   (a) /resources_one/{id}/resources_many
   (b) /resources_one/{id}/resources_many/{id}
3. For each many-to-many relationship, locate the master resource and execute the previous step taking the master resource as the main one.
4. Complete the URIs adding to the query string any control parameter that appear in the original requests.

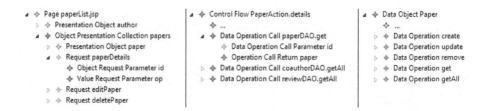

Fig. 6. Operation identification on a MIGRARIA-MVC Model

Identifying Available Operations. Considering that our modernization process takes as input a previously implemented legacy application, obviously the set of operations for each resource that the REST API must provide is limited by the operations available in the original system. Therefore, we need to identify the operations previously defined over these resources to be modernized in order to properly filter the set of possible REST requests to be provided. Again, this information is obtained by the modernization engineer by analyzing and querying the MIGRARIA MVC model. This analysis allows, in this case, obtaining all the requests related with the set of views that compose the subsystem to be modernized. Although most of such requests are included in these views, there may be other ones not included in the views but being responsible for generating a concrete view, e.g. a request generated by a menu link. Note that the MIGRARIA MVC model provides enough information to identify the controller handling a particular request and moreover the controller responsible for the generation of a particular view. The Controller component of a MIGRARIA MVC model permits the engineer to specify the operation call sequence executed by a controller to manage the data objects of the legacy application. Based on the analysis of this sequence, the operations being performed over a resource within a controller may be identified. A comprehensive analysis of the controllers that handle the set of requests related with the modernization provides, as result, the list of available operations for each resource.

To illustrate the operation identification process, we consider here a specific request contained in one of the views to be modernized of the running example, concretely the *paperDetails* request of the *paperList* view. Based on this request, the controller (ControlFlow) that handles it is identified by means of the existing relationships between the *View.Request* and *Controller.ControlFlow* elements. In this case, the *paperDetails* request is handled by the *paperAction.details Con-trolFlow* which contains the operation call sequence described in figure 6. In this case, for example, the operation *get* is invoked over the data object *Paper*, pass-ing as parameter the *id* of the paper (request parameter) to fetch and receiving a *Paper* object as result. As shown, in this model excerpt, all the operation calls are related to concrete data operations defined in a concrete data object. In a MIGRARIA MVC model, all the data operations are classified according to its defined mission among the following categories: create, update, remove, get, getAll and getFilter. Such classification provides the modernization engineer with a common vocabulary to identify unequivocally the list of data operations performed by a controller. Such identification is necessary to match properly those operations with the correct HTTP method to use in a REST REQUEST. The table 2 shows such mapping.

Generating REST Requests Mappings. Following a similar approach to the generation of REST URIs, our process generates all the possible combinations of URIs and HTTP methods, producing four different request mappings for each REST URI. Next, that collection is filtered by the set of available operations, so only the REST requests with a proper matching with a legacy controller is maintained, while the rest is removed. Table 2 summarizes the results obtained for the REST URIs selected in our illustrative example.

Delegating REST Requests Processing to Legacy Struts Actions. It comprises the following steps:

1. The definition of the mappings between REST requests and existing con-trollers. This mapping is derived from the previously obtained information regarding the relation request-controller. Therefore, for instance and accord-ing to table 2 , the management of an HTTP GET request for the path */paper/{id}* will be delegated to the *paperAction.details* controller.
2. The conversion of the request input data (parameters or message body) to the corresponding data format expected by the controller. Since legacy controllers are reused in the process, the context that they expect must be built in order to ensure a right execution. Thus, it could be needed, for instance, that a particular object that represents the information sent by an HTML form (expected by the controller) must be populated with the data obtained from the REST request (e.g. in JSON format). The generation of this context needed by the controller requires to know, on the one hand, the parameters of the source request and, on the other hand, the presentation objects related with the source request. All this information may be also

Table 2. REST configuration process result summary

URIs	Operations	Actions	REST Requests
/paper	Create	paperAction.new	POST
	Read	paperListAction	GET
	Update		
	Delete		
/paper/{id}	Create		
	Read	paperAction.details	GET
	Update	paperAction.save	PUT
	Delete	paperAction.delete	DELETE
/paper/{id}/coauthor	Create	coauthorAction.new	POST
	Read	paperAction.details	GET
	Update		
	Delete		
/paper/{id}/coauthor/{id}	Create		
	Read		
	Update	coauthorAction.save	PUT
	Delete	coauthorAction.delete	DELETE

easily gathered from the MIGRARIA MVC model of the legacy application by analyzing the structure of the view that contains the source request. In our running example, the *new* request contained in the *paperCreated* view is related with the input presentation object named *paperForm*. Therefore, the object expected by the controller must be generated to handle that input presentation object. Figure 7 presents, on its left side, the structure of the JSON message for the creation of a new paper, and on its right side, the expected object by the Action *paperCreate* which will be created and initialized conveniently from the JSON message received.

3. The generation of the response in a particular data format (e.g. in JSON format) instead of generating an HTML page as response, REST API clients usually expect responses in a particular data format (JSON, XML) in order to properly manage them at client tier. Therefore, the response generated by the legacy application, as an HTML page, is not useful in this case and it must be replaced by a response generated in the previously accorded data format. In MVC-based Web development frameworks, controllers used to delegate to a different framework component the composition of the final response, i.e. a presentation template management system. Thus, controller main responsibilities are to generate the needed output objects to populate the template selected to compose the response. Based on this approach, we may know the presentation objects that a particular controller will generate (and their structure) just analyzing the MIGRARIA MVC model. As an example, the *paperActions.details ControlFlow* generates the *paper* output presentation object to compose the response by means of the template view *paperDetails*. The structure of the *paper* presentation object, defined within

```
{                                      public class PaperForm extends ActionForm {
  "paperForm" : {
    "id" : ""                              private Long id;
    "title" : "My New Paper"               private String title;
    "abst" : "Abstract..."                 private String abst;
    "fileLocalPath" : "mypaper.pdf"        private String fileLocalPath;
    "author" : "5"                         private long author;
    "track" : "3"                          private long track;
  }
}
```

Fig. 7. JSON input to form bean

```
<h2>Paper <bean:write name="paper" property="id" /> details</h2>       {
<table id="paperDetailsTable">                                          ...
    <tr>                                                                "paper" : {
        <th>Title</th>                                                    "id" : "12"
        <th>Abstract</th>                                                 "title" : "Example Paper"
        <th>Track</th>                                                    "abst" : "Abstract..."
    </tr>                                                                 "track.name" : "Example Track"
    <tr>                                                                }
        <td><bean:write name="paper" property="title" /></td>           ...
        <td><bean:write name="paper" property="abst" /></td>        }
        <td><bean:write name="paper" property="track.name" /></td>
    </tr>
</table>
```

Fig. 8. Output bean to JSON

the *paperDetails* template view, is shown in Figure 8 (left side). Based on this information the final response is generated in the agreed data format, JSON in this example.

Generating REST API Configuration. As previously stated, our approach consists on extending the base Web development framework to incorporate REST capabilities and automatically configuring it to provide an API to the underlying legacy system. The above sections describe in detail both. In this work, the (semi)automatic configuration is generated by means of a model to model transformation described in ATL [5]. That transformation implements the process depicted above and generates an XML file as output. The schema of such file has been defined as an extension of the one used by the configuration file of Struts v1.3, so its deserialization can be implemented as an extension of the actual Struts configuration module. For the shake of brevity, we do not explain the concrete extensions performed.

5   Related Work

Although other model-based approaches have been proposed to define a REST API from a legacy application [6,3,11], to our knowledge none of them is contextualized within a complete model-driven modernization process and nor provides extensions of legacy technology, i.e. Struts v1.X, as the approach presented in this work.

Different approaches and case studies exist about generating a REST API from a legacy application. [6] describes a common process for re-engineering legacy systems to RESTful services which is focused on data-driven systems. The process description is performed at a conceptual level. Parts of their process have been used to derive the process presented in this work. Our approach has extended and adapted that process to a concrete scenario of the modernization of a web application. We also provide a realization of this process in a specific web development technology. Both approaches share a common focus on URIdefinition. [3] describes the case study of an existing legacy application for Internet bidding generalized and replaced by a RESTful API. Instead of reusing existing implementations the auhtors designed a new protocol and implemented it in different languages. The main common points is the focus on data-centric CRUD operations. Finally,[11] develops an API oriented to resources and CRUD operations, by the transformation of an object-oriented model of a legacy application into a resource-oriented one, hereafter generating the URIs is a simple step (M2M transformation on the contrary to our M2T translation).

6   Conclusions and Future Work

This work tackles a part of the modernization process defined within the MI-GRARIA project which faces the evolution of the presentation of a legacy Web system towards a Web 2.0 new RIA client. This process requires not only the generation of the new RIA client but also the creation of a new connection layer for enabling the data interchange between the client and the original system functionalities. In this paper we have presented how this connection layer is generated. In particular, the generation of a REST service layer is described that provides the client with an API to handle the user requests. By means of a running example (excerpt of a fully-functional case study) we have detailed the activities that comprise the process that are mainly divided into two main steps: a) framework-dependant REST API specification and b) application-dependant REST API specification. While the former is performed just once and reused for applications developed in the same MVC Web framework, the latter depends on the particular application being modernized so that, in this case, model-driven techniques come to scene to systematically automate the process providing benefits regarding reusability and effort reduction. Note that the work presented here takes as input the results obtained in the previous steps of MIGRARIA that generates a conceptual representation of the legacy system in terms of models (conformed to a new defined metamodel).

As main lines for future work on MIGRARIA we consider the following: 1) improve the tool support by developing a visualization tool integrated into the MIGRARIA tool chain and that eases the developer's intervention in the process; 2) enrich the process with domain semantic information to improve the resource and relations identification and the REST request generation.

References

1. Barros, A.P., Dumas, M.: The rise of web service ecosystems. IT Professional 8(5), 31–37 (2006)
2. Ceri, S., Fraternali, P., Matera, M., Maurino, A.: Designing multi-role, collaborative web sites with webml: a conference management system case study. In: 1st Workshop on Web-oriented Software Technology (2001)
3. Engelke, C., Fitzgerald, C.: Replacing legacy web services with RESTful services. In: Proceedings of the First International Workshop on RESTful Design - WS-REST 2010, vol. 5, p. 27 (2010)
4. Fielding, R.T.: Architectural Styles and the Design of Network-based Software Architectures. PhD thesis, University of California, Irvine (2000)
5. Jouault, F., Kurtev, I.: Transforming models with ATL. In: Bruel, J.-M. (ed.) MoDELS 2005. LNCS, vol. 3844, pp. 128–138. Springer, Heidelberg (2006)
6. Liu, Y., Wang, Q., Zhuang, M., Zhu, Y.: Reengineering Legacy Systems with RESTful Web Service. In: 2008 32nd Annual IEEE International Computer Software and Applications Conference (2100219007), pp. 785–790 (2008)
7. Mesbah, A., Van Deursen, A.: An architectural style for ajax. In: The Working IEEE/IFIP Conference on Software Architecture, WICSA 2007, p. 9. IEEE (2007)
8. Rodríguez-Echeverría, R., Conejero, J.M., Clemente, P.J., Pavón, V.M., Sánchez-Figueroa, F.: Model Driven Extraction of the Navigational Concern of Legacy Web Applications. In: Grossniklaus, M., Wimmer, M. (eds.) ICWE 2012 Workshops. LNCS, vol. 7703, pp. 56–70. Springer, Heidelberg (2012)
9. Rodríguez-Echeverría, R., Conejero, J.M., Clemente, P.J., Preciado, J.C., Sánchez-Figueroa, F.: Modernization of legacy web applications into rich internet applications. In: Harth, A., Koch, N. (eds.) ICWE 2011. LNCS, vol. 7059, pp. 236–250. Springer, Heidelberg (2012)
10. Rossi, G., Pastor, O., Schwabe, D., Olsina, L.: Web Engineering: Modelling and Implementing Web Applications (Human-Computer Interaction Series) (October 2007)
11. Szymanski, C., Schreier, S.: Case Study: Extracting a Resource Model from an Object-Oriented Legacy Application (2012)
12. Ulrich, W.: Modernization Standards Roadmap, pp. 46–64 (2010)

Towards an Access-Control Metamodel for Web Content Management Systems

Salvador Martínez[1], Joaquin Garcia-Alfaro[3], Frédéric Cuppens[2],
Nora Cuppens-Boulahia[2], and Jordi Cabot[1]

[1] ATLANMOD, & École des Mines de Nantes, INRIA, LINA, Nantes, France
{salvador.martinez_perez,jordi.cabot}@inria.fr
[2] Télécom Bretagne; LUSSI Department Université Européenne de Bretagne, France
forename.surname@telecom-bretagne.eu
[3] Télécom SudParis; RST Department CNRS Samovar UMR 5157, Evry, France
joaquin.garcia_alfaro@telecom-sudparis.eu

Abstract. Out-of-the-box Web Content Management Systems (WCMSs) are the tool of choice for the development of millions of enterprise web sites but also the basis of many web applications that reuse WCMS for important tasks like user registration and authentication. This widespread use highlights the importance of their security, as WCMSs may manage sensitive information whose disclosure could lead to monetary and reputation losses. However, little attention has been brought to the analysis of how developers use the content protection mechanisms provided by WCMSs, in particular, Access-control (AC). Indeed, once configured, knowing if the AC policy provides the required protection is a complex task as the specificities of each WCMS need to be mastered. To tackle this problem, we propose here a metamodel tailored to the representation of WCMS AC policies, easing the analysis and manipulation tasks by abstracting from vendor-specific details.

1 Introduction

Web Content Management Systems (WCMSs) is the technology of choice for the development of millions [1] of Internet sites and increasingly, becoming a framework widely used for the development of Web applications. They provide an integrated environment for the definition of the design, layout, organization and content management of the application and, because of its relative ease of use, they enable users with little technical knowledge to develop fully functional systems.

This widespread use highlights the importance of security requirements, as WCMSs may manage sensitive information whose disclosure could lead to monetary and reputation losses. Due to the nature of the users, the focus has been often put in facilitating the WCMSs configuration. Although this systems are easy to use, a proper configuration is needed to minimize the introduction of vulnerabilities. As a consequence, tools for checking the configuration of WCMSs have been provided and analysed by the scientific communities. However, this tools are focused in low-level security aspects like management of cookies or prevention of SQL injection vulnerabilities [5,8].

---

[1] http://trends.builtwith.com/cms (15 April 2013)

Q.Z. Sheng and J. Kjeldskov (Eds.): ICWE 2013 Workshops, LNCS 8295, pp. 148–155, 2013.

Moreover, despite some approaches for extracting AC information from dynamic web applications source code[3,2], little attention has been brought to the analysis of how developers use the content protections mechanisms provided by WCMSs systems. Particularly, Access-control techniques, integrated in most WCMSs and capable of enforcing confidentiality and integrity of data must be analyzed so that no logical flaws are present in the security policy. Unfortunately knowing if an implemented AC policy on a WCMS provides the required content protection is a complex and error-prone task as the specificities of each WCMS vendor AC implementation must be mastered (e.g. the set of roles and permissions that can be defined vary largely among the different WCMSs).

In order to tackle this problem, we propose to raise the level of abstraction of the AC implementation so that it gets represented acording to a vendor-independent metamodel. This WCMS security metamodel must be able to represent WCMS specific information along with AC concerns. We can regard such a metamodel as an extension of typical AC models[6] specially tailored to the representation of security in WCMSs.

Ideally, this models should be automatically obtained from existing WCMS AC configurations. Therefore, here, along with the description of the metamodel for the representation of WCMS AC policies, we describe the process to automatically extract them from a Drupal[1] WCMS, one of the three most popular WCMSs. Note however, that the extraction from other WCMSs like Wordpress or Joomla will follow the same process. Once these models are available, they can be analysed in a generic way, focusing in the security aspects and disregarding the specificities of concrete vendors. Moreover, Model-driven tools for querying, performing metrics, provide visualizations, etc, become automatically available, easing the analysis tasks.

Combining the vendor-independent representation and the extraction process, migration and reengineering tasks are facilitated. Recovered AC policies represented in our metamodel can be used, after its analysis, correction, etc., as a pivot representation for automatically generating correct configurations or configurations for other WCMSs.

The rest of the paper is organized as follows. In Section 2 previous concepts are introduced whereas is Section 3 we describe our proposed WCMS AC metamodel. In Section 4, the extraction approach over a Drupal system is described. Applications of the extracted model are summarized in Section 5. Finally, Section 6 concludes the paper and discusses some future work.

2   Background and Motivation

WCMSs are Content Management Systems (CMSs) specially tailored to the authoring of content in the Internet. They integrate facilities for the definition of the design, layout, organization and collaborative content management of web sites and can also be used, due to the wide range of features they offer, as a framework basis for the development of web applications. They are, due to its relative ease of use (they allow users with little knowledge of web markup and programming languages to create and manage fully functional web sites) and low cost, the technology of choice for the development of millions of web sites.

In general, they are composed by a back-end, comprising the repository of contents and administrative tools and a front-end that displays this information to web clients.

Access-control[7] is a mechanism aiming at the enforcement of the Confidentiality and Integrity security requirements. Basically, AC defines the Subjects, Objects and Actions of a system and provides the means to describe the assignment of permissions to subjects. This permissions declare which actions the subject is authorized to perform on the objects of the system. It is, due to its conceptual simplicity w.r.t. other techniques, like cryptography, heavily used in multiple domains and it has been integrated, among others, in file systems, databases, network filtering languages and WCMSs.

There exist different models for the specification of Access-control policies, where the current trend is Role-based access control (RBAC)[6], as it simplifies the administration of security policies by granting privileges to roles and not directly to users.

Motivation. As discussed in the introduction, security is a critical concern in WCMSs as they may manage sensitive information. Therefore, security mechanisms have been integrated in most WCMSs where access-control mechanisms play a prominent role. However, WCMSs users often lack depth technical and security knowledge, so that the implemented access-control policies may contain security flaws. For instance, in Drupal, the permission *Delete any content* of type Article could be, by mistake, granted to the default role *Authorized User*. As all user-defined roles inherit by default from this role, this mistake will give them the capacity of deleting the content of the application. Furthermore, the frequent need of migrating from one WCMS to another, also highlights the need for understanding the current security policy so that it can be accurately translated especially, since the security concepts in each WCMS differ. Failing at doing so will often imply putting the new system under risk.

In this scenario, analysing and understanding the security policy enforced by a WCMSs turns up as a critical necessity. Unfortunately, each WCMSs vendor provides its own access-control model and management tools so that this analysis tasks requires in-depth knowledge of the concrete system in hand.

We believe that, in order to tackle this problem, the level of abstraction of the AC policies enforced in WCMSs needs to be raised, so that the information is represented in a vendor-independent manner. We propose thus to represent the AC policies as models corresponding to a WCMS access-control metamodel. In the rest of the paper, we will detail the proposed metamodel and extraction approach.

3   WCMS Access-Control Metamodel

Central to the process of recovering and analysing the access-control information of WCMSs is the definition of a metamodel able to concisely represent the extracted Access-control information in the domain of WCMSs. This metamodel must also be platform-independent, so that we can analyse the access-control information disregarding the especificities of the concrete WCMS security features and implementation.

Figure 1 depicts our proposal for such a metamodel. It is an RBAC-inspired metamodel, thus, containing all RBAC basic concepts along with WCMS specific information. It consists basically of four kind of elements. Contents, i.e., the information

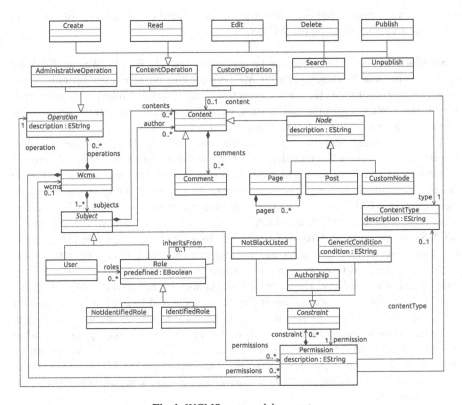

Fig. 1. WCMS metamodel excerpt

hosted by the system, Actions, i.e., operations that can be performed on the WCMS, Permissions, i.e., the right of performing these Actions and Subjects, i.e., the triggers of Actions. In the following, we will detail the metamodel concepts of these categories along with its rationale.

Content. The content of a WCMS is the information it manages. This is represented in our metamodel by the *Content* metaclass. Each WCMS defines its own kinds of content. To be able to represent that eventuality, our *Content* elements have a *ContentType* that identifies its type. This also allows for the representation of fine-grained and coarse grained access-control. Effectively, some WCMS access-control models allow for the definition of different permissions for individual content elements, while others only allow the definition of global permissions on all the contents of a type.

Then, we provide the users of our metamodel with some predefined kinds of content. In one side we have *Node*, representing the principal contents of the WCMSs. We have specialised them in two subclasses: *Page* that represents full content pages (that can contain other pages) and *Post* that represents individual blog posts. We also provide a *CustomNode* metaclass so that additional types of nodes ca be integrated. On the other side, we have *Comments* that represents comments that can be posted in any other content element. We do not represent pages in the back-end of the WCMS used to administer content. That behaviour will be represented by permissions of executing administrative operations on the WCMS.

Operations are the actions than can be performed over the *WCMS*. We can divide all operations that can be done over a WCMS between two types, content operations and administration operations (e.g., operations to manage users and roles). The latter category is more WCMS specific and as such, we will uniquely represent the permissions on that category with the metaclass *Administration Operation*.

W.r.t. the content operations, in our metamodel, all CRUD actions are available: *Create* for the creation *Content* elements; *Edit* for the modification of already created *Content* elements; *Read* for reading/viewing created *Content* elements; *Delete* for the deletion of *Content* elements. The *Search* operation is also available. It is a very common action in WCMSs and, as it can be expensive, it is usually restricted only to certain users (e.g., logged users). Additionally, there are two special actions the *Subjects* of WCMSs can perform. *Publish* and *Unpublish*. In WCMSs it will not be surprising to find that some *Subjects* can create and manage contents using CRUD operatios while not being authorized to make it publicly available without revision-moderation from another authorized *Subject*. These two actions support this behaviour. *Publish* is the action of making available some created *Content* element and *Unpublish* is the action of removing a piece of *Content* from its place of publication without internally deleting it.

Finally, we also consider the possibility of new operations that may appear e.g., when extending the WCMS. In order to be able to represent these possible new operations, we provide the *Custom Operation* metaclass. This way, if the WCMS is extended with the capability of e.g., doing polls, an eventual new operation, vote, could be represented by this metaclass.

Permissions are the right of performing actions on the WCMS. They can define *constraints* that restrict the *Permission* to execute the corresponding action only when certain conditions hold. In our metamodel, we have identified two kinds of *Constraints* that typically appear in WCMSs: *Authorship* and *NotBlacklisting*. The former expresses that the permission is effective only if the *Subject* is the author of the *Content* whereas the latter restricts the applicability of the permission to the condition of not being blacklisted. Other conditions may exist and therefore, we provide the means to represent them by the *GenericCondition* metaclass. It holds in a text field the condition of the *Constraint*. The nature of the contents of this text field is left open to the metamodel users, so that in can hold conditions expressed in natural language or in more formal constraint languages like OCL. Similarly, in [4] the authors added the constraints to permissions represented by triggers to a metamodel tailored to represent Relation Database Management Systems (RDBMS) access-control by adding the source code of the triggers. As in there, the representation and extraction of the meaning of such custom constraints will require a further analysis. We leave such analysis as future work.

Subjects are the elements interacting with the contents of the WCMS by performing actions (note that a *Subject* can be the author of a piece of *Content* and that this may influence the Access-control of the information. Thus, this is represented in our

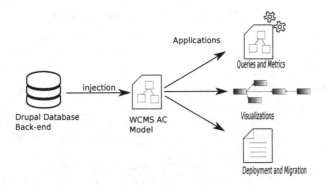

Fig. 2. Drupal AC extraction and analysis approach

metamodel). Following a RBAC approach, in our metamodel we have two kinds of Subjects: *Users* and *Roles* where *Users* get *Roles* assigned. However, unlike RBAC we are more flexible in the permission assignment by allowing both *User* and *Role* to get permissions granted.

Depending of the WCMS in hand, *Roles* are predefined by the application or can be defined by the developer. Both cases can be discerned in our metamodel by using the *predefined* attribute of the *Role* metaclass. Moreover, we have identified two specific roles that often appear in WCMSs. *IdentifiedRole* and *NotIdentifiedRole* are often present in WCMS to discriminate between not logged and logged users. As such, we have decided to add them to the metamodel so that this behaviour can be easily modeled. Finally, role inheritance is also supported.

4 Approach

Although our metamodel could be manually filled by inspecting the AC information using the WCMS administration tools, ideally, it should be filled by an automatic reverse-engineering approach. In the following, we present such an automatic process for a Drupal WCMS although it can be easily adapted to work with other WCMSs. The process in depicted in Figure2.

In Drupal, contents, along with the corresponding access-control information (i.e., users, roles and permissions) are stored in a database back-end. Thus, in order to obtain a model conforming to our WCMSs metamodel with this information, an injection process need to be launched. This process performs SQL queries over the database back-end while creating, as output, the corresponding model elements. Note that, additionally, extra access-control rules could be defined or modified programatically, in the source code of plugins, etc. Techniques as the ones in [3,2] could be used to as a further step to complement our approach.

Note however, that this first step will require a previous step, i.e., the discovery of the data model of the WCMSs as each WCMS defines its own. For doing so, we can rely on the WCMS available documentation or in worse cases, to schema extraction tools. In the case of drupal, the relevant tables are the following ones: USERS, that contains all

Table 1. Mapping from drupal to our metamodel

DRUPAL	WCMS Metamodel
User	User
Default Role	Role
User-defined Role	Role with inheritance relation to the Authenticated Role
Page and Article types	ContentType for Page and Article
Node	If the type is page or article, Page with the proper ContentType. If it is blog post, Post. If there is another type of node, CustomNode
Content actions	ContentOperation.
Comment	Comment pointing to the corresponding Content
Permission	Permission with the corresponding links to the subject, object and operation. For content permissions, link to Content or ContentType (for permissions granted on all content of a given type). For administrative permissions, link to the WCMS instance.

system users; ROLE, containing all roles; USER_ROLES relating users with assigned roles; PERMISSION connecting roles with permissions; COMMENT for the special content of the type comment and NODE for all the other content types.

Drupal AC. Extraction Evaluation: In drupal, there exist three main kinds of content, Pages, Articles and Comments and three roles by default, *Anonimous*, *Authenticated* and *Administrator*. By default, any new user-created role, what is allowed, inherits the permissions from the *Authenticated* one. Thus, to create roles more restricted than the *Authenticated* role, the *Authenticated* role needs to get permissions removed. Using the default modules, permissions can not be granted in concrete content, e.g., concrete pages but on content types. This way, permission to edit content can be granted and all Pages but not on individual pages (apart from the distinctions made wrt to ownership and publish/unpublished).

Our metamodel is capable of representing the AC information of Drupal by using an injector performing the mappings summarized in Table 1.

5 Applications

Once the injection process is finished, we can start analysing and manipulating the obtained model in a vendor-independent way. We summarize here some applications.

Visualization: Visual data is often easier and faster to analyze than textual or tabular data. Using MDE tools we can easily provide a visualization of our WCMS AC model so that the relation between subjects, objects and permissions can be easily grasp.

Queries: The most basic thing we may want to do with a security model is to query it to learn more about specific details of the security policies currently enforced in the WCMS. As an example, we could want to know what elements can be accessed by a given user, taking into account its assigned roles and also the permissions inherited from parent roles. This is very complex to do directly on the WCMS itself since this information is scattered among a number of database tables which are completely vendor-specific. Instead, when using our model we can just use a standard model query language to traverse the information in the extracted model classes. The model query is defined just once and can be executed on security models extracted from any relational vendor.

WCMS Migration: New requirements to be met by the application, discovered security vulnerabilities, technological choices, etc., may impose the migration from one WCMS to another. In this scenario, properly migrating the access-control information (users, roles, permissions) becomes critical. Our metamodel can be used as a pivot representation. Representing the AC information of the old WCMS in a model corresponding with our metamodel will facilitate its understanding and analysis, thus, helping to provide a good translation towards the AC model in the new WCMS.

6 Conclusions and Future Work

We have presented a metamodel specially tailored for the representation of Access-control policies of WCMSs in a vendor-independent manner along with an automatic process for extracting it from Drupal WCMSs. This model facilitates de analysis and manipulation of the implemented policies by isolating them from the specific details of each WCMS system.

As future work we plan to extend our reverse engineering process for the other major WCMSs. Moreover, we intend to continue working on the applications sketched in Section 4 and to investigate the benefits of a translation from our metamodel to XACML specifications to benefit from existing general security tools and research. Finally, we would also like to explore how Digital Rights Management (D.R.M.) concepts could be integrated in our metamodel as DRM appears to start becoming a common requirement for WCMSs under specific scenarios.

References

1. Drupal Open-source CMS (2013), http://drupal.org/
2. Alalfi, M.H., Cordy, J.R., Dean, T.R.: Recovering role-based access control security models from dynamic web applications. In: Brambilla, M., Tokuda, T., Tolksdorf, R. (eds.) ICWE 2012. LNCS, vol. 7387, pp. 121–136. Springer, Heidelberg (2012)
3. Gauthier, F., Letarte, D., Lavoie, T., Merlo, E.: Extraction and comprehension of moodle's access control model: A case study. In: PST, pp. 44–51. IEEE (2011)
4. Martínez, S., Cosentino, V., Cabot, J., Cuppens, F.: Reverse Engineering of Database Security Policies. In: Decker, H., Lhotská, L., Link, S., Basl, J., Tjoa, A.M. (eds.) DEXA 2013, Part II. LNCS, vol. 8056, pp. 442–449. Springer, Heidelberg (2013)
5. Meike, M., Sametinger, J., Wiesauer, A.: Security in open source web content management systems. IEEE Security & Privacy 7(4), 44–51 (2009)
6. Sandhu, R., Ferraiolo, D., Kuhn, R.: The NIST model for role-based access control: towards a unified standard. In: Proceedings of the Fifth ACM Workshop on Role-Based Access Control, RBAC 2000, pp. 47–63. ACM (2000)
7. Sandhu, R.S., Samarati, P.: Access control: principle and practice. IEEE Communications Magazine 32(9), 40–48 (1994)
8. Vaidyanathan, G., Mautone, S.: Security in dynamic web content management systems applications. Communications of the ACM 52(12), 121–125 (2009)

A Model-Based Approach for Supporting Offline Interaction with Web Sites Resilient to Interruptions

Félix Albertos Marco[1], José Gallud[1], Victor M.R. Penichet[1], and Marco Winckler[2]

[1] Escuela Superior de Ingeniería Informática de Albacete
Campus Universitario, 02071 Albacete, Spain
{felix.albertos, jose.gallud, victor.penichet}@uclm.es
[2] Université Paul Sabatier, ICS-IRIT team
118 route de Narbonne, 31062 Toulouse CEDEX, France
winckler@irit.fr

Abstract. Despite the wide availability of Internet connections, situations of interrupted work caused by accidental loss of connectivity or by intentional offline work are very frequent. Concerned by the negative effects of interruptions in users' activities, this work investigates a new approach for the design and development of Web applications resilient to interruptions. In order to help users to recover from interruptions whilst navigating Web sites, this paper proposes a model-based approach that combines explicit representation of end-user navigation, local information storage (i.e. Web browser caching mechanism) and polices for client-side adaptation of Web sites. With this model, we are able to provide users with information about which Web site's contents are available in an offline mode and how they can get easy access to local cache content. Moreover, the model can also be used to set proactive mechanism such as pre-caching Web pages that are likely to be looked at by users. Such a model-based approach is aimed at being used to build new Web sites from scratch but it can also be used as a mapping support to describe offline navigation of existing Web sites. This paper presents the conceptual model, a modeling case study and a tool support that illustrates the feasibility of the approach.

Keywords: work interruption, caching modeling, model-based approach, local storage, navigation model.

1 Introduction

Despite the wide availability of Internet connections, situations of interrupted work caused by accidental loss of connectivity or by intentional offline work are very frequent. Several studies have demonstrated negative effects of interruptions in users activity: resuming the task after an interruption is difficult and can take a long time [20], interrupted tasks are perceived as harder than uninterrupted ones [12], interruptions cause more cognitive workload and they are annoying and frustrating quite often because they disrupt people from completing their work [11, 12]. Interruptions can be particularly dreadful when navigating the Web because they often cause users to be

Q.Z. Sheng and J. Kjeldskov (Eds.): ICWE 2013 Workshops, LNCS 8295, pp. 156–171, 2013.

disconnected from the applications, so that users should restart tasks from the beginning rather than simply resuming them. Interruptions can also be very annoying when navigating Web sites that do not even require a connection because most Web browsers do not allow a natural navigation through content already stored in the local cache.

The study of interruptions is relatively new and there is very little information about how interruptions affect users' activity on the Web. However, some studies in the field of Human-Computer Interaction can provide some clues about how to tackle this kind of problem. Formally speaking an interruption can be defined as a (intentional or unexpected) switch between two tasks; when an interruption occurs, users are forced to do something else (the secondary task) until the primary task can be resumed [19].It has also been shown that interruptions will ultimately affect users' ability to complete tasks but the disruptive effect varies according to the type of interruption (e.g. system alarms and notification, denial of service, loss of connectivity...)[14]. Thus, there is no universal solution for dealing with interruptions. Nonetheless, an interruption is not a fate. Indeed, previous works [6, 14,18] have shown that it is possible to design interactive applications resilient to interruptions. The term resilient is often used to name systems that are able to recover from failures, but in the present context it is used to qualify applications that can prevent from the occurrence of interruptions, help users to resume from interrupted tasks, and/or ensure a minimum level of service for performing a task in spite of the interruption [14].

This work investigates a new approach for the design and development of Web applications resilient to interruptions. We specifically address interruptions caused by the loss of connectivity. Our goal is to ensure as much as possible a continuity of services to users that chose or are forced to work offline until their connection can be restored. For that, we propose a model-based approach that combines explicit representation of end-user navigation, local information storage (i.e. Web browser caching mechanism) and policies for supporting client-side adaptation of the Web site. With this model we are able to provide users with information about which Web site's contents are available in an offline mode and how they can get easy access to local cache content. The approach encompasses mechanisms for pre-caching Web pages that are likely to be looked at by users. It is fully supported by a set of tools that have been specially designed to illustrate its feasibility. These tools explore the full potential for local storage management provided by HTML5; they include an editor for modeling the Web site navigation and a player for managing the navigation in offline mode. The approach and the tools can also be used with existing Web sites. The rest of the paper is organized as follows: section 2 provides an overview of the state of the art of interruptions, Web technologies, solutions for local storage (i.e. cache) and Web navigation models; this section is aimed at providing the necessary technical background to understand our approach, which is presented at the section 3; the following section4 presents a case study and a set of tools that have been specifically conceived to illustrate our approach; then, at section 5 we present our conclusions and we discuss the perspective for such as an approach.

2   Review of the Literature

2.1   Interruptions in Interactive Applications

Most of the research about interruptions has been done by conducting empirical studies with users either on controlled conditions (i.e. usability labs) or on working environment. The current knowledge [19] suggests the following strategies for reducing the disruptive effects of interruptions: i) *human training:* it has been shown that trained users can recover from interrupted work by rehearsing and/or by learning how to use environmental clues; ii) *design guidelines* may help to conceive user interfaces that might reduce the effects of interruptions; for example, where to place visual clues to help users to resume from interrupted tasks; and iii) *tool support* such as GroupBar [6] can help people to save and retrieve applications and window management setups when switching between tasks.

2.2   Caching Models for Web Application

Cache management is one of the most important mechanisms to improve the performance of Web services [5]. Cache and proxies help users to retrieve documents from a nearby server, reducing so the request response time, network bandwidth consumption and server load. A side-border effect of cache is that the information stored locally is available even in case of interrupted connectivity with the remote server.

Disconnection is common in particular in mobile environments. For that Chang et al. [4] propose a standard browsing model that is aimed at supporting user work in disconnected mode by making the cache model transparent to both Web browsers and Web (proxy) servers. This tool contains a list of all HTML entries in the cache with a hyperlink to the corresponding contents stored locally, so it may be used for browsing local pages when disconnected. Other similar tools for supporting cache management are Web-Based Teamwork [21] and BITSY [13]. However, all these tools don't allow tuning the Web application for working in offline mode.

Most browsers do not have mechanisms for managing Web sites in offline mode. Recently, Cannon and Wohlstadter [2] have proposed a framework for offline storage that introduces automated persistence of data objects for JavaScript. Google Gears allow browsers with the ability to persist data for offline use. However, the management of persistent data in the browser is not straightforward due to the need of synchronization, management of throughput, latency and existence of non-standards browser.

The development of Web applications supporting offline work is complex [8]. Existing applications are harder to adapt with offline support, usually implying writing alternate versions of its code [9]. Tatsuboriand Suzumura [17] propose a development method that speeds up the implementation of offline work in a Web application by deploying server functionalities on the local machine. However, replicating all data to the local server is not practical for all applications. They overcome this by enhancing the local server with an adaptive pre-fetcher mechanism that keeps fetching useful data from the remote server. Benson et al. [1] propose the synchronization of a relational database between the browser and the web server and a client-side template library. Although work [1] can reduce the transfer between the client and the server it does not necessarily improve the navigation into local storage.

2.3   Client-side Technologies for Supporting Local Cache Management

Most of the approaches for cache management rely on server-side technologies such as proxy and server-side templates. However, technologies such as Gears-monkey [9], HTML5 [22] and Web storage [23] allow to envisage new strategies for storing locally information from Web applications. Gears-monkey [9] allows the injection of code into third-party Web sites that are visualized in browsers. Client-side scripts developed by users can thus be injected to support offline information management. Nonetheless, this solution is limited to a few platforms and cannot be executed in most of them, such as in mobile phones. Moreover, it requires experienced users to write the required scripts.

Web storage [23] introduces two mechanisms similar to HTTP session cookies for storing name-value pairs on the client side. Despite the fact that Web storage is useful for storing pairs of keys and values, it does not provide in-order retrieval of keys, nor efficient searching over values or storage of duplicate values for a key.

World Wide Web Consortium (W3C) has recently proposed to integrate local storage management into their recommendations [22]. Indeed, the candidate recommendation of HTML5 fully integrates functions for local cache management and offline work, which was completely neglected in previous versions. Using HTML5's application Cache technology allows us to address the requirement of being always connected to use the web. However, one of the main issues about the Application Cache proposed in HTML5 is that there is no underlying model.

2.4   Model-Based Approach for Dealing with Interruptions

There have been several attempts to formalize cognitive models describing the impact of interruptions on human behavior [20]. The unpredictability of interruptions would favor the use of declarative models to describe what should be accomplished by the user system (whatever it happens) rather than describe the steps required (i.e. control flow) to accomplish it. Notwithstanding, there are some situations where the interruption of present task can be predicted - in particular when users decided to get interrupted -, so that the systems should provide an alternative representation of the interrupted tasks.

Only a few works in the literature have addressed the description of interruptions in system specifications [14]. It is interesting to notice that despite the fact that model-based approaches [15] are prominent in the field of Web engineering, as far as we could investigate there is no clear proposal for using Model-Driven Approaches for building Web sites resilient to interruptions.

Most of Web engineering methods such as UWE [10], WebML [3], WSDM [7], OOHDM [16] and SWC [24] are useful to describe the structure of Web applications that are aimed at deploying on a Web server and run online. The occurrence of interruptions during the execution of the Web application is not a matter of concern of currently existing MDA approaches; they assume that interruptions should be treated by the browser alone. As a consequence, there is no construct in such models to describe an alternative navigation for the Web application when the connectivity is lost.

3   A Model-Based Approach for Supporting Offline Interaction

This section presents our model-based approach for supporting the user interaction with Web sites in offline mode. In case of loss of connectivity, user experience with Web sites can be improved this way by providing users with an explicit representation of an alternative offline navigation of contents previously stored in the cache. The offline navigation doesn't provide all functions and contents available online. Nonetheless, our model can control the way users can interact with Web sites' offline contents.

3.1   The Approach in a Nutshell

Our approach combines explicit representation of user navigation and local information storage. For that we define an *offline navigation* model that is able to cope with two basic requirements: i) to determine a set of information resources available in every state of the user navigation; and ii) to be able to describe the transitions linking the states. The focus of the model relies on the hypertext level of Web applications as illustrated by Fig. 1. States in the navigation models correspond to containers for the information units featuring a Web page. Transitions correspond to links that allows users to navigate between pages. Transitions might contain conditions that decide about links activation, thus providing the means to control the navigation between Web pages. Mappings are established so between states and content embedded into Web page and then, between transitions and links.

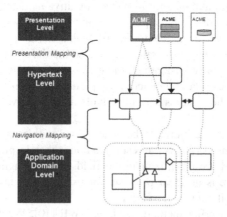

Fig. 1. Modeling levels of Web applications

States in the *offline model* represent *resources* that are stored in the *local cache*; therefore unavailable remote resources should not be described as part of the model. Transitions in the *offline model* are described in the *local storage* as paths to the *local cache*; the information carried out by transitions is used to replace URLs encoded into the original Web pages. Our approach relies on a *local storage* to establish mappings policies for accessing information stored in the local cache. Fig. 2 provides a view at glance on how the key components of our approach, i.e. *resources, offline mode, local storage* and *cache*, are distributed between the client and the server. As we will see, *resources* (i.e. current Web site content) are delivered to the client in conjunction with an *offline model*. However, the *offline model* is only activated when the user is offline.

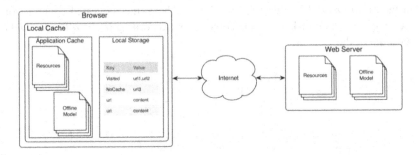

Fig. 2. Overview of the architecture of our approach describing local cache storage places

Hereafter we describe the basic concepts used for building *offline models*. It is noteworthy that the *offline model* can be used even over Web sites that were not built according to a model-based approach.

3.2   Basic Concepts of the Offline Model

The basic concepts of the *offline model* are derived from the SWC notation [24], which is dedicated to the modeling of Web sites navigation. The *offline model* is represented as a graph - called project - that contains the following elements:

- **Project** corresponds to a set of *contents, nodes* and *connections* of the Web site; The information needed to define a *project* includes the identification of the Web site, the location of the Web site and the status (online/offline) that is used to check the URL base for determining if the *offline model* must be activated or not.
- **Content** refers to the many kinds of elements, such as textual, visual and audio information, that are available in a Web site. Contents are usually organized by information units. Some contents are embedded into the HTML code while others are encoded into external files (e.g.CSS, images, videos, etc.) or are only accessible after connecting to a database. We assume that Web pages can be static, with fixed content, or dynamic, when generated on the fly.
- **Node** is the basic element in the model; a node usually refers to a Web page. Nodes correspond to states that constitute the graph representing the navigation

in the Web site. Each node is associated with a list of *contents* that are available when the users access a particular Web page. When dealing with dynamic pages, nodes in the *offline model* correspond to a snapshot of the content delivered by the site in a given moment of time and, as long as the user is disconnected, that node is treated as a static Web page. It is noteworthy that, within a web project, navigation may go beyond the boundaries of the site. In such cases, nodes are used to represent external states that appear in the navigation model; however, such nodes have no content associated with them.

- **Mapping between nodes and contents:** nodes should be considered containers of a set of contents, either static or dynamic. A mapping function describes which the content that a state must contain is. The mapping between contents and nodes in the *offline model* is illustrated by Fig. 3. There, the requested content from a web page, *Cx*, is translated to the content *Cx'*, according to the *offline model* and the *state* of the web site.

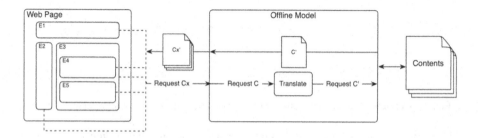

Fig. 3. Mapping between contents and web pages

- **States** are used to describe three different properties (*static*, *navigational* and *data*) that characterize the state of a node:
  o *Static:* it describes how the node is defined in the model. Possible values are: *internal, external, initial, precacheable, nocacheable* and *normal. Internal* means the node that represents an element of the web site, whilst *external* represent a node for a connecting third part web site. The case *normal* refers to a node that is part of the navigation model. An *initial* node indicates the state for starting the navigation; only one *initial state* is allowed in *offline mode*. Nodes marked as *Precacheable* are always cached when the web site is visited. Conversely, *nocacheable* nodes will never be stored.
  o The property *navigational state* is used to set the current dynamics of Web site navigation; so they will change according to the user navigation. Possible values for nodes are: *nonvisited* and *visited*.
  o The property *data* state defines what the cache is able to store with respect to the user navigation and the expected behavior set for the model. As a result, a node can be *cached* or no *cached*. When a node is *cached*, it will be available when the site is interrupted. When a node is *nocached*, it will not be available when the site is interrupted.

- **Connections**: this refers to the links that allow the navigation between nodes. Connections are set by identifying a source and a target node. Moreover, the navigation between nodes is defined by the attribute type that might contain one of the following values: *normal* (is an usual link), *online* (works when the site is online), *offline* (works when the site is offline and points to content that is available on the local cache, and which is used to avoid dangling links in the offline mode) and *alternative* (is a link created in the model to provide alternative navigation when the site is in offline mode).
- **Storage places**: it refers to possible locations for the contents (e.g. *web*, *proxy*, *local cache*). The approach can combine access to distant resources only available on the Web server and contents available on local or distant caches. The storage contains: web pages, with all the associated resources, and the *offline model* that recreate the navigation through content for offline operations. Within this local cache, two techniques are used: application cache and local storage, as illustrated by Fig. 2. Application cache is used to store elements of the offline model and Web contents locally. The local storage stores annotated web pages and information about the offline model, such us visited nodes and related properties.

3.3   Runtime Concepts of the Model

If an interruption occurs, the information encoded in the *offline model* can be used to perform a client-side adaptation of the Web site. Then, when the connection is restored, users should be able to resume the navigation online and eventually synchronize the actions performed offline with the Web server. Thus, users should be informed constantly about the status of the connection and what is actually available on the local cache and how such contents can be navigated.

Mechanisms for client-side adaptation of Web pages
The local cache is dynamic and the contents stored locally may evolve overtime. Moreover, certain nodes may lack the access to remote resources that thus cannot be shown during offline navigation. In order to make a fair description of what is available in the local cache and what is not, we propose small modifications in the DOM structure of locally stored Web pages. The policies for modifying the DOM are derived from the information provided by the offline model. Such transformations should include: i) replacing link's labels to indicate if the target resource is local or external; ii) removing links and resources from pages that are not available in offline mode; iii) providing alternative contents to links; iv) add a navigation map to inform users what resources are available while offline.

Fig. 4 and Fig. 5 illustrate some of these DOM modifications on Web pages to cope with offline navigation. Fig. 4 illustrates how links have been replaced in the source page (Fig. 4.a) to prevent users from navigating to a page that contains a video streaming only available online (Fig. 4.b). Instead of the video, users working offline will see a static picture and a descriptive text, but the rest of the content of that page remains intact (see Fig. 4.c).

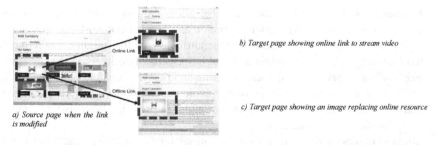

b) *Target page showing online link to stream video*

c) *Target page showing an image replacing online resource*

a) *Source page when the link is modified*

Fig. 4. Example of link transformation and content replacement to cope with offline navigation

Fig. 5 shows another example of adaptation where DOM elements have been disabled to prevent users to try to access external resources such as databases or interactive maps (Fig. 5.a). Removing DOM elements is a possible, yet drastic, solution that could be alleviated by adding alternative content; for example, when offline users cannot search products in a database they could be diverted to a simple page featuring a PDF catalogue. Using similar client-side adaptation techniques, DOM elements can be inserted in Web pages to users informed about the nodes and resources available in *offline mode*. Fig. 5.b shows a new element depicting the graph of the corresponding *offline model* for navigating the Web site.

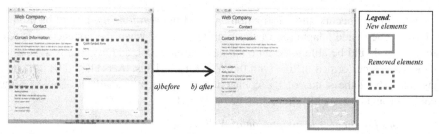

a)*before*   b) *after*

Fig. 5. Example of before-after DOM modifications to cope with offline navigation

Client-side adaptations and user interactions in offline mode
All client-side adaptations proposed in our approach are driven by the *offline model*. Fig. 6 provides a short excerpt of the algorithm that performs the adaptations by removing contents and changing link destination according to the underlying *offline model*. In this example, a Web page is parsed; if the *data-offline status* attribute value is "disabled" in the *offline* model then the element is removed from the Web page. If the element is a hyperlink, the *data-offline URL* value is checked to determine if the destination should be replaced, which is done by changing the *href* attribute.

```
for (every Element in WebPage) do {
    // Content removal
    if (Element.attributes.data-offlineStatus=="disabled"){
    Element.remove();
    } else {
        // Change Link Destination
if ((Element.represents(hyperlink)) && (Element.attributes.data-offlineURL.hasValue())){
    Element.attributes.href = Element.attributes.data-offlineURL.getValue();
        }
    ...
}
```

Fig. 6. Excerpt of the algorithm for adapting Web pages to cope with offline navigation

The client-side adaptation algorithm also takes into account the present user navigation over the Web. Table 1 shows the availability of connections and the corresponding status; for example, *normal* connections are available in the *online* as well as in the *offline* mode; *online* and *offline* connections are only available in the eponym modes; finally, *alternative* connections are added as an independent mechanism to navigate in the model when the site is *offline*.

Table 1. Connection availability according to the status of the site

Mode\ Connection types	Normal	Online	Offline	Alternative
Online	X	X	-	
Offline	X	-	X	X

Table 2 shows other properties that determine the accessibility of nodes in the *offline model*. The access to nodes also depends on the existence of *connections* between nodes and the *type of the target node*. The property *cache* can be assigned to a node that is likely to be visited during a Web site navigation; by setting this property in a node it is possible to request the storage (i.e. *precache*) of the corresponding contents in the local cache; the *offline connection* can reach that node regardless of if the user has visited the web page or not. Fig. 7.a illustrates the decision process for determining node accessibility; notice that initial states are always accessible.

Table 2. Node properties determining whether or not the content is accessible when offline

Target node properties/Connections types	Normal	Online	Offline	Alternative
External	Yes	No	Yes	Yes
Initial	Yes	Yes	Yes	Yes
Cached	Yes	No	Yes	Yes
No cached	No	No	No	No

Other properties determining the accessibility of nodes depend on whether or not the user has actually visited the Web page. This aspect is defined by the property *data* associated with each node. The user navigation over the Web site changes dynamically the value of the property *data* of nodes. Table 3 shows the effect on local storage according to the type of the node and the user navigation on the Web site. The decision process for determining if content is accessible or not is illustrated by Fig. 7.b.

Table 3. Effects on local storage of user navigation

Node data status/Node type	Normal	Initial	Precacheble	Nocacheable
Novisited	Nocached	Cached	Cached	Nocached
Visited	Cached	Cached	Cached	Nocached

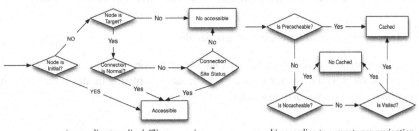

a) according to online/offline scenarios   b) according to current user navigation

Fig. 7. Decision process for determining node accessibility

Synchronization mechanisms

Our approach defines mechanisms for synchronizing contents to use offline, allowing the use of the web until the connection is back. Synchronization is done in two levels within the local cache: the application cache manager and the offline model, as illustrated by Fig. 8. We assume that the application cache manager is implemented in HTML5. It is in charge of keeping up to date web content associated with the application cache storage. The application cache version included in the *offline model* allows updating the content if it is out of date. When an online page is loaded or the site status changes to online, the offline model is responsible of checking if all the content associated with the offline model is stored locally.

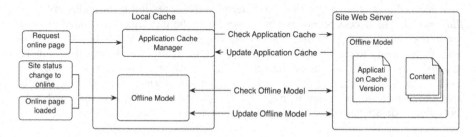

Fig. 8. Illustration on how synchronization mechanisms can be integrated into the approach

4   Tool Support and Case Study

Hereafter we present the tools that we have developed to demonstrate the feasibility of our approach. The *Offline Model Editor* is dedicated to designers and it is aimed at supporting the design of the model for existing Web sites; this tool runs in a browser using jQuery and jQuery UI 1.8. It is divided in two applications: the *Site Editor* and the *Node Editor*. The *Site Editor* is used to define the Web site offline behavior, set web pages properties and connections. The *Node Editor* is used to annotate individual web pages in order to define the rules for content transformation; it allows designers to include the available transformation only by means of making a click over the desired elements. These tools appear on the Web client as a graphical element that provides users with information about the pages available, the corresponding links and the state of the connection. Fig. 9 provides the overall architecture of the tools.

4.1   Demonstration of Tools by a Case Study

Hereafter we present a set of scenarios that illustrate the usage of the tools. We assume two users: a web designer who aims to create the offline model for a Web site; and an end user who uses offline model.

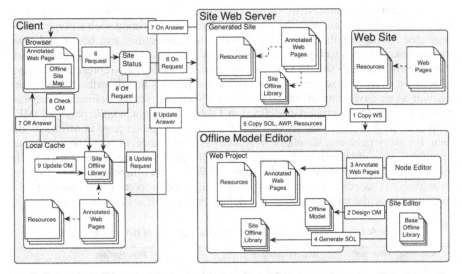

Fig. 9. Overall architecture of the tools developed to support the approach and the interaction with the Client browser and third-party web site

4.2 Creating the Offline Model

Let us assume a very simple Web site. After designing the entire site, as depicted in the Fig. 10.a, the designers are asked to create an *offline model* for allowing users to access in disconnected mode. The first restriction is to remove elements that would crash if users use an offline mode, such as the map from the "CONTACT" web page and the Google's search bar. The second issue is to replace the entire "PROJECT I" web pageby another one, featuring only textual information and an image instead of the original video. Finally, the page "NEWS" should not be accessible when offline. Instead, the "NEWS" page should refer to the page "ABOUT" when offline.

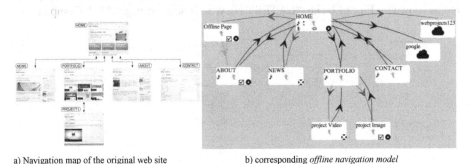

a) Navigation map of the original web site   b) corresponding *offline navigation model*

Fig. 10. Site map and *offline model* for the case study

Using the tool *Site Editor,* we create a navigation model as illustrated in Fig. 10.b by defining nodes and connections. Part of the process of creating such a graph can be automated by parsing the pages of the Web site: connections can be created from existing links between web pages; external pages can also be represented automatically by inferring the web site domain. At this point, the model only represents the original web site. The next step consists in adding the policies that describe the Web site behavior when navigating offline to the model. Such policies are defined by decorating the model with the properties defined in Table 4. For example, the page "HOME" receives an icon *initial* to inform that it is the initial navigation page in offline mode. Then, for every page that should be available in offline mode, the designers associate a property *cacheable* such as the page "ABOUT" and the page "project image". In order to prevent the navigation to the page "NEWS" in an offline mode, the property *nocacheable* is associated with it. Only when all static properties have been set, the designer can use the tool *Node Editor* to define internal policies for the content.

Table 4. Icons representing policies on node elements of the *offline* model

Element in the node	Representation	Description
Name	Text value	The name of the node
Accessible	*j*	The node could be visited from the actual one
Initial	:	The node has been set as initial
Current	🏃	The user is visiting this node
Visited	◉	The node has been visited
Precacheable	☑	The node has been set as "precacheable"
Cached	◐	The node has been locally cached
No Cacheable	✕	The node has been set as "nocacheable"
External	▲	The node is external to the web site

The tool *Node Editor* allows to visualize the Web page and to modify DOM elements as shown by Fig. 11. This is a visual tool, so it is possible to select the DOM elements and click on them and select "remove element". It is worthy of notice that all nested elements to the DOM will be removed. Removed elements are marked in yellow in the *Node Editor*, as depicted Fig. 11.a. To change a link destination, the designer has to select the link and then select a different node in the model as a new destination. Connections that have been modified in the *offline model* are marked in red as shown by Fig. 11.b (i.e. "LATEST NEWS" link at the page "Web Company").

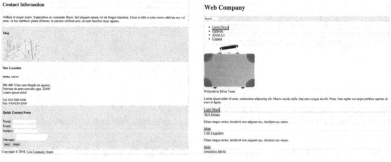

a) Elements removal from page "CONTACT"   b) Changing links destination

Fig. 11. Edition of DOM elements of a Web page with the tool *Node Editor*

In order to create an alternative connection between the page "OFFLINE PAGE" and the page "ABOUT", the designer just needs to draw a new connection between these pages. As shown in Fig. 10.b, the *offline model* represents normal connections (which means connections that match to existing hyperlinks on the Web site) in black; online connections (those that are available online only) in green; offline connections are represented in red and alternative connections are depicted in orange.

Once finished, the *offline model* is published with the original Web site. The *offline model* is downloaded so that the users connect to the Web site. The activation of the *offline model* only occurs when the users got interrupted and the connection is lost. In such case the parser starts transforming the local Web pages according to the predefined constraints. Then, the graph featuring the *offline model* is shown as in Fig. 12. To navigate, users can click on the modified links embedded into pages or by selecting the nodes directly on the graph.

Fig. 12. Visualization of the Web site and tool in offline mode (with zoom at right-side)

5   Discussion and Future Work

In this paper we have discussed some problems caused by interruptions whilst working with the Web application and, in particular, the interruptions caused by loss of connectivity. For that we have proposed a model-based approach that is delivered with a tool support for helping to build Web sites resilient to interruptions. The overall approach is quite simple: we combine a navigation model to exploit resources that are already stored in the local cache. The navigation model is tuned to work in a specific way when users are offline. It is worthy of notice that the so-called *offline navigation model* is a piece of design that is affected by the designers' intentions when designing the offline navigation. Moreover, the model is subject to the actual user interaction with the Web site. The current implementation exploits resources from HTML5, in particular the API Web storage and the Offline Web Applications.

The model and the tools presented here are a proof of concept. Despite the evident limitations, it allows the discussion about the problems related to the loss of connectivity and poses fundamental questions about whether or not we can provide solutions to make Web sites more resilient to interruptions. The use of the *offline model* as presented in this paper has several implications:

i) First of all, the *offline model* embeds the main concepts for describing the dynamic aspects of local cache and Web site navigation. These aspects are duly represented by our model, which extends the SWC navigation model. As we have seen, the model takes into account not only the structural aspects of the Web site navigation, but all the actual behavior over the Web site and the constraints imposed by the designer to create a specific user experience when the users are navigating the Web site offline.

ii) Secondly, the *offline model* can be used as a domain specific language that is used as input for the tools we have developed to access the local cache and Web storage. Indeed, it is the *offline model* that drives our tools to perform the client-side adaptations required to enable users to navigate local cache. It is by the means of such an *offline model* that designers can express their constraints on the navigation;

iii) Thirdly, the graph representation of the *offline model* allows the reconstruction of a navigation site map (as shown by Fig. 12) that explicitly shows the users the available resources. Such a visual aid fulfills two main goals: first of all it explicitly shows to users that the navigation proposed corresponds to an offline mode of interaction (as the online version does not show that graph); then, it visually explains users the sub-set of information available on the local cache.

The approach can be used to build new Web sites from scratch, but it also can be used as a mapping support for describing offline navigation of existing Web sites. For the purposes of this work, we have built our *offline model* as an extension of the SWC navigation model. We think that other model-based approach could be extended to support offline navigation; however, this hypothesis remains to be investigated.

Indeed, despite the fact that we consider the *offline model* a powerful tool for building Web sites resilient to interruptions, this paper only provides the foundations and much more remain to be done. Currently, it only works with static Web pages but the overall model can be extended to work with dynamic pages. We only have provided a partial solution for dynamic content and just presented the issue of synchronization with the Web site when the connection is restored. We assume that dynamic content can be "frozen" in the local cache and manipulated as static Web pages when the user is offline. Nevertheless, further investigation is required to test our model and tools with more complex scenarios. Moreover, despite the fact that the tools presented are operational this work requires empirical studies with end-users. All these aspects will be subject of our future work.

References

1. Benson, E., Marcus, A., Karger, D., Madden, S.: Sync kit: a persistent client-side database caching toolkit for data intensive websites. In: WWW 2010, pp. 121–130. ACM (2010)
2. Cannon, B., Wohlstadter, E.: Automated object persistence for JavaScript. In: WWW 2010, pp. 191–200. ACM (2010)
3. Ceri, S., Brambilla, M., Fraternali, P.: The History of WebML Lessons Learned from 10 Years of Model-Driven Development of Web Applications. In: Borgida, A.T., Chaudhri, V.K., Giorgini, P., Yu, E.S. (eds.) Conceptual Modeling: Foundations and Applications. LNCS, vol. 5600, pp. 273–292. Springer, Heidelberg (2009)
4. Chang, H., Tait, C., Cohen, N., Shapiro, M., Mastrianni, S., Floyd, R., Housel, B., Lindquist, D.: Web browsing in a wireless environment: disconnected and asynchronous operation in ARTour Web Express. In: ACM/IEEE MobiCom 1997, pp. 260–269. ACM (1997)

5. Che, H., Tung, Y., Wang, Z.: Hierarchical Web Caching Systems: Modeling, Design and Experimental Results. IEEE Journal on Selected Areas in Communications 20(7) (2002)
6. Czerwinski, M., Horvitz, E., Wilhite, S.: A diary study of task switching and interruptions. In: CHI 2004, pp. 175–182. ACM (2004)
7. De Troyer, O., Casteleyn, S., Plessers, P.: WSDM: Web Semantics Design Method. In: Web Engineering, pp. 303–351 (2008)
8. Gutwin, C., Graham, N., Wolfe, C., Wong, N., de Alwis, B.: Gone but not forgotten: designing for disconnection in synchronous groupware. In: CSCW 2010, pp. 179–188. ACM (2010)
9. Kao, Y.-W., Lin, C., Yang, K., Yuan, S.-M.: A Web-based, Offline-able, and Personalized Runtime Environment for executing applications on mobile devices. Comput. Stand. Interfaces 34(1), 212–224 (2012)
10. Koch, N., Knapp, A., Zhang, G., Baumeister, H.: Uml-Based Web Engineering - An Approach Based on Standards. In: Web Engineering, pp. 157–191 (2008)
11. McFarlane, D.C.: Coordinating the interruption of people in human-computer interaction. In: INTERACT 1999, pp. 295–303. IOS Press, Amsterdam (1999)
12. Mark, G., Gudith, D., Klocke, U.: The cost of interrupted work: more speed and stress. In: SIGCHI 2008, pp. 107–110. ACM (2008)
13. Mehta, N., Swart, G., Divilly, C., Motivala, A.: Mobile AJAX Applications: Going Far Without the Bars. In: 2nd IEEE Workshop on Hot Topics in Web Systems and Technologies (2008)
14. Palanque, P., Winckler, M., Ladry, J.-F., terBeek, M., Faconti, G., Massink, M.: A Formal Approach Supporting the Comparative Predictive Assessment of the Interruption-Tolerance of Interactive Systems. In: ACM EICS 2009, pp. 211–220. ACM Press (2009)
15. Rossi, G., Pastor, O., Schwabe, D., Olsina, L. (eds.): Web Engineering: Modelling and Implementing Web Applications. Human-Computer Interaction Series. Springer (2008)
16. Rossi, G., Schwabe, D.: Modeling and Implementing Web Applications with Oohdm. In: Web Engineering, pp. 109–155 (2008)
17. Tatsubori, M., Suzumura, T.: HTML templates that fly: a template engine approach to automated offloading from server to client. In: WWW 2009, pp. 951–960. ACM (2009)
18. ter Beek, M.H., Faconti, G.P., Massink, M., Palanque, P.A., Winckler, M.: Resilience of Interaction Techniques to Interrupts: A Formal Model-Based Approach. In: Gross, T., Gulliksen, J., Kotzé, P., Oestreicher, L., Palanque, P., Prates, R.O., Winckler, M. (eds.) INTERACT 2009. LNCS, vol. 5726, pp. 494–509. Springer, Heidelberg (2009)
19. Trafton, J.G., Monk, C.A.: Task Interruptions. Reviews of Human Factors and Ergonomics 3, 111–126 (2007)
20. Trafton, J.G., Altmann, E.M., Brock, D.P., Mintz, F.E.: Preparing to resume an interrupted task: Effects of prospective goal encoding and retrospective rehearsal. International Journal of Human-Computer Studies 58(5), 583–603 (2003)
21. Yang, Y.: Supporting Online Web-Based Teamwork in Offline Mobile Mode Too. In: WISE 2000, vol. 1. IEEE Computer Society, Washington, DC (2000)
22. W3C. A vocabulary and associated APIs for HTML and XHTML. W3C Candidate Recommendation (December 17, 2012), http://www.w3.org/TR/2012/CR-html5-20121217
23. W3C. Web Storage (February 13, 2013), http://dev.w3.org/html5/webstorage/
24. Winckler, M., Palanque, P.: StateWebCharts: A Formal Description Technique Dedicated to Navigation Modelling of Web Applications. In: Jorge, J.A., Jardim Nunes, N., Falcão e Cunha, J. (eds.) DSV-IS 2003. LNCS, vol. 2844, pp. 61–76. Springer, Heidelberg (2003)

A Method for Integrating Process Description and User Interface Use during Design of RIA Applications

Hernán Casalánguida and Juan Eduardo Durán

Facultad de Matemática, Astronomía y Física, Universidad Nacional de Córdoba, Medina Allende s/n, Córdoba, Argentina
hcasalan@hal.famaf.unc.edu.ar, duran@mate.uncor.edu

Abstract. During design of rich internet applications (RIA) it is important to integrate in one model the description of both the interactions of the user with the system, and the processes (considering data flow, control flow, and possibly, detailed autonomous task descriptions), for having a very rich set of relations between modeling elements that can be inspected. Such integrated models consider both UI aspects, and user interaction aspects; therefore, their construction needs the participation of both graphic designers and analysts, leading possibly to communication problems, less productivity, and perhaps to introduce errors. To treat these problems, we propose a method consisting of: process requirements description, traces definition from requirement elements into either UI elements (UIE)/events on UIEs (provided by UI designers), or to autonomous actions design (provided by analysts); in addition, we present a transformation from the deliverables of this process onto an integrated model.

1 Introduction

There exist in the literature some RIA methods considering notations that treat in the same diagram both aspects of the UI, and aspects related with the interaction: WebML [1,2], notations based on state machine concepts (see OOH4RIA [3], ADVs [4]), and notations considering event condition action (ECA) rules (see RUX [5], OOWS 2.0 [6], MARIA [7]). In [8] it is said that "A general limit of ECA rules is that they do not always reflect the procedural, imperative way of thinking familiar to many people from imperative or object-oriented programming". State Machines are much better to understand control flow, but they are not much adequate for describing ECA rules (see [9], page 16, for an explanation). Therefore, a modeling notation allowing to express data and control flow, ECA rules, and possibly to describe UI elements will be useful for expressiveness and understandability.

In [6] (page 78) it is stated that: "to treat in the same model together visual aspects of the UI (e.g. its organization in terms of UIEs) with aspects related with the interaction (e.g. the events that initiate the communication with the system, or the information to introduce) has as a direct consequence more complex models that need to be defined by both analysts and graphic designers". To build such kind of models without considering an appropriate development process may lead to the following

Q.Z. Sheng and J. Kjeldskov (Eds.): ICWE 2013 Workshops, LNCS 8295, pp. 172–186, 2013.
© Springer International Publishing Switzerland 2013

problems: inconsistency introduction and/or the construction of such models by analysts and UI designers working at the same time. These problems are important, because complex models tend to be more difficult to understand, and problems of the interaction between analysts and UI designers may impact productivity and the quality of the product.

Integrated modeling notations contemplating both user interaction in the UI and process description also consider both UI aspects and user interaction aspects, with the addition of process aspects (i.e. data flow, control flow, and, possibly, detailed autonomous action description - i.e. tasks executed by the system without user participation); therefore, their construction has the same kind of problems. Hence, it is necessary to simplify in some ways such kind of modeling notations, and to have an appropriate development process to construct models respecting them to avoid problems concerning the interaction of both analysts and UI designers.

To construct models comprising user interaction in the UI and process description, we propose the following development process to treat the described problems: First, to use a requirements model for describing the process that must be respected by both graphic designers and analysts. Next, the data mentioned in the requirements model is designed in detail and must be known by graphic designers and analysts, because such data impact both the UI and autonomous actions considered by analysts. Following, a design notation is used by graphic designers to describe UIEs and event patterns on them, and simultaneously analysts use a design notation for the definition of autonomous actions. Finally, from these three notations a model integrating the processing of events over the UI with processes is automatically generated.

Our proposal is possible if we start from our UML activity diagram (AD) requirements notation for RIAs in [10]: such ADs have modeling elements that need to be described in design by UI designers (concerning output, input request, and input); there are also other modeling elements in them that need to be described in design by analysts (i.e. autonomous actions); and there are also modeling elements that refer to the data managed by the application (i.e. pins and object nodes) that need to be described in detail in design.

The minimum information necessary to generate a model integrating UI use and process description is: an AD using our notation in [10] for describing process requirements, and trace relationships of two kinds: a) traces between these AD's actions and design elements that can be either UIEs, or event patterns, or activities for autonomous actions; b) traces between AD's object nodes and design elements for representing data in detail. In this paper we assume that we have available this information, and we are not worried about how to obtain these trace relationships.

In this work, we present a development process that starts with RIA requirements modeling using the UML profile in [10] (see Sec.2). Next, actions related to input and output in such ADs are associated with either UIEs or events (to provide more details about them). UIEs respect a UML profile called *RIAAD* presented in Sec. 3; RIAAD consists of two notations: one extending class diagrams to represent UIE , and another extending UML ADs for describing autonomous actions. Finally, these ADs and their trace relationships are mapped onto *user interface use and process description models (UIUPDM)*; these transformations are implemented in ATL, and presented in Sec. 5.

2   Activity Diagrams for Rich Internet Application Requirements

In [10] an action inside an AD for a use case (UC) can be of one the following stereotypes: «search» (it represents database queries), «job» (it represents a call behavior action, whose activity performs an autonomous action), «input» (it represents the provision of an input by an human actor), «output request» (it represents the request by the system for the provision by a human actor of some inputs), «output content» (it represent the system displaying content), «input and suggest» (it represents the provision of an input by a user, and the use of automatic suggestions for input that are selectable), and «output message» (it represents the system showing a message to the user – e.g. a message of error, success, status, a help, or warning). In addition, we consider the stereotype: «output media» (the system shows content by playing a media file – e.g., image, video, audio, animation, and presentation – and also shows the controls of the player for user interaction). Icons:

$\mathcal{P}$ («search»), $\text{\ding{42}}$ («job»), $\textcircled{\Xi}$ («input»), $\boxed{?}$ («output request»), and $\boxed{\text{NEWS}}$ («output message»).

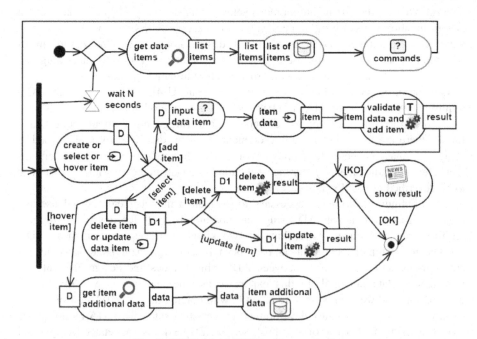

Fig. 1. UC Enriched CRUD of items of a list

Fig. 1 shows an AD for an *enriched CRUD of items of a list* UC – http://trirand.com/blog/jqgrid/jqgrid.html is an example of such a kind of application. Some of the features of this UC are: it permits collaborative edition of the list, because the list is redisplayed every *N* seconds (N ≤ 5) showing the changes in the list made by other people; item registers can be updated by editing their fields; by hovering an item of the list you can read additional data about it.

3   RIA Application Abstract Design (RIAAD)

In this section we present the RIAAD notation, consisting of design elements that will be used when defining trace relationships from requirement's actions. Our desire is that RIAAD for UIE description have a rich set of UIEs to allow design decision taking; this part of RIAAD, to our knowledge, fills some gaps we have found in existing abstract design notations for RIA: the representation of *editable* UIEs, being them either elementary or content structures; the abstraction of special UI patterns for navigation in RIA like breadcrumb, alphanumeric filter links, and navigation bar, and the appropriate representation of suggest field; the representation of UIEs for the edition of multimedia objects (audio, video, etc.), and of documents -i.e. presentations, spreadsheets – (e.g. youTube allows editing videos https://www.youtube.com/editor, and Google Drive allows editing documents). RIAAD part for UIE modeling is based on UWE [11], UWE-R [12], and MARIA [7] metamodels, with some additions necessary to fill the mentioned holes.

The UIEs of RIAAD are presented in Figs. 2 and 3. A *UiStructure* respects some structuring rule, and are classified into: ContentStructure, AccessStrucure, UiInputStructure, and UiOutputStructure. *ContentStructure* (CS) represents an UIE with a structure used for content presentation. A CS can be *editable* (i.e. allowing the edition of some of its contents) or not (it is only used to present content to the user). CSs are classified into: List, Table, Tree, and Record.

AccessStructure represents an UIE used for accessing other UIEs (i.e. navigation) or performing an action. *LinksBased* represents a link grouping to access either other UIEs or performing an action; it is classified into: Menu, Breadcumb, and ANFilterLinks. *Breadcumb* represents a UIE containing a list of steps; each step has a link, a name, and a level number. Breadcumbs are used to represent navigation paths, whose nodes can be visited by selecting steps. *ANFilterLinks*: (alphanumeric filter links) represents a list of items ordered alphanumerically; each item has a link, and an alphanumeric character as name. ANFilterLinks are used to organize a set of named objects S in the following way: by selecting an item i, we access to the objects whose identifier starts with the name of i. *NotLinksBased* represents access to UiStructures and/or functionality not based exclusively on links; for some NotLinksBased structures the user may fill input structures – e.g. forms – for gathering of parameters for UiStructure generation or functionality execution. We considered three kinds of NotLinksBased elements: NavigationBar, NavList and NavAltBlocks.

NavigationBar represents a set of Anchors and Forms (at least one form must be present). Usually a navigationBar behaves in the following way: after a Press event (i.e. anchor selection or form submission) a UiStructure is shown, or a command is executed. For instance, see the last line of site http://www.vodahost.com/partner/.

NavList (navigation list) represents an UIE containing a set of items; each item contains: optionally an anchor corresponding with content displayed for this item, optionally a navigationBar for parameters providing and/or functionality access, and one or more BasicUIElements for describing an item. Typical examples of NavList are indexes (only the navigationBar is excluded), inbox in Gmail (NavigationBar containing an UiInputStructure with only checkboxes, and anchors to mails), Koha library management system (http://manual.koha-community.org/3.6/en/opac.html) bibliographic search the catalog functionality (a NavigationBar consisting of a check box, and of forms and anchors for accessing commands; and an anchor to a bibliographic record). *NavAltBlocks* represents an object containing a collection of Blocks in which only one block at a time is visible; each block contains one or more UiStructures, has a name, and an order.

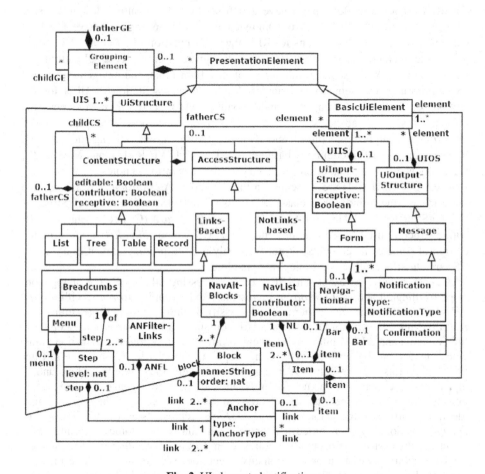

Fig. 2. UI element classification

UIInputStructure represents a UIE used for user input; a special kind of UiInputStructure is a form; a UiInputStructure contains BasicUiElement instances with typeOfEdition="input". *UIOutputStructure* represents a UIE used for presenting information to the user, and contains BasicUiElements having typeOfEdition="no-editable". A kind of UiOutputStructure element is *Message*, and is classified into: *Notification* (e.g. of some event) and *Confirmation* (i.e. a confirmation request).

A CS/NavList can be a *contributor* (it can pvovide elements to a CS/UiInput-Structure). A CS/UiInputStructure can be *receptive* (it can receive elements from other CS/NavList).

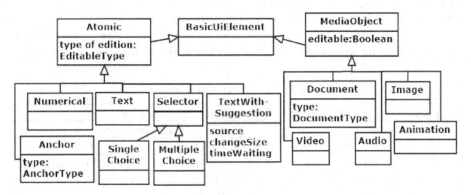

Fig. 3. Classification of BasicUiElement

Atomic elements can be used for different purposes according to their *type of edition*: *input* (for information input), *editable* (for information editing), and *no_editable* (for the presentation of information in a specific modality). *textWithSuggestion* represents editing text with suggestion (its type of edition can be *editable* or *input*) and has as tagged values: *search* (the value is the name of a search action), *change size* (values can be "char" | "word" | "sentence"), *time waiting* – i.e. before suggesting - (the value is in Nat; 0 means not waiting). *AnchorType* can have as values: *classical-Link* (link to another web page/document), *bookmarkLink* (a link to a position in the same web page), and *commandLink* (its selection initiates an action or task). *MediaObject* represents a media file; if a mediaObject is editable then it also includes the edition widget according to the specific media; else it only represents the playing of a media file. We considered mediaObjects of kinds: *document, image, video, audio* and *animation*. *DocumentType* can have as values: *PlainText, RichText* (an enriched text document), *Presentation* (a document consisting of slides), *SpreadSheet*.

All the above UIEs with the exception of UiComponent, PresentationElement, UiStructure, and BasicUiElement are stereotyped, extend Class, and their stereotype names are: "«"++ element name ++ "»".

An *atomic event* consists of its name, its source (an UIE instance), and its data. We assume that in any given time of a web application execution, there exists a stream of the atomic events that happened; in addition, for each atomic event in the stream there is a time stamp of its occurrence. Table 1 shows the atomic event classification considered in this paper. For each event type we list the event contained in it and the UIEs that act as sources of such events. An *event pattern* (EP) represents a set of events respecting the pattern and can be used for querying the stream of atomic events (i.e. a list of events that belong to the event stream can respect or not an EP). Now we provide a BNF grammar for event patterns. An *atomic EP* consists of: a name of event, the source, and optionally event data. A *composite* EP is described by providing all composition operations (given by non-terminals <OP> and <REP>) and atomic events participating. The composition operators were taken from [13, 14].

```
<EP> ::= <CEP>| <AEP> ,
<CEP> ::= <EP> <OP> <EP> | <REP> <N> <EP> ,
<OP> ::= AND | OR | SEQ , <N>::= <nat> times ,
<REP> ::= exactly | at least | at most ,
<AEP> ::= <NAME> on <SOURCE> (with <DATA>)?
<NAME> ::= <str>, <SOURCE> ::= <str>, <DATA> ::= <str>
```
`<str>` is used for alphanumeric strings and `<nat>` is used for natural numbers.

Table 1. Atomic Event Classification

Event Type	Event name	Source of the event
User interface events	Press	Anchor, Form (submission)
	Over, moveOut	BasicUiElement, elements of CS.
	enter, edited	CS (element edition), BasicUiElement
	select	LinksBased, Selector, Selector in Form. Block in NavAltBlocks.
	remove, add, move	CS (modification)
	select to share	contributor CS/NavList
	Put	receptive CS/UiInputStructure
Data events	update, delete, insert,	relations, XML document.
Transaction	commit, abort, request	Transaction
Timer events	start, timeout	Timer
Service events	start, finish	web service
Developer defined	Given by the developer	The actual web application or an external application.

«event» - ⚡- extends Action and represents an event list occurrence in the event stream respecting an EP. An «event» action has a tagged value called *expr,* whose value is an EP expression or an identifier of an EP expression; in addition, an «event» action has an output pin whose tokens can represent an event list matching the EP or data of the event list.

Now, we describe the part of RIAAD consisting of elements to be used for describing «job» Actions. To our knowledge, our classification of actions for modeling autonomous actions not only serves for changing UIE content values (like OOWS 2.0 [6], and RUX [5]), but also adds facilities for automatically change the structure of UiInputStructures and add/delete elements in CS, and we introduced «data process» actions. To describe «job» Actions with an activities, we consider the stereotypes: *«insert»* (⊟) /*«delete»* (⊟) /*«update»* (⊟): represents the insertion/ deletion/update of either data elements, or relations between data elements, or a view of a database (e.g., a relational database or XML document). *«insertUI»* (⊞) /*«deleteUI»* (⊡): represents the insertion/deletion of either an element inside a UI CS. *«updateUI»* (⊡): represents the automatic update by the application of information of either a CS, or a UIBasicElement, or a UIBasicElement in a

UiInputStructure. For changing the structure of a UiInputStructure (i.e. adding and removing some UiBasicElements and maintaining the rest with the same values) we use actions with setereotype *«change UiIS»*. *«dataRetrieve»* (🔍): represents the search of information from a given source that can be a text file, a relational database, an XML document, a view of a database. *«getUIContent»* (☐➔): represents the collection of content from one or several UI elements. *«UIPropertyChange»* (☐:=) represents an action that alters a UIE properties (e.g., *accessible* - i.e. if the UIE is visible, audible, etc. depending on the modality –, *enabled* - i.e. is true if and only if events on the UIE are enabled by the system-, and *focus* – UIE on focus -; it has a tagged-value *property,* whose value is the property name, and a *value* tagged value, whose value is the property's value. *«validation»* ($\sqrt{}$|×): represents the validation of information or business rules (in the client side – e.g. UIE content validation - or in the server side). *«dataProcess»*: it represents information processing (e.g. data coming from a database, content coming from an UIE). *«generateEvent»*: it represents the generation of an atomic event over a UIE; it has a tagged value *expr*, with an atomic EP expression as value. *«external job»*: represents the invocation of either an external task (e.g. the invocation of a web service or the treatment of an application generated event by another application), or the collection of information not belonging to the application (e.g. mashups). *«external notification»*: represents a notification to the application coming from an external job (e.g., a web service notification message, or the notification of an event from an external application to be processed).

4   Relating Actions in an AD UC with Modeling Elements

Actions whose stereotypes start with the word "output" are associated with UIEs (e.g. from RIAAD metamodel). An *«input»* action is associated usually with an *«event»* action representing the occurrence of an EP. A *«job»* action is associated with an AD describing the activity performed by the job and using the stereotypes explained at the end of Sec. 3. A *«search»* action is associated with a *«data retrieve»* action.

Fig. 4 shows the associations to some actions of the AD in Fig. 1 with UI elements and with *«event»* actions: *«output request» commands* is associated with an «UiInputStructure» *commands* containing three «anchor» elements of type command-Link; action «output content» *list of items* is associated with «List» *items* being editable; «input» *create or select or hover item* is associated with «event» *create or select or hover*, where *E* is the identifier of the expression: *Press on create item OR enter on items OR Over on items;* «input» *delete item or update item data* action is associated with «event» *delete or update item,* where E_1 is the identifier of the expression: *Press on delete item OR (change on item SEQ Press on update item);* and action *«output request» input item data* is associated with «Form» *new item popup.*

«job» validate data and add item is associated with the activity described in Fig. 5: first, the information about the item is validated; next, a checking for business rules violation is performed; following, item is inserted into the database, and finally, the presentation of the items list is updated to reflect the item insertion.

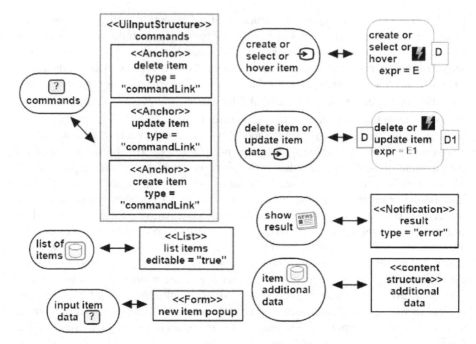

Fig. 4. Association of design elements to actions for CRUD operations on lists

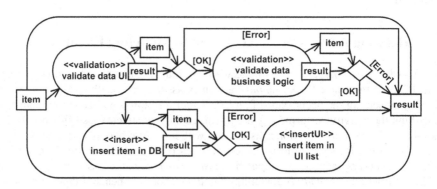

Fig. 5. Refinement of validate data and add ítem job

5   User Interface Use and Process Description Models (UIUPDM) and Their Automatic Generation

At least an UIUPDM should describe which UI components are presented and when, and have *«event»* actions with meaningful names; to have less than that is too few, because we need to talk about UI use. For this purpose, we consider the following stereotypes: *«synch»* (→▣) extends Action, and represents the synchronization of some data with an existing presentation element - to present this data-; for the representation of the data we use inputPins; the name of a «*synch*» action has the form "to" ++ *PE*, where *PE* is a UIE name; in addition, if *PE* is not yet visible then it is shown. «*present*» (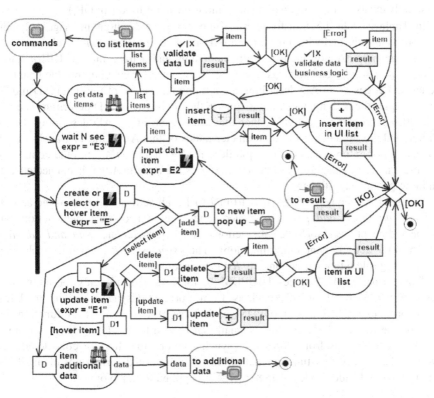) extends Action, and represents the presentation of UIEs that do not exhibit content coming from object nodes.

For the definition of UIUPDMs we decided not to show EP expressions inside the diagrams to make them less overcharged. We suggest instead writing EPs associated to identifiers in event actions of a UIUPDM model outside the diagram. In addition, we decided not to show in a UIUPDM the description of objects/data structures associated with tokens for object nodes. We consider three kinds of UIUPDMs: a) to show job descriptions, and avoid showing UIE descriptions; (this is useful when there are actions inside job descriptions that access/modify the UI); b) To show UIE descriptions, and avoid showing job descriptions (it is easy to inspect descriptions about user interaction in the UI, and UIEs presentations); c) to show details only of UIEs and job descriptions of small size. We propose to be able to generate automatically the three kinds of UIUPDM models; the user needs only to decide, which possibilities are appropriate for the situation at hand. In this section we will illustrate in detail the automatic generation of UIUPDM case a), and for the other two cases we only explain how to define the transformation.

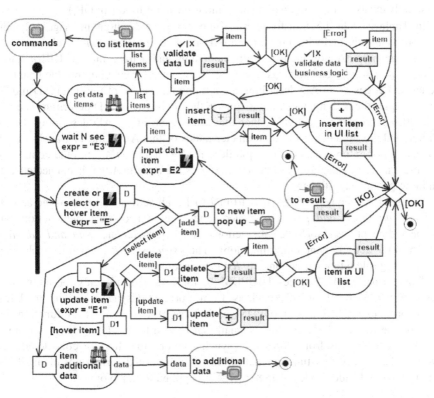

Fig. 6. UIUPDM for enriched CRUD of items of a list use case

Fig.6 shows an example of an UIUPDM model for case a), for enriched CRUD of items of a list case study; E and E_l are defined in Fig. 4, E_2 is the identifier of event *Press on submit of new item pop up* and E_3 is the identifier of event *timeout N sec on timer*. In addition, we use *«synch» to notification* action to obtain a result notification from creation, delete and update item operations results; *«synch» to list items* action is used to present the *list of items* CS and *«present» commands* is used to present the *commands* UiInputStructure.

For the automatic generation of UIUPDM we consider transformations defined in ATL language that map requirements for UCs and trace relations for these ADs onto a UIUPDM by applying some rules. For explaining transformation rules we used the following nomenclature: IP for inputPin, OP for outputPin, *a*.name for the name of element a, $n \lozenge n'$ to say that node n is related to node n' in its AD (related means either an activityEdge or a Pin association); a: outputAction means a is either of stereotype «output content», or «output message», or «output media», or «output request»; a: ForJobDesc means that a is a RIAAD stereotype used for describing jobs; IPar means an input parameter node; OPar means an output parameter node. We consider the following operations from activity edges to activity nodes: $-(e)$ returns the origin of e and $+(e)$ returns the target of e. Finally, [p: IP$\lozenge$] a means that it optionally exists an input pin p of a (the similar meaning for a [$\lozenge$p: OP]).

In Table 2, rule 4/5 transforms an «output request»/«output message» element without input pins and with a trace to an UIE u onto a *«present» u.name* element; rule 6 maps an outputAction element with input pins and a trace into an UIE u into a *«synch» to u.name* element; rules from 7 to 12 are used for copying into the result the nodes and edges of an AD describing an autonomous action of the input AD model; rule 7 copies the action nodes (and its pins if they exist) in the AD describing the job; rule 10 only copies the activity edges that are present in the AD describing the job action, and are not connected to parameter nodes of this AD. Rule 11 transforms the connection of an object node i to a job described with an AD A, onto the connection of object node i to an activity node n, where n is the node in A that is connected with an input parameter with name i.

In Fig 6.with the help of the rules from 7 to 12, all actions and pins of the activity *validate data and add item* are copied, and if it is necessary such actions are connected to predecessor/successor actions of the job *validate data and add item* action in the activity containing this «job». The *«synch» list items* action is obtained by applying rule 6 to «output content» *list items* action.

Transformation AD&Traces2UIUPDM_b) for case b) needs only the addition to rules from 1) to 7) of relationships from «present»/«synch» actions to UIEs. Transformation AD&Traces2UIUPDM_c) for case c) uses an auxiliary function that returns true iff an UIE description is small that is used to decide inside rules from 1) to 7) if relationships from «present»/«synch» actions to UIEs are considered; and there is also an auxiliary function that returns true iff a job description is of small size that is used to decide if rules from 8) to 12) are applied for a job or not.

Table 2. Transformation rules of AD&Traces2UIUPDM case a)

rule	Maps	Onto
1	«input» a trace «event» e	«event» e
2	«input and suggest» a trace «event» e	«event» e
3	«search» a trace a': action	a': action
4	«output request» *a* trace *u* :UIE	«present» *u*.name
	Condition: *a* has not input pins	
5	«output message» *a* trace *u* :UIE	«present» *u*.name
	Condition: *a* has not input pins	
6	p: IP → a: outputAction trace *u* : UIE	p: IP → «synch» to *u*.name
7	[p: IP →] a: ForJobDesc [→p': OP]	[p: IP →] a: ForJobDesc [→p':OP]
	Condition: «*job*» a' trace A: AD ∧ a in A	
8	*o* : objectNode	*o* : objectNode
	Condition: «*job*» a' trace A: AD ∧ *o* in A ∧ *o* is not a Pin	
9	*n* : controlNode	*n* : controlNode
	Condition: «*job*» a' trace A: AD ∧ *n* in A	
10	*f*: activityEdge	*f*: activityEdge $-(f) =$ n, ∧ $+(f) =$ n'
	Condition: «*job*» a' trace A: AD ∧ $-(f) =$ n ∧ $+(f) =$ n' ∧ n, n': activity-Node ∧ *f*, n, n' in A ∧ *f* is not connected with a parameter node	
11	i: ON → «*job*» a' trace A: AD	i: ON → n : activityNode
	Condition: i: IPar → n : activityNode ∧ i, n in A	
12	«*job*» a' trace A: AD ∧ a' → o: ON	n : activityNode → o: ON
	Condition: n : activityNode → o: OPar ∧ o, n in A	

6   Related Work

Table 3 shows a comparison of our approach with other methods we found in the literature. Before explaining this table, we define some concepts: *integrated models* are models integrating user interaction with the UI and the response of the system to these interactions; integrated models can be: based on ECA Rules - ECA -, state machines –SM-, or integration of UI use with process modeling, permitting the definition of ECA rules - UIUP -; *role* means either analyst or UI designer. The column with title "two roles involved" means that to construct the integrated model at least one role has to understand diagram aspects that concern the other role (this may lead to one role interfering/involving with the other or to understandability reduction).

Table 3. Method Comparison

Method	Integrated model	Notation type	Two roles involved	Way of obtaining integral model
WebML	Hypertext model	partially a UIUP	Yes	Semi-automatic from BPMN, or manually
OOH4RIA	Orchesta-tion model	SM	Yes, to define interaction dependences	Semi-automatic from OOH presentation and navigation models
RUX	Interaction presentation	ECA	Yes	Manually
OOHDM	ADV	SM	Yes	Manually
OOWS 2.0	Event rules	ECA	Yes	Manually
MARIA	Dialog model	ECA	Yes	Some guides to obtain it from CTTs
our approach	UIUPDMs	UIUP	No	Automatic generation from RIA requirements and traces

Only two of the methods are UIUPs: WebML ([2]) only partially, and our approach. WebML does not consider event patterns; the extension of WebML for Ajax technology ([1]) considers elements for modeling only typical Ajax events, and the treatment of such events do not consider all kinds of actions necessary for RIA applications (they do not consider operations modifying the structure/content of UIEs). Only our approach considers the construction of integrated models, without the necessity of a role having to read and understand details corresponding to the other role; OOH4RIA ([3]) alleviates partially this problem, because it semi-automatically generates an orchestration model skeleton that needs to be completed with the definition of interaction dependencies that need the involvement of analysts, who needs to comprehend UI details. Our development process generates automatically a complete integrated model, using design decisions from UI designers and analysts (captured by traces); WebML generates first versions of hypertext models from BPMN models that probably need to be refined or modified by designers. ECA approaches tend to be the less complex, followed by SMs, because SMs (in Table 3) approaches, in addition to ECA rules, consider UIEs with some details, and also control flow details. An UIUP must have at least the complexity of ECA rules, because it must describe ECA rules; we consider WebML more complex than our UIUPDMs, because it considers all kind of aspects: UIEs details, autonomous action description, and some relations of UIEs with the data model.

7   Conclusion

Our UIUPDM models contemplate several RIA needs presented in [16]: data management, definition of complex autonomous actions, validation of information, event handling, UIEs abstracting several widgets, the work with multimedia content, permits data synchronization, UIEs content/structure modification, UIE presentation, the possibility of the participation of several actors in a UIUPDM of a functionality, the communication with external Jobs, definition of tasks/business processes.

Our UIUPDMs abstract from details concerning: the size and positioning of UIEs, style of UIEs showing content, platform details, and device details; such details should be considered during concrete design or implementation. Our UIUPDM notations do not consider: a) the container hierarchies inside pages (only basic UIEs are considered in trace relationships); these can be defined using RIAAD for UI presentation; to know how basic visible UI components inside a container/page dynamically change, read the UIUPDMs; b) if the following operations are performed in the client side or the server side: CRUD operations on data, event processing, and validation of data; this can be considered during concrete design, or by adding more details to UIUPDMs operations (i.e. using a tagged value *source,* whose values can be *'client'* or *'server'*).

The necessity of looking at other diagrams to understand UIUPDMs in more depth can be mitigated if we consider UIUPDMs as maps: by clicking on non-detailed modeling elements, they are expanded by using movable popups containing their descriptions (the UIUPDM does not disappear after these expansions). For UIUPDM_a) «synch»/«present» actions can be expanded, for UIUPDM_b) «job» actions can be expanded, and for UIUPDM_c) not detailed «synch»/«present»/«job» actions can be expanded. Building a tool supporting this idea is a task for the future.

To find RIAAD modeling elements, we have considered some case studies: the ones of URLs in Sec. 3, case studies of the next sentence, and the approaches for RIA in the literature. We have applied our development process to the following case studies: enriched collaborative CRUD of items of a list, image editing with auto-save, live feed update, hover detail, on demand scrolling, state information update, book return, and the e-Learning platform in www.parleys.com.

Concerning the problems that would arise if UIUPDMs are built without using a carefully designed development process, we have taken the following preventive measures against them: a) *inconsistency introduction*: analysts and UI designers respect: business process description by using traces to refine actions, and detailed data description during trace relationship definition; in addition, data and control flows of requirements are copied into UIUPDMs; b) *the construction of UIUPDMs by analysts and/or UI designers*: it is avoided, because UIUPDMs are generated automatically from trace relationships; c) *complex UIUPDMs*: we decided to abstract from several details (see the 2nd paragraph in this Sec.), and to have different kinds of UIUPDMs concentrating on some aspects and avoiding others.

The development of a tool supporting de development process of this paper is a task for the future.

The necessary effort during abstract design is at least the effort that takes building trace relationships; there is one trace relation per action in a UC AD; UIEs in trace relationships are UIEs necessary for performing input or output, and do not involve entire pages or complex container hierarchies; we think that the biggest effort is required by describing complex autonomous actions.

The process for obtaining UIUPDs does not depend on: a) the abstraction level of UI design elements and event patterns; b) the particular set of UI design elements.

References

1. Brambilla, M., Fraternali, P., Molteni, E.: A Tool for Model-driven Design of Rich Internet Applications based on AJAX. In: Murugesan, S. (ed.) Handbook of Research on Web 2.0, 3.0, and X.0: Technologies, Business, and Social Applications, ch. 31, pp. 96–118. IGI Global (2010) ISBN: 9781605663845
2. Fraternali, P., Comai, S., Bozzon, A., Toffetti, G.: Engineering rich internet applications with a model-driven approach. ACM Trans. Web 4(2), Article 7, 47 pages (2010)
3. Melia, S., Gomez, J., Perez, S., Diaz, O.: A Model-Driven Development for GWT-Based Rich Internet Applications with OOH4RIA. In: Proceedings of the 8th Intl. Conf. on Web Engineering, pp. 13–23. IEEE (2008)
4. Urbieta, M., Rossi, G., Ginzburg, J., Schwabe, D.: Designing the Interface of Rich Internet Applications. In: Proccedings of Latin American Web Congress 2007, pp. 144–153. IEEE (2007)
5. Linaje Trigueros, M.: Rux-method: modelado de interfaces de usuario Web multi-dispositivo, multimedia, interactivas y accesibles. Sánchez Figueroa, F. (dir.) (2009)
6. Valverde Giromé, F.: OOWS 2.0: Un Método De Ingeniería Web Dirigido Por Modelos Para La Producción De Aplicaciones WEB 2.0. Pastor López, O. (dir.) (2010)
7. Paternò, F., Santoro, C., Spano, L.D.: MARIA: A universal, declarative, multiple abstraction-level language for service-oriented applications in ubiquitous environments. ACM Trans. Comput.-Hum. Interact. 16(4), 1–30 (2009)
8. Bry, F., Eckert, M., Pătrânjan, P.-L., Romanenko, I.: Realizing business processes with ECA rules: Benefits, challenges, limits. In: Alferes, J.J., Bailey, J., May, W., Schwertel, U. (eds.) PPSWR 2006. LNCS, vol. 4187, pp. 48–62. Springer, Heidelberg (2006)
9. Eckert, M., Bry, F., Brodt, S., Poppe, O., Hausmann, S.: A CEP Babelfish: Languages for Complex Event Processing and Querying Surveyed. In: Helmer, S., Poulovassilis, A., Xhafa, F. (eds.) Reasoning in Event-Based Distributed Systems. SCI, vol. 347, pp. 47–70. Springer, Heidelberg (2011)
10. Casalánguida, H., Durán, J.E.: Requirements Engineering of Web Application Product Lines. In: Proceedings of the 7th Intl. Conf. on Web Information Systems and Technologies, pp. 418–425. SciTePress (2011)
11. Koch, N., Knapp, A., Zhang, G., Baumeister, H.: UML-Based Web Engineering. An Approach Based on Standards. In: Web Engineering: Modelling and Implementing Web Applications. Human Computer Interaction Series, pp. 157–191. Springer (2008)
12. Filho, O., Ribeiro, J.: UWE-R: An Extension to a Web Engineering Methodology for Rich Internet Applications. WSEAS Trans. Info. Sci. and App. 6(4), 601–610 (2009)
13. Mbaki, E., Vanderdonckt, J., Guerrero, J., Winckler, M.: Multi-level Dialog Modeling in Highly Interactive Web Interfaces. In: Proceedings of the 8th Intl. Conf. on Web Engineering, pp. 44–49. IEEE Computer Society, Los Alamitos (2008)
14. Bry, F., Pătrânjan, P.: Reactivity on the Web: Paradigms and Applications of the Language XChange. J. Web Eng. 5(1), 3–24 (2006)
15. Manolescu, I., Brambilla, M., Ceri, S., Comai, S., Fraternali, P.: Model-driven design and deployment of service-enabled web applications. ACM Trans. Internet Techn. 5(3), 439–479 (2005)
16. Toffetti, G., Comai, S., Preciado, J.C., Linaje Trigueros, M.: State-of-the Art and trends in the Systematic Development of Rich Internet Applications. J. Web Eng. 10(1), 70–86 (2011)

Recommendation of Text Tags
in Social Applications Using Linked Data

Andrea Calì[1,2], Stefano Capuzzi[3], Mirko Michele Dimartino[1],
and Riccardo Frosini[1]

[1] Dept. of Computer Science and Inf. Syst., Birkbeck, University of London, UK
[2] Oxford-Man Institute of Quantitative Finance, University of Oxford, UK
[3] Dipartimento di Ingegneria dell'Informazione, Università di Brescia, Italy

Abstract. We present a recommender system that suggests geo-located
text tags by using linguistic information extracted from Linked Data sets
available on the Web. The recommender system performs tag matching
by measuring the semantic similarity of natural language texts. Our approach evaluates similarity using a technique that compares sentences
taking into account their grammatical structure.

1 Introduction

Presently, large RDF data sets are available, which offer a large amount of
machine-processable information for a wide range of applications. In October
2007, the Linked Open Data (LOD) data sets consisted of over two billion RDF
triples, interlinked by over two million RDF links. By September 2011 this had
grown to 31 billion RDF triples, interlinked by around 504 million RDF links [4].
In spite of its success, the Semantic Web may contain several poor quality data
and numerous unsolved data management problems, related both to the concept
as well as the implementation [2,6]. Several dictionaries and Thesauri have also
been recently published in RDF format, for instance WordNet and Wiktionary.

We have designed a social application that allows end-users to retrieve geo-
tagged text snippets which are semantically related to natural language queries.
To achieve this goal we exploit the above mentioned Linked Data sets. As a first
step, we to compare English words and establish a similarity measure using the
properties extracted from the Linked Data resources. With such word similarity
measure at hand, we use it as a building block to compare whole text snippets.
Sentences are compared by considering their syntactic structure, so as to capture
their semantics at a somewhat detailed level.

In this paper we describe the main features of our first prototype offering semantic search of natural language text tags. In our system, the user is able to submit
geo-tagged text snippets, describing anything related to the location, by a mobile
application; the application stores the tags, sharing them with other users. A user
can query the system using a natural language text snippet, in order to retrieve semantically related, as well as geographically close, tags submitted by other users.

Q.Z. Sheng and J. Kjeldskov (Eds.): ICWE 2013 Workshops, LNCS 8295, pp. 187–191, 2013.

2   Background and Related Work

Linked Data is a way of publishing and interlinking web data using standard web technologies such as RDF and URIs. The Linked Data initiative aims also at gathering resources to which semantic meaning can be attached, as well as an interlinked structure that connects resources [1].

The amount of available data is nowadays extremely large, hence the necessity of systems that aid users to find relevant information. Functionalities such as flexible querying [12,7] or recommendation systems [11,3] do aid users in searching Linked Data. Flexible querying helps the user to retrieve information without knowing the structure of the underlying RDF dataset. Recommender systems are widely used to predict preferences of the user, usually related to a certain domain.

As of today, the corpus-based approach is the most used technique for semantic text similarity [8,14]. In such an approach, word similarity is computing by counting the frequency of occurrences of two words in a document. This approach relies on the number of documents, and the accuracy increases as the number of documents increases [14].

An example of a recommender system is aided by the analysis of natural languages is [5].

3   Techniques

Our recommender system relies on the word semantic similarity and sentence similarity to retrieve semantically related text snippets. In this section we briefly explain how we address new efficient approaches that cope this limitations, leveraging the widespread information underlying the Linked Open Data (LOD) cloud.

Word-to-word Semantic Similarity. To date, the corpus-based approach is the most used technique to retrieve word-to-word semantic similarity. The corpus-based word similarity uses a large set of documents to compute the semantic of terms and can be very accurate [8]. Despite its effectiveness, the corpus-based approach requires a large number of samples of written and spoken language from a wide range of contexts (i.e., huge memory space in real world applications) so as to compute adequately accurate results. Also, it is difficult to create statistical unbiased samples that are representative of a language, thus once the corpus is created it cannot be updated, for instance, according to the fast and dynamic progression of the urban language [9].

Our aim is to evaluate word-by-word semantic similarity by querying Linked Data sets, thus retrieving accurate and up-to-date information, exploiting the vast amount of semi-structured data in the LOD cloud.

As a first step, we have designed a distance-based method over the RDF triples in Wordnet, which is a large lexical database of English. Nouns, verbs, adjectives and adverbs are grouped into sets of cognitive synonyms (synsets), each expressing a distinct concept. Synsets are interlinked by means of conceptual-semantic and lexical relations (e.g., *Synonym, Antonym, Hypernym*). To quantify

Word 1	Word 2	Similarity	Word 1	Word 2	Similarity
sea	water	0.142	rock	stone	0.6433
sea	ocean	0.6	woman	girl	0.6165
arm	leg	0.1295	man	woman	-0.8133
arm	hand	0.619	window	wall	0.1323
chest	body	0.0342	window	door	0.0343
arm	body	0.5908	rescue	save	0.6247
print	printer	0.734	place	square	0.0343
first	last	-0.7251	feel	sense	0.6284
first	position	0.1210	red	blue	0.1323
student	teacher	0.0972	black	white	-0.7693
teach	teacher	0.7346	recall	remember	0.6419
class	room	0.1246	hiccup	cough	0.1323
similar	twin	0.1323	forget	remember	-0.9124
tinkle	sparkle	0.153	end	finish	0.6117
estate	property	0.622	rust	iron	0.0448

Fig. 1. Word similarity: first experiments

the similarity between two words, we assign to the relevant predicates of Word-Net a value between -1 and 1, where -1 indicates that the connected words are opposite and 1 indicates that the words are equivalent. If two words are not directly connected we navigate the RDF dataset as a graph in order to find paths that connect words, and the similarity is given by the weighted sum of the product of all weights in each path.

Structured Sentence Similarity Matching. The semantic word similarity measure above sketched is used as a subroutine to compare text snippets and sentences. To evaluate the semantic similarity between two sentences our system analyses the syntactic and grammatical structure of the sentences. According to this method, the system generate the sentence-to-sentence similarity and compares the sentences between two text snippets to compute the semantic similarity of full tags, which may contain more than just one sentence.

The system parses the text snippets, and represents them as RDF trees. Roughly speaking, to compute the similarity between two sentences, we compare their trees and match the lexical components (nodes); for instance, the *Subject* of the first sentence with the *Subject* of the second, and so forth. Then we compare the subtrees of each element recursively. When the algorithm reaches the leaves of the tree (i.e. not a grammatical component but a single term) it calls the word similarity procedure above explained.

4   First Experiments and Discussion

We show in Figure 1 some preliminary results on the word-to-word similarity algorithm previously described. What we have achieved depends heavily on how WordNet is accurate in terms of connections between terms; moreover, the weights of the algorithm are set to "reasonable" values, but they will be learned

Query: "A tall guy is walking around Oxford Street"	Similarity
Hot guy on train and I look like death from running around oxford street	0.49024059
some guy with a megaphone was saying random stuff on oxford street today, spoke the truth real talk!	0.47607129
When a guy barks at you on Oxford Street #standard	0.44464286
On Oxford Street there is a Starbucks guy giving out free coffee! And who said Wednesdays can't be exciting #coffeefix	0.42439007
When your walking down oxford street and a guy barks at you #woof	0.38843864

Fig. 2. Sentence similarity: first experiments

from user feedback in future versions of the system. This said, the initial results are encouraging as the system, for instance, correctly finds similarity between *rust* and *iron*, or *arm* and *leg*.

For the sentence similarity we have used sentences extracted from Twitter via its APIs. Some results are shown in Figure 2.

Future Work. As future work, we plan to extend our technique in order to capture the context of words in sentences, and to use it in the ranking. In order to do so, we envision the use of Semantic Web languages to express more expressive ontological information. We also plan to make use of a learning algorithm in order to adjust the similarity computation according to user feeeedback.

Acknowledgments. Andrea Calì acknowledges support by the EP-SRC project "Logic-based Integration and Querying of Unindexed Data" (EP/E010865/1). The authors would like to thank Alexandra Poulovassilis and Peter Wood for their valuable comments on this research.

References

1. Bizer, C.: Evolving the web into a global data space. In: Fernandes, A.A.A., Gray, A.J.G., Belhajjame, K. (eds.) BNCOD 2011. LNCS, vol. 7051, p. 1. Springer, Heidelberg (2011)
2. Bizer, C., Heath, T., Berners-Lee, T.: Linked data - the story so far. Int. J. Semantic Web Inf. Syst. 5(3), 1–22 (2009), http://eprints.soton.ac.uk/271285/
3. Di Noia, T., Mirizzi, R., Ostuni, V.C., Romito, D., Zanker, M.: Linked open data to support content-based recommender systems. In: Proceedings of the 8th International Conference on Semantic Systems, I-SEMANTICS 2012, pp. 1–8. ACM, New York (2012), http://doi.acm.org/10.1145/2362499.2362501
4. Fensel, D., Facca, F.M., Simperl, E.P.B., Toma, I.: Semantic Web Services. Springer (2011)
5. Fleischman, M., Hovy, E.: Recommendations without user preferences: a natural language processing approach. In: Proceedings of the 8th International Conference on Intelligent User Interfaces, IUI 2003, pp. 242–244. ACM, New York (2003), http://doi.acm.org/10.1145/604045.604087

6. Hassanzadeh, O., Kementsietsidis, A., Velegrakis, Y.: Data management issues on the semantic web. In: 2013 IEEE 29th International Conference on Data Engineering (ICDE), pp. 1204–1206 (2012)
7. Huang, H., Liu, C., Zhou, X.: Computing relaxed answers on RDF databases. In: Bailey, J., Maier, D., Schewe, K.-D., Thalheim, B., Wang, X.S. (eds.) WISE 2008. LNCS, vol. 5175, pp. 163–175. Springer, Heidelberg (2008), http://dx.doi.org/10.1007/978-3-540-85481-4_14
8. Islam, A., Inkpen, D.: Semantic text similarity using corpus-based word similarity and string similarity. ACM Trans. Knowl. Discov. Data 2(2), 10:1–10:25 (2008), http://doi.acm.org/10.1145/1376815.1376819
9. Marcus, M.P., Marcinkiewicz, M.A., Santorini, B.: Building a large annotated corpus of English: the penn treebank. Comput. Linguist. 19(2), 313–330 (1993), http://dl.acm.org/citation.cfm?id=972470.972475
10. Miarka, R., Zacek, M.: Knowledge patterns for conversion of sentences in natural language into RDF graph language. In: Ganzha, M., Maciaszek, L.A., Paprzycki, M. (eds.) FedCSIS, pp. 63–68 (2011), http://dblp.uni-trier.de/db/conf/fedcsis/fedcsis2011.html#MiarkaZ11
11. Ostuni, V.C., Di Noia, T., Mirizzi, R., Romito, D., Sciascio, E.D.: Cinemappy: a context-aware mobile app for movie recommendations boosted by dbpedia. In: SeRSy, pp. 37–48 (2012)
12. Poulovassilis, A., Wood, P.T.: Combining approximation and relaxation in semantic web path queries. In: Patel-Schneider, P.F., Pan, Y., Hitzler, P., Mika, P., Zhang, L., Pan, J.Z., Horrocks, I., Glimm, B. (eds.) ISWC 2010, Part I. LNCS, vol. 6496, pp. 631–646. Springer, Heidelberg (2010), http://dl.acm.org/citation.cfm?id=1940281.1940322
13. Socher, R., Bauer, J., Manning, C.D., Ng, A.Y.: Parsing With Compositional Vector Grammars. In: ACL (2013)
14. Turney, P.D., Pantel, P.: From frequency to meaning: vector space models of semantics. J. Artif. Int. Res. 37(1), 141–188 (2010), http://dl.acm.org/citation.cfm?id=1861751.1861756

Query Answering in Datalog+/– Ontologies under Group Preferences and Probabilistic Uncertainty

Thomas Lukasiewicz, Maria Vanina Martinez,
Gerardo I. Simari, and Oana Tifrea-Marciuska

Department of Computer Science, University of Oxford, UK
{thomas.lukasiewicz, vanina.martinez,
gerardo.simari, oana.tifrea}@cs.ox.ac.uk

Abstract. In the recent years, the Web has been changing more and more towards the so-called Social Semantic Web. Rather than being based on the link structure between Web pages, the ranking of search results in the Social Semantic Web needs to be based on something new. We believe that it can be based on user preferences and underlying ontological knowledge. Modeling uncertainty is also playing an increasingly important role in these domains, since uncertainty can arise due to many uncontrollable factors. In this paper, we thus propose an extension of the Datalog+/– ontology language with a model for representing preferences of groups of users and a model for representing the (probabilistic) uncertainty in the domain. Assuming that more probable answers are more preferable, this raises the question how to rank query results, since the preferences of single users may be in conflict with the probability-based preferences and also with each other. We thus propose preference merging and aggregation operators, respectively, and study their semantic and computational properties. Based on these operators, we provide algorithms for answering k-rank queries for DAQs (disjunctions of atomic queries), which generalize top-k queries based on the iterative computation of classical skyline answers, and show that, under certain reasonable conditions, they run in polynomial time in the data complexity.

1 Introduction

In the recent years, the Web has been shifting more and more away from data on linked Web pages towards less interlinked data in social networks relative to underlying ontologies, called the *Social Semantic Web*. This requires new technologies for search and query answering, where the ranking of search results is not based on the link structure between Web pages anymore, but on the information in the Social Semantic Web, in particular, the preferences of the users and the underlying ontological knowledge.

Modeling the preferences of a group of users is also an important research topic in its own right. With the growth of social media, people post their preferences and expect to get personalized information. Moreover, people use social networks as a tool to organize events, where it is required to combine the individual preferences and suggest items obtained from aggregated user preferences. For example, if there is a movie night of friends, family trip, or dinner with working colleagues, one has to decide which is the ideal movie or location for the group, given the preferences of each member. In addition, collaborative search [18] has recently started to play an important role.

Q.Z. Sheng and J. Kjeldskov (Eds.): ICWE 2013 Workshops, LNCS 8295, pp. 192–206, 2013.

Modeling group preferences comes with two challenges. The first one is to define a group preference semantics that solves the possible *disagreement* among users. For example, people (even friends) often have different tastes on how they prefer to spend their holidays. Therefore, a system should return results in such a way that each individual benefits from the result. The second challenge is to allow for efficient algorithms, e.g., to compute efficiently the answers to queries under aggregated group preferences [2].

There are many studies that are addressing the area of group modeling, which is indirectly related to the area of social choice (group decision making, i.e., optimal decisions for a user given the opinion of a collection of users), studied in mathematics, economics, politics, and sociology [21,23]. Other areas related to social choice are meta-search [16], collaborative filtering [14], and multi-agent systems [24]. Group preferences have especially been studied in the area of recommender systems [2,20], which focus on quantitative preferences. However, in many real-world scenarios, the ordering of preferences is incomplete. This appears due to privacy issues or an incomplete elicitation process (for example, because users may not want to be asked too many questions). Furthermore, it is often difficult to determine the appropriate numerical preferences and weights that maximize the utility of a decision [5]. For example, it is difficult for a user to determine a numerical value (e.g., 0.7 or 0.9) to rate a certain activity. Therefore, there is a growing interest in formalisms for representing and reasoning with qualitative incomplete preferences [22,13,1]. These approaches, however, do not have underlying ontologies, which are an important ingredient of the Semantic and the Social Semantic Web, and which also provide useful information for the ranking of query results.

The presence of uncertainty in the Web in general is undeniable [12,15,19,9]. Different sources of uncertainty that must be dealt with in answering queries in the Social Semantic Web are, for example, information integration (as in travel sites that query multiple sources to find touristic tours), automatic processing of Web data (analyzing an HTML document often involves uncertainty), as well as inherently uncertain data (such as user comments or tight relationships between users).

The current challenge for Web search is therefore inherently linked to:

(1) leveraging the social components of Web content towards the development of some form of semantic search and query answering on the Web as a whole, and (2) dealing with the presence of uncertainty in a principled way throughout the process. In this paper, we develop a novel integration of ontology languages with both preferences of groups of users and uncertainty management mechanisms. We do this by developing an extension of the Datalog+/– family of ontology languages [7] with a preference model over the consequences of the ontology, as well as a probabilistic model that assigns probabilities to them. The preference and the probabilistic model are assumed to model the preferences of a group of users and the uncertainty in the domain, respectively.

The main contributions of this paper can be summarized as follows.

– We introduce GPP-Datalog+/–, which combines the Datalog+/– ontology language with both group preferences (a generalization of preference handling in relational databases) and probabilistic uncertainty. To our knowledge, this is the first combination of ontology languages with group preferences and probabilistic uncertainty.
– We present operators for merging single-user and score-based (probability-based) preferences (in the form of a strict partial and a weak order, respectively), to

produce a new single-user preference relation satisfying certain basic properties. We also present several ways to compute group preferences as an aggregation of sets of single-user preferences, based on social choice theory [17].

– Based on an algorithm for the above preference merging and aggregation, we give algorithms for answering k-rank queries for DAQs (disjunctions of atomic queries), which generalize top-k queries based on the iterative computation of classical skyline answers. We show that answering DAQs in GPP-Datalog+/– is possible in polynomial time in the data complexity modulo the cost of computing probabilities.

The rest of this paper is organized as follows. In Section 2, we recall some basics on Datalog+/–. Section 3 introduces the syntax and the semantics of GPP-Datalog+/–, in particular, the general group preference model and the probabilistic model, along with preference merging and aggregation operations. In Section 4, we present algorithms for k-rank query answering, along with correctness and data tractability results. Section 5 summarizes the main results of this paper and gives an outlook on future research.

2   Preliminaries

We first recall some basics on Datalog+/– [7], namely, on relational databases, (Boolean) conjunctive queries ((B)CQs), tuple- and equality-generating dependencies (TGDs and EGDs, respectively), negative constraints, the chase, and ontologies in Datalog+/–.

Databases and Queries. We assume (i) an infinite universe of *(data) constants* Δ (which constitute the "normal" domain of a database), (ii) an infinite set of *(labeled) nulls* Δ_N (used as "fresh" Skolem terms, which are placeholders for unknown values, and can thus be seen as variables), and (iii) an infinite set of variables $\mathcal{V}$ (used in queries, dependencies, and constraints). Different constants represent different values (*unique name assumption*), while different nulls may represent the same value. We assume a lexicographic order on $\Delta \cup \Delta_N$, with every symbol in Δ_N following all symbols in Δ. We denote by $\mathbf{X}$ sequences of variables $X_1, \ldots, X_k$ with $k \geqslant 0$. We assume a *relational schema* $\mathcal{R}$, which is a finite set of *predicate symbols* (or simply *predicates*). A *term* t is a constant, null, or variable. An *atomic formula* (or *atom*) $\mathbf{a}$ has the form $P(t_1, \ldots, t_n)$, where P is an n-ary predicate, and $t_1, \ldots, t_n$ are terms.

A *database (instance)* D for a relational schema $\mathcal{R}$ is a (possibly infinite) set of atoms with predicates from $\mathcal{R}$ and arguments from Δ. A *conjunctive query (CQ)* over $\mathcal{R}$ has the form $Q(\mathbf{X}) = \exists \mathbf{Y}\, \Phi(\mathbf{X}, \mathbf{Y})$, where $\Phi(\mathbf{X}, \mathbf{Y})$ is a conjunction of atoms (possibly equalities, but not inequalities) with the variables $\mathbf{X}$ and $\mathbf{Y}$, and possibly constants, but without nulls. A *Boolean CQ (BCQ)* over $\mathcal{R}$ is a CQ of the form $Q()$, often written as the set of all its atoms, without quantifiers. Answers to CQs and BCQs are defined via *homomorphisms*, which are mappings $\mu\colon \Delta \cup \Delta_N \cup \mathcal{V} \to \Delta \cup \Delta_N \cup \mathcal{V}$ such that (i) $c \in \Delta$ implies $\mu(c) = c$, (ii) $c \in \Delta_N$ implies $\mu(c) \in \Delta \cup \Delta_N$, and (iii) μ is naturally extended to atoms, sets of atoms, and conjunctions of atoms. The set of all *answers* to a CQ $Q(\mathbf{X}) = \exists \mathbf{Y}\, \Phi(\mathbf{X}, \mathbf{Y})$ over a database D, denoted $Q(D)$, is the set of all tuples $\mathbf{t}$ over Δ for which there exists a homomorphism $\mu\colon \mathbf{X} \cup \mathbf{Y} \to \Delta \cup \Delta_N$ such that $\mu(\Phi(\mathbf{X}, \mathbf{Y})) \subseteq D$ and $\mu(\mathbf{X}) = \mathbf{t}$. The *answer* to a BCQ $Q()$ over a database D is *Yes*, denoted $D \models Q$, iff $Q(D) \neq \emptyset$.

Given a relational schema $\mathcal{R}$, a *tuple-generating dependency (TGD)* σ is a first-order formula of the form $\forall \mathbf{X} \forall \mathbf{Y}\ \Phi(\mathbf{X}, \mathbf{Y}) \rightarrow \exists \mathbf{Z}\ \Psi(\mathbf{X}, \mathbf{Z})$, where $\Phi(\mathbf{X}, \mathbf{Y})$ and $\Psi(\mathbf{X}, \mathbf{Z})$ are conjunctions of atoms over $\mathcal{R}$ (without nulls), called the *body* and the *head* of σ, denoted $body(\sigma)$ and $head(\sigma)$, respectively. Such σ is satisfied in a database D for $\mathcal{R}$ iff, whenever there exists a homomorphism h that maps the atoms of $\Phi(\mathbf{X}, \mathbf{Y})$ to atoms of D, there exists an extension h' of h that maps the atoms of $\Psi(\mathbf{X}, \mathbf{Z})$ to atoms of D. All sets of TGDs are finite here. Since TGDs can be reduced to TGDs with only single atoms in their heads, in the sequel, every TGD has w.l.o.g. a single atom in its head. A TGD σ is *guarded* iff it contains an atom in its body that contains all universally quantified variables of σ. The leftmost such atom is the *guard atom* (or *guard*) of σ.

Query answering under TGDs, i.e., the evaluation of CQs and BCQs on databases under a set of TGDs is defined as follows. For a database D for $\mathcal{R}$, and a set of TGDs Σ on $\mathcal{R}$, the set of *models* of D and Σ, denoted $mods(D, \Sigma)$, is the set of all (possibly infinite) databases B such that (i) $D \subseteq B$ and (ii) every $\sigma \in \Sigma$ is satisfied in B. The set of *answers* for a CQ Q to D and Σ, denoted $ans(Q, D, \Sigma)$, is the set of all tuples $\mathbf{a}$ such that $\mathbf{a} \in Q(B)$ for all $B \in mods(D, \Sigma)$. The *answer* for a BCQ Q to D and Σ is *Yes*, denoted $D \cup \Sigma \models Q$, iff $ans(Q, D, \Sigma) \neq \emptyset$. Note that query answering under general TGDs is undecidable [3], even when the schema and TGDs are fixed [6]. Decidability of query answering for the guarded case follows from a bounded tree-width property. The data complexity of query answering in this case is P-complete.

Negative constraints (or simply *constraints*) γ are first-order formulas of the form $\forall \mathbf{X}\ \Phi(\mathbf{X}) \rightarrow \bot$, where $\Phi(\mathbf{X})$, called the *body* of γ, denoted $body(\gamma)$, is a conjunction of atoms (without nulls). Under the standard semantics of query answering of BCQs in Datalog+/– with TGDs, adding negative constraints is computationally easy, as for each constraint $\forall \mathbf{X}\ \Phi(\mathbf{X}) \rightarrow \bot$, we only have to check that the BCQ $\Phi(\mathbf{X})$ evaluates to false in D under Σ; if one of these checks fails, then the answer to the original BCQ Q is true, otherwise the constraints can simply be ignored when answering the BCQ Q.

Equality-generating dependencies (or *EGDs*) σ, are first-order formulas of the form $\forall \mathbf{X}\ \Phi(\mathbf{X}) \rightarrow X_i = X_j$, where $\Phi(\mathbf{X})$, called the *body* of σ, denoted $body(\sigma)$, is a conjunction of atoms (without nulls), and X_i and X_j are variables from $\mathbf{X}$. Such σ is satisfied in a database D for $\mathcal{R}$ iff, whenever there exists a homomorphism h such that $h(\Phi(\mathbf{X}, \mathbf{Y})) \subseteq D$, it holds that $h(X_i) = h(X_j)$. Adding EGDs over databases with TGDs along with negative constraints does not increase the complexity of BCQ query answering as long as they are *non-conflicting* [7]. Intuitively, this ensures that, if the chase (see below) fails (due to strong violations of EGDs), then it already fails on the database D, and if it does not fail, then the EGDs do not have any impact on the chase with respect to query answering.

We usually omit the universal quantifiers in TGDs, negative constraints, and EGDs, and we implicitly assume that all sets of dependencies and/or constraints are finite.

The Chase. The *chase* was first introduced to enable checking implication of dependencies, and later also for checking query containment. By "chase", we refer both to the chase procedure and to its output. The TGD chase works on a database via so-called TGD *chase rules* (see [7] for an extended chase with also EGD chase rules).

TGD Chase Rule. Let D be a database, and σ be a TGD of the form $\Phi(\mathbf{X}, \mathbf{Y}) \rightarrow \exists \mathbf{Z}\ \Psi(\mathbf{X}, \mathbf{Z})$. Then, σ is *applicable* to D if there exists a homomorphism h that maps the atoms of $\Phi(\mathbf{X}, \mathbf{Y})$ to atoms of D. Let σ be applicable to D, and h_1 be a homomorphism that extends h as follows: for each $X_i \in \mathbf{X}$, $h_1(X_i) = h(X_i)$; for each $Z_j \in \mathbf{Z}$, $h_1(Z_j) = z_j$, where z_j is a "fresh" null, i.e., $z_j \in \Delta_N$, z_j does not occur in D, and z_j lexicographically follows all other nulls already introduced. The *application of* σ on D adds to D the atom $h_1(\Psi(\mathbf{X}, \mathbf{Z}))$ if not already in D.

The chase algorithm for a database D and a set of TGDs Σ consists of an exhaustive application of the TGD chase rule in a breadth-first (level-saturating) fashion, which outputs a (possibly infinite) chase for D and Σ. Formally, the *chase of level up to* 0 of D relative to Σ, denoted $chase^0(D, \Sigma)$, is defined as D, assigning to every atom in D the *(derivation) level* 0. For every $k \geqslant 1$, the *chase of level up to* k of D relative to Σ, denoted $chase^k(D, \Sigma)$, is constructed as follows: let $I_1, \ldots, I_n$ be all possible images of bodies of TGDs in Σ relative to some homomorphism such that (i) $I_1, \ldots, I_n \subseteq chase^{k-1}(D, \Sigma)$ and (ii) the highest level of an atom in every I_i is $k-1$; then, perform every corresponding TGD application on $chase^{k-1}(D, \Sigma)$, choosing the applied TGDs and homomorphisms in a (fixed) linear and lexicographic order, respectively, and assigning to every new atom the *(derivation) level* k. The *chase* of D relative to Σ, denoted $chase(D, \Sigma)$, is defined as the limit of $chase^k(D, \Sigma)$ for $k \to \infty$.

The (possibly infinite) chase relative to TGDs is a *universal model*, i.e., there exists a homomorphism from $chase(D, \Sigma)$ onto every $B \in mods(D, \Sigma)$ [7]. This implies that BCQs Q over D and Σ can be evaluated on the chase for D and Σ, i.e., $D \cup \Sigma \models Q$ is equivalent to $chase(D, \Sigma) \models Q$. For guarded TGDs Σ, such BCQs Q can be evaluated on an initial fragment of $chase(D, \Sigma)$ of constant depth $k \cdot |Q|$, which is possible in polynomial time in the data complexity.

Datalog+/– Ontologies. A *Datalog+/– ontology* $O = (D, \Sigma)$, where $\Sigma = \Sigma_T \cup \Sigma_E \cup \Sigma_{NC}$, consists of a database D, a set of TGDs Σ_T, a set of non-conflicting EGDs Σ_E, and a set of negative constraints Σ_{NC}. We say O is *guarded* iff Σ_T is guarded. The following example shows a simple Datalog+/– ontology.

Example 1. Let $O = (D, \Sigma)$ be an ontology describing travel activities:

$$\Sigma = \{museum(X) \to SS(X), park(A) \to SS(A), SS(A) \to act(A),$$
$$relax(X) \to act(X), adv(X) \to act(X), sport(X) \to act(X)\};$$

$$D = \{sport(s_1), sport(s_2), relax(r_1), relax(r_2), adv(a_1),$$
$$adv(a_2), museum(m_1), museum(m_2), park(p_1)\}.$$

This ontology models a very simple travel itinerary domain, which may be used as the underlying model in an online travel agency. Activities can be either sightseeing (e.g., visiting museums or parks), relaxing (e.g., sauna), adventure (e.g., bungee jumping), or sport. The database D provides some instances for each kind of activities.   ∎

3   GPP-Datalog+/–

In this section, we introduce the GPP-Datalog+/– language, an extension of Datalog+/– with both a group preference model and a probabilistic model. To this end, we assume the following sets giving rise to the logical languages for ontologies, preferences, and probability models: Δ_{Ont}, Δ_{Pref}, and Δ_M are finite sets of constants, $\mathcal{R}_{Ont}$, $\mathcal{R}_{Pref}$, and $\mathcal{R}_M$ are finite sets of predicate names such that $\mathcal{R}_M \cap \mathcal{R}_{Ont} = \emptyset$, and $\mathcal{V}_{Ont}$, $\mathcal{V}_{Pref}$, and $\mathcal{V}_M$ are infinite sets of variables. In the following, we assume w.l.o.g. that $\mathcal{R}_{Pref} \subseteq \mathcal{R}_{Ont}$, $\Delta_{Pref} \subseteq \Delta_{Ont}$, $\mathcal{V}_{Pref} \subseteq \mathcal{V}_{Ont}$. We denote the corresponding *Herbrand bases* (the sets of all possible ground atoms) with $\mathcal{H}_{Ont}$, $\mathcal{H}_{Pref}$, and $\mathcal{H}_M$, respectively. Clearly, we have $\mathcal{H}_{Pref} \subseteq \mathcal{H}_{Ont}$, meaning that preference relations are defined over a subset of $\mathcal{H}_{Ont}$.

Group Preference Model. A *preference relation* is any binary relation $\succ \subseteq \mathcal{H}_{Pref} \times \mathcal{H}_{Pref}$. In this paper, we are interested in strict partial orders (SPOs), which are irreflexive and transitive relations — we consider these to be the minimal requirements for a preference relation to be useful in the applications that we envision. One way of specifying such relations that is especially compatible with our approach is the preference formula framework of [8]. A *user preference model* U induces a preference relation over a subset of $\mathcal{H}_{Ont}$, denoted $\succ_U$; in general, we treat $\succ_U$ as a set of ordered pairs. A preference relation $\succ$ is *score-based* iff it is induced by an assignment of a numeric score to each element in such a way that $a_1 \succ a_2$ iff $score(a_1) > score(a_2)$.

In this work, we assume the existence of a *group preference model*, where we intuitively have a group of n users, and each user has an associated preference model.

Definition 1. A *group preference model* $\mathcal{U} = (U_1, \ldots, U_n)$ for $n \geqslant 1$ users is a collection of n user preference models.

Example 2. In the running example, a user may specify a preference relation over the *act* atoms, such as, e.g., shown in Fig. 1 (where we assume the transitive closure of the graphs). For instance, the preferences reflect that the user u_1 is a more sporty person and prefers sport and adventure activities above all other activities. His most preferred activity is $act(s_1)$, i.e., he prefers to practice sport s_1 over all other activities. The group preference model consists of the preferences models of the users u_1, u_2, and u_3. ∎

Probabilistic Model. For modeling uncertainty, we assume the existence of a probabilistic model M that represents a probability distribution $\Pr_M$ over some set $X = \{X_1, \ldots, X_n\}$ of Boolean variables such that there is a 1-to-1 mapping from X to the set of all ground atoms over $\mathcal{R}_M$ and Δ_M. Examples of the type of probabilistic models that we assume in this work are Markov logic and Bayesian networks. The probabilistic extension adopted here was first introduced in [11,10].

We use the standard notions of substitutions and most general unifiers. More specifically, a *substitution* is a mapping from variables to variables or constants. Two sets S and T *unify* via a substitution θ iff $\theta S = \theta T$, where θA denotes the application of θ to all variables in all elements of A (here, θ is a unifier). A *most general unifier (mgu)* is a unifier θ such that for all other unifiers ω, there is a substitution σ such that $\omega = \sigma \circ \theta$.

Definition 2. Let M be a probabilistic model. Then, a *(probabilistic) annotation* λ relative to M is a (finite) set of expressions of the form $A = x$, where (i) A is an atom over $\mathcal{R}_M$, $\mathcal{V}_M$, and Δ_M, and (ii) $x \in \{0, 1\}$. A probabilistic annotation is *valid* iff for any two different $A = x$, $B = y \in \lambda$, there exists no substitution that unifies A and B.

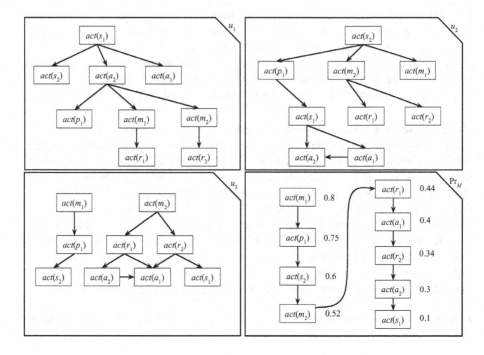

Fig. 1. Group preferences for Example 1

Intuitively, a probabilistic annotation is used to describe the class of events in which the random variables in a probabilistic model M are compatible with the settings of the random variables described by λ, i.e., each X_i has the value x_i. A *(probabilistic) scenario* is a valid probabilistic annotation λ for which $|\lambda| = |X|$ and all $A = x_i \in \lambda$ are such that A is ground. We use $scn(M)$ to denote the set of scenarios in M.

Example 3. Continuing with the running example, suppose that an online trip booking system consults a probabilistic model that assigns probabilities specifying how likely it is that certain events happen. This uncertainty could arise for instance from the fact that the system is aggregating information from multiple sources, which may contain conflicting information, as well as uncertainty due to other factors. Such a system could inform the user of the probability of an activity being recommended at the time of the query by taking into account reviews, crowds, season, etc. The following is an example of how the ontology from Example 1 may be extended by replacing the atoms in the database with formulas of the form: $act(X): \{recommended(X, d) = 1\}$, where $recommended(X, d)$ denotes the probabilistic event that activity X is suitable for the specified date d. Fig. 1 gives an example of such a probability assignment, along with the preference relation as a graph that is induced by these values, assuming that higher probabilities are more preferable. The probabilistic model Pr_M assigns to $act(m_1)$ the highest probability, while it assigns to $act(s_1)$ the lowest. ∎

Preference Merging and Aggregation. There are two challenges encountered in GPP-Datalog+/– ontologies, as seen in Fig. 1. The first challenge is that each user preference model yields a certain precedence relation that might be in disagreement with the one induced by the probabilistic model. The second challenge is that the user preference models may be in disagreement with each other. To address the first challenge, we introduce the notion of *preference merging operators*, which take two preference relations and produce a third one satisfying two basic properties as stated below.

Definition 3. Let $\succ_U$ be an SPO and $\succ_M$ be a score-based preference relation. A *preference merging operator* $\otimes(\succ_U, \succ_M)$ yields a relation $\succ^*$ such that (i) $\succ^*$ is an SPO, and (ii) if $a_1 \succ_U a_2$ and $a_1 \succ_M a_2$, then $a_1 \succ^* a_2$.

The two properties required by Definition 3 are the minimal required to produce a "reasonable" merging of the two relations. To address the second challenge, we define *preference aggregation operators*, which take a set of preference models and produce a new preference model. We next define aggregations of single-user preference models.

Definition 4. Let $\mathcal{U} = (U_1, \ldots, U_n)$ be a group preference model, where every U_i is an SPO. A *preference aggregation operator* $\uplus$ on $\mathcal{U}$ yields an SPO $\succ^*$,

We are now ready to define GPP-Datalog+/– ontologies.

Definition 5. A *GPP-Datalog+/– ontology* has the form $KB = (O, \mathcal{U}, M, \otimes, \uplus)$, where O is a Datalog+/– ontology, $\mathcal{U} = (U_1, \ldots, U_n)$ is a group preference model with $n \geqslant 1$, M is a probabilistic model (with Herbrand bases $\mathcal{H}_{Ont}$, $\mathcal{H}_{Pref}$, and $\mathcal{H}_M$, respectively, such that $\mathcal{H}_{Pref} \subseteq \mathcal{H}_{Ont}$), $\otimes$ is a preference merging operator, and $\uplus$ is the preference aggregation operator. We say that KB is a *guarded* iff O is guarded.

Semantics. The semantics of GPP-Datalog+/– ontologies $KB = (O, \mathcal{U}, M, \otimes, \uplus)$, with $\mathcal{U} = (U_1, \ldots, U_n)$, arises as a direct combination of the semantics of Datalog+/–, the group preference model, and the probabilistic model. As for the probabilistic model, we have that $\Pr_{KB}(a) = \sum_{\lambda \in scn(M),\, O_\lambda \models a} \Pr_M(\lambda)$, and we refer to the score-based preference relation induced by $\Pr_{KB}$ as the *probabilistic preference relation* associated with KB, denoted $\succ_M$. Then, $KB \models a_1 \succ^* a_2$ iff $O \models a_1, a_2$ and $a_1 \succ^* a_2$, where $\succ^* = \uplus(\otimes(\succ_{U_1}, \succ_M), \ldots, \otimes(\succ_{U_n}, \succ_M))$. Intuitively, the consequences of KB are computed in terms of the classical consequences of O, and for each user i, a preference merging operator establishes a new preference over atoms in $\mathcal{H}_{Ont}$ that takes into account both $\succ_{U_i}$ and $\succ_M$; the final preference relation over pairs of atoms in $\mathcal{H}_{Ont}$ is then defined via the preference aggregation operator $\uplus$. In the next section, we study different methods for answering k-rank queries under this aggregation operation.

4   Query Answering in GPP-Datalog+/–

In this section, we concentrate on skyline queries [4], a well-known class of queries that can be issued over preference-based formalisms, and the iterated computation of skyline answers that allows us to assign a *rank* to every atom; we refer to these as k-rank answers. We focus on a special kind of classical queries, called disjunctive atomic queries

(DAQs), which are disjunctions of atoms. We analyze two approaches to computing an answer to a k-rank query that are suitable for partially ordered sets of preferences. In the first one, called *collapse to single user (CSU)*, we reduce the group modeling problem to a single-user problem by creating a single virtual user that is constructed by aggregating the preferences of the individuals from the group – the k-rank is computed over the collapsed preference relation. In the second approach, called *voting-based aggregation*, we first compute the k-rankings according to each individual user and then apply aggregation techniques based on voting strategies (originally developed for quantitative preferences [17]) to aggregate the answers and obtain a single k-ranking.

We now define skyline and k-rank answers to a DAQ in GPP-Datalog+/– ontologies.

Definition 6. Let $KB = (O, \mathcal{U}, M, \otimes, \uplus)$ be a GPP-Datalog+/– ontology, where $\mathcal{U} = (U_1, \ldots, U_n)$, and $Q(\mathbf{X}) = q_1(\mathbf{X}_1) \vee \cdots \vee q_n(\mathbf{X}_n)$ be a DAQ. Then, a *skyline answer* to Q relative to $\succ^* = \uplus(\otimes(\succ_{U_1}, \succ_M), \ldots, \otimes(\succ_{U_n}, \succ_M))$ is any θq_i entailed by O such that no θ' exists with $O \models \theta' q_j$ and $\theta' q_j \succ^* \theta q_i$, where θ and θ' are ground substitutions for the variables in $Q(\mathbf{X})$. For transitive relations, a k-rank answer to Q (where $k \geqslant 0$) is a sequence $S = \langle \theta_1, \ldots \theta_{k'} \rangle$ of maximal length of ground substitutions for the variables in $\mathbf{X}$, built by subsequently appending the skyline answers to Q, removing these atoms from consideration, and repeating the process until either $S = k$ or no more skyline answers to Q remain.

In the sequel, we adopt the following preference merging operator $\otimes_t$ (or simply $\otimes$) to combine individual preferences with those based on scores. Given a relation $\succ_U$, score-based relation $\succ_M$, and value $t \in [0, 1]$ (that allows the user to choose how much influence the probabilistic model has on the output preference relation), the operator works by iterating through all pairs (a, b) of elements in $\succ_U$ and, if (i) $\succ_M$ disagrees with $\succ_U$, (ii) the difference in score is greater than t, and (iii) changing (a, b) to (b, a) does not introduce a cycle in the associated graph then the pair is inserted in reverse order into the output; otherwise, the output contains the same pair as $\succ_U$. Finally, the operator outputs the transitive closure of this relation. The following result shows that the $\otimes_t$ is indeed a preference merging operator.

Proposition 1. Let $\succ_U$ be an SPO, $\succ_M$ be a score-based preference relation, and $t \in [0, 1]$. Then, $\otimes_t$ as defined above is a preference merging operator.

We now explore two different approaches to a preference aggregation operator $\uplus$.

4.1 Collapse to Single User

Under the CSU strategy, the preference relation for all users, along with the probabilistic preference relation, are taken into account in the generation of a new preference relation that encodes the dominant preferences. This single-user preference relation is then used to compute the answers to queries. In the following, for $a, b \in \mathcal{H}_{Ont}$ and SPOs $U_1, \ldots, U_n$, let $\#(a, b) = |\{(a, b) \mid a \succ_{U_i} b \text{ with } 1 \leqslant i \leqslant n\}|$.

Definition 7. Let $U_1, \ldots, U_n$ be $n \geqslant 1$ SPOs. Then, $\uplus(U_1, \ldots, U_n)$ is a set of pairs of ground atoms $a, b \in \mathcal{H}_{Ont}$ such that: (i) $\#(a, b) > \#(b, a)$, and (ii) there does not exist

---

Algorithm 1: AggPrefsCSU($\succ_M, \succ_{U_1}, \ldots, \succ_{U_n}, t$)
Input: SPOs ($\succ_{U_1}, \ldots, \succ_{U_n}$), score-based $\succ_M$ over $\mathcal{H}_{Ont}$, and $t = (t_1, \ldots, t_n) \in [0, 1]^n$.
Output: Preference relation $\succ^* \subseteq \mathcal{H}_{Ont} \times \mathcal{H}_{Ont}$.

  1. Initialize G as an empty graph;
  2. Add as nodes in G all elements appearing in the preference relations $\succ_{U_i}$;
  3. For every user $i \in \{1, \ldots, n\}$ do
  4.   Initialize $currUserG$ as the graph corresponding to $\succ_{U_i}$;
  5.   For every pair $(a, b) \in \succ_{U_i}$ do
  6.   if $(score(b) - score(a) > t_i)$ and changing (a, b) to (b, a)
             in $currUserG$ does not introduce a cycle then
  7.   remove edge (a, b) from $currUserG$ and add edge (b, a);
  8. $currUserG := transitiveClosure(currUserG)$;
  9.   For every edge (s, t) in $currUserG$ do
 10.   if there is no edge (s, t) in G then
 11.   add edge (s, t) to G and label it with 1;
 12.   if there is an edge (s, t) in G and it is labeled with $n \geqslant 1$ then
 13.   increase the label of edge (s, t) in G by 1;
 14.   if there is an edge (t, s) in G and it is labeled with 1 then
 15.   remove edge (s, t) from G;
 16.   if there is an edge (t, s) in G and it is labeled with $n > 1$ then
 17.   decrease the label of edge (t, s) in G by 1;
 18. return $inducedPreferenceRelation(removeCycles(transitiveClosure(G)))$.

Fig. 2. An algorithm for combining the relations in a group preference model with a probabilistic preference relation

$c, d \in \mathcal{H}_{Ont}$ such that $\#(c, d) > \#(d, c)$ and the graph associated with $\uplus(U_1, \ldots, U_n) \cup \{(c, d)\}$ is cycle-free.

Intuitively, $\uplus$ compares the numbers of users in $\mathcal{U}$ that prefer a over b with those that prefer b over a. The following algorithm computes the $\uplus$ operator; below, we provide an algorithm that uses this operator for answering k-rank queries to GPP-Datalog+/– ontologies in polynomial time in the data complexity (modulo the cost of computing probabilities with respect to the probabilistic model M).

Algorithm AggPrefsCSU. The algorithm in Fig. 2 implements a preference aggregation operator using a vector of values $t = (t_1, \ldots, t_n) \in [0, 1]^n$, where t_i defines how much influence user i wishes to assign to the probabilistic model. The output is a new preference relation consisting of the collapsed preferences of all the users. A graph is used as an intermediate data structure representing the collapsed preferences; the nodes of this graph are all the atoms that appear in the preference relations, while the edges are labeled with an integer representing the number of users that have this edge in their individual preference relation. The algorithm iterates through all the users i and, by inspecting all pairs of elements (a, b) in their preference relations, builds the graph output by the $\otimes_t$ operator (lines 6–8), called $currUserG$. Then, before continuing with the next user, the algorithm looks at all the edges in $currUserG$ and updates the general graph G by incrementing or decrementing the edge labels and introducing or removing

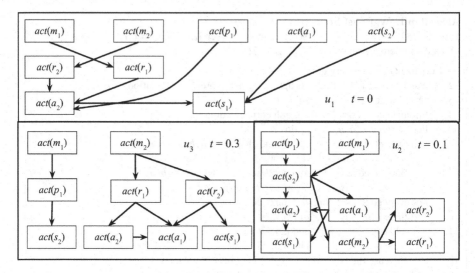

Fig. 3. The merged preference relation obtained for each user. The three graphs show the merging of each individual preference with the probabilistic preference.

edges. After the final iteration of the `for` loop in line 3 the edge labels of G correspond to the number of users that have that edge in their preference relation after combining it with the probabilistic one according to t. The final step of the algorithm computes the transitive closure of the graph and eliminates any cycles by applying the procedure *removeCycles* (note that cycles can arise even though all individual relations are cycle-free). We say that this subroutine does not unnecessarily remove edges if there does not exist an edge e in G such that *removeCycles*$(G) \cup \{e\}$ does not contain cycles.

Example 4. Consider again the running example. Fig. 3 shows the result of the individual mergings of the preference relation for each user with the score-based relation using $t = 0$ for u_1, $t = 0.1$ for u_2, and $t = 0.3$ for u_3. Fig. 4 shows the final collapsed graph. Consider the atoms $act(a_1)$ and $act(a_2)$ in this graph. Observe that the user u_2 prefers $act(a_1)$ to $act(a_2)$ after merging with $\succ_M$, but the user u_3 maintains that $act(a_2)$ is preferable (although $act(a_1) \succ_M act(a_2)$, the threshold for u_3 is higher than the difference in probability). Therefore, there is no edge between $act(a_1)$ and $act(a_2)$ in the final graph, since these two results cancel each other out. ∎

The following theorem states several properties satisfied by the output of AggPref-sCSU under certain conditions: (i) the output is an SPO, (ii) if all preference relations (including the probabilistic one) agree on the ordering of a pair of atoms, then the same ordering appears in the output, and (iii) for $t = 0^n$, the output only depends on the ordering given by $\succ_M$ (and not on the actual probabilities).

Theorem 1. *Let* $KB = (O, \mathcal{U}, M, \otimes, \uplus)$ *be a GPP-Datalog+/– ontology, where* $\mathcal{U} = (U_1, \ldots, U_n)$, *let* Q *be a DAQ,* $k \geqslant 1$, *and* $t = (t_1, \ldots, t_n) \in [0,1]^n$. *Let* $\succ^* =$ Agg-PrefsCSU$(\succ_M, \succ_{U_1}, \ldots, \succ_{U_n}, t)$. *Then, (i) if removeCycles preserves transitivity, then*

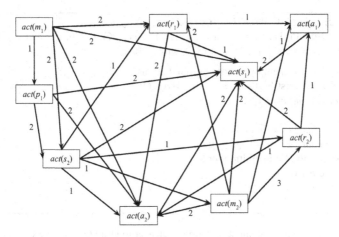

Fig. 4. Collapse to single user graph

$\succ^*$ *is an SPO; (ii) if removeCycles only removes edges* (v_1, v_2) *whenever there does not exist another edge in the cycle labeled with a lower number then, given* $a_1, a_2 \in \mathcal{H}_{Ont}$ *such that for all* $U_i \in \mathcal{U}$, *it holds that* $(a_1, a_2) \in \otimes_{t_i}(\succ_{U_i}, \succ_M)$, *then we have that* $a_1 \succ^* a_2$; *and (iii) if* M' *is a probabilistic model such that* $\succ_M = \succ_{M'}$ *and* $t = 0^n$, *then* $\succ^* = \mathsf{AggPrefsCSU}(\succ_{M'}, \succ_{U_1}, \ldots, \succ_{U_n}, t)$.

Algorithm k-Rank-CSU. We now present an algorithm to compute k-rank answers according to Definitions 6 and 7; we also analyze its correctness as well as running time when used in conjunction with the $\mathsf{AggPrefsCSU}$ algorithm. Fig. 5 shows the pseudocode for the algorithm, which begins by computing for every user the combination of the two preference relations in the GPP-Datalog+/– ontology and the necessary finite part of the chase relative to Q. The main while-loop iterates through the process of computing the skyline answers to Q relative to this new relation by using a *computeSkyline* subroutine (which can be implemented by means of a linear-time scan of C), updating the result by appending these answers in arbitrary order, and removing the atoms in the result from C. Once the loop is finished, the algorithm returns the first k results, since the last iteration may add superfluous elements.

Example 5. Consider the running example, with $Q = act(X)$, $k = 5$, and $(t_1, t_2, t_3) = (0, 0.1, 0.3)$. One possible k-rank answer to Q (in atom form) as computed by the algorithm is: $\langle act(m_1), act(p_1), act(s_2), act(m_2), act(r_2) \rangle$. ∎

The following theorem proves the correctness of the k-Rank-CSU algorithm, and it shows that it runs in polynomial time under certain conditions.

Theorem 2. *Let* $KB = (O, \mathcal{U}, M, \otimes, \uplus)$ *be a GPP-Datalog+/– ontology, Q be a DAQ, and $k \geqslant 0$. If O is a guarded Datalog+/– ontology and the removeCycles subroutine does not unnecessarily remove any edges, then Algorithm k-Rank-CSU correctly computes k-rank answers to Q in $O(poly(|D|) \cdot S + C)$ time in the data complexity, where S is the cost of computing $score(a) = \Pr_{KB}(a)$ for any atom a such that $O \models a$, and C is the cost of removeCycles.*

Algorithm 2: k-Rank-CSU$(KB = (O, \mathcal{U}, M, \otimes, \uplus), Q, k, t)$
Input: Guarded GPP-Datalog+/– ontology KB, DAQ $Q(\mathbf{X})$, $t \in [0,1]^n$, and $k \geqslant 0$.
Output: k-rank answer $\langle a_1, \ldots, a_{k'} \rangle$ to Q, with $k' \leqslant k$.

 1. Initialize Res as an empty vector of ground atoms;
 2. Set $\succ^* :=$ AggPrefsCSU$(\succ_M, \succ_{U_1}, \ldots, \succ_{U_n}, t)$;
 3. $C :=$ computeChase(O, Q);
 4. $i := k$;
 5. While $i > 0$ and $C \neq \emptyset$ do
 6. $S :=$ computeSkyline$(C, Q, \succ^*)$;
 7.   Append S to Res in arbitrary order;
 8.   Remove S from C;
 9. $i := i - |S|$;
10. Return $truncate(Res, k)$.

Fig. 5. An algorithm for computing a k-rank answer to DAQ Q using the CSU strategy

Note that the running time depends on the cost of the *removeCycles* subroutine. Though cycles can be removed in polynomial time, depending on the properties that we wish the output of this subroutine to satisfy, the actual cost may vary considerably.

4.2 Voting-Based Preference Aggregation

As an alternative to the approach described in the previous section, we now briefly discuss specific strategies that can be used to combine the answers to k-rank queries computed individually for each user based on a small set of well-known voting mechanisms from the social choice literature. Recall that this is essentially different from the CSU approach above, where a single k-ranking is computed from a preference relation distilled from all the users' individual preferences. We consider the following voting mechanisms: *plurality voting*, where each user votes for their top-preferred items, the items' frequency for all the users are summed up, and the items with highest number of votes win; the *least misery* strategy first removes from consideration the elements that are the least preferred by each user, and then applies plurality voting — the idea behind it is that a group is as happy as its least happy member; in the *average without misery* strategy, the least misery approach is generalized by removing the t least liked elements for each member (instead of just one); and the *fairness strategy*, which is often applied when people try to fairly divide a set of items — one person chooses first, then another, until everyone has made one choice, and next, everybody chooses a second item, often starting with the person who had to choose last on the previous round; an advantage of this strategy is that the top items from all individuals are always selected.

Integrating the voting-based aggregation strategies presented above into an algorithm for computing k-rank answers can be done by leveraging the k-Rank-CSU algorithm from the previous section: an answer can then be computed by calling k-Rank-CSU for each individual user (this will only merge the individual preferences of each user with the score-based relation — i.e., this step implements the application of the $\otimes_t$ merging operator). Since rankings are total orders, we can think of them as preference relations; therefore, the aggregation strategy chosen will lead to a specific implementation of the

⊎ preference aggregation operator: plurality voting will simply tally the number of votes received for each atom from the individual rankings. If a *misery* strategy is used, then it is necessary to identify all the nodes that are undesired for each user and mark them as unavailable before obtaining the individual rankings. On the other hand, if *fairness* is adopted, it is necessary to iterate through the 1-rank answers to the query for each user, and directly build the output k-tuple. The following corollary to Theorem 2 states that k-rank answers to DAQs using voting-based aggregation, as discussed above, can be computed in polynomial time in the data complexity.

Corollary 1. *Let $KB = (O, \mathcal{U}, M, \otimes, \uplus)$ be a GPP-Datalog+/− ontology, Q be a DAQ, and $k \geqslant 0$. If O is guarded, and the voting-based aggregation $\uplus$ can be computed in polynomial time in the data complexity, then a k-rank answer to Q using voting-based aggregation can be computed in $O(poly(|D|) \cdot S)$ time in the data complexity, where S is the cost of computing $score(a) = \Pr_{KB}(a)$ for any atom a such that $O \models a$.*

Here, the computational cost depends on the implementation of the voting strategies, which can clearly be computed in polynomial time in the data complexity for the strategies discussed above, and the computational cost of calling k-Rank-CSU for each user. Since k-Rank-CSU is only ever called with a single user, cycles can never arise; this is why the C factor from Theorem 2 does not appear.

5   Summary and Outlook

In this paper, we have proposed an extension of the Datalog+/− ontology language that allows for dealing with both partially ordered preferences of groups of users and probabilistic uncertainty. We have focused on answering k-rank queries in this context. In detail, we have presented different operators to compute group preferences as a merging and an aggregation of the preferences of single users with probability-based preferences and with each other, respectively. We have then provided algorithms to answer k-rank queries for DAQs (disjunctions of atomic queries) under these group preferences. We have shown that, under certain reasonable conditions, such DAQ answering in Datalog+/− can be done in polynomial time in the data complexity.

Current and future work involves implementing and testing the GPP-Datalog+/− framework. Furthermore, we want to explore which of the merging/aggregation operators is similar to human judgment and thus well-suited as a general default merging/aggregation operator for search and query answering in the Social Semantic Web.

Acknowledgments. This work was supported by the Engineering and Physical Sciences Research Council (EPSRC) grant EP/J008346/1 "PrOQAW: Probabilistic Ontological Query Answering on the Web", the European Research Council (FP7/2007-2013)/ERC grant 246858 ("DIADEM"), by a Yahoo! Research Fellowship, and by a Google European Doctoral Fellowship.

References

1. Ackerman, M., Choi, S.Y., Coughlin, P., Gottlieb, E., Wood, J.: Elections with partially ordered preferences. Public Choice (2012)

2. Amer-Yahia, S., Roy, S.B., Chawla, A., Das, G., Yu, C.: Group recommendation: Semantics and efficiency. Proc. VLDB Endow. 2(1), 754–765 (2009)
3. Beeri, C., Vardi, M.Y.: The implication problem for data dependencies. In: Even, S., Kariv, O. (eds.) ICALP 1981. LNCS, vol. 115, pp. 73–85. Springer, Heidelberg (1981)
4. Börzsönyi, S., Kossmann, D., Stocker, K.: The skyline operator. In: Proc. ICDE 2001, pp. 421–430. IEEE Computer Society (2001)
5. Brafman, R.I., Domshlak, C.: Preference handling — An introductory tutorial. AI. Mag. 30(1), 58–86 (2009)
6. Calì, A., Gottlob, G., Kifer, M.: Taming the infinite chase: Query answering under expressive relational constraints. In: Proc. KR 2008, pp. 70–80. AAAI Press (2008)
7. Calì, A., Gottlob, G., Lukasiewicz, T.: A general Datalog-based framework for tractable query answering over ontologies. J. Web Sem. 14, 57–83 (2012)
8. Chomicki, J.: Preference formulas in relational queries. ACM Trans. Database Syst. 28(4), 427–466 (2003)
9. Finger, M., Wassermann, R., Cozman, F.G.: Satisfiability in $\mathcal{EL}$ with sets of probabilistic ABoxes. In: Proc. DL 2011. CEUR-WS.org (2011)
10. Gottlob, G., Lukasiewicz, T., Martinez, M.V., Simari, G.I.: Query answering under probabilistic uncertainty in Datalog+/– ontologies. Ann. Math. Artif. Intell. (in press, 2013)
11. Gottlob, G., Lukasiewicz, T., Simari, G.I.: Answering threshold queries in probabilistic Datalog+/– ontologies. In: Benferhat, S., Grant, J. (eds.) SUM 2011. LNCS, vol. 6929, pp. 401–414. Springer, Heidelberg (2011)
12. Jung, J.C., Lutz, C.: Ontology-based access to probabilistic data with OWL QL. In: Cudré-Mauroux, P., et al. (eds.) ISWC 2012, Part I. LNCS, vol. 7649, pp. 182–197. Springer, Heidelberg (2012)
13. Lang, J., Pini, M.S., Rossi, F., Salvagnin, D., Venable, K.B., Walsh, T.: Winner determination in voting trees with incomplete preferences and weighted votes. Auton. Agent. Multi-Ag. 25(1), 130–157 (2012)
14. Linden, G., Smith, B., York, J.: Industry report: Amazon.com recommendations: Item-to-item collaborative filtering. IEEE Distributed Systems Online 4(1) (2003)
15. Lukasiewicz, T., Martinez, M.V., Orsi, G., Simari, G.I.: Heuristic ranking in tightly coupled probabilistic description logics. In: Proc. UAI 2012, pp. 554–563. AUAI Press (2012)
16. Manoj, M., Jacob, E.: Information retrieval on internet using meta-search engines: A review. Journal of Scientific and Industrial Research 67(10), 739–746 (2008)
17. Masthoff, J.: Group modeling: Selecting a sequence of television items to suit a group of viewers. User Modeling and User-Adapted Interaction 14(1), 37–85 (2004)
18. Morris, M.R.: Collaborative search revisited. In: Proc. CSCW 2013, pp. 1181–1192. ACM Press (2013)
19. Noessner, J., Niepert, M.: ELOG: A probabilistic reasoner for OWL EL. In: Rudolph, S., Gutierrez, C. (eds.) RR 2011. LNCS, vol. 6902, pp. 281–286. Springer, Heidelberg (2011)
20. Ntoutsi, I., Stefanidis, K., Norvag, K., Kriegel, H.-P.: gRecs: A group recommendation system based on user clustering. In: Lee, S.-G., Peng, Z., Zhou, X., Moon, Y.-S., Unland, R., Yoo, J. (eds.) DASFAA 2012, Part II. LNCS, vol. 7239, pp. 299–303. Springer, Heidelberg (2012)
21. Pattanaik, P.K.: Voting and Collective Choice: Some Aspects of the Theory of Group Decision-making. Cambridge University Press (1971)
22. Pini, M.S., Rossi, F., Venable, K.B., Walsh, T.: Aggregating partially ordered preferences. J. Log. Comput. 19(3), 475–502 (2009)
23. Taylor, A.D.: Social Choice and the Mathematics of Manipulation. Cambridge University Press (2005)
24. Wooldridge, M.: An Introduction to Multiagent Systems. Wiley (2009)

Towards an Integrated Social Semantic Web

Antonio Maccioni

Università Roma Tre, Rome, Italy
maccioni@dia.uniroma3.it

Abstract. The Social Semantic Web is the data space on the Web where human produced information are enriched and modeled using Semantic Web standards. This vision is enabled by the convergence between Web 2.0 and Web 3.0 but still, it's far from be put into practice. Moreover, this miss causes drawbacks such as data redundancies and overhead in the development of social applications. In this paper we discuss how, in pursuing the Social Semantic Web vision, a different approach for opening social data to the Semantic Web should be adopted. Furthermore, without reinventing the wheel, we will use existing technologies to define a framework for integrating Social Web and Semantic Web. This would help to reengineer or extend the Social Network infrastructures in order to fully benefit from a social Semantic Web.

1 Introduction

Social networking provides services that we could not even imagine few years ago. A Social Network (SN) is commonly intended as a communication platform such as Facebook,[1] Twitter[2] or Linkedin[3] but, more generally, they are all the applications that foster collaborative and participative behaviour of profiled human users. Users in a SN can easily interact to each other in order to achieve a goal. For example, let us consider a Social CRM[4] where customer care activities are managed by customers themselves.

The interactions within a SN produce huge amount of meaningful data. The aim to formalize the meaning of such data in order to allow machines to understand and process the data has led to the concept of Social Semantic Web (SSW) [3]. SSW inherits principles and methodologies from Semantic Web (SW), the global knowledge base where data is freely available on the Web and semantically organized through the so called ontologies of reference, described with RDF and "linked" to other data. The Semantic Web is fed by organizations and practitioners that transform or, in rare cases, produce natively RDF data to publish on the Web following the Linked Data principles [2]. This approach works well if conducted by Semantic Web experts, but it is impractical for non

---

[1] www.facebook.com
[2] www.twitter.com
[3] www.linkedin.com
[4] Customer Relationship Management.

Q.Z. Sheng and J. Kjeldskov (Eds.): ICWE 2013 Workshops, LNCS 8295, pp. 207–214, 2013.

expert users (e.g., also SN users). Efforts have been made by people to make social Data available on the Web, but they make the data loose of authenticity and become easily obsolete. In fact, the common approach works well on static data (e.g., historical data) as it is noticeable from the Linked Open Data initiative[5] , but it is not the best option for dynamic and evolving social data.

For social data we can count, at most, on series of APIs that SNs expose to engage developers. In this way we can obtain social data that is usually structured by using JSON or XML formats. These data are rarely compliant to Semantic Web standards and, if published, generate ambiguities and replications. For example, let us consider when a user has to add the same personal information in all the social networks he registers to. Another paradoxical case is when SNs refer to each other as when we insert on the Linkedin profile our Twitter ID and vice versa. By using the identification principle of Semantic Web, we could easily refer to the same resource identifier (i.e. an URI representing ourself) when inserting our personal information and an application can get from the Web our public information including related profiles. This is possible when the application knows a reference ontology (e.g., FOAF) to model and query such kind of information.

In this paper we review the current state of the Social Semantic Web, showing its main drawbacks and we depict a framework where Social Web and Semantic Web are integrated with each other using existing technologies. Very little efforts can be made by SN players to implement the forementioned framework. These efforts may consist on: (i) refining data and application standards for SNs, (ii) extending and adopting existing ontologies and (iii) deploying a Semantic Web infrastructure for each SN. Then, this framework can be used to reengineer SN infrastructures in order to natively take advantage of the Semantic Web. Note that, at the current state of the art, there are interesting attempts, such as the Social Graph[6] (promoted by Facebook and implemented through the Open Graph), to enrich the SSW but they are not very effective as our proposed framework.

The main benefits to share a SSW framework of reference are:

- easier integration among SN applications;
- higher social data quality;
- empowering of Social Network Analysis (SNA) that is the area which tries to infer information from SN data (e.g., a classic example of SNA is the problem to find, over a SN, a team of experts on a certain topic). If the SN data are available in a public space and connected to other related available data, SNA can exploit the surrounding information to infer more knowledge;
- enabling the creation of services in the context of smart cities, where applications exploit data in a smart way to provide useful services to citizens. Let us imagine services like automatic recruitment (that can be done by matching people's info with job requests), personalized event or activity recomendation, etc.

---

[5] lod-cloud.net/

[6] en.wikipedia.org/wiki/Social_graph

We will show, by analysing real case scenarios, the validity of the proposed solution.

The rest of the paper is organized as follows. Section 2 discusses the current state of the Social Semantic Web pointing out its drawbacks. In Section 3 we illustrate the proposed framework to integrate Web 2.0 with Web 3.0 and in Section 4 we show how this SSW framework is beneficial in real case scenarios. Finally, Section 5 sketches conclusions and future works.

2   The Current Social Semantic Web

In this section we review the current state of the Social Semantic Web in the perspective of whom, in order to design new services, has to exploit SSW data.

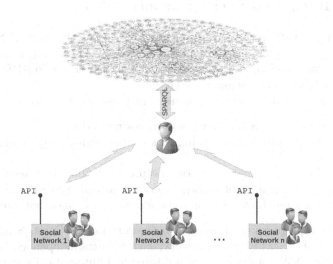

Fig. 1. The current Social Semantic Web

Fig. 1 helps to understand the scenario. We have many social networks (i.e. SocialNetwork$_1$, SocialNetwork$_2$, ... SocialNetwork$_n$) providing a set of APIs. An user (i.e. in the middle of Fig. 1) can use these APIs to retrieve social network's data. The user can also exploit the Semantic Web (i.e. the graph cloud on the top of Fig. 1) information and integrate them with API calls' results. Actually, the user is implementing an ad-hoc integration of the Social Semantic Web consisting in the following steps:

1. query all the SNs through API calls and retrieve data from the SW (e.g., through SPARQL);
2. transform data into a common interoperable format;
3. integrate data by using matching and similarity techniques.

For instance, let us consider the concrete case in which a user wants to mashup social and encyclopedic information from three data sources: Flickr[7] , Facebook and DBPedia[8] [1] (i.e., the linked data extracted from Wikipedia[9]). To do so, we have to query the Flickr APIs[10] to return data in one of the following formats: REST, XML-RPC, SOAP, JSON or serialized PHP. Facebook data can be extracted in several ways: with the Open Graph APIs[11] or through the FQL[12] (Facebook Query Language). The user can obtain DBPedia data from its SPARQL endpoint[13] in different formats (e.g., XML, CSV, JSON). Finally, the integration of all the data is computed to employ the service.

It is easy to notice that the computational load of this process is heavy and the software engineer has to learn different API usages. He could use a single SPARQL query over the Semantic Web to obtain in one shot all the useful data for the service. This integrated vision will be explained in the next section.

3   The Integrated Social Semantic Web

In the previous section we have seen that, to exploit the current SSW, it is required to go through many subsequent steps. To avoid this long chain of steps, volunteer users transform data that they get from SN APIs into RDF data, that then they publish on the Semantic Web.

This approach, led by volunteer users, fails under many aspects:

- social data evolves faster than these transformed data;
- infrastructures provided by volunteers cannot manage high computational load;
- most of the times a single user does not provide a "fully furnished" SW platform (e.g., exploiting content negotiation or providing SPARQL endpoints);
- data coming from different social networks are, sometimes, not interoperable.

This section proposes an integrated framework for the Social Semantic Web as depicted in Fig. 2. In this framework, each SN acts independently from the others but the SSW data is natively produced and automatically integrated.

The technologies and tools that we use for this framework are:

- OpenSocial[14] : it is a formal model to represent social application primitives. It was initially proposed by Google[15] and MySpace[16] in order to standardize back-ends of social applications.

---

[7]   www.flickr.com
[8]   dbpedia.org/
[9]   www.wikipedia.org/
[10]   www.flickr.com/services/api/
[11]   developers.facebook.com/docs/reference/opengraph/action-type
[12]   developers.facebook.com/docs/technical-guides/fql/
[13]   dbpedia.org/sparql
[14]   opensocial.org/
[15]   www.google.com/
[16]   www.myspace.com/

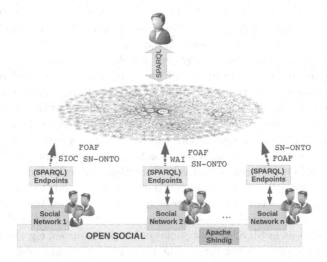

Fig. 2. The Integrated Social Semantic Web

- Apache Shindig[17] : it is the reference implementation of OpenSocial. It is a container for hosting social applications (both client and server side) which implements primitives to manage: user profiles, user relationships, user activities, user authentications, user authorizations, etc.
- FOAF ontology: is a very famous ontology to represent personal data and relationships among people.
- WAI (Who Am I) Ontology[18] : is an ontology that extends FOAF considering that a person can have multiple roles and multiple profiles.
- SIOC [4] ontology: is an ontology to represent information of online communities (blogs, wikis, forums, mailing lists, etc.) and their relationships.
- VCARD ONTOLOGY[19] : is an ontology derived from the IETF standard for business cards and, therefore, it allows to represent personal information such as company affiliations.
- SPARQL endpoint: is a Web service that is able (i) to receive SPARQL queries over HTTP, (ii) to process them and (iii) to convey the answers back to the user.

Social Network players should agree on this framework and on these technologies in order to extend their own existing infrastructures. This is analogous to the schema.org[20] project where search engine players formed a consortium to define common metadata to embed within Web pages (by using microformats or RDFa) in order to make understand the Web contents to the crawlers.

---

[17] shindig.apache.org/
[18] vocab.ctic.es/wai/wai.html
[19] www.w3.org/TR/vcard-rdf/
[20] schema.org/

By adopting this framework, SN players can natively feed the Semantic Web with their social data. Still, a little effort has to be made in the development of a common model to represent Social Web data.

Let us call this model *Social Network ontology* (`sn-onto`). We propose, in order to agree on the specifications of `sn-onto`, the way tracked by SIOC-A (SIOC in Action) [5]. SIOC-A extends SIOC considering active communities. Basically, it embeds the concept of *action* (i.e. `sioca:Action`) within SIOC. Since OpenSocial primitives already consider the dinamicity and the actions performed within a social application, the Social Network ontology should join (re-using the existing concepts, when possible) concepts from: SIOC, SIOC-A, FOAF and the OpenSocial primitives. Note that an activity-centric ontology reflects the dinamicity of SNs and SN data, in opposition to the staticity of other domains where the current approach to open data on the Semantic Web works well. In particular, the elements connected to `sioca:Action` should not be general artifacts as in SIOC-A, but social network resources, e.g., instances of a possible class `sn-onto:SNResource`. Then, each SN can implement subconcepts of `sn-onto:SNResource` according to its domain. For example, these resources can be posts, tweets, etc. Similarly, also the actions (i.e. `sioca:Action`) can be specialized according to the domain of reference, e.g., like, comment, retweet, etc.

Furthermore, SNs could exploit the SSW very smartly, exploiting and computing linking of data already on the Web. For example, let us consider a SN user that likes a Wikipedia page. From this action, we can automatically extract the DBPedia [1] resource corresponding to the Wikipedia page and then link the SN user URI to the DBPedia resource by using a property of `sn-onto`. Then, for example, another SN can exploit this information to recomend readings to the user.

A similar case can happen georeferencing objects: they can be automatically linked to geographic datasets such as Geonames[21] . Note that these linkings would be impossible to obtain if left to be generated by single users.

4   Real Case Scenarios

In this section we consider real case scenarios in order to validate our framework with a proof of concept. In particular, two scenarios will be considered as follows.

4.1   Music Domain

Nowadays many musical social networks and musical applications exist: Last.fm[22] , Spotify[23] , Jamendo[24] , SoundCloud[25] , Deezer[26] just to mention

---

[21]   www.geonames.org/

[22]   www.lastfm.it/

[23]   www.spotify.com

[24]   www.jamendo.com/

[25]   soundcloud.com/

[26]   www.deezer.com/

the most famous. They have data representing artists (name, origin, members, genre, etc.) and their production (albums, songs, etc.). All of these SNs provide APIs to developers in order to make them implement additional features. Even if some of the SNs built its own database gathering metadata of user's MP3 files, noone of those SNs provide directly their datasets.

The DBTune project[27] has published on the Semantic Web data extracted from Last.fm and Jamendo. The project has also published an RDF version of MusicBrainz [10], the open music encyclopedia, that is now considered an hub within the SW, since several music datasets refer to it. DBTune datasets have been linked to other famous datasets such as Geonames and DBPedia.

Another important step in the music domain of the Semantic Web has been already accomplished: the creation of an ontology of reference, the Music Ontology [9]. DBTune already uses this ontology to model the data.

In this scenario, we can notice that each SN creates the database from scratch and that the content of these databases are not aligned. Moreover, they do not make use of the music ontology. Clearly, all of them would benefit from the use of a common dataset with a common data model. For example, since they exploit users listenings in order to provide suggestions on similar artists, they could, sharing the data, recomend an artist that a user has listened from another social network.

4.2 Research Publications Domain

There exists social networks that make use of scientific publications, e.g., Linkedin (the SN for professionals) and ResearchGate[28] (the SN for researchers). The author has to add his publications manually in each SN.

This is quite absurd because there exist a large number of databases of scientific publications that could be exploited: Arnetminer[29] , DBLP[30] , the ACM repository[31] , the IEEE repository[32] , Google Scholar[33] . All of them work as data silos and are not officially shared on the Semantic Web. Moreover, they are also highly inconsistent among each other as we can notice by the number of publications that an author has in each database. As a result, for each author, the number of citations and parameters such as the h-index change across the databases.

Some of the above mentioned databases have a non-official RDF version, but if there was a common official database on the Web, publications and authors could be addressed with the same URI and exploited by all the applications, including SNs.

---

[27] dbtune.org/
[28] www.researchgate.net/
[29] arnetminer.org/
[30] www.informatik.uni-trier.de/~ley/db/
[31] www.acm.org/
[32] www.ieee.org/
[33] scholar.google.it/

5   Conclusions and Future Work

In this paper, we showed that existing technologies can be employed to pursue the vision of the Social Semantic Web. In this vision Social Web and Semantic Web are integrated to exploit benefits of both of them at the same time. There exists other aspects of the SSW left outside the framework presented in this paper such as the management of folksonomies (e.g., folksonomies generated from SNs, such as delicious[34] , to be integrated automatically on the SW) or the semantic extraction from text [8] (e.g., extraction of knowledge from SNs such as Quora[35]). They will be considered in future work. Other future work are represented by the adaptation of new emerging applications based on social data such as RandomDB [6] or the use of social aspects applied to existing Semantic Web problems such as the keyword search [7].

References

1. Auer, S., Bizer, C., Kobilarov, G., Lehmann, J., Cyganiak, R., Ives, Z.G.: DBpedia: A nucleus for a web of open data. In: Aberer, K., et al. (eds.) ASWC 2007 and ISWC 2007. LNCS, vol. 4825, pp. 722–735. Springer, Heidelberg (2007)
2. Berners-Lee, T.: Design issues: Linked data (2006)
3. Breslin, J., Passant, A., Decker, S.: The Social Semantic Web. Springer, Heidelberg (2009)
4. Breslin, J.G., Harth, A., Bojars, U., Decker, S.: Towards semantically-interlinked online communities. In: Gómez-Pérez, A., Euzenat, J. (eds.) ESWC 2005. LNCS, vol. 3532, pp. 500–514. Springer, Heidelberg (2005)
5. Champin, P.A., Passant, A.: Sioc in action representing the dynamics of online communities. In: I-SEMANTICS (2010)
6. De Virgilio, R., Maccioni, A.: Generation of reliable randomness via social phenomena. In: Cuzzocrea, A., Maabout, S. (eds.) MEDI 2013. LNCS, vol. 8216, pp. 65–77. Springer, Heidelberg (2013)
7. De Virgilio, R., Maccioni, A., Cappellari, P.: A linear and monotonic strategy to keyword search over RDF data. In: Daniel, F., Dolog, P., Li, Q. (eds.) ICWE 2013. LNCS, vol. 7977, pp. 338–353. Springer, Heidelberg (2013)
8. Gangemi, A.: A comparison of knowledge extraction tools for the semantic web. In: Cimiano, P., Corcho, O., Presutti, V., Hollink, L., Rudolph, S. (eds.) ESWC 2013. LNCS, vol. 7882, pp. 351–366. Springer, Heidelberg (2013)
9. Raimond, Y., Abdallah, S.A., Sandler, M.B., Giasson, F.: The music ontology. In: ISMIR, pp. 417–422 (2007)
10. Swartz, A.: Musicbrainz: A semantic web service. IEEE Intelligent Systems 17(1), 76–77 (2002)

---

[34]   delicious.com/

[35]   www.quora.com/

Recommending Experts
for Collaboration in Mashup Development

Valeria De Antonellis and Michele Melchiori

Dept. of Information Engineering, University of Brescia
Via Branze, 38 - 25123 Brescia, Italy
{deantone,melchior}@ing.unibs.it

Abstract. Mashup development is currently powered by Web sites, as ProgrammableWeb and Mashape, that offer large, continuously updated and growing, catalogues of software components accessible through Web APIs. Developing Web mashup is becoming attracting for developing Web and enterprise applications, but it requires specialized knowledge about Web APIs, their technologies and the way to combine them. In this paper, firstly we discuss how social-based semantic approaches can support the phases of mashup development. Then, we describe our framework LINKSMAN (LINKed data Supported MAshup collaboratioN) for expert search in enterprise mashup development based on integrating knowledge both internal and external to enterprises.

1 Introduction

Web mashup is nowadays a popular approach for implementing Web applications leveraging on third party functionalities and data. The approach is powered by Web sites offering large, ever growing, catalogues of software components accessible through Web APIs (e.g., ProgrammableWeb, Mashape). On the one hand, this availability of Web APIs makes mashup interesting also for enterprises [5]. On the other hand, developing mashups requires specialized knowledge about Web APIs, their technologies and the way to combine them in a meaningful way. This kind of knowledge can be available in an organization, but distributed among various experts. An opportunity in this sense is to take advantage of Enterprise 2.0 that is a recent specialization of the Web 2.0 social-based technologies to the enterprise needs and requirements.

In this paper, firstly we discuss how social-based semantic approaches can support the different mashup development phases. Then, we discuss the specific role of our framework LINKSMAN (LINKed data Supported MAshup collaboratioN) for expert search in enterprise mashup development.

In general, expert search systems aim at identifying candidate experts with respect to a topic of interest and ranking them with respect to the expertise level based on available sources of evidence, typically document contents. On the contrary, the work [8] discusses the potential benefits and drawbacks of using Linked Open Data (LOD) as sources for expert search. The authors analyze what is currently present and missing in various LOD datasets w.r.t. different

Q.Z. Sheng and J. Kjeldskov (Eds.): ICWE 2013 Workshops, LNCS 8295, pp. 215–222, 2013.
© Springer International Publishing Switzerland 2013

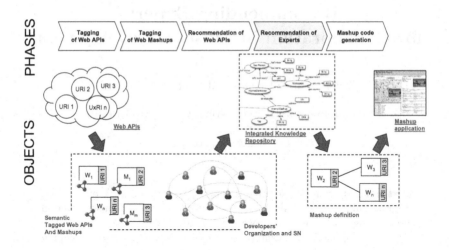

Fig. 1. Integrated Development of Mashups

kinds of expert search. The authors in [6] remark that in the existing expert search approaches there are several flaws related to the lack of focus on realistic applications and limitations to consider a single data source. Supporting the collaboration inside organizations modeled as P2P networks and the contribution that semantics can give to the problem have been tackled in the framework proposed in [7]. With respect to expert search approaches for general purposes, LINKSMAN specializes in enterprise mashup development and exploits in an integrated way knowledge that is both private internal to the enterprise and external. In LINKSMAN, the internal knowledge mainly concerns developers, their organization inside the enterprise, their social connections and software artifacts they have developed. To this purpose, we adopt ProgrammableWeb[1] as external source because this site is actually one of the most updated and popular for mashup development. External knowledge concerns mashups and Web APIs from public Web APIs repositories.

This paper is organized as it follows. In Section 2 we present a the integrated development scenario and identify its use cases. In Section 3 the models for the internal and external knowledge are given. In Section 4 we identify the collaboration patterns and provide suitable metrics for implementing them. Finally, Section 5 provides final remarks and future work.

2   Integrated Mashup Development Scenario

In order to clarify the problem, let us consider a developer working for the marketing department of an enterprise, who has to build an application to visualize,

---

[1] See http://www.programmableweb.com: the last access on May 20th, 2013 counts more than 9,100 Web APIs and 7000 mashups.

on an interactive map, information about potential markets, sales and demographic data. This application can be obtained by composing functionalities and data that are made available by means of Web APIs. To this aim suitable Web APIs have to be selected (for example, the GeoData Demographics API, that provides demographic data for a given zone) from public repositories and possibly integrated with private components. This selection activity may exploit advanced search techniques [1,3]. However, using the selected Web APIs in order to build an application may be difficult because of the need to understand their syntax, semantics and data formats. In this context, it is frequent that a developer searches for advices and collaboration with other developers of the same enterprise. Moreover, it is reasonable to assume that her preference is for experts that she can contact/involve because some social or organizational contacts exist with them.

Integrated Development Approach. In our approach we identify different phases of development of mashups and involved objects as represented in Fig. 1. Our purpose is to support the developer along the mashup lifecycle represented by these phases. In a repository like ProgrammableWeb, Web APIs and mashups are described in terms of URIs, descriptions, categories, tags and technical features (protocols, data formats and security features). This characterization is further enriched in our approach by associating Web APIs and mashups with semantic tags (*Tagging of Web APIs* and *Tagging of Mashups* phases, in the figure) according to the framework described in [2]. The approach has been extended in [4] where we provided a framework based on different Web API features to support Web API search and reuse in enterprise mashup design. Based on semantically tagged Web APIs and Mashups we define different kinds of Web API request, as detailed in the use cases described below, to support the *Recommendation of Web APIs* phase. Concerning involved developers, we model their organization and social network. This knowledge is integrated with knowledge about Web APIs and mashups and made available as *Integrated Knowledge Repository*. On this repository, we define a framework for the *Recommendation of Experts*, that is the focus in this paper, with the purpose to advice the developer with experts inside the organization that can be involved or give advices on the design and code writing of the mashup.

Use cases. Concerning supporting a developer in the phases above described, we identified three main use cases for mashup development (see Fig. 2): (i) developing a new mashup, (ii) completing an existing mashup with functionalities provided by additional Web APIs, and (iii) substitution of a Web API in an existing mashup with a functionally equivalent one (e.g., to improve the quality or replacing a no more available API). These cases are supported by specific kinds of Web API request as detailed in [3], that here we summarize:

– *single Web API selection*, when the designer is developing a new mashup and aims at finding a Web API by specifying the Web API category and semantic tags; optionally, the designer may also specify the desired technical features for the Web API to search for;

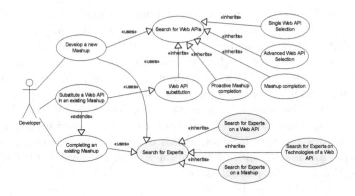

Fig. 2. Use cases for mashup development

- *advanced single Web API selection*, it is a variant of the previous one; in this case, the designer has also in mind the kind of mashup where the Web API has to be included, that is specified through a set of semantic tags;
- *mashup completion*, the mashup is already partially specified and the designer desires adding a new Web API; in this case, the request includes the set of Web APIs already in the mashup; the category for the requested Web API, semantic tags featuring it and the mashup can be optionally specified;
- *proactive mashup completion*, it is a variant of the previous use case; the designer does not specify the category and the semantic tags of the Web API to search for, since she does not know exactly what APIs are available, what to look for and using what tags for the request; therefore, she relies on suggestions of the system, which proposes candidate Web APIs based on existing mashups that includes Web APIs similar to the one already in the mashup;
- *Web API substitution*, when the designer desires to substitute a Web API in an existing mashup; in this case, the category and the tags are automatically extracted from the Web API to substitute;.

Example 1. A request to find a Web API in the category `Mapping` to be used for plotting data on maps together with the `Data-Planet` and `GeoData Demographics` APIs (*mashup completion* request) can be expressed by specifying the desired category, a set of semantic tags {`plot`, `geographic map`} and the set of Web APIs already in the mashup.

The use cases related to the *Search for Experts* (see Fig. 2) to support recommendation of experts are discusses in the following Sect 4.

3   Data Model for Integrating Public and Enterprise Knowledge

We model as linked data (LD) both the public knowledge about Web APIs, based on ProgrammableWeb and the knowledge about the organization and

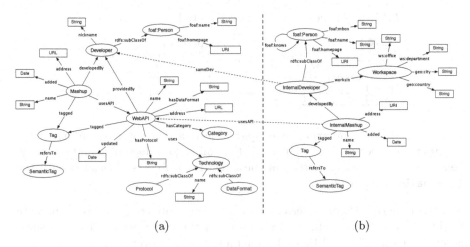

Fig. 3. Data models: (a) `PW repository`; (b) `developer organization`

social network of developers. The models are represented ad RDF vocabularies and are linked to provide an integrated data set.

Design of the Vocabularies. The representation of the linked RDF vocabularies concerning ProgrammableWeb (PW) and Developers Organization (DO) is shown in Figure 3. The former vocabulary has been obtained by analyzing the content of PW. The DO vocabulary keeps into account and estends the content of a well know Enterprise 2.0 platform, that is IBM Connections. Developers in the DO vocabulary have social and collaboration relationships inside the organization through the `foaf:knows` property. The PW and DO data sources are linked (see dashed links in Figure 3) according to the following criteria: (i) a `sameDev` link is established between a DO resource `InternalDeveloper` and a PW resource `Developer` when an internal developer is also registered as developer in PW; (ii) a DO mashup (instance of the `InternalMashup` class) is linked through a `usesAPI` property to each PW `WebAPI`.

Descriptors for expert search. In the PW and DO data models we identify the classes that are most suitable sources of expertize evidence (see Table 1). Moreover, we establish perspectives that can be applied on these classes: *Organization perspective, Social perspective, Web APIs perspective* and *Technologies perspective.* A perspective is a set of elements (classes or properties) that are related to a specific aspect of the domain represented in the data models. Table 1 shows applicability of each perspective to classes. For example, the `InternalDeveloper` class has an *Organization perspective* in order to indicate that there is a set of elements in the vocabularies that provides organization related information about an internal developer, such as office and department.

Descriptors are associated with the objects of these classes based on the applicable perspectives. A descriptor for an object o_i according to a perspective p is defined as a set of terms, $des_p(o_i) = \{t_{i1}, t_{i2}, ..., t_{in}\}$.

Table 1. Applicability of perspectives to DO and PW classes

Class	Perspectives			
	Organization	*WebAPIs*	*Technologies*	*Social*
InternalDeveloper	ok	ok	ok	ok
InternalMashup , Mashup		ok	ok	
WebAPI			ok	

Example 2. For an `InternalDeveloper` object, a descriptor according to the *Organization* perspective is built as the union of values of `country`, `city`, `department`, `office` properties of the `workplace` objects associated with the `InternalDeveloper` object.

Similarity of Descriptors. Because the descriptors are set of terms, a measure of similarity between pairs of descriptors on the same perspective is defined according to the classical Dice's formula for similarity over sets:

$$Sim(des_p(o_i), des_p(o_j)) = \frac{2 \cdot |des_p(o_i) \cap des_p(o_j)|}{|des_p(o_i)| + |des_p(o_j)|} \tag{1}$$

The similarity ranges in $[0..1]$.

4   Expert Search Use Cases

An expert search use case specifies a type of request in order identify experts about a specific kind of problem. We define in a general way a request R submitted by a developer D_R as follows.

$$R = < T_R, D_R, WA_R > \tag{2}$$

where T_R is the type of request, $WA_R = \{W_{Ri}\}$ is a set of Web APIs W_{Ri} specified by the developer D_R for implementing a mashup. We distinguish three different types of request R corresponding to the use cases in Fig. 2 that specialize the *Search for Experts* one:

R1) search for experts on a specific Web API W_R, where $WA_R = \{W_R\}$;
R2) search for experts on the technologies of a Web API W_R, where $WA_R = \{W_R\}$;
R3) search for experts on a mashup whose component APIs are $WA_R = \{W_{Ri}\}$.

In the third case D_R is looking for developers that have experience in mashups built from the set of Web APIs WA_R or at least with a not empty subset if it.

In the literature, different assumptions are made on what makes an expert and how to assess her expertise [8]. In order to answer to R we focus on content/activities and formulate the expertize assumptions as in the following: (i) if a developer has developed a mashup containing a Web API W_{Ri}, then she might have competencies about the W_{Ri} Web API; (ii) if a developer has developed a mashup containing a Web API W_{Ri}, then she might have competencies about the technologies of W_{Ri}; (iii) if a developer has developed a mashup including a subset of the Web APIs in $\{W_{Ri}\}$, then she might have competencies on how to compose these APIs.

Table 2. Definition of metrics for the collaboration patterns

Pattern	Definition of $m(R, D_i)$
P1	$\alpha \cdot Sim(des_{pO}(D_R), des_{pO}(D_i)) +$ $\beta \cdot Sim(des_{pS}(D_R), des_{pS}(D_i)) \in [0, 1]$, with $\alpha, \beta \in [0..1]$ and $\alpha + \beta = 1.0$
P2	$\alpha \cdot Sim(des_{pO}(D_R), des_{pO}(D_i)) +$ $\gamma \cdot Sim(des_{pT}(D_R), des_{pT}(W_R)) \in [0, 1]$, with $\alpha, \beta, \gamma \in [0..1]$ and $\alpha + \beta + \gamma = 1.0$
P3	$\alpha \cdot Sim(des_{pO}(D_R), des_{pO}(D_i)) +$ $\beta \cdot Sim(des_{pS}(D_R), des_{pS}(D_i)) +$ $\gamma \cdot Sim(des_{pW}(D_R), des_{pW}(\{W_{Ri}\})) \in [0, 1]$, with $\alpha, \beta, \gamma \in [0..1]$ and $\alpha + \beta + \gamma = 1.0$

4.1 Definition of Collaboration Patterns

We define a collaboration pattern in a general way as:

$$CP = <R, m, \delta, \prec> \tag{3}$$

where R is the request, m is the metric used to measure the matching between
a candidate developer and R, using the similarity between descriptors as in
Equation (1). Application of a collaboration pattern CP to a dataset described
according to the data models of Section 3 produces a set of developers matching
the request R. The developers are then ordered according to the ranking function
$\prec$, that is $D_i \prec D_j$ if $m(R, D_i) \leq m(R, D_j)$. A threshold δ is used to filter out
less relevant search results.

The generic collaboration pattern is specialized for each type of request. In
particular, based on a suitable expertise assumption, each type of request deter-
mines the structure of R, m and a set of considered perspectives. The definitions
of the metrics $m()$ for each specialization of the collaboration pattern are given
in Table 2.

Pattern p1 (searching for expertize on a given Web API) if the developer D_i
has used the Web API W_R in some mashups (that is, $W_R \in des_{pW}(D_i)$), then
$m(R, D_i) \neq 0$ and it is based on a weighted sum of two terms: i) similarity of D_i
and D_R w.r.t. the *Organization* perspective, ii) similarity of D_i and D_R w.r.t.
the *Social* perspective. So, developers that are closer to D_R w.r.t. the *Social* and
Organization perspectives will be ranked better, because it is supposed to be
easier for the developer D_R to contact them and to get their collaboration. In
the current version of LINKSMAN, we set $\alpha = \beta = 0.5$.

Pattern p2 (searching for expertize on the technologies of a given Web API)
if developer D_i has used APIs that share technologies with the Web API W_R
(that is, $Sim(des_{pT}(D_i), des_{pT}(W_R)) \neq 0$), then $m(R, D_i) \neq 0$ and it is based on
a weighted sum of three terms: i) similarity of D_i and D_R with respect the
Organization perspective, ii) similarity of D_i and D_R with respect to the *Social*
perspective, iii) similarity between technologies that D_i has used in developer's
mashups and technologies featuring W_R. Also in this case and in the following
p3, we set equally the values of α, β and γ.

Pattern p3 (searching for expertize on a given mashup) if developer D_i has
used at least one of the APIs $\{W_{Ri}\}$ specified in the request (that is, $Sim(des_{pT}$
$(D_i), des_{pT}(W_R)) \neq 0$), her evaluation is not zero and it is based on a weighted
sum of three terms: i) similarity of D_i and D_R with respect the *Organization*

perspective, ii) similarity between D_i and D_R with respect to the *Social* perspective iii) similarity between the set of APIs used by D_i in her mashups and $\{W_{Ri}\}$ (*WebAPIs* perspective). In the Table 2, pW denotes the WebAPIs perspective.

5   Conclusions and Future Work

In this paper, we described a social and semantic based approach to support enterprise mashup development. In particular, we discussed how different use cases can be supported by Web API search techniques that are based on social semantic tagging. Then, we presented the LINKSMAN framework for expert search of mashup developers based on collaboration patterns. Future work includes identification of additional collaboration patterns, using additional external sources of knowledge (e.g., Mashape, `http://www.mashape.com`) and performing evaluation based on the prototype we are developing.

References

1. Bianchini, D., De Antonellis, V., Melchiori, M.: Service-based Semantic Search in P2P systems. In: ECOWS 2009 - 7th IEEE European Conference on Web Services, pp. 7–16 (2009)
2. Bianchini, D., De Antonellis, V., Melchiori, M.: Semantic Collaborative Tagging for Web APIs Sharing and Reuse. In: Brambilla, M., Tokuda, T., Tolksdorf, R. (eds.) ICWE 2012. LNCS, vol. 7387, pp. 76–90. Springer, Heidelberg (2012)
3. Bianchini, D., De Antonellis, V., Melchiori, M.: A Linked Data Perspective for Effective Exploration of Web APIs Repositories. In: Daniel, F., Dolog, P., Li, Q. (eds.) ICWE 2013. LNCS, vol. 7977, pp. 506–509. Springer, Heidelberg (2013)
4. Bianchini, D., De Antonellis, V., Melchiori, M.: A Multi-perspective Framework for Web API Search in Enterprise Mashup Design. In: Salinesi, C., Norrie, M.C., Pastor, Ó. (eds.) CAiSE 2013. LNCS, vol. 7908, pp. 353–368. Springer, Heidelberg (2013)
5. Hoyer, V., Fischer, M.: Market overview of enterprise mashup tools. In: Bouguettaya, A., Krueger, I., Margaria, T. (eds.) ICSOC 2008. LNCS, vol. 5364, pp. 708–721. Springer, Heidelberg (2008)
6. Hristoskova, A., Tsiporkova, E., Tourw, T., Buelens, S., Putman, M., De Turck, F.: Identifying experts through a framework for knowledge extraction from public online sources. In: 12th Dutch-Belgian Information Retrieval Workshop (DIR 2012), Ghent, Belgium, pp. 19–22 (2012)
7. Montanelli, S., et al.: The ESTEEM platform: Enabling P2P Semantic Collaboration through Emerging Collective Knowledge. Journal of Intelligent Information Systems 36(2), 167–195 (2011)
8. Stankovic, M., Wagner, C., Jovanovic, J., Laublet, P.: Looking for Experts? What can Linked Data do for You? In. In: Proc. of Linked Data on the Web (LDOW) at WWW 2010 (2010)

Crowdsourcing Mobile Web Applications

Cecilia Challiol[1,2], Sergio Firmenich[1,2], Gabriela Alejandra Bosetti[1,2],
Silvia E. Gordillo[1,3], and Gustavo Rossi[1,2]

[1] LIFIA, Facultad de Informática, UNLP. La Plata, Argentina
{ceciliac,sergio.firmenich,gabriela.bosetti,gordillo,
gustavo}@lifia.info.unlp.edu.ar
[2] CONICET
[3] CIC

Abstract. Building Mobile Web or Hypermedia Applications is usually difficult since there is a myriad of issues to take into account. Moreover adding support for personalized or context-aware behaviors goes far beyond the possibilities of many kinds of organizations that intend to build this kind of software (museums, city halls, etc). In this article we present a novel approach to delegate part of the effort in building mobile Web software to developers outside those organizations or even to final users. We show that this approach is feasible, light and practical and present a set of experiments we developed to verify our claims.

Keywords: Mobile Web Applications, Client-Side Adaptation, Crowdsoursing, Mobile Hypermedia.

1   Introduction

Mobile Web applications cover a great variety of domains (tourist, marketing, entertainment, etc.) to provide different services to the users, ideally considering his/her actual location. These applications must be "evolvable" and "adaptable" due to their particular characteristics. These characteristics may be classified from the point of view of the software: intensive use of users' preferences, great variety of services, etc. or the hardware: wide variety of platforms and availability of devices. Many authors have researched on these topics [12], most of them consider the task of building this kind of software very complex.

Web applications have been evolving to provide services with different purposes, for example, for shopping, banks, museums, etc… The majority of these applications are not built considering the user's location to provide services or content and of course they do not consider more sophisticated services such as providing mobile guides [7] and much less other well known features of Mobile Hypermedia [2] such as for example walking links [11].

To solve this problem, at least partially, many organizations, such as museums, tend to use their own existing websites to provide location-based information, for example, through barcodes which once read by the mobile device point the user to the

Q.Z. Sheng and J. Kjeldskov (Eds.): ICWE 2013 Workshops, LNCS 8295, pp. 223–237, 2013.
© Springer International Publishing Switzerland 2013

correspondingly defined url. Another popular strategy is to use QRpedia[1] codes to provide Wikipedia pages associated to that code (which is in a particular location). This mechanism does not consider mobility aspects since the Web application (in this case, Wikipedia) is not designed to assist the mobile user.

One possibility, to solve this problem, such as is mentioned in [1], is to extend crowdsourcing technology to enrich mobile applications. So, each user can develop new services associated with a specific physical location, allowing the crowd to share the solution.

Inspired in part by the mentioned research we propose an approach to augment Web applications with mobile features, specifically implementing most interesting mobile hypermedia concepts such as mobile guides, walking links, etc. Our approach allows users to create their own tours according to their interest and eventually share them with others. The approach only requires an existing Web application and a mechanism to map locations to application objects (such as barcode or other kind of sensing strategy).

To create these augmentations, we use a client-side approach in the typical style of crowdsourcing; users create their personalized scripts that once run in the mobile device, enrich Web applications with mobile hypermedia functionality. Since the task of scripting might prove to be difficult we have develop a set of tools to improve and ease the process.

The structure of the paper is the following: Section 2 introduces a background of both mobile hypermedia and Web augmentation. In Section 3 we compare our approach with other related works. Section 4 explains our approach and presents our framework. An evaluation is presented in Section 5 in order to validate our approach. Finally, in Section 6 we present the conclusions and mention some further works.

2   Background

2.1   Mobile Hypermedia

Mobile Hypermedia Applications [2] are a particular kind of Mobile Application that extends the concept of navigation (used in the traditional Hypermedia) to the real world. In these applications, there are two ways to access to the information: digitally (as in typical hypermedia applications) and physically, based on the users' location. Corresponding with these types of information access we have digital links (the usual hypermedia links) and "walking" links, those links which connect two different physical objects (or real world object) and require the user to walk to reach the target object. Figure 1 shows digital and physical information access, and links in two levels and the association between them; real world objects are related with their hypermedia information, that we call digital counterpart (other author call as "digital-physical link" [10] or "physical hyperlink" [16]). The "mechanics" of mobile hypermedia is the following; when users are sensed in front of a physical object, its digital counterpart is shown; it might exhibit digital links which are navigated as usual or walking links (which point to others physical objects). When a walking link (or

---

[1] QRpedia page: http://qrpedia.org/

real-world link as mentioned in [13]) is triggered the application assumes the user intention to walk to this target; at this moment a map may be displayed in order to guide the user to the selected object; when he arrives, the user will be sensed to be in front of the object, and show information about it.

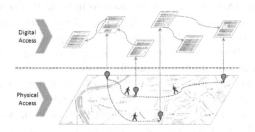

Fig. 1. Levels related with Mobile Hypermedia

Digital and walking links trigger different kind of navigation: the first one has a defined semantic for concepts like back and forward. The second one implies the user movement and, in this context, the user may change his decision to go to the target, she/he may get lost, etc; back and forward are more difficult to establish.

We have been working on different aspects related with Mobile Hypermedia Applications. These aspects cover different areas, such as, for example, context-aware assistance to the traveler [15], browsing behavior in these kinds of applications [5], modeling aspects [6]. In these works we mainly discuss issues related with the application of software engineering principles to the development of mobile systems.

We have been using separation of concerns to create Mobile Hypermedia applications in a model-based approach. The separation between pure hypermedia and mobility aspects allowed us to think in other ways to create mobile hypermedia applications, by using existing Web applications and adding the physical concern, e.g. positioning information. In this paper we are interested in light and user-centered ways of enriching Web applications to create mobile applications with those features of mobile hypermedia that improves the user experience.

2.2 Web Augmentation

Web augmentation [3] is a well-known technique for manipulating existing Web applications in order to improve them with new features. These approaches manipulate Web pages DOM (which is an object-based representation of HTML pages), since this is the only resource which is perceivable from outside of the application server. By changing the DOM we can alter what users perceive of the applications. We have successfully used Web augmentation for supporting users' concerns in traditional desktop Web applications [9]. In this paper we show a new approach used for building mobile applications running on mobile clients. As usual in the context of Web augmentation, our approach follows the idea of crowdsourcing: it allows users to define their own applications (or applications extensions) by developing specific scripts which respond to their own requirements; they may eventually share these scripts with the community.

3   Related Work

[8] describes an approach allowing Web applications to access context information in an easy and fast way. To do that, they create their own context-aware Web browser and a list of specific XML tags which are used to indicate that some particular page needs some context information, for example, location. In addition, each page requires implementing some mechanism to refresh the page with the current context. Their context-aware Web browser is designed in three layers: the standard Web browser, the context tag manager and the context information scheduled task manager. The context tag manager analyzes each requested page and if it has a specific context-aware XML tag, it activates the corresponding task to obtain the required context. The context information scheduled task manager, defines different tasks to obtain contexts of the user or of the mobile devices (using, for example, sensor information). When a specific task is called, the context information is encapsulated and it is sent using a web server to the web application (through some mechanism, the web page is updated with the current context). The authors present in [8] a context-aware Web browser defined specific for Android platform.

[17] presents a generic approach to enhance existing Websites with context-aware features on-the-fly. This work enriches a priori unknown, third-party Websites by using a semantic mechanism to extract information from these sites. Semantic information is used to enhance (through DOM manipulation) each page with the according context. This approach uses three methods of adaptation: context-aware recommendations, injection of contextual information and aids, and Websites user guides. The authors present in [17] a concrete application, using Android based on the SCOUT framework (which offers support to context-aware mobile application development). In this Android application each adaptation and the mechanism to enhance each page are defined.

Both approaches, [8] and [17] require users to install native applications in their devices; meanwhile in our proposal the user "just" installs browser plugins. Furthermore, our approach allows creating complex adaptations by only merging simple scripts; this users can combine these scripts easily (only activating them) or they can create their own scripts. Providing the same functionality with native applications is more complex, because these applications would need to provide a platform to create new adaptations.

Additionally [8] and [17] have defined specific adaptations types while in our approach each user may define his/her own personalized adaptations.

In [14], the authors present a crowdsouring approach to adapt mobile Web interfaces. The authors provide a toolkit for deployment adaptations, and then these adaptations are shared through a specific server. The adaptation are related only with those aspects associated with viewing context as, for example, size, position of websites elements, etc. This approach captures the context in which each adaptation takes place to increase the quality of adaptation scenarios. Then, this information is used to recommend the best-matching adaptations for a given context. This approach allows user to personalize (adapt) mobile web interfaces; when these adaptations are shared with the crowd, these can be used in a particular context. Adaptations are reviewed and rated by others users.

Our approach shares the same philosophy of [14], i.e. encouraging users to create their own adaptations, but while [14] focuses on interfaces, we focus on mobile features.

4   Our Approach

Our aim is to augment existing Web applications with mobile features, in particular with mobile hypermedia features such as walking links, active guided tours, etc. Our approach is client-side oriented with the typical style of crowdsourcing; in this sense we envision two different user roles: developers and end-users. Developers are JavaScript programmers who can create their own personalized scripts (which run in mobile devices) to enrich existing Web applications. End-users install and use scripts generated by some developer. In this section, we focus on the role of the developers and how our approach simplifies the task of augmenting Web applications, particularly, with mobile hypermedia features.

As previously indicated, we only assume the existence of Web pages and some mechanism (such as barcodes or other kind of sensing strategy) to map locations to those pages. One possible scenario is a museum, which uses QRpedia to provide Wikipedia pages in specifics locations to visitors. Figure 2 shows the user's view of an object in La Plata Museum.

Fig. 2. User reads a QRpedia in a museum

While the Wikipedia page might have links to explore, they may not relate the object with other physical objects in the museum, nor give the user any cue about mobility through the museum rooms.

The same museum, meanwhile, may provide in its site a *Darwin tour*[2] which connects chronologically different animals of the museum providing information about each animal from the point of view of *Darwin*. An interesting augmentation of the current QRpedia-based "guide" results from implementing a mobile *Darwin tour*. A script developer may take the information from the *Darwin tour* site and augment, for each animal, the corresponding Wikipedia article (by manipulating the DOM in the client). Additionally, he may add walking links among museum's specimens to

---

[2] Darwin tour: http://www.fcnym.unlp.edu.ar/museo/educativa/
darwin/darwinenmuseo.html

follow them chronologically; eventually he can add mechanisms for orienting the users in case they get lost or a warning if they reach a different target (not the one in the tour). For example, when such a link is selected a map with the path to the target object is shown. Figure 3 shows a general scheme of the relation between the script, the existing information and how it is connected with QRpedia (as a layer that is only active when the script is running).

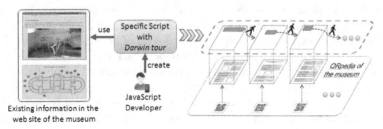

Fig. 3. A developer creates a script with the *Darwin tour*

Figure 4 shows the results as perceived by the user. It can be appreciated that the user not only receives the Wikipedia page but also information related with the *Darwin tour*. In particular, a walking link is shown; when it is selected a map is displayed.

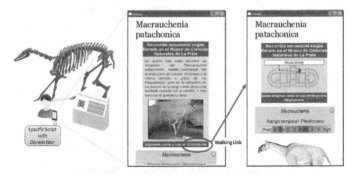

Fig. 4. The script with the *Darwin tour* is running

Different developers may create scripts implementing varied mobile functionality, e.g. personalized for different profiles (young students, disabled people, etc); the approach has two interesting benefits: first, it relieves the host institution (e.g. the Museum) from a task that might be outside its scope, and also allows arbitrary customization of the user experience with minimum effort.

However, in the example described above the developer needed to create all the mechanisms related with mobile hypermedia features as part of the script. The complexity might grow when, for example, there are other sensing mechanisms (e.g. in outdoor settings). For example, a script which uses GPS, needs to access the internal information of the mobile device in order to obtain the location. Additionally (though not further discussed in this paper), developers would want to generate visual adaptations of the original pages if they do not fit well with mobile devices (See [14]).

As part of our approach and to simplify the developers' tasks we have built a framework providing script skeletons for most mobile hypermedia features. Thus developers only need to instantiate the framework with the specific augmentations, e.g. concrete data and walking links. In Section 4.1 we summarize the characteristics of our framework and in Section 4.2 we briefly detail how users create scripts that use the framework. To run scripts generated by our framework, we provide a plugin, which is described in Section 4.3.

4.1   The Development Framework

Our framework, called MoWA (*Mobile Web Augmentation*), addresses the general functionality (or mechanisms) of mobile hypermedia applications. In addition, MoWA provides concrete functionally for specific domains. In this paper, we will focus on presenting the more general mobile hypermedia features. When developers use MoWA they only need to create a script which extends one of the framework's extension points. A further goal is helping developers to create the script in an easy way.

In Figure 5, we present a reduced schema of MoWA to understand its principal concepts. In the figure we use modules to group functionalities to show a more abstract overview.

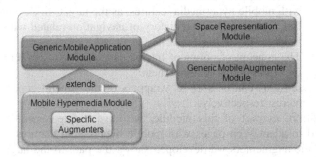

Fig. 5. Reduced schema of MoWA framework

We next present a more detailed explanation of the core functionalities provided by each module presented in Figure 5:

- *Generic Mobile Application Module.* This module implements generic concepts existing in all mobile hypermedia applications (in particular, we focus on those that consider the user's position to offer information). Some of these concepts are, for example, the information related with the user or with the points of interest.
    - o For the user, it is important to represent his/her current position (sometimes the history of these positions is also important). Another aspect, as we focus on mobile web applications, is to save the navigation history.
    - o For each point of interest its location and properties (which are used to augment the point of interest) are represented. These properties are

defined by each developer according to each specific augmentation. In MoWA they are represented in a general way. In addition, for each point of interest, a URL associated to it is defined (the URL can be expressed, for example, as a regular expression). This URL is used to resolve which page needs to be enhanced when the user is in front of the target physical object.

- *Space Representation Module.* In this module concepts related with the space are represented; this information is useful to eventually show a map or, for example, to find a specific path to an object of interest.
- *Generic Mobile Augmenter Module.* In this module generic augmenters, which help developers to enhance each point of interest defined in their scripts, are defined. For example, we provide augmenters to:
  - o Show information about the point of interest in the corresponding page.
  - o Show a map with the current location of the user.
  - o Show some properties defined for the point of interest (in the *Generic Mobile Application Module*).
- *Mobile Hypermedia Module.* In this module the specific mobile hypermedia features are defined. The concepts represented in this module extend those defined in the *Generic Mobile Application Module*. For example:
  - o The concept of user is extended to save specific information related with mobile hypermedia features, as the target (in case that a walking link is selected) or the history of navigation related with the walking links.
  - o The concept of points of interest is extended to be able to represent the walking link between them.

These extensions can be seen as wrappers of the general concept of user or point of interest respectively.

In addition, as part of this module, we have defined specific augmenters oriented to adapt Web pages with mobile hypermedia features. For example, one of the augmenters we developed shows the path to the target in the map when a walking link is selected, which corresponds to the functionality shown in Figure 4.

MoWA can be used not only by developers who want to create specific scripts but also by the institutions, for example a museum, to provide suitable space representations. These space representations can be later used by developers in the scripts. In this case, developers create scripts using not only the "bare" framework but also the additional information offered by the institution (which is created using MoWA too).

In the following sub-section, we detail the steps that developers need to follow to create their scripts.

4.2   Creating Scripts Using MoWA

Developers with programming skills may use MoWA by programming JavaScript scripts. For doing it, developers need to follow these guidelines:

- Create a new concrete application, for example, one with the mobile hypermedia features. To do that, he/she only needs to create a new class which extends on, for example, *AbstractMobileHypermedia*.
    o Define the mechanisms of sensing which are relevant for the application, for example, barcode, GPS, etc. This information is used afterwards when the script is running in the browser.
- Create the instances of each point of interest which will be considered by the application. For each point of interest it is required to define:
    o Its properties (which will be used to enhance the page).
    o Its associated url (used to resolve which page is enhanced).
    o Its position (used to handle when and where the augmentation should be triggered)
- Define the walking links related with each point of interest. These links define the mobile hypermedia which users (of the script) rely on in order to "navigate" the real world.
- Create the space representation which can consist of complex structures or a simple image map. The developer needs to indicate where each point of interest in the defined space is located.
- Define an augmentation method for each point of interest. This method will be run when the user is positioned in the location associated with the point of interest. It is in this method where DOM manipulations may be defined (for a particular point of interest). Developers can use the augmenters defined in MoWA; for example to show walking links associated to the point of interest. If all the Web pages corresponding with each point of interest are augmented in the same way, developers may use a unique method for all points of interest.

Following the mentioned guidelines, we show in Figure 6 a *Darwin tour* specifies as an extension of *AbstractMobileHypermedia*. Figure 7 shows a simplified schema for the *Darwin tour* script.

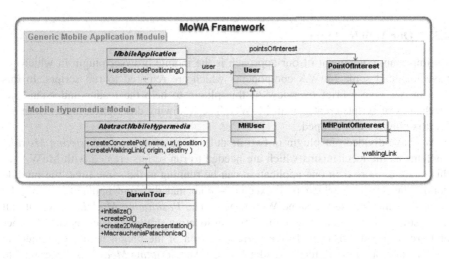

Fig. 6. Darwin *tour* application using MoWA

```
...
DarwinTour.prototype = new AbstractMobileHypermedia();
DarwinTour.prototype.initialize = function() {
  this.useBarcodePositioning();
  this.createPoI();
  this.create2DMapRepresentation();
};
DarwinTour.prototype.createPoI = function() {
  var nameM = 'Macrauchenia Patachonica';
  var url = 'http://es.m.wikipedia.org/wiki/Macrauchenia_patachonica';
  var position = url;
  var macrauchenia = this.createPoI(nameM, url, position);
  ...
  var nameG = 'Gliptodonte';
  ...
  var gliptodonte = this.createPoI(nameG, ..., ...);
  ...
  this.createWalkingLink(macrauchenia, gliptodonte);
};
DarwinTour.prototype.MacraucheniaPatachonica = function(){
  this.insertAfterDOMElement("section_0");
  this.augmenters["showPoI"].execute();
  this.augmenters["showWalkingLinks"].execute();
};
...
```

Fig. 7. Darwin *tour* script using MoWA

For creating the script related to the *Darwin tour*, developers do not need to define specific mechanisms to handle the involved objects; he should only define information related to each point of interest or related to the space; and in addition, he/she could use the augmentation methods provided by MoWA. So, his/her task to create scripts is easy. As said before the museum could offer its own space representation, so, the developer could use this representation, without the need to define this representation as part of his/her script.

To run these scripts, we provide a plugin to the mobile browser. A brief description of this plugin is detailed in the next sub-section.

4.3   Our Mobile Plugin

An important component of our approach is the mobile browser plugin in which we have included some MoWA components which are required to run scripts. In this section, we give a brief overview of this plugin to help the reader understand the mechanics of scripts created with MoWA. The following description is based on the Firefox plugin we developed.

We have divided our plugin in two modules. One of them, the *Scripting Module*, implements the mechanisms which are needed to run scripts created with MoWA. In this module, more than one application can be running at the same time; the module defines the order in which they execute – note that different applications may be defined to manipulate the same Web page -. The *Positioning Module* represents all the abstraction needed to handle the different location strategies, such as GPS listener or Barcode Reader listener. In the current version of the plugin we have created an implementation of the Barcode Reader listener. The *Scripting Module* is "listening" to the positioning events (triggered by the *Positioning Module*). Every time that the user's location changes, the *Scripting Module* is notified, and executes, for each application, the corresponding augmentation (if it is defined for this location).

Figure 8 shows a simplified sequence diagram of the *Darwin* tour script running our plugin. Suppose that this sequence occurs when the user reads the same barcode that has been showed in Figure 2. Then the *PositionManager* (which is included in the *Positioning Module*) detects that a barcode reader read a new code; it sends a notification to the *Scripting Module*, in particular to the *Darwin* tour application. As the url detected by the barcode reader matches with the url defined for a particular point of interest, then the augmentation method is executed and the page will be augmented with information related with this point of interest.

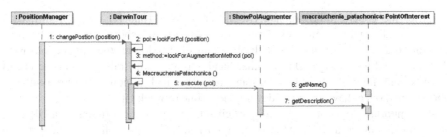

Fig. 8. *Darwin tour* script running in our plugin

5   Evaluation

In order to evaluate our approach, we have conducted an experiment whose main goal was to explore how easy is to build mobile Web applications using our approach compared to a more traditional development approach (i.e. programming an entire application that runs on the server-side). Specifically, we wanted to determine if this kind of applications are developed faster and more effectively using client-side adaptation than with a traditional mobile Web development style.

With this purpose, we convened developers with different skills in Web development. A total of 16 developers participated in the experiment, all of them computer science students, aged between 20 and 39. We collected the programming experience of the participants with a preliminary digital questionnaire about: back-end technology experience (PHP, Spring, Python, etc.) and front-end experience (JavaScript, DOM manipulation, HTML, etc.). According to this information, we divided the participants into two groups of 8 participants each (to balance the knowledge in both groups): Group 1 (for developing a mobile Web application in a traditional way) and Group 2 (for developing a mobile Web application with our approach).

The rest of the experiment was performed during a week with two in-person meetings. This part of the experiment started with a meeting in which all 16 participants were asked to fill another questionnaire about Mobile Hypermedia background. Then, they were instructed about Mobile Hypermedia concepts, which took around 30 minutes. Afterwards we presented the task to be developed:

*"La Plata Museum has several pieces exposed with an associated QRpedia code. We need a Mobile Web Application that supports a specific tour among specific pieces. The tour, called **Darwin tour**, is based on the relationships Darwin found between these pieces. The application has to contemplate the current information provided for each piece plus new information about Darwin research (R1). Besides, the application must support users with walking links for showing them the following piece to be visited (R2) and correct them if they are in a wrong piece (R3). The application must allow users to visit the Museum in two ways (normally and with Darwin Tour) as well as allow users to cancel the Darwin tour. If the user finishes the Darwin tour, then a message must be shown informing this situation."*

After the general talk, we had two different talks (one for each Group); each separated talk took 20 minutes. Group 1 was instructed about tools for QR code generation and was advised about the freedom of developing the application using their preferred technology. On the other hand, Group 2 was trained about the use of MoWA and how it should be instantiated. We had a new meeting (with all participants) once they ran out of development time (a week later).

It is important to mention that all participants got the same artifacts: i) a QR code simulator running as a GreaseMonkey Script, ii) an HTML page showing the Museum map with an identified piece (from this HTML page participants could locate the pieces of the Museum and draw walking links between two pieces), iii) a full detail of the pieces contemplated by the *Darwin tour*: pieces, QRpedia codes, map location, etc. All of them were advised about the time available for developing the application: one week starting from the first in-person meeting. Besides, we asked them to register all their activity by using activity diaries, making a new entry for each work session (time used, tasks performed, problems founded, suggestions, etc.). Finally, we specified the concrete artifact to be delivered: the developed application, documentation about both, installation and use, the activity diary and a video showing the application.

At the beginning of the second meeting, we asked Group 1 participants to answer some questions about the development process; meanwhile Group 2 participants completed a SUS [4] questionnaire about the use of MoWA. Besides, we defined a general questionnaire (for all 16 participants) whose goal was to get the requirements satisfied for each participant, and the difficulty level found for the task.

Figure 9 summarizes the results in terms of effectiveness. From each requirement (R1, R2, R3) the figure shows how many participants of each group have satisfied it. Note that only four participants of the Group 1 could finish all requirements, meanwhile the rest of the same group did not finish any. Participants of the Group 2, however, were much more successful: seven of them finished the application completely, while the eighth finished R1, R2 but could not satisfied R3.

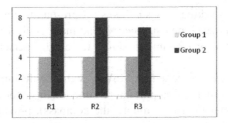

Fig. 9. Effectiveness of each group by requirements

Regarding the time took for developing the application: if we take into account only successful cases (4 from Group 1 and 7 from Group 2, where successful means all requirements satisfied), we found that Group 2 was faster. The average time of Group 1 was of 18 hours and 52 minutes (with a standard deviation of 7 hours 28 minutes), and Group 2's average time was of 5 hours and 17 minutes (standard deviation = 3 hour).

Though this is a first evaluation of our approach, the first conclusion is that developing this kind of applications is much faster and effective with our approach than using traditional Web application development.

As a complementary result of our approach, the SUS questionnaire score was quite motivating for us, MoWA got a score of 81,3 which is an acceptable score for our first version of the tool.

6   Concluding Remarks and Further Work

In this paper we have proposed a novel approach for building Mobile Web Applications that reduce the intrinsic complexity involved in the development process of this kind of applications. Our approach takes into account personalization since users are able to install and use their preferred scripts. We made only two assumptions for applying our approach: i) a Web application exists, and ii) there is a mechanism to map locations to application objects.

Based on the concepts of crowdsourcing and client-side augmentation, our approach supports two roles for users: developers and end-users. For developers we provide a framework that can be used for specifying augmentations (for adapting Web pages in a particular way) and new Mobile Web applications (which coordinate these augmentations for making concrete the new applications over the original Web pages). For the two kinds of artifacts our MoWA framework provides extension points that make easier their development.

Meanwhile, end users are supported with a plugin to run these scripts inside the mobile browser plugin. Personalization is achieved by allowing end-users to install their preferred artifacts (scripts).

We performed an evaluation that shows that our approach is feasible. Moreover, according with the first results presented in this paper, we can figure out that developing using our approach is faster and more effective than using traditional Web development techniques.

Currently, we are working on visual tools for pre-building a specific application in order to simplify the development process. The main goal of these tools is to allow users with minimum programming skills to create personalized Mobile Web applications.

In the same line, we are extending MoWA with new features related with mobile Web application in order to support more functionality, for example, considering others sensing mechanisms (for example, the compass), providing more augmenters as part of MoWA, etc.

As part of our future work, we are planning to perform new experiments with users, but in contraposition with the experiment presented in this paper, we want to evaluate usability aspects of the Mobile Web application generated with our approach, which would involve the point of view of the end-users.

References

1. Alt, F., Shirazi, A.S., Schmidt, A., Kramer, U., Nawax, Z.: Location-based Crowdsourcing: Extending Crowdsourcing to the real world. In: 6th Nordic Conference on Human-Computer Interaction: Extending Boundaries, pp. 16–20. ACM, New York (2010)
2. Bouvin, N.O., Christensen, B.G., Gronbaek, K., Hansen, F.A.: HyCon: a framework for context-aware mobile hypermedia. Journal of the New Review of Hypermedia and Multimedia 9(1), 59–88 (2003)
3. Bouvin, N.O.: Unifying Strategies for Web Augmentation. In: 10th ACM Conference on Hypertext and Hypermedia, pp. 91–100. ACM, New York (1999)
4. Brooke, J.: SUS: a 'quick and dirty' usability scale. In: Usability Evaluation in Industry, pp. 189–194. Taylor and Francis, London (1996)
5. Challiol, C., Muñoz, A., Rossi, G., Gordillo, S.E., Fortier, A., Laurini, R.: Browsing Semantics in Context-Aware Mobile Hypermedia. In: Meersman, R., Tari, Z., Herrero, P. (eds.) OTM 2007 Workshop, Part I. LNCS, vol. 4805, pp. 211–221. Springer, Heidelberg (2007)
6. Challiol, C., Rossi, G., Gordillo, S.E., Fortier, A.: Separation of Concerns in Mobile Hypermedia: Architectural and Modeling Issues. In: Alencar, P., Cowan, D. (eds.) Handbook of Research on Mobile Software Engineering: Design, Implementation and Emergent Applications, vol. 1, pp. 211–233. IGI Global (2012)
7. Emmanouilidis, C., Koutsiamanis, R., Tasidou, A.: Mobile guides: Taxonomy of architectures, context awareness, technologies and applications. Journal of Network and Computer Applications 36(1), 103–125 (2013)
8. Espada, J.P., Crespo, R.G., Martínez, O.S., Pelayo, G., Bustelo, B.C., Lovelle, J.M.C.: Extensible architecture for context-aware mobile web applications. Journal Expert Systems with Applications 39(10), 9686–9694 (2012)
9. Firmenich, S., Winckler, M., Rossi, G., Gordillo, S.: A Framework for Concern-Sensitive, Client-Side Adaptation. In: Auer, S., Díaz, O., Papadopoulos, G.A. (eds.) ICWE 2011. LNCS, vol. 6757, pp. 198–213. Springer, Heidelberg (2011)
10. Hansen, F.A., Bouvin, N.O.: Mobile Learning in Context - Context-aware Hypermedia in the Wild. Journal of Interactive Mobile Technologies 3(1), 6–21 (2009)
11. Harper, S., Goble, C., Pettitt, S.: Proximity: Walking the Link. Journal of Digital Information (JODI) 5(1) (2004)

12. Hong, J.-Y., Suh, E.-H., Kim, S.-J.: Context-aware systems: A literature review and classification. Journal Expert Systems with Applications 36(4), 8509–8522 (2009)
13. Millard, D.E., De Roure, D.C., Michaelides, D.T., Thompson, M.K., Weal, M.J.: Navigational hypertext models for physical hypermedia environments. In: Fifteenth ACM Conference on Hypertext and Hypermedia, pp. 110–111. ACM, New York (2004)
14. Nebeling, M., Norrie, M.C.: Context-Aware and Adaptive Web Interfaces: A Crowdsourcing Approach. In: Harth, A., Koch, N. (eds.) ICWE 2011. LNCS, vol. 7059, pp. 167–170. Springer, Heidelberg (2012)
15. Rossi, G., Gordillo, S., Challiol, C., Fortier, A.: Context-Aware Services for Physical Hypermedia Applications. In: Meersman, R., Tari, Z., Herrero, P. (eds.) OTM 2006 Workshops. LNCS, vol. 4278, pp. 1914–1923. Springer, Heidelberg (2006)
16. Schmalstieg, D., Schall, G., Wagner, D., Barakonyi, I., Reitmayr, G., Newman, J., Ledermann, F.: Managing Complex Augmented Reality Models. Journal of IEEE Computer Graphics and Applications 27(4), 48–57 (2007)
17. Van Woensel, W., Casteleyn, S., De Troyer, O.: A generic approach for on-the-fly adding of context-aware features to existing websites. In: 22nd ACM Conference on Hypertext and Hypermedia, pp. 143–152. ACM, New York (2011)

Vision Based Page Segmentation Algorithm: Extended and Perceived Success

M. Elgin Akpınar[1] and Yeliz Yeşilada[2]

[1] Middle East Technical University
Ankara, Turkey
[2] Middle East Technical University
Northern Cyprus Campus
Mersin 10, Turkey
{elgin.akpinar,yyeliz}@metu.edu.tr

Abstract. Web pages consist of different visual segments, serving different purposes. Typical structural segments are header, right or left columns and main content. Segments can also have nested structure which means some segments may include other segments. Understanding these segments is important in properly displaying web pages for small screen devices and in alternative forms such as audio for screen reader users. There exist different techniques in identifying visual segments in a web page. One successful approach is Vision Based Segmentation Algorithm (VIPS Algorithm) which uses both the underlying source code and also the visual rendering of a web page. However, there are some limitations of this approach and this paper explains how we have extended and improved VIPS and built it in Java. We have also conducted some online user evaluations to investigate how people perceive the success of the segmentation approach and in which granularity they prefer to see a web page segmented. This paper presents the preliminary results which show that, people perceive segmentation with higher granularity as better segmentation regardless of the web page complexity.

Keywords: Web Accessibility, Web Page Segmentation, Reverse Engineering, User Study.

1 Introduction

Web pages are typically designed for visual interaction. They include many visual elements such as header, footer, menu, etc that guide the reader. One can easily look at the visual rendering and can differentiate the segments which typically differs in background color, font styles, borders or margins around the segments. On the other hand, the underlying source code typically does not provide such kind of clear segmentation or pattern. Therefore, when web pages are automatically processed by assistive technologies or adapted for mobile devices this kind of information is not available.

In order to address this problem, there exist different techniques for identifying visual segments in a web page [3,1,7]. These approaches differ in the techniques they use for automating the process, some use machine learning techniques, some uses heuristics, etc. Once a web page is automatically segmented, web pages are then typically

Q.Z. Sheng and J. Kjeldskov (Eds.): ICWE 2013 Workshops, LNCS 8295, pp. 238–252, 2013.

re-engineered for better presenting them on mobile devices [28,12,19] and for screen reader users [14,4,27]. Reengineering approaches include variety of techniques, for example allowing user to directly read the main content, or allowing user to skip the menu or diving a web page into several small pages, etc. (see Section 2).

A well known segmentation technique is Vision Based Segmentation Algorithm (VIPS Algorithm) [7]. VIPS uses both the underlying source code and also the visual rendering of a web page. This technique is very popular and has been used to segment web pages for mobile devices as well as improving the precision and recall of information retrieval results. When a web page is segmented by VIPS, it generates a block tree of a web page. This tree is structurally similar to the underlying DOM tree, but it includes the hierarchy of visual elements on web pages. Nodes in the top levels represent higher level segments and nodes in the lower levels include the lower level, higher granularity segments. This approach therefore gives a segment tree that can be used in different levels (see Section 3).

Even though VIPS is proven to be a very successful approach [7], there are some limitations. These limitations consist of poorly defined order of precedence for the rule set and tresholds which are applied on DOM elements in segmentation and adatibility problems to new technologies such as HTML 5 and dynamic web contents. This paper explains how we have extended and improved VIPS and built it in Java (see Section 4). We have also conducted an online user evaluation to investigate how people perceive the success of the segmentation approach and in which granularity they prefer to see a web page segmented. In particular, we have investigated the following two research questions: (1) What is the perceived success of our extended segmentation algorithm? How does this differ based on the web page complexity? ; (2) Which level of segmentation is the most preferred?. This paper presents the preliminary results which show that, people perceive segmentation with higher granularity as better segmentation regardless of the web page complexity (see Section 5). This finding is very important for being able to decide how to segment a web page automatically and display it to mobile and disabled users for better interaction experience.

2   Related Work

Web page segmentation has been primarily used to re-engineer pages so that they are easier to access by mobile web users [28,12,19] and by visually impaired users who access web pages in audio [14,4,27]. Our literature review also shows that the segmentation process has been proposed and used in different fields, for example, information retrieval [7,6], image retrieval [5], etc. Here, we briefly present related work in mobile web and web accessibility fields.

There are still many problems associated with mobile web access. Web pages are typically designed for certain screen sizes [11,28] and therefore scaling down for small screen devices or scaling up for large displays can be difficult [16], some mobile devices also do not have keyboard or mouse [24], they have limited processing capabilities [24] and they tend to have problems with multimedia data [12,19]. Furthermore, the information need is very different for mobile web users, people focus more on getting direct answers to specific questions, and expect more relevant and clear results instead of browsing through large amount of data [24]. Most important of all of these is that the relationship between web page segments and elements are not semantically explicit so one cannot easily display a page on another or alternative platform [20,28]. Therefore, segmentation process provides a good way of identifying segments in a web page such that they can be used to better display a web page to mobile and screen reader users.

When we look at the existing work, there are different approaches that make use of segmentation for reengineering web pages. [28] aims to extract and present only the important parts of the web page for mobile web access. [17] similarly aims to discover the importance of segments in a web page – block-importance information can be used to decide which part of the page need to be displayed first to the user. [29,24] focus on identifying the main content of the page so that it is directly presented to the user. [1,22,10,9] split a web page several pages. [1] aims to identify information blocks so that a web page can be divided into smaller pages and represented to the user with a table of contents. [12,19] propose a reengineering technique called the indexed segmentation, which transforms segments or components of web pages into a sequence of small sub-pages that fit the display of a hand-held device, and binds them with hyperlinks. [11] proposes to segment the web page into several smaller pages and then displays a table of contents called "object lists" and provides a link to each segment from this table of contents.

There are also some other work that uses segments to provide zoom in and out of a web page [16], identify the navigation and content blocks, and then filter the relevant ones and show the summarizes to the user[1], identify the segments and filter out the irrelevant or unnecessary ones [22], identify the navigation bar and do not display it if the page is a content page [8]. [8] similarly proposes to remove decoration and special objects such as adverts, logo, contact, copyright, reference, etc. [12,19] propose a transcoding technique for outlining the sections by using the section headers. In summary, the page is kept the same but the section header is converted to a link that points to the content of that section. Highlights the importance of blocks/segments in a web page with different color. It shows a thumbnail view of the page with the importance of the blocks highlighted [24].

[21] presents the complete web page to the user and the user then clicks on regions on the web page to retrieve sub-pages. Similarly, [23] aims to show the user the thumbnail view of the page and when the users move their mouse over a section, they asynchronously retrieves that block and displays it to the user. [10,9] also aim to present the thumbnail view of the page and then the user can move to sub-pages. [25,3] present the thumbnail view of the page and the full screen information about a segment, the user can move from one block to another to retrieve the content.

When we look at web accessibility field, we also see that visually impaired users also experience similar problems to mobile web users and similar approaches have also been proposed for web accessibility [26].

When the page is visually segmented but this is not encoded in the source code, applications such as screen readers cannot access that information. Therefore, the page becomes very inaccessible to screen reader users. [2,18] aim to identify visual segments in a web page such that the page can be re-engineered to better support accessibility. They propose to manually annotate the page to identify the role of segments in a page.

Similar approach is proposed by [27] in the Dante project, where the visual segments in a web page is annotated by an ontology and that ontology is then used to re-engineer web pages for visually impaired web users. Similar approach has the been proposed by [13] where the segmentation of visual elements have been automated by using the underlying CSS of a web page. [14,4] indicates that the applications such as screen readers process a web page sequentially (i.e., they first read through menus, banners, commercials, etc) therefore this makes browsing time-consuming and strenuous for screen reader users. Therefore, with the specialized audio browser called Hearsay or CSurf what they try to do is that when the user clicks on a link they aim to retrieve the target page and point the user to the relevant block to that link. They do this by segmenting a web page into several blocks and then identifying the context and the relevant block to that link.

When we investigate the approaches used to segment a web page, we see that they can be grouped into two: top-down and bottom-up page segmentation. Top-down web page segmentation approach starts with the root node of a page and segments this node into smaller blocks iteratively, using different features obtained from the content of the page [3]. Bottom-up web page segmentation approach, on the other hand, starts with atomic content units such as the leaf nodes of the DOM representation [3]. Different algorithms have been also proposed to automate the process of segmentation which includes heuristics approach [1], machine learning [3], clustering, etc. One successful approach is the VIPS algorithm that combines the analysis of both the underlying source code and the visual rendering of a web page [7]. However, there are some limitations of this approach. Therefore, in our work we have extended VIPS. In the following sections, we first introduce VIPS and then discuss our improvements.

3   VIPS: A VIsion Based Page Segmentation Algorithm

Web pages are based on a hierarchical DOM structure which consists of both significant and insignificant nodes having contextual or representational purpose in the page layout. DOM structure includes all the nodes and their relationships in a web page. Visual rendering of the page, on the other hand, eliminates insignificant nodes and restructure the page layout with respect to the representation of the nodes. It helps to disregard invisible nodes, differentiate various tag types and group bulk content by using visual attributes, such as font size, background color or margin. Most segmentation algorithms focus on the DOM structure but visual rendering is also an important factor in segmentation for differentiating blocks of visual elements in a web page.

Figure 1 represents two segmentation approaches. The first in Figure 1.a is based only on the DOM structure of the page. The figure shows that, it highlights invisible nodes as content blocks and disregards some visual cues, such as background color, which are used to group content. For example, although DB.3 is invisible and insignificant, it is in the content structure as it appears in the DOM structure. Moreover, DB.4 and DB.5 have the same background color, which is different from the background color of both DB.1 and DB.2. The color differentiation implicitly indicates that they are related, but DB.4 and DB.5 are represented as different blocks. In combination of both DOM structure and visual rendering, on the other hand, provides much richer information and therefore provides better segmentation.

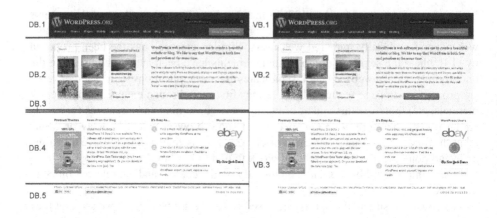

Fig. 1. 1st level of segmentation based on a) DOM structure (left) and b) both DOM and visual rendering (right)

In brief, DOM structure on its own does not provide sufficient segmentation results as contains invisible nodes and it provides only structural organization of the nodes. In order to segment pages to detect coherent blocks, visual representation need to be also used in coordination with the underlying DOM structure. VIPS Algorithm achieves this by examining a set of visual cues of each node in the DOM structure. Therefore, it provides a much more convenient technique for web page segmentation. However, VIPS Algorithm still has some limitations. In the following sections, we summarize the VIPS Algorithm and explain its limitations.

3.1   VIPS Algorithm

VIPS Algorithm first labels all the nodes in a web page with respect to their visibility in the page layout, the line-breaks they produce and their children nodes [7]. It labels the nodes which are displayed in a page layout as valid nodes. It divides the blocks according to whether they produce a line-break in rendering. If a node has a HTML tag which only affects the textual appearance (such as italic or bold font) and if it is applied to a textual content without introducing a line-break, then this node is labeled as inline node. Otherwise, if the HTML tag produces a line-break before or after its representation, it is labeled as line-break node. Free text nodes, which does not have a HTML tag are labeled as text nodes. The nodes which only consist of text nodes or inline nodes are labeled as virtual text nodes.

After labeling the nodes in a web page, VIPS Algorithm aims to find visual blocks in a web page in three main steps which are: (1) visual block extraction, (2) visual block separation and (3) content structure construction. In visual block extraction part, some visual cues of the nodes are examined to decide whether create a block for the node on some predefined rules. In visual block separation, using the visual cues further, VIPS Algorithm tries to find the relevance between two blocks. Finally, in content structure construction, VIPS constructs a block tree of visual blocks in a hierarchical structure.

Visual block extraction is the major part of the algorithm, since visual segments are defined in this part. Some predefined rules are applied on nodes to decide whether to construct a block or not. This decision is mainly taken on the label of the node (valid, inline or line-break) and labels, background colors, font styles and sizes of its children. Also, in each visual block extraction step, a Degree of Coherence (DoC) value is assigned to each block. When a block is assigned bigger DoC value than a predefined value, the algorithm stops segmenting for the corresponding node. After one iteration of visual block extraction process, the algorithm returns a set of visual blocks which are related to some of the nodes in the DOM structure of the web page.

In visual block separation, the algorithm first detects the separators between the blocks extracted in the previous step. These separators are the spaces which surround the visual blocks. Then, the algorithm assigns a weight to each separator, by examining background color and font size of the blocks at both sides and height and width of the separator. This weight initiates the relevance of the content of two blocks.

In the third, all extracted visual blocks are appended to a tree of visual blocks. The root of this block tree is the visual block which represents the root node of the DOM. The algorithm jumps to visual block extraction and repeats the 3 steps for the children of nodes which examined in previous iteration. Finally, the algorithm terminates when there is no other node to examine.

At the end of the execution of the algorithm over a web page, it produces a tree of visual blocks in a hierarchical structure. This tree is different from the DOM structure of the page, since the algorithm eliminates the invalid nodes and group the adjacent virtual text nodes and inline nodes into one single visual block. Therefore, the tree of visual blocks is simpler when it is compared to the DOM structure of a web page. Figure 2 represents an example segmentation result for the Wordpress.org. Firstly, the page is divided into larger visual blocks, such as VB1.1, VB1.2, VB1.3 in Figure 2. Then, these blocks are further divided into smaller visual blocks. For instance, VB1.3 is further divided into VB1.3.1, VB1.3.2 and VB1.3.3. In our ACTF implementation, the visual element identifier generates the tree of visual elements and creates an XPATH[1] for each visual block with respect to its corresponding node.

3.2   VIPS Limitations

The algorithm is very effective since it combines both the tag attributes of the nodes and visual properties to detect the visual blocks of the page. However, this method of segmentation has several limitations. One major drawback of this approach is that, in the rule set which was defined for visual block extraction, precedence of the rules and thresholds are not well defined. Another problem with this approach is that, the tag set mentioned in the rules are narrow and does not contain HTML5 tags, and the rule set needs to be extended with additional visual attributes. Finally, VIPS has no detailed understanding and detection of dynamic contents.

Although the rule set in the study covers many visual aspects of web pages, the precedence of the rules, the application order on a node is not well defined. This causes some ambiguities in implementation of the algorithm. The order of the representation of

---

[1] http://www.w3.org/TR/xpath/

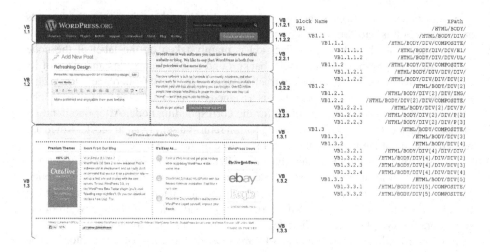

Fig. 2. Visual blocks for Wordpress.org and its corresponding block structure

the rules also conflicts with the given example in the context of visual block extraction. Moreover, the criteria of defining thresholds for size of the nodes to apply for some rules, is not also defined. Therefore, some of the rules need to be clarified, and some additional rules should be defined in the rule set.

Although the nodes are classified under categories with respect to their visual representation in a web page, HTML tags given in the study are very limited. The list of tags contains six tag types, which are inline text nodes, TABLE, TR, TD, P and other tags. However, this list is so narrow that, it does not cover neither all HTML tags nor any of HTML5 tags, which was released after VIPS was introduced [7]. Other tags than TABLE, TR, TD and P have different properties and behaviors in a web page so that they should not be used in the same category. Also, some of the tags produce unnatural visual representation when they are not used as they should be. For example, a TABLE node consists of TR nodes, which also consists of TD nodes. If we append a TD node without a TR node directly to the TABLE node, it results in a representation that does not result in a line-break. On the other hand, some of the tags produce longer line-breaks than the others. For example, P nodes have top and bottom margins longer than those of a DIV node. Line break tags need to be further classified according to their representation in the page.

Modern web pages also contain many dynamic contents which is updated frequently or with a user interaction, without reloading the whole page. This type of content is usually invisible at the initial page load and becomes visible after an event or a AJAX call appends some additional content to the existing nodes. However, these invisible nodes are considered as invalid; therefore, they are not taken into consideration when they become valid later. The algorithm applies only on a state of a web page, in order to catch the dynamic content, it requires further execution of segmentation process.

In summary, VIPS Algorithm is a very popular and functional algorithm to segment a web page according to its both visual layout and the underlying DOM structure.

However, the algorithm needs to be improved to implement a segmentation mechanism on modern web pages.

4   VIPS Improvements and Implementation

In order to solve the limitations explained in the previous section, we have implemented an extended version of the VIPS algorithm on Accessibility Tools Framework (ACTF) on Java platform[2]. ACTF is a framework and extensible infrastructure, which enables developers to build a variety of utilities for improving the accessibility of applications and content for people with disabilities. ACTF provides a IE based browser and interfaces to control this browser, such as changing textual content of an element. Using these interfaces, DOM structure of a web page and its visual rendering properties are retrieved.

First of all, we extended the set of tags by including HTML5 tags and classifying them under tag sets which are defined in the original algorithm. Then, we have further classified line break nodes with respect to the spaces which they produce around their borders. For example, a DIV node and a P node produce different size of spaces in their visual representation. Moreover, we added some visual cues to detect separate contents in a web page. These cues include font size and font weight, background color as already exist in the original algorithm and additionally margin, padding and float attributes. These visual attributes are generally used to separate different content with titles and empty spaces between the content and create coherent content by grouping sub-blocks in the page layout. We have also implemented embedded objects such as video players and widgets in the web pages.

Another ambiguity in the original algorithm is about invisible nodes. Although there is a basic method to make a node invisible in visual representation, some designers refer different techniques which need to be explained in detail. The most general technique for invisible nodes is to set its display attribute to 'none', or visibility attribute to 'hidden'. However, in some web pages, invisible nodes are created by setting the absolute position of the node to out of page borders with either high negative left or negative top values. Another possibility for invisible nodes is that, their text-indent attribute is set to a negative value to prevent them being represented in the web page. Also, some leaf nodes without textual or graphical content has either zero width or height. These nodes are only represented in the page layout as separators between significant content.

By using the above definitions and visual cues, we traversed the nodes in DOM structure and examined the visual styles of each node. Following rules are applied on the nodes in this structure for visual block extraction:

1. Remove all the invalid nodes. Note that, valid nodes without any child must be kept, since, although they do not have a valid content, they appear in the page layout and might be used as a separator between two different topics. Also, although invalid nodes are not taken into consideration, they may be significant when dynamic content segmentation is handled and criteria for ignoring invisible nodes may be changed in future extensions.

---

[2] http://www.eclipse.org/actf/

2. If a node has only text node or invalid children, no block extracted.
3. If node has only one child,
   (a) If child is a text node or virtual text node, then no block extracted.
   (b) If child is line-break node, then same rules are applied to the child node.
4. If all the children are virtual text nodes of a node, node is put into block pool and we do not divide this rule in next turns.
5. If some of the children has full page width and some of the children are in the same horizontal axis and their total width is equal to the page width, divide this node so that, each full width node is a separate block and the nodes in the same horizontal axis are grouped into one single block.
6. If node is a table and some of its columns have different background color than the others, divide the table into the number saparate columns and construct a block for each piece.
7. If one of the child node has bigger font size than its previous siblings, divide node into two blocks. Put the nodes before the child node with bigger font size into the first block, and put the remaining nodes to the second block.
8. If the first child of the node has bigger font size than the remaining children, extract two blocks, one of which is the first child with bigger font size, and the other contains remaining children.
9. If a node contains a child whose tag is HR, BR or any of line-break nodes which has no children, then the node is divided into two as the nodes before the separator and after the separator. For each side of the separator, two new blocks are created and children nodes are put under these blocks. Note that, separator does not extract a block under the main block, it just serves to extract two blocks which other nodes are put into.
10. If a node has some nodes whose line-break spaces are different than each other, divide this node. Each node having larger line-break space will be a separate block, and other nodes next to each other create a block as a whole.
11. If node has at least one child with float value "left" or "right", create three blocks. For each children,
   (a) If child is left float, put it into the first block.
   (b) If child is right float, put it into the second block.
   (c) If child is not both left and right float, put it into the third block. If first block or second block have children, create new blocks for them. Also, create a new block for the child without float.
12. If a node has a child, whose at least one of margin-top and margin-bottom values are nonzero, divide this node into two blocks. Put the sibling nodes before the node with nonzero margin into the first block and put the siblings after the node with nonzero margin into the second block.
   (a) If child has only nonzero margin-top, put the child into second block.
   (b) If child has only nonzero margin-bottom, put the child into first block.
   (c) If child has both nonzero margin-top and nonzero margin-bottom, create a third block and put it between two blocks.
13. If a node has a line-break child containing an image or object, divide node into two blocks. Put the nodes before the child with image or object into the first block, and put the remaining children into the second block.

14. If the first child of the node contains an image or image, put this child as a block, and create a new block for the remaining children.

The application precedence of the rules are the same as their definition order. In each iteration of visual block extraction mechanism, each visual block is appended in a block pool with respect to their hierarchical position in the page layout. Finally, a content structure is built by using these visual blocks in a tree structure. Our implementation concerns only on visual block extraction and content structure construction parts in the original algorithm, since visual separator detection process is not relevant with our usage area of web page segmentation.

We also committed our implementation to ACTF and it is available under the terms of the Eclipse Public License v1.0³, so that, anyone can benefit from our contribution.

5   Evaluation

We have conducted a user evaluation to better understand how people perceive the success of our extended and implemented VIPS algorithm. In order to reach more people from different countries with different demographic properties, such as level of expertise in web design and development, age group and education, our user evaluation was conducted online which is available at http://emine.ncc.metu.edu.tr/eval/survey/.

Procedure

Regarding the segmentation, our online study included three main parts:
Information Sheet: First page in our study included an information sheet about the study. This page mainly included an overview of the study, and some information about the anonymity and the tasks to be completed.
Demographics: When somebody participated in our study, we collected some demographics information about them, for example their gender, experience in web design, education, age range, etc.
Visual Elements Identification: In this part, participants were shown a web page in top five levels of segmentation, and they were asked to rate these levels and also rank the levels of segmentation. In overall, the survey application was designed to repeat this step for randomly selected nine pages.

Materials

In order to group web pages with respect to their sizes and complexities, we have used the Visual Complexity Rankings and Accessibility Metrics (VICRAM) framework [15]. For a given web page, VICRAM assigns a Visual Complexity Score (VCS) which represents the complexity of the web page. We have selected top 100 web pages from Alexa and calculated their VCS values. By grouping these pages into three, we then randomly

---

³ http://www.eclipse.org/legal/epl-v10.html

selected ten pages from each complexity group and 30 overall pages. The first group is low complexity pages with VCS value lower than three. The other group consists of medium complexity pages with a VCS value between three and seven. Final group includes high complexity pages with a VCS value above seven. However, when we were preparing the data for our evaluation, we could not take a screenshot of one of the low complexity pages because it was too dynamic therefore we have 29 pages at the end. This approach gave us a systematic method for choosing pages with different levels of complexity. Our evaluation aims to retrieve data of pages from each complexity group for each participant, so that, ranking and rating task were repeated for nine randomly selected pages, which includes three pages from each complexity group.

Research Questions

Regarding the segmentation, our study focused on investigating the following two research questions:
1. What is the perceived success of our extended segmentation algorithm? How does this differ based on the web page complexity? With the first part of the question, we aim to investigate how people view the segmentation success and in the second part we try to understand whether complexity has any effect on the perceived success of our algorithm.
2. Which level of segmentation is the most preferred? As explained above our segmentation algorithm segments a web page in different levels, therefore this question aims to understand which level would people think be appropriate level for segmentation.

Results

Our online study was released on the 7th of February 2013, and here we present the preliminary analysis of our results based of the data collected in two weeks after the survey was announced. In overall, 220 participants completed our study and 25 of them have completed at least three pages. Since our study was designed to include pages with different complexity levels, we wanted to make sure that data that we analyze come from participants who evaluated at least one page from each complexity level. Of our 25 participants, ten were female and 15 were male. Seven participants were aged between 18-24, eight of them were 25-34, eight of them were 25-54 and two of the participants were aged over 55. Five participants completed high/secondary school, two completed associate's degree, six completed bachelor's degree, seven completed master's degree and five completed doctorate. 18 participants have worked in web design and development, four of them studied this subject and three of them are interested in web design as a hobby. Seven participants describe their level of expertise in web design and development as professional, 13 as intermediate and five as novice/beginner. All of the participants use internet daily.

In overall, 259 pages and 1,295 levels have been evaluated. Among these pages and levels, 148 pages and 740 levels were considered in our evaluation as valid evaluations since their participants satisfied the minimum requirement of evaluating at least three pages from different complexity levels. Evaluated pages consist of 49 pages and 245

Table 1. Rating results

	Level 1	Level 2	Level 3	Level 4	Level 5
Low Complexity	47.2	58.4	66.4	70.45	72.22
Medium Complexity	42.4	52	66	73.6	74
High Complexity	40.8	51.6	62	68.4	76

Table 2. Ranking Results

Level No	High Complexity					Medium Complexity					Low Complexity				
	Best L.				Worst L.	Best L.				Worst L.	Best L.				Worst L.
Level 5	38	4	1	2	6	31	3	1	2	11	17	1	1	1	6
Level 4	5	35	2	4	5	6	30	2	7	3	5	15	1	2	3
Level 3	2	5	36	5	3	5	5	33	2	3	1	4	13	5	3
Level 2	2	2	8	33	5	3	4	5	28	8	1	3	6	15	1
Level 1	2	5	4	7	32	3	6	7	9	23	2	3	5	3	13

levels from high complexity, 48 pages and 240 levels from medium complexity, and 51 pages from low complexity.

Table 1 represents the ranking results of the participants for three complexity groups and five segmentation levels. For each value in the table, we have detected the overall view of each participant on a particular level and calculated the average result over participants' responses weighted by their population variance. The rating results indicate that, for all complexity groups, the 1st level of segmentation has the lowest success rate and 5th level of segmentation has the highest success rate.

Table 2 shows the ranking results of the participants for five segmentation levels. In this table, best level column represents the level which has been selected by the majority of participants as best level of segmentation among the first five levels in a particular web page. According to the level ranking results, the best level among first five levels of segmentation is the 5th level, in which segmentation is more detailed. The worst level of segmentation is the 1st level, where the web page is segmented into its basic segments.

Discussion

In brief, user evaluation results on levels of segmentation shows that the success rate in the 5th level is the most successful segmentation, which has a value around 74% and success rate decreases when the segmentation level decreases, down to approximately 40%. The growth in success rates, when we look at the upper levels, is the same and success rates are very similar for each level in three complexity groups. However, there is a significant difference between the success rates of 1st and 5th levels in each complexity groups.

According to the ranking results of the participants in our user evaluation shows that, when we pick the most selected level among each column in Table 2, the best level of segmentation among the first five levels in a particular web page is selected to be the

5th level, which represents the visual blocks appearing in the highest depth in the block structure. Moreover, 5th level has smaller visual blocks and more detailed segmentation when it is compared to the preceding levels. Participants also ranked the 1st level of segmentation as the worst level. This may be because the first level of segmentation does not have enough granularity and people perceived them as not so useful.

When we compare the results of rating and ranking procedures, we see that, the results are parallel in growth, so that, 5th level which is selected as the best level is also rated as the most successful level. Similarly, the 1st level which is selected as the worst level is also rated as the most unsuccessful level. However, the same rules apply on each node in every level of a web page, therefore, we expect to have similar rates for each level. This may be explained with our method of evaluation. Since we have conducted an online survey, and the pages which the participants evaluated are very limited, there is a possibility that most of the participants applied the same task of ranking the levels. Therefore, the results in the rating part of our survey may also reflect the ranking of segmentation levels rather than the success of our segmentation approach.

6 Summary and Future Work

This paper presented how we have extended VIPS algorithm for automatically segmenting web pages. The paper also presented our online user evaluation which was conducted to investigate how people perceive the success of the segmentation approach and in which granularity they prefer to see a web page segmented. Finally, the paper presented the preliminary results which show that people perceive segmentation with higher granularity as better segmentation regardless of the web page complexity. This finding is very important for being able to decide how to segment a web page automatically and display it to mobile and disabled users for better interaction experience.

Our current implementation of the extended VIPS Algorithm on the ACTF framework does not include a specific mechanism in detecting and understanding dynamic content in web pages. Many pages for example contain auto-suggest lists, dropdown menus, calendars, notification boxes, tickers, tabs, slideshows (carousels). These blocks are typically invisible at the initial load of the page and become visible after a certain event, such as the mouse comes over a menu item for dropdown menus, user types some characters in a text box for auto-suggest lists, user clicks on a node for calendars and after some events, the result of the event is displayed in the page for notifications. The invisible content is either loaded initially as set to be invisible (as in dropdown menus and calendars) or appended to an existing node in the DOM structure after an AJAX call (as in auto-suggest lists). Therefore, we need to detect the invisible content and the event which turns these content to visible. After their detection, the content should not be divided further to its sub-blocks, rather represent a single visual block as a whole.

Content expansion is also very popular in modern web pages. In this type of dynamic content, a visible content is expanded after user interaction, such as, expansion buttons and accordion menus. Another type of content expansion is page expansion, in which, new content is retrieved with an AJAX call and appended to the bottom of the page, when user scrolls down to the bottom. In page expansion, new content is not included in the initial DOM structure and has the same visual structure with existing content. These kind of dynamic content is important for users who are accessing web pages in constraint environments. One might need to display only the new expanded material to the user, however the our extended VIPS algorithm does not explicitly focus on these expanded content and web pages need to be segmented all together. Therefore, in our future work we are planning to address this by dynamically segmenting the new content without completely reprocessing a web page.

Acknowledgements. The project is supported by the Scientific and Technological Research Council of Turkey (TÜBİTAK) with the grant number 109E251 (http://emine.ncc.metu.edu.tr/). As such the authors would like to thank to (TÜBİTAK) for their continued support.

References

1. : Efficient web browsing on small screens. In: Proceedings of the Working Conference on Advanced Visual Interfaces, AVI 2008, pp. 23–30. ACM, New York (2008)
2. Asakawa, C., Takagi, H.: Annotation-based transcoding for nonvisual web access. In: ASSETS 2000, pp. 172–179. ACM Press (2000)
3. Baluja, S.: Browsing on small screens: recasting web-page segmentation into an efficient machine learning framework. In: WWW 2006: Proceedings of the 15th International Conference on World Wide Web, pp. 33–42. ACM, New York (2006)
4. Borodin, Y., Mahmud, J., Ramakrishnan, I.V., Stent, A.: The hearsay non-visual web browser. In: Proceedings of the 2007 International Cross-disciplinary Conference on Web Accessibility (W4A 2007), pp. 128–129. ACM, New York (2007)
5. Cai, D., He, X., Li, Z., Ma, W.Y., Wen, J.R.: Hierarchical clustering of www image search results using visual, textual and link information. In: Proceedings of the 12th Annual ACM International Conference on Multimedia, MULTIMEDIA 2004, pp. 952–959. ACM, New York (2004)
6. Cai, D., He, X., Wen, J.R., Ma, W.Y.: Block-level link analysis. In: Proceedings of the 27th Annual International ACM SIGIR Conference on Research and Development in Information Retrieval, SIGIR 2004, pp. 440–447. ACM, New York (2004), http://doi.acm.org/10.1145/1008992.1009068
7. Cai, D., Yu, S., Wen, J.R., Ma, W.Y.: Vips: a vision based page segmentation algorithm. Tech. Rep. MSR-TR-2003-79, Microsoft Research (2003)
8. Chen, J., Zhou, B., Shi, J., Zhang, H., Wu, Q.: Function-based object towards website adaptation. In: Proceedings of the Tenth International World Wide Web Conference. ACM, Hong Kong (2001)
9. Chen, Y., Ma, W., Zhang, H.: Detecting web page structure for adaptive viewing on small form factor devices. In: Proceedings of the Twelfth International World Wide Web Conference (2003)
10. Chen, Y., Xie, X., Ma, W.Y., Zhang, H.J.: Adapting web pages for small-screen devices. IEEE Internet Computing 9, 50–56 (2005), http://portal.acm.org/citation.cfm?id=1053547.1053593
11. Hattori, G., Hoashi, K., Matsumoto, K., Sugaya, F.: Robust web page segmentation for mobile terminal using content-distances and page layout information. In: WWW 2007: Proceedings of the 16th International Conference on World Wide Web, pp. 361–370. ACM Press, New York (2007)
12. Hwang, Y., Kim, J., Seo, E.: Structure-aware web transcoding for mobile devices. IEEE Internet Computing 7(5), 14–21 (2003)
13. Lunn, D., Harper, S., Bechhofer, S.: Identifying behavioral strategies of visually impaired users to improve access to web content. ACM Trans. Access. Comput. 3(4), 13:1–13:35 (2011), http://doi.acm.org/10.1145/1952388.1952390

14. Mahmud, J.U., Borodin, Y., Ramakrishnan, I.V.: Csurf: a context-driven non-visual web-browser. In: Proceedings of the 16th International Conference on World Wide Web, WWW 2007, pp. 31–40. ACM, New York (2007),
http://doi.acm.org/10.1145/1242572.1242578
15. Michailidou, E.: ViCRAM: Visual Complexity Rankings and Accessibility Metrics. Ph.D. thesis (2010)
16. Milic-Frayling, N., Sommerer, R.: Smartview: Flexible viewing of web page contents. In: Poster Proceedings of the Eleventh International World Wide Web Conference (May 2002)
17. Song, R., Liu, H., Wen, J.R., Ma, W.Y.: Learning block importance models for web pages. In: Proceedings of the 13th International Conference on World Wide Web, WWW 2004, pp. 203–211. ACM, New York (2004),
http://doi.acm.org/10.1145/988672.988700
18. Takagi, H., Asakawa, C., Fukuda, K., Maeda, J.: Site-wide annotation: Reconstructing existing pages to be accessible. In: ASSETS 2002, pp. 81–88. ACM Press (2002)
19. Whang, Y., Jung, C., Kim, J., Chung, S.: Webalchemist: A web transcoding system for mobile web access in handheld devices. In: Optoelectronic and Wireless Data Management, Processing, Storage, and Retrieval, pp. 102–109 (2001)
20. Xiang, P., Shi, Y.: Recovering semantic relations from web pages based on visual cues. In: Proceedings of the 11th International Conference on Intelligent User Interfaces, IUI 2006, pp. 342–344. ACM, New York (2006),
http://doi.acm.org/10.1145/1111449.1111531
21. Xiao, X., Luo, Q., Hong, D., Fu, H.: Slicing*-tree based web page transformation for small displays. In: Proceedings of the 14th ACM International Conference on Information and Knowledge Management, CIKM 2005, pp. 303–304. ACM, New York (2005),
http://doi.acm.org/10.1145/1099554.1099638
22. Xiao, Y., Tao, Y., Li, Q.: Web page adaptation for mobile device. In: Wireless Communications, Networking and Mobile Computing (2008)
23. Xiao, Y., Tao, Y., Li, W.: A dynamic web page adaptation for mobile device based on web2.0. In: Proceedings of the 2008 Advanced Software Engineering and Its Applications, pp. 119–122. IEEE Computer Society, Washington, DC (2008),
http://portal.acm.org/citation.cfm?id=1487741.1488145
24. Xie, X., Miao, G., Song, R., Wen, J.R., Ma, W.Y.: Efficient browsing of web search results on mobile devices based on block importance model. In: Proceedings of the Third IEEE International Conference on Pervasive Computing and Communications, pp. 17–26. IEEE Computer Society, Washington, DC (2005),
http://portal.acm.org/citation.cfm?id=1048930.1049752
25. Yang, X., Shi, Y.: Enhanced gestalt theory guided web page segmentation for mobile browsing. In: Proceedings of the 2009 IEEE/WIC/ACM International Joint Conference on Web Intelligence and Intelligent Agent Technology, vol. 03, WI-IAT 2009, pp. 46–49. IEEE Computer Society, Washington, DC (2009),
http://dx.doi.org/10.1109/WI-IAT.2009.227
26. Yesilada, Y., Chuter, A., Henry, S.L.: Shared Web Experiences: Barriers Common to Mobile Device Users and People with Disabilities. W3C (2008),
http://www.w3.org/WAI/mobile/experiences
27. Yesilada, Y., Harper, S., Goble, C.A., Stevens, R.: Screen readers cannot see (ontology based semantic annotation for visually impaired web travellers). In: Koch, N., Fraternali, P., Wirsing, M. (eds.) ICWE 2004. LNCS, vol. 3140, pp. 445–458. Springer, Heidelberg (2004)
28. Yin, X., Lee, W.: Using link analysis to improve layout on mobile devices. In: Proceedings of the Thirteenth International World Wide Web Conference, pp. 338–344 (2004)
29. Yin, X., Lee, W.S.: Understanding the function of web elements for mobile content delivery using random walk models. In: Special Interest Tracks and Posters of the 14th International Conference on World Wide Web, WWW 2005, pp. 1150–1151. ACM, New York (2005),
http://doi.acm.org/10.1145/1062745.1062913

Relating User Experience with MobileApp Quality Evaluation and Design

Philip Lew[1] and Luis Olsina[2]

[1] School of Computer Science and Engineering, Beihang University, China
[2] GIDIS, Web Engineering School at Universidad Nacional de La Pampa, Argentina
philiplew@gmail.com, olsina@ing.unlpam.edu.ar

Abstract. Designing quality into web applications (WebApps) and evaluating WebApp quality and usability have been the subject of abundant research. However, both the design and evaluation of traditional WebApps cannot account for the particular features and usage contexts of mobile applications (MobileApps). MobileApps have several characteristics that pose challenges in their design and evaluation regarding current quality models and their included characteristics and sub-characteristics. For instance, the operability of a user interface has a much different and greater influence when evaluating MobileApp usability and user experience due to the context of the user. Characteristics such as multi-touch gestures, button size, and widget usage have a magnified impact on task completion rates. We propose in this paper utilizing our previously developed ISO 25010-based quality models and framework so-called 2Q2U (*Quality, Quality in use, actual Usability* and *User experience*) for MobileApps. Specific MobileApp task screens and attributes are illustrated in order to show our evaluation approach applicability.

Keywords: MobileApp, Quality models, User Experience, Usability, QinU.

1 Introduction

WebApps, a combination of information, integrated functionalities and services have become the most predominant form of software delivery today with users and businesses choosing to rent or use software rather than buy it. This has led to increased and focused attention in software quality models that facilitate understanding, evaluating, and especially improving their quality.

With respect to software quality models, ISO 25010 [7] outlines a flexible model with product/system quality –also known as internal and external quality (EQ)-, and system-in-use quality –also referred to as quality in use (QinU). Product quality consists of those characteristics that can be evaluated in early development stages, for instance, design documents, code quality, etc., while system quality consists of those characteristics and attributes that can be evaluated in late stages, with the application in execution state. On the other hand, system-in-use quality consists of characteristics as evaluated by an end user when actually executing application tasks in a real context. An example would be a nurse or a doctor entering patient record and diagnosis information into an electronic health records system. A doctor even while

Q.Z. Sheng and J. Kjeldskov (Eds.): ICWE 2013 Workshops, LNCS 8295, pp. 253–268, 2013.
© Springer International Publishing Switzerland 2013

doing the same task, may have different error and completion rates than a nurse for whatever reason. Doctors may also take longer and have less efficiency in completing tasks simply because they don't do as many. In addition, system QinU is heavily dependent on the context of the task and user. For instance, a user in a dim warehouse doing inventory will have a different viewpoint than a doctor in a well-lit hospital.

ISO 25010 also delineates a relationship between the two quality views whereby system quality 'influences' system-in-use quality and system-in-use quality 'depends' on system quality. We recently have developed 2Q2U version 2.0 [12], which ties together all of these quality concepts by relating system quality characteristics and attributes with QinU and user experience (UX). Using 2Q2U, evaluators can select the quality characteristics to evaluate and conduct a systematic evaluation using the 'depends' and 'influences' relationships [9].

Today, for MobileApps, more robust network infrastructures and smart mobile devices have led to increased functionality and capability thereby warranting special attention in comprehending how they are different from the UX point of view because user requirements, expectations, and behavior can be somewhat different. For instance, the quality design and evaluation of operability from a system viewpoint has a much different and greater influence for MobileApp usability and UX due to the size of the screen and context of the user. Characteristics such as button size, placement, contextual help, and widget usage for example have a much greater impact on task completion rates and task error rates [1, 3, 4, 15]. Ultimately, UX characteristics are very often neglected in quality modeling or seldom placed appropriately in quality views and this is magnified in a mobile context [10, 12].

Given this, there is a need for a characterization of MobileApps considering non-functional aspects in both UX and EQ. Consequently, the particular features of MobileApps –regarded both as a system and a system-in-use entity- pose new challenges regarding current quality models and their included and more relevant characteristics and sub-characteristics, as well as the particular attributes or properties to be measured and evaluated. Additionally, for MobileApps, there is an increased emphasis on many contextual elements related to the task and therefore the QinU. So, starting with the task at hand, and applying our 2Q2U model [12], we can incorporate the importance of task and particular MobileApp UX factors into the design of MobileApps. Starting with MobileApp UX, we can outline practical guidelines to design a MobileApp with optimal EQ characteristics based on UX goals.

Ultimately, the specific contributions of this research are: (a) Analyzing UX and usability for MobileApps in the light of 2Q2U v2.0 quality models; (b) Characterizing relevant quality features of MobileApps with regard to context, system-in-use and system; and (c) Illustrating MobileApp features and their potential impact in MobileApp quality design and evaluation.

Following this introduction, Section 2 outlines our nonfunctional requirements component and 2Q2U quality framework for better understanding where context, UX and usability fit in, among other issues. Section 3, discusses relevant features of MobileApps (both as a system and a system-in-use entity category) useful for designing and evaluating UX and usability. In Section 4, we discuss the usefulness of the proposed framework, while examples of UX/usability attributes and screens for MobileApps are illustrated. Section 5 describes related work and, finally, Section 6 draws our main conclusions and outlines future work.

2   Nonfunctional Requirements and the 2Q2U Quality Framework

In [12] we have updated the ISO 25010 standard [7] regarding quality models for evaluating new generation WebApps. The new quality models and framework is called 2Q2U v2.0, which also relies on the C-INCAMI (*Contextual-Information Need, Concept model, Attribute, Metric* and *Indicator*) measurement and evaluation conceptual framework [13]. C-INCAMI is structured in six components, namely: i) *Measurement and Evaluation Project*; ii) *Nonfunctional Requirements*; iii) *Context*; iv) *Measurement;* v) *Evaluation*; and vi) *Analysis and Recommendation*.

Of particular interest to illustrate in this article for understanding and instantiating MobileApp quality models are C-INCAMI's Nonfunctional Requirements and Context components, both shown in Fig. 1 –below, key words in the figure are highlighted in italic. The Nonfunctional Requirements component (labeled *requirements*) specifies the *Information Need* of any measurement and evaluation project; that is, the *purpose* (e.g. "understand", "improve") and the *user Viewpoint* (e.g. "developer", "mobile final user"). In turn, it *focuses* on a *Calculable Concept* (whose *name* is for instance "External Quality", "User Experience", etc) and *specifies* the *Entity Category* to evaluate –e.g. a system, system-in-use *super Category*-, by means of a concrete *Entity* –e.g., the "United flight booking".

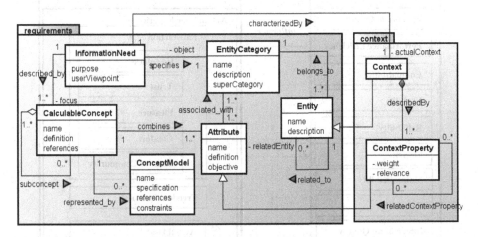

Fig. 1. C-INCAMI Nonfunctional Requirements and Context components

On the other hand, a calculable concept and its *sub-concepts* (e.g. "Usability") can be *represented by* a *Concept Model* (e.g. in "External Quality model") where the leaves of an instantiated model (requirements tree) are *Attributes associated with* an entity category. In fact, the concrete entity *belongs* to an entity category whose *name* is e.g. "Flight MobileApp".

The context component (labeled *context* in Fig.1) delineates the state of the situation of the entity to be assessed with regard to the information need (see *characterized By* relationship). *Context,* a special kind of *Entity* in which related relevant entities are involved, can be quantified through its related entities such as the environment of a mobile user, location, user age, user tasks, device type and screen size, etc. or even networking environment and performance.

To describe the context, properties of the relevant entities, which are also attributes called *Context Properties* are used. Context is particularly important regarding QinU requirements as instantiation of requirements must be done consistently in the same context so that evaluations and improvements can be accurately compared. But also context in a given project can be important regarding EQ requirements, as we discussed in [12], in which also we have proposed to delete the ISO 25010 *Context Coverage* characteristic from its QinU model, since as shown here the context specification can be represented independently of quality models.

Regarding *Concept* (quality) *Models* we have recently enhanced the ISO 25010 external quality and quality in use models, while maintaining many characteristics and the 'depends' and 'influences' relationships between both views. Fig. 2 depicts the quality model enhancement named 2Q2U, which was used in different studies [8, 9, 12].

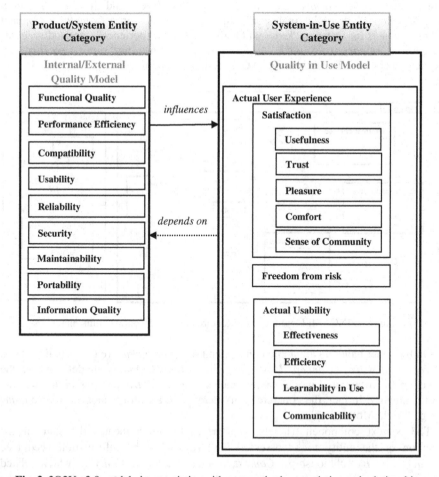

Fig. 2. 2Q2U v2.0 model characteristics with some sub-characteristics and relationships

Table 1. Definitions of QinU characteristics and sub-characteristics that are absent in ISO 25010 or were rephrased in 2Q2U v2.0

2Q2U v2.0 QinU Characteristic or Sub-characteristic Definition	ISO 25010 QinU Definition
Actual User Experience: Degree to which specified users can achieve actual usability, freedom from risk, and satisfaction in a specified context of use	Note: Absent calculable concept
Actual Usability (synonym *usability in use*):Degree to which specified users can achieve specified goals with effectiveness, efficiency, learnability in use, and without communicability breakdowns in a specified context of use	Note: Absent calculable concept, but similar concept (i.e. *usability in use*) was in the ISO 25010 draft
Effectiveness: Degree to which specified users can achieve specified goals with accuracy and completeness in a specified context of use	*Effectiveness*: Accuracy and completeness with which users achieve specified goals
Efficiency: Degree to which specified users expend appropriate amounts of resources in relation to the effectiveness achieved in a specified context of use	*Efficiency*: Resources expended in relation to the accuracy and completeness with which users achieve goals
Learnability in use: Degree to which specified users can learn efficiently and effectively while achieving specified goals in a specified context of use	Note: Absent calculable concept
Communicability: Degree to which specified users can achieve specified goals without communicative breakdowns in the interaction in a specified context of use	Note: Absent calculable concept
Sense of Community: Degree to which a user is satisfied when meeting, collaborating and communicating with other users with similar interest and needs	Note: Absent calculable concept

On top of each column (Fig. 2) the entity category is shown. For the QinU focus the *Entity Category* is named "System in Use", while for the EQ focus the *Entity Category* is named "System". For the QinU model we have added two main characteristics which are absent in the ISO standard viz. Actual User Experience, and Actual Usability. These concepts are related hierarchically as shown in Fig. 2 and also defined in Table 1.

For the EQ model we have added a new characteristic named Information Quality (which includes sub-characteristics such as Information Accuracy and Information Suitability), and rephrased others such as Functional Quality (which includes sub-characteristics such as Functional Accuracy and Functional Suitability) instead of the ISO functional suitability name. Also, we have also rephrased Usability as the *"degree to which the product or system has attributes that enable it to be understood, learned, operated, error protected, attractive and accessible to the user, when used under specified conditions"*. Ultimately, the rationale of these adaptations is in [12].

In using the ISO 25010 quality models for MobileApps, it is assumed that the software quality models, definitions, and concepts in the standard were intended for application to software information systems as a whole and therefore are also applicable to a great extent to MobileApps, a type of software application. Moreover, we have built up 2Q2U on top of ISO standards in order to consider new features of new generation WebApps. We argue that using 2Q2U is sufficient for instantiating quality models for either native MobileApps or web-oriented MobileApps, as we see later on.

Next, we examine several features and entities relevant for the quality design and evaluation of MobileApps. In doing so, we consider three main aspects of the above C-INCAMI framework, namely: i) Context; ii) Entity Category, regarding both system and system in use; and iii) Calculable Concepts, i.e. quality characteristics, sub-characteristics and attributes, regarding both the EQ and QinU focus. The rationale for considering these aspects relies on a previous work [9], where we instantiated QinU and EQ models for the purpose of understanding and then combined these instantiations with SIQinU (*Strategy for Improving Quality in Use*) to carry out evaluations to ultimately accomplish improvement in a WebApp.

3   Featuring MobileApp Usability and UX

QinU, UX and Usability have all recently come to the research forefront due to a general shift in emphasis to satisfying the end user as part of the customer experience. For MobileApps (including native MobileApps and Mobile WebApps), they become even more important due to the significance of the user context. In particular the user's activity at the time of usage, location, and time, amongst other influencing factors have significant impact on the quality of the user's experience.

This section examines several features and entities relevant for designing and evaluating UX, Usability, Information Suitability, etc. for MobileApps. For doing this, we consider the above three main aspects: i) Mobile contextual factors; ii) Mobile system-in-use (QinU) factors; and iii) Mobile system (EQ) factors.

3.1   Mobile Contextual Factors

The context of a MobileApp user is much different than a traditional WebApp or desktop user not only due to the size of the screen but other factors that influence the user's environment and therefore their behavior. A few of these factors include:

- *Activity*: What the user is doing at the time of usage has a significant influence on the user's attention span. For example, if they are driving, then they have a very short attention span, maybe 1 second, versus if they are in the middle of a conversation, perhaps they have an attention span of 3 seconds. On the other hand, if they are at home sitting on the sofa, then the user may have other distractions as well;

- *Day/time of day*: The day and time can impact what a user is doing, and the level of natural light. Unlike desktop or WebApps which are typically accessed indoors, the usage of MobileApps is particularly sensitive to this contextual factor influencing visibility;
- *Location*: The location of the user influences many elements. For instance, indoors, outdoors, in a car, in an elevator, train or factory all of which can also be related to the user activity;
- *User profile*: The increasing complexity of software combined with an aging user demographic has an interesting effect on the usability of MobileApps. For aging users, usually their close range vision capability has diminished along with their dexterity. On the other hand, applications have become complex, and therefore function and content simple-ness and understandability are also critical and influenced by the particular user group. Not only are there more aging users, there are also more younger users as children these days begin using computing devices as toddlers;
- *Device*: The size and type of the device and its physical characteristics influences what the user can see (or not see) as well as the placement and number of controls and widgets in reduced real-estate displays. This shortage of resources combined with the amount of text (information conciseness) all impact the usability and UX of the MobileApp; and
- *Network performance*: Obviously the speed at which an application uploads and downloads data is going to have a great impact because of the decreased attention span. It may also be compounded by other contextual elements such as *Activity* as a user engaged in a time sensitive activity will have decreased tolerance for poor network performance.

These contextual elements in turn heavily influence the QinU of a MobileApp with the degree of influence dependent on the task being executed. By understanding these contextual factors, and defining the task at hand, those EQ characteristics and the design decisions that determine the system quality can be optimized to account for the MobileApp user's experience.

3.2   Mobile System-in-use Factors

As seen in Fig. 2, system-in-use quality has UX, Actual Usability, and Satisfaction as sub-concepts. UX is determined by the satisfaction of the user's be goals (hedonic), and do goals (pragmatic) as noted by Hassenzahl [5]. On the one hand, do-goals relate to the user being able to accomplish what they want with Effectiveness and Efficiency while be-goals relate to the user's satisfaction. Satisfaction [7] includes those 'soft' and subjective sub-characteristics including Usefulness, Trust, Pleasure and Comfort.

While completing a task, the user's experience depends on much more than just completing the task itself. The task, the context of the task, including the conditions under which the task is undertaken and the user's background have a strong influence on the user's experience. Different tasks for the same user as well as different users for the same task will cause totally different user experiences.

Hence, the MobileApp UX must be evaluated with respect to a real user performing a real task that includes several key system-in-use factors that have significant impact on the effectiveness and efficiency of the user. For example:

i) *Task Workflow*: For MobileApps design, Pareto's 80/20 rule (80 percent of the usage goes toward 20 percent of the functionality) applies more than ever because applications need to be designed with the most common tasks in mind that would be suited to mobile usage. Because of the context of use of a mobile user, and the mobile user's limited attention span, task workflow and length of the workflow is extremely important for this limited task set. As noted by Budiu [3], tasks most suited for mobile devices include a) tasks that have a deadline such as paying a bill or buying a gift at the last minute, b) tasks that require rapidly changing information such as bank balances, flight information, movie schedules, directions, and c) tasks that require privacy as small screens are ideal for privacy. Given these activities, if task workflows are not designed to be short, there is a higher probability of error and a lower rate of completion -see effectiveness definition in Table 1. Workflows therefore need to be compressed by combining several steps into one through careful task definition and analysis. Reduced workflows, in turn, reduce task times and increase Efficiency (see definition in Table 1) while at the same time, reducing error rates and error rate reduction is extremely critical for users with short attention spans. If you are driving and executing a task and get an error, do you continue trying?;

ii) *Learnability*: For those applications that are more complex, Learnability in use (see definition in Table 1) is critical. Users that cannot learn how to quickly become masters of your application with soon look for and find another one by the competition. The App Store paradigm has created this behavior because so many applications in the same domain are either extremely inexpensive or free.

Using 2Q2U v2.0 in conjunction with a measurement and evaluation strategy documented in [9], we can define the task, and start with the QinU, noting the importance of task for the particular MobileApp and work backwards to determine the system characteristics and attributes that are necessary to achieve high UX performance. With this process, we can derive some key aspects of design from the system quality point of view while specifically taking QinU into account.

3.3   Mobile System Factors

Regarding system factors, because of these aforementioned contextual and system-in-use aspects, designing a MobileApp —as a system from the entity standpoint- needs to incorporate several elements. These elements include sub-entities (e.g. widgets, menus, forms, etc.) and their associated attributes and characteristics (e.g. Operability, Understandability, Functional Suitability, etc.). Some of the typical sub-entities for MobileApps that should to be considered for quality design and evaluation are:

- *Typing/input*: which includes search bars, and other data entry fields whereby the users should be assisted as much as possible to reduce errors and the 'cost' of typing. This includes such measurable attributes as default values, default value removal and shortcuts.

- *Entry widgets* such as carousels, drop down boxes and lists. System designers need to prevent the need for typing and reduce error rates by using widgets.
- *Sort, search and filter*: Special considerations are needed for MobileApps in order to reduce the workload and typing input. In addition, the small screen size makes it easy for the user to lose context, so attributes like typo tolerance, predictive contextual help would be desirable.
- *Menus* should be limited, simple and easily navigated with a clear breadcrumb path showing where the user has come from and where they can go. This is mostly applicable to Mobile WebApps where a small screen limits the users' context or field of vision in navigating from one place to another.
- *Forms and registration*: Forms need be clear with context sensitive help. The last thing you want is a user unable to complete a form because they didn't quite understand one particular mandatory field. Either defaults, or help within the entry field giving an example of what goes in the field should be provided.

Regarding the aforementioned sub-entities of typical MobileApps, we can now consider some examples of sub-characteristics of Usability, Information and Functional Quality that are particular to MobileApps, for example:

i) *Learnability*: Through its various entities listed above such as menus and widgets, learnability can be designed into the MobileApp through defaults, facilitating predictive actions, context sensitive help, and so on;

ii) *Navigation*: The MobileApp's ability to enable to a user to easily find the functionality or information that they need is critical. Not only do they need to easily find it, they need to do it fast. These are sometimes in alignment but not necessarily;

iii) *Operability*: This is a central sub-characteristic of usability. It means the degree to which a MobilApp has attributes that make it easy to operate and control. For example, controllability represents the degree to which users can initiate and control the direction and pace of the task until task completion. Easy to operate is related to those provided mechanisms which make entering data as easy and as accurate as possible while maintaining consistent usage and placement of controls even in different contexts and platforms of use;

iv) *Error handling*: Error prevention, error awareness, and error status are key attributes that need to be designed correctly to not only prevent errors, but enable the mobile user to recover with minimal effort. In addition, errors should be easily and quickly understood so that the user can move forward with their task;

v) *Understanding*: For MobileApps, because the screen is so small, it requires special consideration for understanding what the application is about, and what it does almost instantly. As mentioned previously, mobile users have a very short attention span so they must glance at the application and understand how it operates. For instance, an airline application, when they open it up, they already know they want to, either check a flight status or make a reservation, so the design must heavily consider this expectation so that there is reduced ramp up time;

vi) *Visibility*: Many factors determine whether or not the application is easily visible to a user. Depending on the context, different text colors and backgrounds can have a positive or negative impact. This sub-characteristic, while related to aesthetics is not identical. Remember that mobile users want to glance quickly and understand almost immediately and there may be glare on their screen if they are outdoors. This means appropriate usage and placement of text in appropriate format can impact the user's speed of comprehension greatly.

Finally, among other sub-characteristics and attributes to take into account for evaluating MobileApps is Information Conciseness, which in few words means shorter is better. In [12] Information Conciseness is an attribute of the Information Coverage sub-characteristic, which in turn is related to Information Suitability, and is defined as *"degree to which the information coverage is compactly represented without being overwhelming"*.

In alignment with the ISO 25010 'influences' relationship (see Fig. 2), each of these system sub-characteristics/attributes can have an influence on the system in use for both the do-goals and be-goals. Depending on the context, user, and task, the influence can impact the user's ability to operate, navigate and use the application efficiently (do-goals) or comfortably and with pleasure and satisfaction (be-goals).

Thus, in designing a MobileApp, one must also take into account the decision to make a native MobileApp versus a Mobile WebApp. For instance, navigability, as described above, and congruence and consistency with the regular WebApp are significant. On the other hand, many widgets and other features of the mobile phone are not accessible to WebApps so they inherently start at a disadvantage regarding widget usage which, depending on the application, can impact system in use greatly.

4   Illustrating Quality Design and Evaluation for MobileApps

Now, given the aforementioned 2Q2U framework and mobile UX and usability concepts we can apply them to MobileApps. This section builds upon Section 3 and demonstrates the importance of a few of the factors through some examples whereby the context, system, and system in use come into play for MobileApps. Note that a systematic instantiation of quality models for MobileApps -as we did in [9] for the JIRA WebApp's QinU and EQ- will be documented in a separate manuscript.

When designing MobileApp tasks for QinU, for example for evaluating Effectiveness and Efficiency characteristics, content and functions are embedded in the task design itself rather than as attributes of the application. And, mentioned previously, UX do-goals for a MobileApp-in-use are heavily influenced by the workflow of the task. Because the most prevalent mobile tasks include deadline oriented, or time sensitive information, the workflow should be short in order to be effective and efficient to make up for the small screen size and user context (in a hurry with short attention span). User's are often executing tasks 'on the spot' and 'in the moment' so a delay, or a mistake is critical at that moment. Can you imagine getting stranded at an airport, and then looking up all the flights going out of an airport and not being able to search effectively because the search menu was designed only with one search parameter?

From this simple example, it is easy to see that QinU depends on many system sub-entities having particular sub-characteristics and attributes depending on the context, user and task. Note that when executing a particular task, there should be very few controls that could lead the user astray or toward a mistake (see for example the Fidelity Investment MobileApp screenshots in Fig. 3.a and b). They purposely design the widgets and controls to be large, thumb friendly, so that the user can complete the task given the information needed as effectively and efficiently as possible. There is contextual help, or a simple drop down menu with limited choices in the fields that need to be filled in.

As mentioned for the typing/input sub-entity, defaults are extremely important to reduce the workload of the user. Defaults can be based on what the user has typed or submitted in the past (e.g., zip codes, names, addresses). Defaults are bound to be wrong sometimes and you don't want to have a default that takes unnecessary effort to change. For example don't use 0 as the default for a telephone number or zip code and don't make users manually erase the text field character by character, by clicking the Delete key. Instead, erasing defaults with a single button that clears the entire field can save several seconds. In Fig. 3.a, the MobileApp shows the default user name as well as the option to save it or not, giving the user a sense of controllability. Also, for typing/input and widget sub-entities, the United Airlines MobileApp shown in Fig. 3.c, shows a carousel for data entry rather than typing. It also gives the user another option for input. Additionally, the screen is very clear for the task at hand. Notice that there is no other input or information not directly related to the task of Finding a flight.

Fig. 3. a) Fidelity Investment MobileApp login screen; b) Fidelity Investments MobileApp find a ticker symbol task; and c) United Airlines MobileApp finding a flight

Examining Fig. 3.b, shows the Fidelity Investment MobileApp for the task of "Finding a stock ticker symbol". Notice the context sensitive help in light grey color symbol or company name, which aids the user. Also, there is a list of past searches which helps the user as well. Both the ticker symbol and company name are shown to eliminate any confusion and prevent using the incorrect ticker symbol. The information is also presented in a clear and concise manner with no other information (information conciseness) to distract from the task at hand while features have been designed to reduce errors and increase efficiencies and task completion rates. The last thing Fidelity wants is for a user to not complete this task which may affect executing a trade.

Figures 4.a and b show the Embark application for the Washington DC Metro train system. Notice that (Fig. 4.a) for the task of "finding a station", the user is given context sensitive help below the search bar. There is also light grey letters in the search bar to make sure the user is not lost, reminding the user what they are trying to do. Also notice that the search bar is quite long, thus providing the user with ample space to type in their desired location. On the other hand, for the same entity, Washington DC Embark application, you can see from Fig. 4.b that the errors are not comprehensible thus very difficult for the user to recover and move forward with their task.

Fig. 4. a) and b) Embark Washington DC Metro MobileApp; c) Apple App Store MobileApp

Lastly, Fig. 4.c shows a search function implemented in the Apple App Store. For the App Store, a user in search of 'tvguide' accidently typed 'tvgiude' and got no results. Thus in terms of typo tolerance and error prevention, it would rate poorly for that particular task.

These examples demonstrate MobileApp sub-entities such as forms, menus and search boxes and why design principles, i.e. mobile system factors can significantly influence the UX and other system in use factors. With a screen so small, it is easy to see why concise information, contextual help, etc. are critical attributes.

5   Related Work and Discussion

Given the evolution of WebApps both as systems and systems in use, characteristics such as QinU and UX, combined with usability and information quality, have all recently come to the research forefront especially for MobileApps due to advances in mobile device capabilities concurrent with cloud technology further jettisoning SaaS-based offerings. In addition, the shift in emphasis to satisfying the customer experience has put greater corporate focus on UX and customer satisfaction. However, based on design and usability guidelines for MobileApps [1, 3, 4, 11], quality standards [7], and related literature [6, 10, 14, 16], it was difficult for us to understand their relationships into quality models.

Hence, it is important in this discussion to highlight definitions given by various researchers to the UX term. For instance, Bevan [2] examined ISO 25010 from the viewpoint of actual usability and UX and drew relationships regarding usability as performance in use, and satisfaction as it relates to UX. Hassenzahl's work [5] in classifying UX in two categories, hedonic and pragmatic is also useful when examining actual usability from the *do*, pragmatic viewpoint and the *be*, or hedonic satisfaction standpoint. To understand the term requires breaking down the word 'user experience' and examining first what experience means.

Experience is a general concept that refers to both immediately-perceived events and the wisdom gained in interpretation of events. In the context of UX, it is a sequence of events over time for a user's interaction with the system. Hassenzahl notes that the time dimension could be either momentary or accumulated and changing over time. Examining the 'user' part of the UX concept, Hassenzahl characterizes a user's goals into pragmatic, do goals and hedonic, be goals and assumes the system-in-use quality is perceived in two dimensions, pragmatic and hedonic. Pragmatic quality refers to the system's perceived ability to support the achievement of tasks and focuses on the system's actual usability in completing tasks that are the 'do-goals' of the user. Hedonic quality refers to the system's perceived ability to support the user's achievement of 'be-goals', such as being happy, or satisfied with a focus on self.

Hassenzahl also argues that the fulfillment of be-goals is the driver of experience and that lack of actual usability or inability to complete do-goals may prevent achieving be-goals, but do-goals are not the end goal of the user. Rather the real goal of the user is to fulfill be-goals such as being autonomous, competent, related to others, stimulated, and popular through technology use. He also states that pragmatic quality enables achieving hedonic quality be-goals and has no value by itself, but only through enabling accomplishment of be-goals.

These two concepts, viz. hedonic and pragmatic have been recently introduced in the ISO 25010 standard to refer to satisfaction and effectiveness/efficiency characteristics respectively. However, UX and actual usability are missing characteristics in the ISO standard, as we discussed in Section 2 for our 2Q2U quality models and framework.

On the other hand, in the Apple [1] and Google [4] design and user interface guidelines, the relationship between system and application design with usability and UX is not explicit, nor is it explained in the well-known usability and UX columns of Nielsen [11], nor in other quality-related researches such as [6, 10]. Budiu [3] lists out many characteristics of MobileApps in that would be desired in certain contexts of use but does not use quality modeling approach and therefore, the capability for consistent application using a framework to systematically apply concepts and evaluate and improve a MobileApp is limited.

In [16] authors discussed how the triangulation of various methods might provide insights about the identification of UX factors that can be detected both in early and later phases of the development process. They pointed out that "*It is important to associate the identifying UX factors with the artifacts used to the design. In our study, we have found that scenarios and task models works as a lingua franca for mapping user requirements and UX factors*" (cf. p. 42). However, this research was not intended to characterize UX in the framework of the QinU view nor its relationship with EQ (system) characteristics.

As discussed elsewhere [9], we can instantiate QinU and EQ models for the purpose of understanding and then combine these instantiations with a strategy to carry out evaluations to ultimately accomplish improvement. As such, based on our examination of existing research, there has been progress in the individual elements such as modeling and evaluation, but limited focus on using a strategy and tailored models for the purpose of improvement considering the QinU/EQ/QinU relationships and cycle.

6   Conclusions and Future Work

As the contributions mentioned in the Introduction Section, we have characterized relevant features of MobileApps with regard to usability and UX analyzed them using previously proposed 2Q2U v2.0 quality models. In the process, we looked at MobileApp usage context and its impact in MobileApp design when considering quality characteristics and attributes for system and system-in-use quality evaluation. Lastly, we illustrated some example MobileApps to show their design features could have a significant influence on the system quality and the user's perception of quality, i.e. system in use and UX.

Our proposal shows the usage of 2Q2U v2.0 as an integrated approach for modeling requirements for external quality and quality in use (i.e., actual usability, satisfaction and user experience), combined with a consistent, and flexible way for representing calculable concepts (characteristics), sub-concepts (sub-characteristics) and attributes used in conjunction with the C-INCAMI measurement and evaluation components and its strategy.

Another manuscript will expand the work further including the definition of attributes, metrics, and indicators for user group types performing specific tasks in real MobileApp context of use.

Ongoing research is focused on further utilizing the 2Q2U v2.0 framework for systematic instantiation of quality models for MobileApps –as we did in [9]- in order to provide foundations when modeling and understanding the relationships among EQ, QinU, actual usability and UX. In doing so, our end goal is improvement. That is, to be able to directly use the system-in-use quality evaluation to directly improve the design of the MobileApp system. This concern has often been neglected in the literature, but may help improve quality design recommendations and ultimately to increase the MobileApp UX as a whole.

Acknowledgments. Thanks to the support given from the Science and Technology Agency, Argentina, in the PAE-PICT 2188 project, and in the 09-F047 project at Universidad Nacional de La Pampa, Argentina. We also thank the State Key Laboratory of Software Development Environment of China under Grant No. SKLSDE-2012ZX-13 and National Natural Science Foundation of China under Grant No. 90818017.

References

1. Apple iOS Human Interface Guidelines, http://developer.apple.com/library/ios/#documentation/UserExperience/Conceptual/MobileH IG/Introduction/Introduction.html (retrieved April 2013)
2. Bevan, N.: Extending quality in use to provide a framework for usability measurement. In: Kurosu, M. (ed.) Human Centered Design, HCII 2009. LNCS, vol. 5619, pp. 13–22. Springer, Heidelberg (2009)
3. Budiu, R., Nielsen, J.: Usability of Mobile Websites, http://www.nngroup.com/reports/mobile (retrieved April 2013)
4. Google User Interface Guidelines: http://developer.android.com/guide/practices/ui_guidelines/index.html (retrieved April 2013)
5. Hassenzahl, M.: User experience: towards an experiential perspective on product quality. In: Proc. 20th Int'l Conference of the Assoc. Francophone d'Interaction Homme-Machine, IHM, vol. 339, pp. 11–15 (2008)
6. Herrera, M., Moraga, M.Á., Caballero, I., Calero, C.: Quality in Use Model for Web Portals (QiUWeP). In: Daniel, F., Facca, F.M. (eds.) ICWE 2010 Workshops. LNCS, vol. 6385, pp. 91–101. Springer, Heidelberg (2010)
7. ISO/IEC 25010: Systems and software engineering. Systems and software Quality Requirements and Evaluation (SQuaRE). System and software quality models (2011)
8. Lew, P., Qanber Abbasi, M., Rafique, I., Wang, X., Olsina, L.: Using Web Quality Models and Questionnaires for Web Applications Evaluation. In: IEEE Proceedings of QUATIC, Lisbon, Portugal, pp. 20–29 (2012)
9. Lew, P., Olsina, L., Becker, P., Zhang, L.: An Integrated Strategy to Understand and Manage Quality in Use for Web Applications. Requirements Engineering Journal 17(4), 299–330 (2012)
10. Nayebi, F., Desharnais, J.-M., Abran, A.: The state of the art of mobile application usability evaluation. In: 25th IEEE Canadian Conference on Electrical Computer Engineering, pp. 1–4 (2012)
11. Nielsen, J.: Mobile Usability Update, Jakob Nielsen's Alertbox (September 26, 2011), http://www.nngroup.com/articles/mobile-usability-update/ (retrieved April 2013)
12. Olsina, L., Lew, P., Dieser, A., Rivera, B.: Updating Quality Models for Evaluating New Generation Web Applications. Journal of Web Engineering, Special Issue: Quality in New Generation Web Applications 11(3), 209–246 (2012); Abrahão, S., Cachero, C., Cappiello, C., Matera, M. (eds.)
13. Olsina, L., Papa, F., Molina, H.: How to Measure and Evaluate Web Applications in a Consistent Way. In: Rossi, Pastor, Schwabe, Olsina (eds.) Springer HCIS Book Web Engineering: Modeling and Implementing Web Applications, pp. 385–420 (2008)
14. Sohn, T., Li, K.A., Griswold, W.G., Holland, J.: A diary study of mobile information needs. In: ACM: Conference CHI 2008, Florence, Italy, pp. 433–442 (2008)

15. Thom-Santelli, J., Hedge, A.: Effects of a multi-touch keyboard on wrist posture, typing performance and comfort. In: Proc. of the Human Factors and Ergonomics Society, 49th Annual Meeting, Santa Monica, USA, pp. 646–650 (2005)
16. Winckler, M., Bach, C., Bernhaupt, R.: Identifying User eXperiencing Factors along the Development Process: A Case Study. In: Lai-Chong Law, E., Abrahão, S., Vermeeren, A., Thora Hvannberg, E. (eds.) Proc. of the 2nd International Workshop on the Interplay between User Experience Evaluation and Software Development (In conjunction with the 7th NordiCHI), Copenhagen, Denmark. CEUR Workshop Proceedings, vol. 922, pp. 37–42. CEUR-WS.org (2012)

Protecting User Profile Data in WebID-Based Social Networks Through Fine-Grained Filtering

Stefan Wild, Olexiy Chudnovskyy, Sebastian Heil, and Martin Gaedke

Technische Universität Chemnitz, Germany
{firstname.lastname}@informatik.tu-chemnitz.de

Abstract. The WebID identification approach allows users to manage their profile data at a self-defined place in the cloud and enables services as well as other requesters to retrieve data stored within these profiles. While existing access control mechanisms can secure entire user profiles from unauthorized access, they lack fine-grained protection of sensitive data within user profiles.

This paper presents an approach for applying requester-specific filters to cloud-stored user profile data in WebID-based distributed social networks. Our approach aims at enabling profile owners to protect sensitive user data within their profiles in a fine-grained manner. We demonstrate our solution by integrating the approach into a WebID identity provider and profile management platform.

Keywords: Security, Privacy, Trust, Identity, Social Web, Semantic Web.

1 Introduction

With increasing presence of social media in daily activities [1], the need for trustworthy collaboration is becoming more and more important [4]. Centralized social networks such as Facebook, Google+ or LinkedIn provide varied possibilities for personal information exchange and networking, but try to bind users within their own domains [15]. Although a growing number of social networks tends to make parts of their collected data available to the public through APIs [9], users are not in full control of their identity data. Avoiding the creation of data silos on the one hand and enabling users to remain in control of their data on the other hand asks for a distributed social network (DSN) [15].

A DSN can be implemented on the basis of W3C's WebID specification [13]. The WebID approach is a universal identification mechanism that enables persons and machines to identify themselves via client certificates, i.e., without entering any user name or password [11]. The client certificate refers via a URI to a resource containing further data about the identity owner. This specific URI is called WebID and the linked resource is called WebID profile. Users can automatically generate a WebID, an appropriate WebID profile, and a client certificate using a WebID identity provider. Data within a WebID profile describes attributes of the identity owner in a machine-readable way via RDF[1] using

---

[1] RDF Primer, http://www.w3.org/TR/2004/REC-rdf-primer-20040210/

Q.Z. Sheng and J. Kjeldskov (Eds.): ICWE 2013 Workshops, LNCS 8295, pp. 269–280, 2013.
© Springer International Publishing Switzerland 2013

domain specific vocabularies like FOAF[2]. While utilizing profile data for creating an improved user experience and optimizing customer services is advantageous, there is also a major problem related to this topic:

An unprotected WebID profile is a potential source of information for known and unknown as well as wanted and unwanted requesters. Since WebID profile documents are parsed during authentication to verify public key information, they have to be accessible for other services or agents. That is, also profile data irrelevant to the authentication procedure per se could be retrieved without further notice. For protecting WebID profiles from unauthorized access, data retrievals or tracking attempts, one could set access control rights to resources representing the WebID profile documents [5,2]. Existing mechanisms only provide coarse access control because they focus on resources instead of represented data. Enabling fine-grained access control with these mechanisms requires outsourcing sensitive WebID profile data to separate resources and set corresponding access permissions. This kind of profile data distribution, however, negatively affects flexibility, ease of maintenance, and portability of user profiles [7].

The paper presents our approach to protect WebID profile data from unauthorized access by providing these main contributions:

1. Theoretical foundation for fine-grained filtering of WebID profile data
2. Practical implementation of our approach using SPARQL
3. Demonstration as part of a WebID identity provider & management platform

The rest of this paper is organized as follows: We describe usage scenarios and derive challenges for a solution in Section 2. We then analyze related work in Section 3. Section 4 presents our approach. We evaluate the solution in Section 5 and show an example in Section 6. We conclude the paper in Section 7.

2   Usage Scenarios

The following scenarios illustrate various aspects of the problem and are used to derive the challenges that need to be dealt with:

Scenario 1. As a WebID identity owner, Alice intends to restrict her profile data's visibility. She wants to do this because all information available could be easily retrieved, if not properly addressed by appropriate access control mechanisms. Sensitive profile data could be used for purposes she does not agree with, e.g., social network analysis or product marketing. Although restricting access to her entire profile would be sufficient, Alice is not interested in losing advantages like authentication or single-sign-on to new yet unknown services. To keep associated services up-to-date, Alice wants to permit monitoring specific profile parts by third-party entities for changes. Alice wants to allow anyone to access profile data she marked as visible, even if Alice is currently unavailable or unauthenticated.

---

[2] FOAF Vocabulary Specification 0.98, http://xmlns.com/foaf/spec/

Scenario 2. A friend of Alice, called Bob, wants to retrieve her current address data. The identity owner Alice knows Bob and has granted him more visibility rights compared to anonymous in Scenario 1. While Bob is allowed to see Alice's private address data, Alice does not want to share this data with Eve, which might be a loose contact. Instead of private address data, only Alice's office address data is visible to Eve. Alice has to be enabled to express whom exactly she wants to make information available to. That is, any agent authenticated via WebID is to be treated differently when accessing data of Alice's profile.

Scenario 3. Alice plans to switch the server hosting her WebID profile. She has distributed her profile data to separate resources for applying access rights at the resource level. For migrating to a new hosting server, Alice has to find, consolidate and transfer all profile data being scattered among various resources as well as adjust access control lists (ACLs) for these resources. Depending on Alice's setup used for securing her personal data, this migration might be a complex undertaking.

Based on these scenarios, we infer following challenges a solution must deal with:

Flexibility. Defining filters on profile data for specific requesters must be flexible and expressive to cover all described scenarios.

Portability. Profile owners must be enabled to easily transfer filter specifications to other systems without making major adjustments. Filter processors have to be either available or easy to implement within new ecosystems.

Maintainability. Filters on profile data have to be standard-compliant to ease maintenance and avoid introducing too much overhead. Both users and machines must be enabled to understand and modify filters on profile data.

3   Related Work

Web Access Control (WAC) is a vocabulary to define access rights to resources at the document level [8]. Requesting agents and agent classes are supported as entities to define access rights to. ACLs specified by WAC are machine-readable through RDF and can be stored independently from the resources they protect. WAC is well-suited for scenarios involving many resources to grant access to [3]. However, WAC does not support directly controlling access to specific data within resources, e.g., data within WebID profiles. Outsourcing specific data as self-contained resources enables more control with WAC. This, however, complicates maintenance because the number of resources required to realize a less coarse-grained control depends on amount and structure of data to apply access rights to. Considering a WebID profile containing many triples to describe diverse attributes of a person, a fine-grained control at its best would result in outsourcing almost each triple to a separate resource. When applying changes, this approach is inflexible. Additionally, such data distribution and related definition of corresponding ACLs comes along with declining portability.

The Access Control Ontology (ACO) is similar to WAC, but adds support for roles and enables directly mapping permissions to HTTP verbs [12]. To protect data within resources with ACO, relevant data has to be outsourced to separate resources. ACO and WAC share the same maintainability and portability issues.

The approach proposed in [14] manipulates WebID profile data for particular profile requesters by introducing sets of triples as alternative information sources in relation to the original profile data. This allows to establish diverse views on profiles depending on specific requesters identified through WebIDs. While WAC and ACO only enable controlling access to resources, this vocabulary facilitates manipulating data represented by resources. These view definitions increase flexibility by providing improved filter expressiveness, e.g., new triples can be directly inserted into the profile view. Due to this facility, it is necessary to resolve alternative triples available in both the view definition and the actual WebID profile. While this resolution can be realized by merging and replacing relevant triples, there is further processing required to prioritize what triples are shown or hidden as part of the view. If view definitions are used as an additional layer of information, profile data would be available in two different places, which are probably conflicting with each other. Consequently, data stored in the user profile as well as in the view definitions must be managed. This decreases maintainability.

4   Protecting User Profile Data by Fine-grained Filtering

For improving the protection of user profiles in WebID-based DSNs, our approach defines a fine-grained filtering of data marked as sensitive by the profile owner. The filtering is applied during a graph-to-graph transformation. As transformation source, graph $G(V, E), G \in \mathfrak{G}$ represents a WebID profile containing data about identity owner $m \in I$, where I is a set of all identities. T is a set of RDF triples each consisting of subject s, predicate p, and object o. As T spans a graph and G defines a set of triples, we formalize this equivalence in (1).

$$T \sim G \Leftrightarrow \forall (s, p, o) \in T : s, p, o \in V \wedge (s, p) \in E \wedge (p, o) \in E \qquad (1)$$

The identity-based graph-to-graph transformation t is defined by (2).

$$t : \mathfrak{G} \times I \to \mathfrak{G} \qquad (2)$$

Transformation t maps graph G to graph G'. Graph G' represents identity owner's m WebID profile filtered by sensitive data requester $r \in I$ is *not* allowed to retrieve. Equation (3) formalizes this transformation.

$$t(G, r) = G' = (V' \subseteq V, E' \subseteq E) \qquad (3)$$

Our approach handles sensitive data as a subset of triples $T \sim G$. While all sensitive data is available in graph G, only data requester r is allowed to see is present in graph G'. Filter function f defines a mapping of a set of triples on $\{0, 1\}$ depending on the identity. While "1" means sensitive data and, therefore, set of triples is present in graph G', "0" means the opposite. Consequently, whitelisting or blacklisting of sensitive WebID profile data for particular requesters can be achieved using filter function f as defined by (4).

$$f : I \times \{(s, p, o)\} \rightarrow \{0, 1\} \tag{4}$$

Function f yields 1 for each triple in graph G and identity owner m. Transformation $t(G, r)$ uses f to create filtered graph G' based on G for requester r. RDF triples $T' \subseteq T$ span graph $G' = (V', E'), T' \sim G'$ as defined in Equation (5).

$$T' = \{(s, p, o)|f_r((s, p, o)) = 1\} \tag{5}$$

To relieve identity/profile owner m from the need to define filter function f_r for each potential r, we introduce fallback function $F(r)$ that yields the best possible fallback entity for a given requester r. Possible fallback entities are:

- *requesters* authenticated using WebID $U \subseteq I$,
- *specific requesters* defined by the profile owner $S \subseteq U$,
- requesters who are *friends* of the profile owner $K \subseteq U$, and
- *anonymous requesters* $A \subseteq I, A \cap U = \emptyset$.

Let $R = \{k, u, a, n\}$ be a set of special entities: k for friend, u for authenticated user, a for anonym, n for null. Equation (6) formalizes fallback function $F(r)$.

$$F(r) = e = \begin{cases} r & \text{if } \exists f_r \\ k & \text{if } \exists f_k \wedge r \in K \wedge r \notin S \\ u & \text{if } \exists f_u \wedge r \in U \wedge r \notin S \wedge r \notin K \qquad e \in (R \cup S) \\ a & \text{if } \exists f_a \wedge r \in A \\ n & \text{if } \nexists f_r \wedge \nexists f_k \wedge \nexists f_u \wedge \nexists f_a \end{cases} \tag{6}$$

Filter function f_n, cf. Equation (7), implements a behavior as if no filtering is active. This enables accessing profiles having no predefined filters.

$$f_n((s, p, o)) = 1 \forall (s, p, o) \in T \tag{7}$$

To use $F(r)$ as part of $t(G, r)$, we refine Equation (5) as shown in Equation (8).

$$T' = \{(s, p, o)|f_{F(r)}((s, p, o)) = 1\} \tag{8}$$

Filter specifications are hidden from anyone but profile owner m. Otherwise, this information is a potential subject to social engineering, e.g., profile analyzers could conclude group affiliations utilizing knowledge about f_r or $F(r)$.

Figure 1 illustrates the theoretical foundation of our solution. When requester r tries to retrieve data from the WebID profile of identity owner m, an appropriate filter is searched for requester r using $F(r)$. Profile owner m has to specify eligible filters prior to this step in order to achieve a protection of sensitive profile data. Filters are stored as filter specifications in the identity owner's WebID profile. Each filter specification (e, t) is a set consisting of entity e and

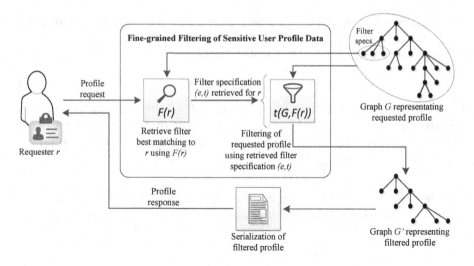

Fig. 1. Approach to Protect Sensitive User Profile Data by Fine-grained Filtering

transformation function t. As soon as a matching filter specification is detected, graph G, representing all WebID profile data of identity owner m, is converted via graph-to-graph transformation $t(G, F(r))$ into graph G', representing this WebID profile filtered by data marked as sensitive by profile owner m. That is, the profile retrieved by requester r only contains data satisfying the constraints defined by filter function $f_{F(r)}$.

While various technologies are suitable for implementing this approach, we introduce the *WebID Profile Filter Language* (WPFL) and use the SPARQL CONSTRUCT query form [6] as transformation and filter function. WPFL defines the proposed filter specification (e, t). It consists of three elements: *entity name* for e, *filter command* for t and a *specification element* to bind them together and connect the filter to the WebID profile. The specification element allows storing filter specifications either in the owner's profile, i.e., graph G, or separately as linked resources. These elements are described by three RDF triples, as exemplarily shown in Turtle[3] syntax below:

```
1  <WebID> filter:specification [
2     filter:entity ENTITY;
3     filter:command COMMAND
4  ] .
```

The SPARQL CONSTRUCT query form facilitates constructing a new graph G' based on an existing graph G, as required by Equation (3). It can include or exclude data during construction of $G' \sim T'$ and, hence, implements

---

[3] Turtle Terse RDF Triple Language, http://www.w3.org/TeamSubmission/turtle/

Equation (5). A whitelisting - as defined by this equation - mentioning all data to be available in graph G' is described by following filter command[4]:

```
1  CONSTRUCT {  ?s  ?p  ?o  } FROM <WebID> WHERE {  ?s  ?p  ?o  .
2     FILTER(?s  in  (Subject1,  Subject2,  [...]))  .
3     FILTER(?p  in  (Predicate1,  Predicate2,  [...]))  .
4     FILTER(?o  in  (Object1,  Object2,  [...]))
5  }
```

As an example, if solely the `foaf:knows` predicate is mentioned, all contacts are copied from G to G'. To increase filtering granularity, it is beneficial to also mention subjects or objects of RDF triples, e.g., in order to include/exclude specific contacts. This all together defines one *filter directive*. SPARQL's `UNION` keywords enable to use several filter directives in one filter command. We utilize SPARQL Property Path [10] to cover filtering of context-dependent data. For instance, street data could be context-dependent as they are element of an address, which in turn could be element of either private or business contact data. Property paths help to address relevant elements in graph G by specifying the routes between them. For example, a filter command to construct a new graph by including name and image of identity owner m as well as city and country of his/her home - but not street, postal code etc. - is described as follows[5]:

```
1  CONSTRUCT {  ?s  ?p  ?o  } FROM <WebID> WHERE {
2     {?s  ?p  ?o  . FILTER(?p  in  (foaf:name,  foaf:img))} UNION
3     {?s  ?p  ?o  . ?t  con:home ?o} UNION
4     {?s  ?p  ?o  . ?t  con:home/con:address ?o} UNION
5     {?s  ?p  ?o  . ?t  con:home/con:address/con:city ?o} UNION
6     {?s  ?p  ?o  . ?t  con:home/con:address/con:country ?o}
7  }
```

A dedicated SPARQL query uses the identity information provided by requester r to select the best-matching available filter specification based on the retrieved filter entity, as formalized in Equation (6). Once an appropriate filter specification is selected, the corresponding filter command is directly passed to a SPARQL processor that executes the graph-to-graph transformation.

5 Evaluation

The proposed approach enables profile owners to create filters on their WebID profile for specific requesters or groups of requesters. Profile owners can independently include or exclude each RDF triple present in their profile. This fine-grained and context-aware filtering allows to create customized profile views for

---

[4] In contrast to whitelisting, blacklisting data is also supported by SPARQL CON-STRUCT queries via `MINUS` statements.

[5] In the example, lines 3 and 4 create the context required for including city and country. Address data is described using the PIM ontology, http://www.w3.org/2000/10/swap/pim/contact#

diverse requesting entities. Unlike WAC and ACO, the proposed solution does not require outsourcing data to separate resources for implementing a flexible filtering. All necessary information can remain in one place. Compared to [14], user profile data and filter specifications are separated from each other in our solution. This simplifies updating, replacing or removing already existing filter specifications. The fallback mechanism $F(r)$ selects the most appropriate filter based on availability and provided identity data. Such a fallback mechanism is not part of any related work known to the authors.

In contrast to related work, both whitelisting and blacklisting of RDF triples are supported by our solution. We recommend whitelisting because it does not show what is hidden from requesters. Otherwise, knowledge about hidden data could be subject to speculations. Additionally, whitelisting eases constructing an empty graph representation of a profile, which might be relevant for identity owners having stringent requirements for privacy and, thus, want to forbid anonymous profile requests. Our solution also allows to create filters that remove all filter specifications during construction of the profile view. Consequently, profile requesters remain unaware of the filtering.

To apply filtering of sensitive profile data by utilizing $t(G, r)$, only the graph representing the WebID profile and the requesting entity are used as input parameters. In comparison to ACO, our approach introduces only minimal overhead with three RDF triples to define a filter specification for a specific requester. The owner's WebID profile can contain all filter specifications, i.e., while separation between profile data and filter specifications is allowed, it is not required. To further ensure maintainability, we did not develop an own language for filter commands, but use SPARQL as a well-established and proven language. SPARQL empowers to create flexible and complex filters, whereas related work tries reducing complexity by defining a restricted vocabulary. We assume that restricted vocabularies offer advantages in terms of usability, but they also limit possibilities of filtering and cause workarounds, like the necessity of outsourcing sensitive user profile data. Independent of the chosen solution, we expect that common profile owners do not have the skills to create and maintain filters without assistance through specialized user interfaces.

For seamlessly integrating our solution into existing systems, filter function f_n implements a behavior as if no filtering is active. This facilitates accessing profiles having no predefined filters. As identity owners are enabled to store all necessary filter details within their WebID profile using our solution, the effort to transfer filter specifications to a new hosting system is reduced. While ACO and the approach proposed in [14] rely on particular processors to execute filters, high availability of SPARQL processors for many platforms and architectures contributes to our solution's interoperability and, thus, filter portability.

6   Example

While our solution is generic and can be implemented in any platform, we demonstrate it using Sociddea. Sociddea is a WebID identity provider and management

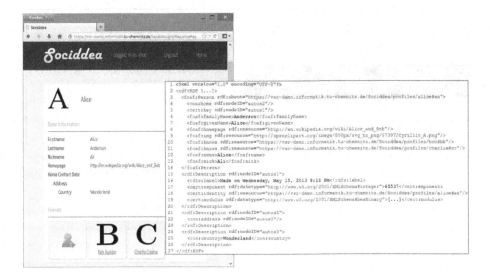

Fig. 2. Representations of a WebID profile hosted on Sociddea

platform developed with ASP.NET MVC4. With Sociddea, a user can automatically create a new WebID, an underlying WebID profile and an associated client certificate. Although Sociddea allows users to host their WebID profiles in the ecosystem provided by Sociddea, there is no constraint to do this. That is, users are also enabled to create new client certificates for profiles hosted somewhere else. Sociddea can represent a WebID profile in various ways. Figure 2 exemplifies an HTML and RDF/XML representation for the same WebID profile hosted on Sociddea.

Sociddea provides a graphical user interface to configure filters for profile data. Profile owners can switch from the common profile authoring to the filter specification mode. All identity attributes presented in the profile authoring mode can be used for specifying filters, i.e., each available identity attribute can be marked as either visible or hidden. At the moment of writing this paper, Sociddea's graphical filter editor supports including/excluding identity attributes through predicates, e.g., first name, last name or phone number. Through selecting an available entity, an already existing filter specification is used to visualize the former identity attribute selection by the user. Once the profile owner completed the selection for a specific entity, this configuration is verified and send to the Sociddea back-end. In order to enable machines to process this yet informal filter configuration, a SPARQL CONSTRUCT statement is automatically created. As whitelisting of attributes has been implemented, this SPARQL statement contains all identity attributes declared as visible for the specific entity. All three RDF triples relevant to specify the filter are stored within the owner's WebID profile. The process of creating such a profile data filter is shown in Figure 3.

Although the implementation generates SPARQL CONSTRUCT statements based on the identity attributes selected by the users, the solution is not limited

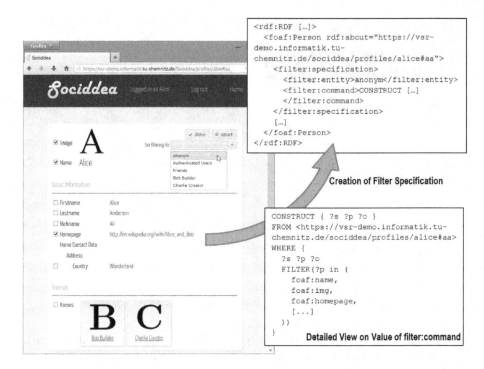

Fig. 3. Creation of Filter Specification Based on User Selection

to this. For generating profiles filtered by certain attributes, a profile owner is allowed to use any valid statement. Our solution's flexibility also allows to filter even identity attributes unsupported by the graphical user interface and facilitates to handle special cases like conditional filtering. Both can be accomplished via appropriate SPARQL commands. Once the filter specification has been created, it is automatically considered during all future attempts to access the particular profile. That is, when a requester tries to retrieve the profile, the solution searches for an appropriate filter specification using the provided identity data and the `filter:entity` triples within the WebID profile. Having found a matching filter entity, the `filter:command` triple belonging to the same `filter:specification` is extracted and directly passed to a SPARQL processor, i.e., no modification is made to the command. While results produced by the SPARQL processor are rendered as defined in the request, rendering as such is not subject to our solution. Figure 4 exemplifies the filtering of a WebID profile for an anonymous requester using the previously created filter specification.

Having no additional logic to be interpreted for filtering, the SPARQL processor can directly apply the filter specification and create a new filtered graph. This allows an efficient execution.

Demonstration. Further information to our solution and a link to the Sociddea WebID identity provider and profile management platform is available at `http://vsr.informatik.tu-chemnitz.de/demo/sociddea/`

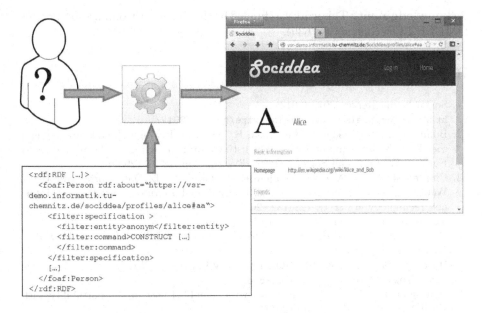

```
<rdf:RDF [...]>
  <foaf:Person rdf:about="https://vsr-
demo.informatik.tu-
chemnitz.de/sociddea/profiles/alice#aa">
    <filter:specification >
      <filter:entity>anonym</filter:entity>
      <filter:command>CONSTRUCT [...]
      </filter:command>
    </filter:specification>
    [...]
  </foaf:Person>
</rdf:RDF>
```

Fig. 4. WebID Profile Data Filtered for Anonymous Requester

7   Conclusion

In this paper we proposed an approach for enabling identity owners to control the way their profile data is exposed to others. We presented typical usage scenarios demonstrating the need for a flexible, portable and maintainable solution. Our solution is substantiated by both a theoretical foundation for fine-grained filtering and a practical implementation using SPARQL. We demonstrated the solution as part of Sociddea - a WebID identity management platform.

Introducing requester-specific filters on WebID profile data allows profile owners to keep control about amount and nature of personal data being presented to entities requesting their profile data. We defined a filter vocabulary to connect the current profile with the filter specification and established a fallback mechanism to automatically select the best-matching filter depending on the requester. To cover almost all scenarios of hiding and showing specifics within profiles, we used SPARQL CONSTRUCT statements as filter commands. We recommend whitelisting non-sensitive profile data per requester and exclude all filter specifications during filtering.

As future work, we plan to conduct a more extensive evaluation of the proposed solution including a user study focusing on creation and modification of filters. From the technical point of view, we will analyze filter cascades to apply several filters and combine protection needs. We also plan to add facilities for reusing filters by sharing them between users of a DSN. Finally, we intend to extend the requester parameter within filter specifications towards a customizable and machine-readable definition of the requesting party.

Acknowledgment. This work was funded by the European Commission (project OMELETTE, contract 257635).

References

1. Social Media Report 2012 (2012),
   http://blog.nielsen.com/nielsenwire/social/2012/
2. Bonneau, J., Anderson, J., Anderson, R., Stajano, F.: Eight friends are enough: social graph approximation via public listings. In: Proceedings of the Second ACM EuroSys Workshop on Social Network Systems, pp. 13–18 (2009)
3. Chudnovskyy, O., Wild, S., Gebhardt, H., Gaedke, M.: Data Portability Using WebComposition/Data Grid Service. International Journal on Advances in Internet Technology 4(3 & 4), 123–132 (2012)
4. European Commission: ICT - Work Programme 2013 (2012)
5. Hackett, M., Hawkey, K.: Security, Privacy and Usability Requirements for Federated Identity (2012)
6. Harris, S., Seaborne, A.: SPARQL 1.1 Query Language (2012),
   http://www.w3.org/TR/sparql11-query/
7. Heitmann, B., Hayes, C.: Achieving privacy-enabled user profile portability with WebID and the Web of Data (2011)
8. Hollenbach, J., Presbrey, J., Berners-Lee, T.: Using RDF Metadata to Enable Access Control on the Social Semantic Web. In: Proceedings of the Workshop on Collaborative Construction, Management and Linking of Structured Knowledge (CK 2009), vol. 514 (2009)
9. Savitz, E.: Welcome To The API Economy - Forbes (2012)
10. Seaborne, A.: SPARQL 1.1 Property Paths (2010),
    http://www.w3.org/TR/sparql11-property-paths/
11. Sporny, M., Inkster, T., Story, H., Harbulot, B., Bachmann-Gmür, R.: WebID 1.0: Web Identification and Discovery (2011),
    http://www.w3.org/2005/Incubator/webid/spec/
12. Tomaszuk, D., Gaedke, M., Gebhardt, H.: WebID+ACO: A distributed identification mechanism for social web (2011)
13. Tramp, S., Frischmuth, P., Ermilov, T., Shekarpour, S.: An Architecture of a Distributed Semantic Social Network. Semantic Web (2012)
14. Tramp, S., Story, H., Sambra, A., Frischmuth, P., Martin, M., Auer, S.: Extending the WebID Protocol with Access Delegation. In: Proceedings of the Third International Workshop on Consuming Linked Data, COLD 2012 (2012)
15. Yeung, C.M.A., Liccardi, I., Lu, K., Seneviratne, O., Berners-Lee, T.: Decentralization: The future of online social networking. In: W3C Workshop on the Future of Social Networking Position, Papers 2 (2009)

Building an Efficient Hadoop Workflow Engine Using BPEL

Jie Liu, Qiyuan Li, Feng Zhu, Jun Wei, and Dan Ye

Technology Center of Software Engineering
Institute of Software, Chinese Academy of Sciences
Beijing, China 100190
{ljie,liqiyuan09,zhufeng10,wj,yedan}@otcaix.iscas.ac.cn

Abstract. Big data processing and analysis techniques can guide enterprises to make correct decisions, and will play an important role in the enterprise business process. The Hadoop platform has become the basis of big data processing and analysis. To satisfy the needs of enterprises to develop data-intensive workflow based on Hadoop and integrate them into existing business processes, we build a Hadoop workflow engine named Pony based on BPEL model. The mapping method from Hadoop Workflow to BPEL process in three levels of the semantic model, deployment model, and execution model is presented. Pony uses a matured and stable BPEL engine to orchestrate Hadoop services. Pony implements a Hadoop job scheduler to collaborate with a BPEL engine to online schedule multiple workflows at runtime. This paper describes the design and implementation of Pony, and the experiment results demonstrate Pony can provide improved performance.

Keywords: MapReduce, Hadoop workflow, BPEL, Data intensive computing, Service oriented architecture.

1 Introduction

Big data processing and analysis techniques will play an important role in the enterprise business process. Hadoop [1] , the open-source implementation of MapReduce [2], is by far the most successful and popular data intensive cloud computing platform due to its remarkable features in simplicity, fault tolerance, and scalability. Users can submit MapReduce jobs consisting of a map function and a reduce function. A master node in the Hadoop cluster performs job scheduling, and distributes work to a number of slaves.

However, more frequently you will have many jobs with dependencies between them. For example, you might want to analyze the accumulated historical sales data to predicate the sale amount next month. You may first need to execute a MapReduce job to import the data to Hadoop, and then you need to execute a MapReduce job to normalize the data to prepare for the following data mining jobs. In this case, we need a Hadoop workflow engine to help us manage the job dependencies.

Q.Z. Sheng and J. Kjeldskov (Eds.): ICWE 2013 Workshops, LNCS 8295, pp. 281–292, 2013.

In Fig.1, it shows a Hadoop workflow example. In this paper we assume Hadoop jobs include MapReduce job, Pig job, Hive job, HDFS job, System commands, Java application, and web service, which can be executed in Hadoop cluster. There are some workflow engines for Hadoop, such as Oozie [3], Cascading [4], Hamake [5], Azkaban [6] and CloudWF [7]. Unfortunately, this diversity of approaches generates a separated growth of best practices and methodologies. First, Hadoop workflow systems lack of a unified, standardized business process specification. Existing workflow systems use their own specification languages. Workflows generated by these systems are unable to communicate with each other, making the combination of business processes and enterprise applications very complex. It usually takes a long time for deployment and implementation, and integration with existing business process in the enterprise. Second, these workflow engines provide limited support for control logic. Existing Hadoop workflows only support these control routers: fork, decision, and join. This makes it hard to design complex data intensive workflow. Third, many data analysis processes need human interaction, we need to model these activities in the workflow model.

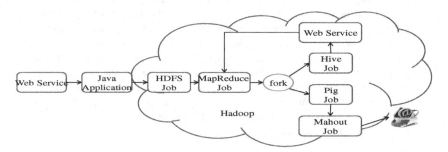

Fig. 1. Hadoop workflow example

BPEL provides a standard language for the specification of executable and abstract business processes [9]. BPEL supports rich control logic and support to model the human activities. BPEL is powerful enough to express complex data processing process. There are also some excellent open source BPEL engines. The benefits of the web service oriented framework are well appreciated.   Therefore, our motivation is to adopt these matured workflow technologies to build an efficient and scalable Hadoop workflow engine.   If we can define a Hadoop workflow with BPEL, we can build a Hadoop workflow engine quickly, and achieve high dependability by adopting a stable BPEL engine. Most enterprises have adopted BPEL as their workflow engine, so this can also make Hadoop workflow easily integrated into existing business process.

Hadoop workflow can be modeled as a Directed Acyclic Graph (DAG). BPEL is a type of block-structured flow definition languages. We should map a Hadoop workflow to a BPEL process at first. BPEL only can orchestrate web service.   We propose to use wrapper service to convert a Hadoop job to a web service. For each job type, one wrapper service is deployed in the service container. The wrapper acts as an intermediary for the Hadoop job by exposing a Web service interface to the client.

The wrapper service is in chief of the job's deployment and execution and response the invoking from BPEL. In this way, we can avoid the service instance explosion.

Existing workflow systems such as Oozie provide no scheduler on workflow level. Instead, they just submit the ready jobs in the workflow to Hadoop cluster. However, the Hadoop job scheduler knows nothing about workflows, the workflows execute in an unpredictable way. In the traditional BPEL process, all the web services may be in different service containers, so it is not feasible to preform global resource scheduling. When multiple Hadoop workflows concurrently execute, all the running jobs of these workflows are in one Hadoop cluster. Therefore, how to efficiently schedule these jobs in Hadoop should be a key feature for the Hadoop workflow engine. In this paper, we propose a method to design a Hadoop job scheduler collaborating with a BPEL engine to implement multiple workflows online scheduling.

The novelty of our work mainly lies in the four aspects.

—   Propose an approach to build a powerful workflow system for Hadoop using BPEL, which can express complex data processing process.

—   Enable Hadoop workflow to easily integrate with existing business process, and enrich business process management with big data processing capability.

—   Present a dynamic scheduling strategy for multiple Hadoop workflow applications, leveraging job dependence information and execution time estimation.

—   Propose the Hadoop workflow benchmark, which can generate various workflows with required properties.

Section 2 describes the architecture of Pony and how to map the Hadoop workflow model with BPEL model. Section 3 introduces how to schedule multiple workflows in Hadoop. Section 4 gives evaluation experiments. Section 5 discussed the related work. Section 6 gives conclusions and describes future work.

2   System Overview

The principle of the architecture of Pony is simple without modification of the BPEL engine and Hadoop cluster. The system should be extensible to easily support other Hadoop job types and data processing activities in future.   Fig.2 is the systematic overview of Pony. BPEL is a little complex for developers to define Hadoop workflow. Therefore, we have developed a graphical design tool to define the dependencies between jobs and the control logics. The tool helps developer design a workflow visually and translates it to BPEL workflow.

The deployment includes deploying BPEL package to BPEL engine and uploading Hadoop Job Java classes to the server where the service container is on. The Hadoop workflow execution engine uses a BPEL engine to orchestrate the jobs by invoking a wrapper in the service container. Only wrapper services interact with Hadoop clusters. Web service wrappers are intended to be an isolated point for the portion of code that does the following: (1) reserializes the operation and parameter data from the parsed

SOAP request. (2) deploys Hadoop Job Java classes to the Hadoop cluster. (3) calls the Hadoop jobs. (4) seializes the return from the jobs and builds the body portion of the SOAP response. This architecture allows the Hadoop jobs to be deployed as a web service while not requiring changes to handle request data in the SOAP format.

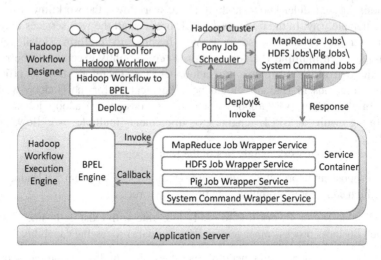

Fig. 2. The Architecture of Pony

3   Mapping Hadoop Workflow with BPEL Process

There are many differences between Hadoop workflow metamodel and BPEL meatmodel. First in the semantic level, two models contain different elements, different semantics for each elements, and different grammatical rules. Second in the deployment and execution level, two models have different activities involved methods, different activities deployment methods and different activities execution methods. Therefore, we must mapping these two model in this two level. Luckily, we find BPEL model can cover the semantic of Hadoop workflow, and we can find the mapping rules between their metamodels.

We first present a method for mapping the metamodel of Hadoop workflow to the metamodel of BPEL. Then, a Hadoop workflow instance can be translated to BPEL instance using the mapping rules. We also describe how to deploy and execute a Hadoop workflow using a BPEL engine.

3.1   Hadoop Workflow Metamodel

A Hadoop workflow is a Directed Acyclic Graph (DAG) of Hadoop jobs and routers. Hadoop workflow can be modeled as HPWFgraph, a graph object. $G = (V, E)$, and $V = (V1, V2, \ldots, Vn \mid Vi \in StartNode \mid EndNode \mid MapReduce Job \mid Pig Job \mid HDFS Job \mid Cmd Shell \mid Router \mid Web service \mid Java program)$.

MapReduce job is denoted as MR= {MRName, {Map} , Reduce, {RMap}, Paramerters, Input, Output}. MRName is the task name, Reduce is the reduced function , RMap processes the output to reduce. {Map} denote a set of map functions ,because one MapReduce job may contains more than one kind Map task. Parameters are the setting properties of tasks, Input is the input data source of task, and Output is the output data source of task. The other job's model is similar to MapReduce Job.

E= (e1, e2,...,en) is a set of directed edges. ei= {ID, WFID, Name, Type, Vs, Vt}. ei denotes one edge and represents the dependencies between two nodes. In Hadoop workflow, most dependencies are data dependencies. ID is the identifier of ei, WFID is the identifier of workflow, Name is the name of ei, Vs is the source node and Vt is the target node.

3.2   BPEL Metamodel

BPEL provides a language for the specification of executable and abstract business processes. BPEL are defined by XML lanaguages. By doing so, it extends the Web Services interaction model and enables it to support business transactions. BPEL defines an interoperable integration model that should facilitate the expansion of automated process integration both within and between businesses.

BPEL2.0 [12] defines the metamodel, and the basic elements include:

—   Partners: An important part of the use of BPEL is the description of the business process interaction between partners communicating with Web Services.

—   Data manipulation: In BPEL it's possible to use variables. A variable is always connected to a message from a WSDL.

—   Basic activities: Every basic activity has several standard attributes and elements that can be used to specify certain properties. In the explanation on this page we will not get into all the options offered by these attributes and elements.

—   Structured activities: Structured activities offer a way to structure a BPEL process. They describe the flow of a process by structuring basic activities. In this way control patterns, data flow, fault handling and coordination of messages can be achieved.

—   Scope: BPEL uses scopes to split the process up into several parts.

3.3   Translating Hadoop Workflow to BPEL Process

We implemented the automatic transformation between the two models by defining mapping rules. The model transformation engine follows a top-down strategy, and translates a Hadoop workflow instance to BPEL definition files with Java class libraries of jobs. A Hadoop workflow instance is modeled as a HPWFGraph (Hadoop Workflow Graph) object, which contains a StartNode as the start node and a EndNode as the end node. First, we define a BPEL process object and variable elements to store all the input information of HPWFGraph. Then, we judge the type of the subsequent node of StartNode. If it is a job node, we translate it to an assign and an invoke activity. If it is a router, we translate it to a switch activity or flow activity. Then we continue to translate the subsequent nodes until the end node. Table 1 shows the mapping rules.

Table 1. Mapping Hadoop workflow metamodel and BPEL metamodel

Hadoop Workflow Metamodel Elements		BPEL Metamodel Elements
HPWFGraph	Hadoop workflow graph object, with the context information.	Process
		Variable
StartNode/ EndNode	The start node and end node of Hadoop workflow graph.	Sequence
		Receive
		Reply
Job (MapReduce Job/ HDFS Job/Cmd Shell/ Pig Job/Java Application/ Web Service)	Job nodes, includes: MapReduce job, Pig job, HDFS job, System command, Java application, web service and so on.	Assign
		Invoke
If/else	Select the path with the condition	Switch
		Sequence
Fork/join	Parallel split/Parallel merge	Flow
		Sequence

3.4   Hadoop Workflow Deployment and Execution

MapReduce job has a property, that it should be deployed to Hadoop only when the input data are ready. The deploy operation will split the input data and distribute map tasks to salve node. So we should deploy a MapReduce job to Hadoop only when its input data are ready. We present a two-phase deployment strategy. In the first phase, we deploy BPEL definition files and Java classes generated from a Hadoop workflow to BPEL engine. In the second phase, when one job is allowed to run, we use the wrapper service to deploy it to the Hadoop cluster. This deployment strategy does not need any modification of BPEL engine.

With an invoke activity a process can call another Web Service that has been defined as a partner. The invoke activity can be either asynchronous or synchronous. A synchronous invoke needs both an input and an output variable. In an executable business process, these input and output variables are required. An asynchronous invoke only needs to specify an input variable, this because there is no direct reaction and thus no output variable. Because most Hadoop job may need a long execution time, we should use asynchronous invoke. When a Hadoop job finishes, the BPEL engine should be notified to invoke the subsequent job.

4   Efficient Workflow Scheduling

4.1   Workflow Scheduling Problem

Job scheduling in Hadoop is performed by a master node, which splits a job to some tasks and distributes them to a number of slaves. Tasks are assigned in response to heartbeats (status messages) received from the slaves every few seconds. Each slave has a fixed number of map slots and reduce slots for tasks. Slot is the logic resource corresponding to CPU core number. Typically, Hadoop tasks are single-threaded, so there is one slot per CPU core [15]. We need to design special scheduler for workflows. User can submit workflow directly to the scheduler and let the scheduler in chief of executing the jobs as their dependency relation. Workflow scheduling is above the job scheduling layer. Workflow scheduler should be in chief of the slot allocation for multiple workflows to achieve best performance in system perspective. Workflow scheduler should plan how to distribute jobs of workflows to nodes in Hadoop cluster.

When a user submits a workflow application, a key question he or she wants to ask is what the turnaround time will be, which is measured by the time difference between submission and completion of the application. In addition, the makespan is used to measure the workflow application performance, the time difference between the start time and completion time of a workflow. In this paper, we focus on how to schedule multiple MapReduce workflows efficiently at runtime.

4.2   Scheduling Strategy

Some research works are about multiple workflows scheduling in a grid. Their goals are also to minimize average makespan of workflows. The principle is to let the workflow with shortest execution time finish as early as first [15]. This is a NP hard problem. We can use a heuristic algorithm to find a better schedule plan. Many algorithms have been developed since, however most static algorithms are designed in the problem domain of scheduling single workflow applications, thus not applied to a common cluster environment where multiple workflow applications and other independent jobs compete for resources. Workflow applications may be submitted at different times by different users.

Online Workflow Management (OWM) has been proposed for the online mixed-parallel workflows [16]. In OWM, there are four processes: Critical Path Workflow Scheduling (CPWS), Task Scheduling, Task Rearrangement and Adaptive Allocation (AA). CPWS manages the task interdependence and submits tasks into the waiting queue according to the critical path in workflows. The task scheduling process in OWM sorts waiting queue. In the task parallel task scheduling, there may have some slacks among the tasks when the free processor are not enough for the first task in the waiting queue. The multi-processor task rearrangement process works for minimizing the slacks with latter tasks in the queue to improve utilization. When there are free resources, AA takes the highest priority task in the waiting queue, and selects the required resources to execute the task.

In a multi-tenant Hadoop cluster, Pony also needs a online scheduling strategy. We use OWM strategy to design an algorithm for Pony. BPEL engine manages the job dependencies and submit ready jobs to the waiting queue in Hadoop cluster. We design a Hadoop job scheduler to manage the waiting queue. We should sort the jobs in the queue to achieve minimize average makespan of workflow. We will estimate the execution time of each job, and sort them using the execution time ascending. When the free processors are not enough for the first job in the waiting queue, we pick a latter job that can be executed. When there are free resources, AA takes the highest priority job in the waiting queue, and selects the required resources to execute the task. So the key step is how to accurately estimate the execution time of MapReduce job.

Compared to workflow scheduling in grid, it is much harder to estimate the execution time of each job in Hadoop. There have been some related works. This is not the scope of this paper. The user can choose a most suitable algorithm for their application scenario and integrated into the scheduling strategy. We implement the algorithm in Pony

4.3   Scheduler Implementation Architecture

In a Hadoop cluster, there are two approaches to implement the workflow scheduler.(1) Implement the workflow scheduler and deploy it along with the job tracker; (2)Implement a workflow scheduler outside the Hadoop, and implement a job scheduler in Hadoop to cooperate with the workflow scheduler to control the resource allocation. However, we hope to achieve the scheduling of the workflow without any modifications of the Hadoop existing structure. The workflow engine is responsible for the job dependencies of each workflow. The Hadoop job scheduler can schedule jobs from different workflows. The existing scheduler does not know the information of the workflow, and therefore cannot effectively carry out the scheduling on workflow level. We propose a method to make jobtracker know the information about workflow, and then we have developed a job scheduler for Hadoop. Please refer to Figure 2. We only put forward architecture specific scheduling algorithm. User can design their workflow scheduler algorithm and implement a Hadoop job scheduler.

5   Experiments

We have implemented Pony base on OnceBPEL, which is developed by our team one year ago and implements BPEL 2.0. We also implemented the algorithm presented in section 4 to a workflow scheduler for Hadoop. We will compare Pony with Oozie [3], which is the most popular workflow engine for Hadoop. When we use Oozie to execute workflows, we can use three kinds job scheduler in Hadoop: FIFO scheduler, Capacity scheduler, and Fair scheduler. When we use Pony to execute workflows, we use our scheduler.

5.1   Experiments Settings

The experiments are conducted in our in-house 10-node Hadoop cluster. Each node has an Intel (R) Core (TM) i7-2600 CPU @ 3.40GHz, 16GB memory, and two 1TB hard drives, connected to a Gigabit switch. The version 0.20.2 of Hadoop is installed on the cluster. One node serves as the master node and the other as the slave nodes. The single master node runs the JobTracker and the NameNode, while each slave node runs both the TaskTracker and the DataNode. Each slave node is configured with eight Map slots and eight Reduce slots. Each Map/Reduce process uses 500MB memory. The data block size is set to 64 MB.

To evaluate Pony with workflow scheduler, we design a bench for workflow scheduling in Hadoop clusters. As we know, this is the first benchmark for Hadoop workflow. We present a method to randomly generated Hadoop workflows structured according to several workflow graph properties as described in [17], including workflow size, meshing degree, edge length, node- and edge-weight.

To generate workflow graph with different properties, we first randomly generated 1000 workflows by randomly connect two jobs. Then we automatically analyze the workflows and tag them with a suitable class name. For example, one workflow may be tagged with {low size, medium meshing degree, high edge length, high Node-weight and high Edge-weight}. When we evaluate the algorithm, we choose workflows with tags as needed.

To generate various MapReduce jobs in workflows, we design a job template whose input and the output are both texts. The computing logic of the job template is to transform the terms by matching with regular expression. The input data size is between 1GB and 10GB. Therefore, we can use the job template to generate job instances and connect them to create workflows.

Besides the graph properties, we add another set of properties to model the dynamic workload: number of concurrent workflows and arrival interval at which the workflows are submitted into the environment.

5.2   Result and Analysis

The experimental results are analyzed with respect to the evaluation metrics described in the previous section. The metrics include workflow graph characteristics and workload dynamic characteristics of arrival interval and concurrency.

We executed 5, 10, 15 number of concurrent workflows respectively in the experiment. Fig. 3 and Fig. 4 show how the algorithms perform with different number of concurrent workflows. Workflows are randomly chosen from candidates. As a result, Oozie with Fair and Capacity have almost identical performance with respect to average makespan and turnaround. When the number of concurrent workflows is 5, Capacity is better than Fair. Because we set fixed number queues in Capacity Scheduler, and fixed pools in Fair Scheduler, so when jobs number grow bigger, they behavior similarly. Surprisingly, FIFO performs better than Fair and Capacity. Because we compute the average makespan and tour around, so with FIFO, which job is waiting would not influence the result. FIFO only harms the users' experience.

Pony is faster than the other three. Because, the scheduler of Pony aware the information of workflow execution status, and the algorithm helps it make the best decision to minimize the makespan. It can be easily seen that the more concurrent workflows are submitted, the Better Pony outperforms other Oozie with three schedulers.

In the experiments, we assume the arrival interval follows a Poisson distribution with mean value of 0, 5, 15, 20, 25 seconds respectively. We use same 10 workflows in this group experiments and let they arrive one by one. Fig 5 and Fig 6 helps us to understand how the algorithms respond to the workload intensity measured by the interval between workflow submissions. It can be seen four system behavior smoothly with different arrival interval. Because the Hadoop cluster processes jobs quickly and most jobs finished in 5 second. However Pony outperforms other Oozie with three schedulers with different arrival interval of workflow.

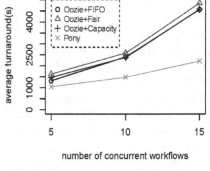

Fig. 3. Average makespan against the total number of concurrent workflows

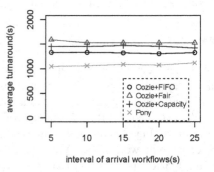

Fig. 4. Average turnaround against the total number of concurrent

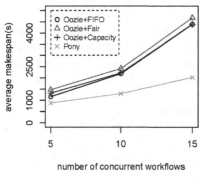

Fig. 5. Average makespan against the arrival interval of workflows

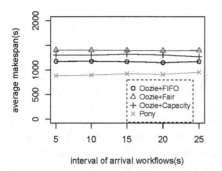

Fig. 6. Average turnaround against the arrival interval of workflows

6   Related Work

There are some Hadoop workflow systems with their own features. Oozie is a coordination system to manage Apache Hadoop jobs. Oozie Workflow jobs are Directed Acyclic Graphs (DAGs) of actions. Oozie Coordinator jobs are recurrent Oozie Workflow jobs triggered by time (frequency) and data availability [3]. Cascading provides a programming language, using the "pipe and the filters to define the data processing process [4]. Hamake is a lightweight client tool, using the "fold" and "foreach" incremental data processing [5]. Azkaban is still not mature, and its goal is to provide a friendly user interface and time trigger [6]. CloudWF supports both MapReduce workflow and legacy non-MapReduce process workflow [7]. Nova is a pig / Hadoop workflow scheduler to handle real-time data [8]. Oozie is most similar to Pony. However, Pony provides a richer model semantic and efficient enactment engine.

Our Hadoop workflow model is directed acyclic graph, which can be mapped to BPEL freely. [11] proposes a platform-independent conceptual model of ETL processes based on the Business Process Model Notation (BPMN) [10] standard. They also show how such a conceptual model can be implemented using Business Process Execution Language (BPEL). We focus on using BPEL to define Hadoop workflow and execute it. [12] proposed how to define scientific workflow using BPEL. [13] proposes using BPEL to support ETL process execution, and they focus on the data transferring.

Now Hadoop provides three job schedulers. Originally, Hadoop employed First in First out (FIFO) scheduling, but such simple schemes cause job starvation. Capacity Scheduler [14] supports for multiple queues, where a job is submitted to a queue. All jobs submitted to a queue will have access to the capacity allocated to the queue. There are also some research works on job scheduling in MapReduce clusters. Workflow based scheduling has always been a core research area in Grid computing. Yu and Buyya [15] surveyed the research on workflow scheduling in grid computing. [16] proposed Online Workflow Management (OWM) for the online mixed-parallel workflows. [17] present a planner-guided scheduling strategy for multiple workflow applications. Hadoop workflow scheduling is very different from grid workflow scheduling, because the execution time estimation of job is much easier for grid workflow. In this paper, our contribution is introducing multiple workflow schedulers to Hadoop platform.

7   Conclusion

We present a method for quickly building a Hadoop workflow engine based on BPEL: Pony. Pony uses BPEL language to define complex Hadoop workflow, which can integrate with existing enterprise business process. Existing workflow engine does not provide workflow scheduler. We present a workflow level scheduler for Pony to improve dynamic scheduling performance by guiding it with information about the workflow resource demanded estimation. A workload benchmark is developed and the experiment shows its great improvement of performance. We present a flexible architecture for user to design their domain specific scheduler.

Big data makes organizations smarter and more productive by enabling people to harness diverse data types previously unavailable, and to find previously unseen opportunities. Hadoop as a most popular big data processing platform will be adopted by more and more enterprises. We will study how to integrate big data analytical workflow with some real business processes. We also would like to study the feasibility of using BPMN to design a business process with big data processing workflow.

Acknowledgements. This work was partially supported by the National Natural Science Foundation of China (61202065, 61173005), the National Grand Fundamental Research 973 Program of China (2009CB320704), the National Key Technology R&D Program (2012BAH05F02, 2012AA011204).

References

1. Hadoop: Open source implementation of MapReduce, http://lucene.apache.org/hadoop/
2. Jeffrey, D., Sanjay, G.: MapReduce: Simplified Data Processing on Large Clusters. In: Proceedings of the OSDI 2004, pp. 1–10 (2004)
3. Apache Oozie, http://yahoo.github.com/oozie/
4. Cascading, http://www.cascading.org/
5. Hamake, http://code.google.com/p/hamake/
6. LinkedIn Azkaban, http://sna-projects.com/azkaban/
7. Zhang, C., De Sterck, H.: CloudWF: A computational workflow system for clouds based on Hadoop. In: Jaatun, M.G., Zhao, G., Rong, C. (eds.) CloudCom 2009. LNCS, vol. 5931, pp. 393–404. Springer, Heidelberg (2009)
8. Olston, C., Chiou, G., Chitnis, L., et al.: Nova: continuous Pig/Hadoop workflows. In: Proceedings of SIGMOD 2011, pp. 1081–1090 (2011)
9. OASIS. Web Services Business Process Execution Language Version 2.0, http://docs.oasis-open.org/wsbpel/2.0/wsbpel-v2.0.pdf
10. OMG. Business Process Modeling Notation (BPMN), http://www.omg.org/docs/formal/09-01-03.pdf
11. El Akkaoui, Z., Zimanyi, E.: Defining ETL workflows using BPMN and BPEL. In: Proceedings of the ACM Twelfth International Workshop on Data Warehousing and OLAP (DOLAP 2009), pp. 41–48 (2009)
12. Emmerich, W., Butchart, B., Chen, L., et al.: Grid Service Orchestration Using the Business Process Execution Language (BPEL). Journal of Grid Computing 3(3-4), 283–304 (2005)
13. Behnen, M., Jin, Q., Saillet, Y., Srinivasan, S.: Supporting ETL Processing in BPEL-Based Processes. Publication number: US 2008/0115135 A1 (Filing date: November 13, 2006)
14. Capacity Scheduler for Hadoop, http://Hadoop.apache.org/common/docs/current/Capacity_scheduler.html
15. Yu, J., Buyya, R.: Workflow Scheduling Algorithms for Grid Computing, Technical Report, GRIDS-TR-2007-10
16. Hsu, C., Huang, K., Wang, F.: Online scheduling of workflow applications in grid environments. Future Generation Computer Systems 27(6), 860–870 (2011)
17. Zhifeng, Y., Weisong, S.: A Planner-Guided Scheduling Strategy for Multiple Workflow Applications. In: Proceedings of the ICPP - Workshops, pp. 1–8 (2008)

Taldea: A Tool for Fostering Spontaneous Communities

Ghada Ben Nejma[1], Philippe Roose[1], Jérôme Gensel[2],
Marc Dalmau[1], and Mohamed Amine Ghorbali[2]

[1] LIUPPA Laboratory / T2I Research Team
2 Allée du Parc de Montaury 64600 Anglet, France
[2] LIG Laboratory / STEAMER Research Team
681 rue de la Passerelle, BP72
38402 Saint Martin d'Hères cedex, France
{gbennej,roose,dalmau}@iutbayonne.univ-pau.fr,
{Jerome.Gensel,mohamed-amine.ghorbali}@imag.fr

Abstract. This paper presents the design and development of a community application that facilitates user's access to communities and exchange information between community members. The application provides multiple services in order to satisfy the needs of users sharing a common interest or practice. We introduce a new type of ephemeral communities with geolocalization, that we call spontaneous communities. Our approach is based on an ontology, which models the different components of a community and their relations. The proposed approach has been validated through a prototype for the visitors of a botanical garden.

1   Introduction

Recent years have witnessed rapid advances in the technological infrastructure. The democratization of mobile devices (e.g. smartphones, touchpads, laptops, sensors, etc.) has made information accessible to anyone at anytime and from anywhere. The idea of ubiquitous computing or computers everywhere has been first proposed by Mark Weiser [8]. In heterogeneous and highly changing environment, ubiquitous applications are progressing to the detriment of distributed systems. Today, ubiquitous applications include more and more the community notion (e.g. Yuback[1], Foursquare[2]). The growth of communities is justified by:

- Social information needs (e.g information for citizenship);
- Social interaction and communion needs (e.g. discussions and sharing of experiences);
- Social recognition needs (e.g political leader recognition).
- Etc.

Yet, social information is not fully exploited as underlined by Deparis *et al.* [1]: *"the organizations begin to realize that they lose a part of their knowledge by not*

---

[1] http://www.yuback.com/
[2] https://fr.foursquare.com/

Q.Z. Sheng and J. Kjeldskov (Eds.): ICWE 2013 Workshops, LNCS 8295, pp. 293–301, 2013.
© Springer International Publishing Switzerland 2013

capitalizing social fragments. Actual knowledge management tools are not able to correctly handle these social fragments and their value is lost for the organizations". Thus, organizations use more and more community applications to facilitate social interaction between users and capitalize the exchanges.

In the MOANO[3] (Models and Tools for Territory Discovery-oriented Nomadic Applications) Project of the ANR (French National Research Agency), we are interested in the design and the development of a spatiotemporal context-sensitive community application in order to facilitate the discovery of a territory. The objective of this work is to propose a community model and to present a tool for fostering spontaneous communities. The ontology-based community modeling allows us to organize and represent the different components of a community and their relationships, to make information search easier for users, to infer new knowledge and capitalize social data. This paper presents our approach for modeling communities using semantic web technologies (e.g. FOAF[4], SIOC[5]). The use of these technologies offers a wide range of benefits such as interoperability, data portability and semantics data interpretation.

The paper is organized as follows. The first section compares the various social tools that can be used by organizations. In the second section, we propose a usage scenario of our community application. It describes how the visitor of a botanical garden can join or create communities in a specific geographic area. In section 3, we describe functional-aspects of our community application. After presenting different modules allowing users access to communities and exchange information, concluding remarks summarize the importance of the presented approach and outline some future work.

2   Social Networks versus Community Applications

The popularity of socials networks and online communities has grown exponentially *"Social networks offer to users interesting means and ways to connect, communicate, and share information with other members within their platforms"* [4]. They are more and more used by organizations to facilitate collaboration between users groups and other aspects of information exchange. Several studies suggest methods for discovering communities in social networks. They consist in identifying groups of users more interconnected than the rest of the network. A comparative analysis of community discovery methods in social networks is addressed by the paper of Sathik et al. [5].

The acquisition, collection and analysis of information spread over social networks are difficult tasks for organizations. Furthermore, with the growing number of social networks, it is often hard to motivate users to join the same network. Some solutions have been proposed for organizations such as enterprise social networking to help employees share their expertise and connect with others, especially in geographically distributed organizations. However, organizations have to face a high number of new challenges such as mobility, ubiquity, and problems of heterogeneity. For all these

---

[3] http://moano.liuppa.univ-pau.fr/
[4] http://www.foaf-project.org/
[5] http://sioc-project.org/

reasons, we consider that context-aware community applications are a solution to adapt to changing situations. We have made a comparative study between social networks, enterprise social networks and community applications and we present the results in the table 1.

The existing applications (e.g. eklaireur[6]) offer services and information related to a specific theme, which has to be defined in advance by developers. The creation of new communities with other themes cannot be spontaneous by user. In our communities' applications, we define a new type of communities as "a spontaneous group of individuals having a common interest related to a circumstantial, accidental, incidental or fortuitous situation that occurs somewhere on a geographical territory". This kind of community can meet specific needs, which are generally not taken into account by perennial communities (e.g. accidents, natural disaster, crisis, fire, etc.).

Table 1. Comparison Table of different social tools in Organizations

	Social Network	Enterprise Social Networks	Community Applications
Share information	Expect no Feedback	Expect some Feedback	Expect some Feedback
Nature of community	Explicit or implicit community	Explicit community	Explicit or implicit community
Similarity between members	May be different	Share a common interest	Share a common interest
Type of relationship	Implicit relationships inferred from user behavior	Explicit relationships between members	Explicit relationships between members
Capitalize social information	No	Yes	Yes
Structure	Network	Network	Overlap
Pervasives systems	Yes	No	Yes
Examples	*Blogs, Wiki, Podcasts, etc.*	*KFET, Yammer, Elgg, etc.*	*Foursquare, Yuback, PassBook, etc.*

3   Use Case

Our work focuses more particularly on temporary, short-lived communities. Indeed, it is the type of community that best matches with unexpected situations. The proposed application intends to help the user in the creation of a spontaneous community with the objective of answering an incidental situation. However, our community application, called *Taldea*, is not only an application that assists user to create a community, but also consists of an environment that supports communities throughout their life cycle. We briefly describe a scenario in a botanical park Mosaïque, located near the French city of Lille. In this park can be found a variety of stakeholders (visitors, gardeners, eco-guards, external participants...). These stakeholders can be equipped with mobile devices. *Taldea* is deployed thanks to a service-based reconfiguration platform we have developed, named *Kalimucho*. This platform implements a contextual-deployment heuristic in order to find a configuration that matches the current context with QoS requirements. *Taldea* is composed of interconnected components supervised by the platform. In this paper, we

---

[6] https://play.google.com/store/apps/details?id=com.eklaireur.ek
ldroid&hl=fr

choose to detail the different ways to access a community. We have implemented the following scenario. A fan of orchid flowers visits the park Mosaïque to discover the local flora of the region. Equipped with his Smartphone, she enters the park. The Smartphone automatically integrates *Taldea* through *Geofencing*[7]. Communities that are semantically related to orchid flowers will be recommended to the visitor. Moreover, she can search for a community by formulating a query. For instance, let us suppose that the visitor connects to the community of interest *'fans of orchids'*. During her tour in the botanical garden, she identifies some rare *'Ophrys apifera'* flowers. She first takes pictures of her discovery. Then, she consults the list of connected members of the "fans of orchids" community. However, at this moment, no member is present in the park or is available for a real time communication. Then, she decides to publish a topic (the unit of exchange within a community) in the community space "fans of orchids" to invite people to admire these flowers. While waiting for an answer from the members, the user of *Taldea* decides to create a spontaneous community named *"fans of rare orchids"*. *Taldea* classifies this new community as a sub-community of the *"fans of orchids"* community. The visitor then creates the topic *"Discover Ophrys apifera"*. This topic is annotated with spatiotemporal data in order to facilitate the location of flowers. The created topic is recommended to all the users of *Taldea* (they can be members of other communities) presents in the park. A short time later, she received several answers for her topic. Several interested persons moved on the scene to discover or to admire these flowers. Other scenarios can be foreseen for other communities such as the communities of practice (e.g. the gardeners of the park). Critical situations (e.g. accidents, disasters, etc.) can highlight the importance of spontaneous communities. In the next section, we describe the different ways to access communities.

4   Taldea: Access Mechanisms to Communities

As shown in the following example, there are three ways to access a community in Taldea: recommendation, search and creation of a community (cf. figure 1). (1) The user logs in, (2) her interests are mapped to the botanical ontology, (3) as well as the interests of existing communities. Then, similarity measures are used in order to identify communities semantically similar to the user's profile. If the user is not satisfied with the proposals (4), *Taldea,* allows her to enter a query using natural language for searching for other communities. (5&6) The query is annotated through the web service TextAnnot[8] .(7) Sparql query is formulated from annotation results to query the ontology by the *Reasoner.*(8) If the user is not satisfied with the search results, she can create a spontaneous community.(9) Inference rules that can be used

---

[7]   The geo-fencing approach is based on the observation that users move in a virtual perimeter for a real-world geographic area. It allow us to track people on a mobile subscriber list based on proximity to a particular retail store and sending them tailored messages relating to that store.

[8]   A web service developed by our research team, it provides information in the form of some annotations based on botanic ontology (http://themat2i.univ-pau.fr:8080/ TextAnnot-WWW/annotation.jsp).

to infer new knowledge for further enrichment of community description. (10) Finally, the community ontology is instantiated with the user- entered information and the inferred information.

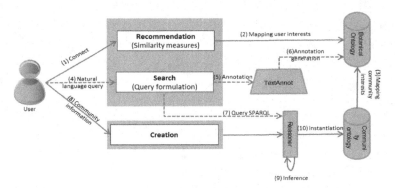

Fig. 1. Access mechanisms to communities

4.1   Creation and Closing of the Community

Nowadays, the social fragments [1] become essential to enrich the knowledge base of organizations. Several ongoing projects aim to use some social information produced by communities such as the projects *SPIPOLL*[9], *operation Escargot*[10], *Sauvage de ma rue*[11]. Referring to the same ontology for different communities (all users refer to the same vocabulary) can enrich the knowledge base of the organization. New knowledge can be reused by other communities.

In this section, we present the ontology for describing formally a community using multiple standards such as FOAF, SIOC, *Owl-Time*[12] and *GeoRSS*[13], etc. These standards make it possible for software agents to understand information exchanged without the ambiguity, complex processing, and rigidity brought by other representation formalisms (e.g. natural language, relational database). Figure 2 shows the community ontology (partial definition of the ontology). The model is structured around a set of abstract entities, each describing physical or conceptual objects including Interest, Member, Lifespan, Resource, Location, Type.

Each creation of a community is an instantiation of the ontology concepts (cf. figure 2). Additional knowledge is provided from user's input annotation and the inferences rules, inferences engines (i.e *Reasoner*) such as the type of community. As illustrated in Table 2, the user enters the following description of the community *"fans of rare orchids"*. This description is automatically annotated. *TextAnnot* attach the created community to the concept '*Orchid*' of the botanic ontology.

---

[9] http://www.spipoll.org/

[10] http://www.noeconservation.org/index2.php?rub=12&srub=31&ssrub= 322&goto=contenu

[11] http://sauvagesdemarue.mnhn.fr/sauvages-de-ma-rue/presentation

[12] http://www.w3.org/TR/owl-time/

[13] http://georss.org/Main_Page

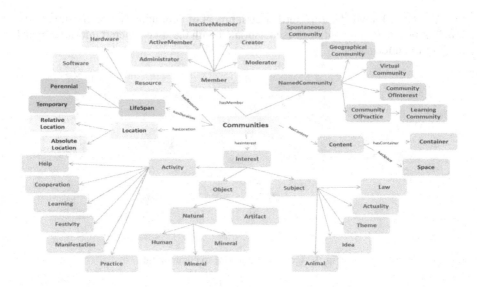

Fig. 2. A part of the community ontology

Table 2. An example of inference

Terminology box associated with the community ontology (Tbox)
Communities: {CommunityOfInterest, CommunityOfPractice, GeographicalCommunity, SpontaneousCommunity, VirtualCommunity} Interest {Activity, Object, Subject} Object {Artifact, Natural} Natural {Animal, Human, Plant, Mineral} CommunityOfInterest ⊆ Communities ⊓∃ hasInterest (Object ∨ Subject)
Assertion box associated with the community ontology(Abox)
Community ⊓ hasInterest (Orchid) Orchid: Plant
Inference
Fans of rare orchids → CommunityOfInterest

A community may be closed when the need for which it was created becomes satisfied or obsolete. After closing a community, the extracted knowledge exchanges between members are capitalized.

4.2   Access to Communities

4.2.1 Community Recommendation
In this paper, we propose a method of community recommendation based on a measure of semantic similarity between the interests of the user and those of communities.

4.2.1.1 User's profile

There are different profile representations in different contexts such as CC/PP[14] (Composite Capability/Preference Profiles), PAPI[15] (Public And Private Information), FOAF (Friend of a friend), etc. All these profile representations are widespread standard. We have chosen the FOAF vocabulary to represent the user's profile because it is simple and enables interoperability among systems. Moreover, given that it is based on RDF, the vocabulary can be extended as needed. Information, in FOAF profile, is categorized as *FOAF basics, Personal info, Online accounts, Projects and groups, Documents and image.* In community recommendation, we are particularly interested in the class *Interest* to perform some semantic matching between the user's profile and communities.

4.2.1.2 Measure of Similarity between the User's Profile and the Community

In the field of information retrieval, semantic similarity measures are used to assess the semantic proximity between the query and the document. In the context of community applications, we evaluate the semantic similarity between the user's profile and communities, by the mapping of user interests and community interests in the domain ontology (i.e the botanic ontology). In different contexts, several approaches have been proposed to measure semantic similarity between concepts in ontology. We can distinguish three major approaches: The first type is based only on the hierarchy or the edge distances, the second type is based on the nodes and the third type is the hybrid approach [6]. For measuring semantic similarity between user profile and communities, we adopted an approach based on arcs because other approaches used the frequency information. This is not significant in the case of community because it is created around infrequent concepts in the corpus. We choose the measure of Wu and Palmer [9]. It is simple to implement, has good performance compared to other similarity measures [6].

The Measure of Wu and Palmer [9] is a measure between concepts in an ontology. Wu and Palmer, similarity metric measures the depth of the two concepts in the ontology, and the depth of the least common subsumer (LCS), and combines these figures into a similarity score:

$$sim\ (concept1, concept2) = \frac{2 * depth(LCS)}{depth(concept1) + depth(concept2)}$$

4.2.1.3 Community Recommendation Algorithm

We propose an approach to recommend communities to users based on their interests. Alg. 1 shows the details of our approach. The key idea is to compute semantic similarity between the user's profile and communities. We first project the user's interests and communities' interests on the domain ontology (Line 1). Secondly, we compare the interests and return communities whose interests match user's ones (Line 2~5). If no match is found, we compute the semantic similarity between each user's interest and each community's interest using Wu and Palmer measure (Line 7~10).

---

[14] http://www.w3.org/Mobile/CCPP/

[15] http://www.cen-ltso.net/main.aspx?put=230

The communities with the highest values of similarity between the user's interests and community's interests are selected (Line10).

Algorithm 1. *Community Recommendation*

1:   *Map user and communities interests on the domain ontology*
2:   **For each** *userInterest*
3:   *Boolean exist := verifyExistence (userInterest, communitiesInterests)*
4:   **If** *(exist = true) then*
5:   *ReturnCommunities (hasInterest, userInterest)*
6:   **Else**
7:   **For each** *communitiesInterests*
8:   *Calculate Sim (userInterest, communitiesInterests)*
9:   **End for**
10: *ReturnCommunities(Sim(userInterest, communitiesInterests)> Threshold)*
11: **End If**
12: **End for**

4.2.2 Community Search

With Taldea, the user can enter queries in natural language to search for communities. The query will be annotated through *TextAnnot*[9]. Using the results of this annotation, a Sparql query is formulated with the concepts results in the clause *Where*.

Table 3. Example of user query

I'm looking for *orchid community*

Table 4. Example of query formulation

```
PREFIX onto : <http://www.communities.org/ontologies/communities.owl#>
Select ?community
Where {
    ?community rdf:type onto:Communities.
    ?community onto: hasInterest onto:"orchid ".
}
```

The two concepts 'orchid' and 'community', result of the annotation process, are used to build the clause *Where* of the Sparql query as shown in Table 4.

This module of the application allows users to query the community knowledge base without using a complex query language.

5   Conclusion

Taldea is a community's application that helps users access to communities and organize social exchanges between users in a geographic territory. In this paper, we present the first module of Taldea allowing user create or find a community. Taldea offers three ways to access a community; recommendation, search and creation of a community. On the one hand, the ontological modeling community adds a semantic layer to information and facilitates the user reach to communities and information retrieval within the community. On the other hand, it infers automatically new knowledge for further enrichment of community description. The use of standards like FOAF for describing the user's profile ensures accessibility and interoperability of data within communities.

Our immediate plan is to enrich the description of the community to include a spatio-temporal contextualization of social exchanges between users. In future work, several issues will be investigated. We plan to include a description of services provided for each kind of community and deploy Taldea in the software platform Kalimucho for deploying reconfigurable distributed applications.

References

1. Deparis, E., Abel, M.H., Mattioli, J.: Modeling a social collaborative platform with standard ontologies. In: International Workshop on Knowledge Acquisition, Reuse and Evaluation, Dijon, France, pp. 167–173 (2011)
2. Leprovost, D., Abrouk-Gouaich, L., Gross-Amblard, D.: Discovering implicit communities in web forums through ontologies. International Journal of Web Intelligence and Agent Systems (2012)
3. Ma, Y., Audibert, L., Nazarenko, A.: Formal Description of Resources for Ontology-based Semantic Annotation. In: The Seventh International Conference on Language Resources and Evaluation (2010)
4. Raad, E., Chbeir, R., Dipanda, A.: User Profile Matching in Social Networks. In: International Conference on Network-Based Information Systems (2010)
5. Sathik, M., Senthamarai, K., Rasheed, A.: Comparative Analysis of Community Discovery Methods in Social Networks. International Journal of Computer Applications 14(8) (2011)
6. Slimani, T., Ben Yaghlane, B., Mellouli, K.: A new similarity measure based on edge counting. In: Proceedings of the Seventeenth International Waset Conference, vol. 17 (2006)
7. Vercoutier, L., Maret, P.: Introducing Web Intelligence for communities. Web Intelligence and Agent Systems Journal (WIAS) 10(1), 89–92 (2012)
8. Weiser, M.: The Computer for the 21st Century. Scientific American Special Issue on Communications, Computers, and Networks (1991)
9. Wu, Z., Palmer, M.: Verb semantics and lexical selection. In: Proceedings of the 32nd Annual Meeting of the Associations for Computational Linguistics, pp. 133–138 (1994)

Identifying User Interests from Online Social Networks by Using Semantic Clusters Generated from Linked Data

Han-Gyu Ko, In-Young Ko, Taehun Kim, Dongman Lee, and Soon J. Hyun

Department of Computer Science, Korea Advanced Institute of Science and Technology
291 Daehak-ro, Yuseong-gu, Daejeon, 305-701, Republic of Korea
{kohangyu,iko,kingmbc,dlee,sjhyun}@kaist.ac.kr

Abstract. Recently, online social network services (SNSs) are being spotlighted as a means to understand users' implicit interests out of abundant online social information. Since SNS contents such as message posts and comments are however less informative comparing with news articles and blog posts, it is difficult to identify users' implicit interests by analyzing the topics of the SNS contents of users. In this paper, we propose a semantic cluster based method of combining SNS contents with Linked Data. By traversing and merging relevant concepts, the proposed method expands keywords that are helpful to understand the topic similarity between SNS contents. By using Facebook data, we demonstrate that the proposed method increases the coverage of potential interests by 28.85% and the user satisfaction by 17.24% compared to existing works.

Keywords: User interest identification, Topic analysis, Social network services, Linked Data, Semantic cluster.

1 Introduction

The proliferation of social network services (SNSs) have encouraged many researchers to investigate on understanding users' potential interests from their social contents and relationships [1]. Unlike the interests that are explicitly specified in each user's personal profile, message posts and conversations among users in SNSs need to be processed and analyzed to extract essential information about users' interests. The phenomenon called 'social correlation' is often used to understand implicit interests of users from their social contents [2, 3]. The core of this phenomenon is that SNS users are often influenced by their social neighbors when they make a decision [4]. Therefore, by identifying the correlation between a set of social neighbors' interests and a target user's SNS contents, we could successfully find and recommend potential interests for the user [5, 6]. These approaches mostly use natural language processing methods to extract keywords from SNS contents.

Despite these efforts, users' satisfaction on recommended interests is quite low – less than 65%. This is because there is a low chance of finding the keywords that represent the interests of social neighbors from SNS contents which are short and less informative in comparison to general Web documents such as news articles and blog

Q.Z. Sheng and J. Kjeldskov (Eds.): ICWE 2013 Workshops, LNCS 8295, pp. 302–309, 2013.

posts. Moreover, some keywords have multiple meanings and the existing approaches cannot deal with the semantic heterogeneity problem effectively.

In order to solve these problems, there are essential requirements to be met. Firstly, there must be a way of expanding the set of keywords extracted from SNS contents so that we can increase the chance of finding them from social neighbors' interests. Secondly, to overcome the semantic heterogeneity problem, it is necessary to identify all potential semantics of a keyword, and match them against social neighbors' interests. Since a user's SNS contents may contain keywords that are about latest issues and trends, it is essential to use ontologies and knowledge bases that reflect those while identifying semantics of a keyword.

In this paper, we propose an approach of using Linked Data[1] as the source of finding the appropriate semantics of the keywords that are extracted from SNS contents. We especially use DBpedia, Freebase and OpenCyc as the primary knowledge bases. In our approach, the concepts that are retrieved from these sources are grouped together as *semantic clusters* based on their similarity and relevance. For efficient retrieval and filtering of Linked Data, we design a concept analysis model by which we can explore Linked Data selectively based on subsumption hierarchies and concept similarity. In addition, to find the most essential concepts from which we can start exploring the relevant concepts to generate semantic clusters, we apply the centrality analysis[2] method. A set of semantic clusters are generated from the keywords that are extracted from a user's SNS contents, and another set of semantic clusters are generated from the representative terms that indicate social neighbors' interests. The correlation between these sets of semantic clusters are identified to find social neighbors' interests that might be relevant to the implicit interests of the user.

We conducted an experiment and a user study by using Facebook. The experiment result shows that our approach contributes to increase the coverage of finding potential interests by around 29%. In addition, the user study result proves that the user satisfaction on recommended interests can be improved by around 17% in comparison to the existing approaches.

In the next section, we introduce existing approaches to infer user interests from SNS contents and social network structures. In Section 3, we describe our approach of generating semantic clusters from Linked Data, and recommending potential interests for users. In Section 4, the effectiveness of the proposed method for identifying users' implicit interests from SNS contents is described, followed by the conclusion and future work in Section 5.

2   Related Works

There have been some researches on inferring user interests from users' activities in SNSs. These researches can be categorized into two types. The first category of works measures the correlation among users by using the structural features of social networks such as popularity, similarity, and interaction strength with social neighbors.

---

[1] http://www.w3.org/standards/semanticweb/data
[2] http://en.wikipedia.org/wiki/Centrality

White et al. [7], Sharma and Cosley [8] are examples. The limitation of these approaches is that they do not consider topics or semantics in social relationships which are essential to accurately infer users' implicit interests.

Another category of works is about analyzing users' SNS contents as well as structural features of social networks. To improve the accuracy of inferring implicit user interests, Zhen et al. [2, 5] and Ahn et al. [6] proposed an approach that combines topic similarity among users' SNS contents with network features such as familiarity with their social neighbors. In these approaches, however, they depend on keyword sets from SNS contents to analyze users' topics, which may be not enough to find the keywords that represent the interests of social neighbors. Hence, their results do not show much improvement in terms of user satisfaction.

3   Identifying User Interests via Semantic Clusters

In this section, we describe a user interest identification method that combines SNS contents with Linked Data. By retrieving concepts that are related to SNS contents and finding and associating more concepts from Linked Data, we can expand the keywords that are extracted from SNS contents and improve the possibility of finding implicit interests of users.

As shown in Figure 1, we handle information from SNSs in two different ways. A *social content* is the combination of a post and its associated comments. An *interest-content* is the content that consists of its name and descriptions. We extract keywords from social contents of a user and interest-contents from his or her social neighbors and retrieve relevant concepts of the topic keywords from Linked Data. We then group semantically relevant concepts together and form semantic clusters. Finally, we identify a list of interest-contents that show high correlation with the user's implicit interests found from their SNS contents.

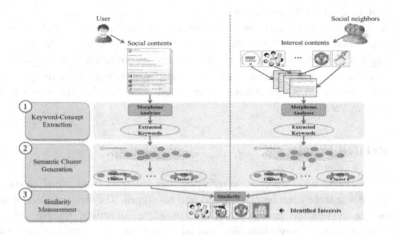

Fig. 1. The process of generating and comparing semantic clusters

The main characteristic of the proposed method is the utilization of semantic clusters rather than using keywords as the source to measure topic similarity between social contents and interest-contents. In the following subsections, we describe the detail steps to generate and analyze semantic clusters from SNS sources and recommend potential interests to users.

3.1   Retrieving Concepts from Linked Data

As the first step to generate semantic clusters, it is necessary to retrieve concepts related to keywords in a user's SNS contents from Linked Data. From Facebook users, we collected all social contents and interest-contents. By using a morpheme analyzer[3], we extracted nouns and noun phrases from those contents as keywords removing stop words and duplicated words.

We then query with each keyword to Linked Data to retrieve the corresponding concept by using SPARQL. We assume that RDF triples which describe the corresponding concept, contain the keyword as one of their property values such as name, title, or label. Because each dataset in Linked Data may use different kinds of predicates to indicate these properties, we handle multiple predicates such as `rdf:label` and `skos:prefLabel` used in target datasets. After that, we query again to retrieve all triples that describe each subject and group them as a concept.

Rather than querying to all the datasets in Linked Data, we selectively query to the datasets that cover various domain knowledge. Because DBpedia is the most central dataset in Linked Data, in which Wikipedia articles are represented as concepts on a large coverage of domains, we use DBpedia and other datasets such as Freebase and OpenCyc, which provide links to DBpedia covering various domains.

3.2   Generating Semantic Clusters

After retrieving all concepts from Linked Data with given keywords, we construct groups of relevant concepts called semantic clusters to filter out irrelevant concepts. We use a concept analysis model shown in Figure 2. Each concept has a label for presentation and a URI for reference. Both properties are literal and connected to the concept through a 'hasKeyword' or 'hadURI' properties, respectively.

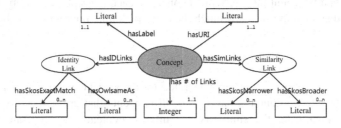

Fig. 2. Concept analysis model

---

[3] http://developer.yahoo.com/search/content/V1/termExtraction.html

Identity-links such as `owl:sameAs` and `skos:exactMatch` are used to consolidate concepts that have the same meaning. We then find and merge semantically relevant concepts by using *similarity-links* such as `skos:broader` and `skos:narrower`. Since those links are used to represent the relative hierarchies of concepts within the same dataset in Linked Data, we need to use similarity-links along with identity-links in a complementary manner to group relevant concepts generated from different datasets. Except for the identity-links and similarity-links which are necessary for analyzing semantic hierarchies among the concepts, others are counted as the number of links.

As the next step, we find and merge more concepts that are semantically relevant to make semantic clusters richer. We apply the breadth-first search method starting from a representative concept for each semantic cluster. The number of hops (the number of edges in the concept graph) from the representative concept is inversely proportional to the semantic relevance. Therefore, it is possible to retrieve concepts that are most semantically relevant by using this method. To select the representative concept, we measure the centrality of concepts and choose the concept that has the highest centrality value as the representative concept in each semantic cluster. We use the PageRank[4] algorithm for measuring the centrality of each concept since it is one of the most effective ways of measuring the relative importance of a node in a set of linked data. We also chose the maximum number of hops as 2 since more than 80% of relevant concepts can be found empirically in the range of 2 hops from the representative concepts [9].

Once the semantic clusters are generated, the ambiguity of a keyword can be resolved by associating it with a set of relevant concepts. For example, the meaning of the keyword "Apple" will become clear when it is associated with the relevant concepts such as "Steve Jobs" and "iPhone".

3.3   Comparing Similarity among Semantic Clusters

By using the semantic clusters generated, we now can measure the similarity between a user's social contents and his or her interest-contents. The interest-contents are from the user's social neighbors in SNS and useful to identify the user's implicit interests.

The similarity measure can be implemented by aggregating the number of overlapped concepts between the semantic clusters of social contents and the interest-contents. When we count the overlapped concepts, each concept's centrality value (C) is considered since it implies how much the concept is important within each semantic cluster.

$$Sim(sc,\ ic_j) = \sum C(k_{sc\text{-}ic}) \tag{1}$$

where sc is the semantic clusters generated for the social contents, ic_j is a semantic cluster for an interest-content, and $k_{sc\text{-}ic}$ is all concepts that are co-occurred in both sides. After measuring the similarity for interest contents, we generate a list of interest-contents as the user's implicit interests ordered by the similarity value in descending manner.

---

[4] `http://ilpubs.stanford.edu:8090/422/1/1999-66.pdf`

4   Evaluation

In order to prove the effectiveness of the proposed method, we performed two different evaluations. First, we measured how many interest-contents from each user's social neighbors were found to validate the effectiveness of the semantic clusters. In addition, we performed a user study to validate the user satisfaction on the interests recommended by the proposed method. Both evaluation results were compared against the keyword based method [6] that is considered as the state-of-the-art approach so far.

For our evaluation, we collected 1,043,000 posts and 123,000 interests from 50 Facebook users who have volunteered provide their account data for this research. The volunteers consist of graduate students in the department of computer science at KAIST. We extracted around 10,000 ~ 250,000 keywords for each user by using the morpheme analyzer.

4.1   Finding Potential Interests from Social Neighbors

We measured the coverage of users' potential interests that were found by analyzing the correlation between social-contents and interest-contents. For each user, we calculated the recall value to measure the coverage of the user's potential interests. The recall value is SOC over INT (SOC/INT), where INT is a set of the interest-contents from each user's social neighbors and SOC is a set of social-contents that have overlapped keywords with the interest-contents from each user.

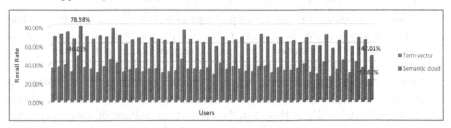

Fig. 3. The coverage of candidate interests

Figure 3 shows the recall rates of the existing approach that uses term vectors and the proposed approach that uses semantic clusters. For all cases, the proposed method shows better results in finding potential interests. The proposed method finds 64.54% of potential interests while the existing approach finds only 35.69% of the interests in average. This result implies that the proposed method is more effective to identify users' implicit interests that can be found by using the semantic similarity measure.

4.2   User Satisfaction on Recommended Contents of Interest

To check if the users actually satisfy with the interests that are recommended by our approach, we conducted a user study. We asked the users to rate the recommended interests in a Likert scale, ranging from 0 to 5. For each participant, we provided two sets of interests, one is recommended by our approach and another is generated from the existing work [6].

We compared the results in terms of the average rating of the users as shown in Figure 4. For 35 cases out of 50, the proposed method shows better user satisfaction than the existing approach (improves the user satisfaction by 17.24%). In addition, the some results from our approach show much higher ratings than the ones from the existing approach. This is because there are many users who rarely reveal their interests in their Facebook pages.

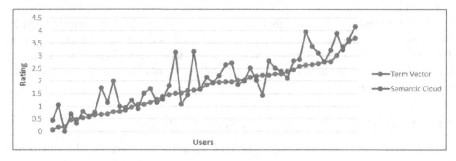

Fig. 4. Ratings on recommended interests (ordered)

4.3   Threats to Validity

Our experiment and user study have the following threats to validity.

1) Limited participants: the number of participants was 50 from a specific area may be insufficient to prove the effectiveness of the propose method to cover various interest domains. However, their social neighbors are not domain-specific people, which may alleviate this threat.

2) Limited datasets: we only used a limited number of datasets such as DBpedia, Freebase and OpenCyc, even there are more than 300 datasets according to the statistics of Linked Data. However, they are a large volume of datasets covering various kinds of interest domains and they are highly interlinked.

3) Outliers in the user study result: an important hypothesis of this research is that users reveal their intentions and interests on their SNS contents. However, there is also a large portion of users who never or rarely do that. This is the reason for the outliers in the user study result.

5   Conclusion and Future Work

In this paper, we proposed a method of identifying and recommending potential interests of a user by analyzing semantically enriched topic keyword sets (semantic clusters) that are generated from the user's SNS contents and social neighbors' interests. In our approach, topic keywords are expended to semantic clusters by associating relevant concepts that are retrieved from Linked Data.

The main contribution of our work are as follows. Firstly, we proposed a framework of utilizing Linked Data to expand topic keywords extracted from SNS contents to semantically enriched sets. Secondly, we developed a method of applying centrality measures and generating semantic clusters to solve the semantic heterogeneity problem of comparing topic keywords. Finally, we proposed a way of comparing semantic clusters to identify the correlation between users' implicit interests extracted from their SNS contents and social neighbors' explicit interests.

In our future research, we will focus on enhancing the quality of semantic cluster generation in terms of scalability, performance, and personalization. In order to access more datasets in Linked Data to cover various topic interests of users, these scalability and performance issues are critical. We are currently working on developing a distributed and iterative approach of accessing and analyzing Linked Data to meet these qualities. In addition, we will produce personalized semantic clusters to improve the users' satisfaction on recommended interests by considering users' preferences.

Acknowledgments. This research was supported by the KCC (Korea Communications Commission), Korea, under the R&D program supervised by the KCA (Korea Communications Agency) (KCA-2013-11913-05005).

References

1. Liu, K., Tang, L.: Large-scale behavioral targeting with a social twist. In: Proceedings of the 20th ACM Conference on Information Knowledge Management, pp. 1815–1824 (2011)
2. Wen, Z., Lin, C.-Y.: On the quality of inferring interests from social neighbors. In: Proceedings of the 16th ACM SIGKDD International Conference on Knowledge Discovery and Data Mining, pp. 373–382 (2010)
3. Mislove, A., Viswanath, B., Gummadi, K.P., Druschel, P.: You are who you know: inferring user profiles in online social networks. In: Proceedings of the Third ACM International Conference on Web Search and Data Mining, pp. 251–260 (2010)
4. Anagnostopoulos, A., Kumar, R., Mahdian, M.: Influence and correlation in social networks. In Proceedings of the 14th ACM SIGKDD International Conference on Knowledge Discovery and Data Mining, pp. 7–15 (2008)
5. Wen, Z., Lin, C.-Y.: Improving User Interest Inference from Social Neighbors. In: Proceedings of the 20th ACM Conference on Information Knowledge Management, pp. 1001–1006 (2011)
6. Ahn, D., Kim, T., Hyun, S.J., Lee, D.: Inferring User Interest using Familiarity and Topic Similarity with Social Neighbors in Facebook. In: Proceedings of the 2012 IEEE/WIC/ACM International Conference on Web Intelligence, pp. 196–200 (2012)
7. White, R.W., Bailey, P., Chen, L.: Predicting user interests from contextual information. In: Proceedings of the 32nd International ACM SIGIR Conference on Research and Development in Information Retrieval, pp. 363–370 (2009)
8. Sharma, A., Cosley, D.: Network-Centric Recommendation: Personalization with and in Social Networks. In: Proceedings of the 2011 IEEE 3rd International Conference on Social Computing, pp. 282–289 (2011)
9. Mirizzi, R., Ragone, A., Di Noia, T., Di Sciascio, E.: Semantic tag cloud generation via dBpedia. In: Buccafurri, F., Semeraro, G. (eds.) EC-Web 2010. LNBIP, vol. 61, pp. 36–48. Springer, Heidelberg (2010)

Supporting Offline Interaction with Web Sites Resilient to Interruptions Applied to E-learning Environments

Félix Albertos Marco

Escuela Superior de Ingeniería Informática de Albacete
Campus Universitario, 02071 Albacete, Spain
felix.albertos@uclm.es

Abstract. Despite the wide availability of Internet connections, situations of interrupted work caused by accidental loss of connectivity or by intentional offline work are very frequent. Concerned by the negative effects of interruptions in users' activities, this work investigates a new approach for the design and development of Web applications resilient to interruptions applied to e-learning environments. In order to help users to recover from interruptions whilst navigating Web sites, this paper proposes a model-based approach that combines explicit representation of end-user navigation, local information storage (i.e. Web browser caching mechanism) and polices for client-side adaptation of Web sites. With this model, we are able to provide users with information about which Web site's contents are available in an offline mode and how they can get easy access to local cache content. Moreover, the model can be also be used to set proactive mechanism such as pre-caching Web pages that are likely to be seen by users. Such model-based approach is aimed to be used to build new Web sites from scratch but it can also be used as a mapping support to describe offline navigation of existing Web site.

1 What is the Setting and History Behind This Project?

The World Wide Web has been used to consume online resources since its inception. But using the Web requires to be connected to the Internet. Unfortunately this connection is not always available: it is susceptible of been interrupted. There are many situations when users may not have or loose temporally connection to the Internet. Some examples are when traveling (e.g. by flight), natural disasters, countries in process of development or situations where the connection is not available or limited (e.g. consumption of educational resources in rural areas). Online learning environments are especially sensible to this issue. Web 2.0 technologies are making it far easier for learning communities to integrate various interests, by facilitating anytime, anywhere, anyone communication [1]. At this point, blended learning arises. There, face-to-face instruction mixes with online strategies. But there is a gap between these approaches. The transition between the classroom and student's home affects students' outcomes. Sometimes, students have to prepare material for late use. They are interrupted while changing the context between home and the class. Moreover, this interruption may be increased because the lack of Internet connection at student's home. To address this

Q.Z. Sheng and J. Kjeldskov (Eds.): ICWE 2013 Workshops, LNCS 8295, pp. 310–314, 2013.
© Springer International Publishing Switzerland 2013

issue are needed means to characterize offline scenarios for helping students to: 1) continue working when the interruption overcomes; 2) recover from the interruption.

2   What Is the Problem to Be Addressed?

Despite the wide availability of Internet connections, situations of interrupted work caused by accidental loss of connectivity or by intentional offline work are very frequent. The study of interruptions is relatively new and there is very little information about how interruptions affect users' activity on the Web. However, some studies in the field of Human-Computer Interaction can provide some clues about how to tackle this kind of problem. Formally speaking an interruption can be defined as a (intentional or unexpected) switch between two tasks; when an interruption occurs, users are forced to do something else (the secondary task) until the primary task could be resumed [2]. It has also been shown that interruptions will ultimately affect users' ability to complete tasks but the disruptive effect varies according to the type of interruption (e.g. system alarms and notification, deny of service, loss of connectivity...) [3]. Thus, there is no universal solution for dealing with interruptions. Nonetheless, an interruption is not a fate. Indeed, previous work [4,3,5] has shown that is possible to design interactive applications to be resilient to interruptions. The term resilient is often used to address systems that are able to recover from failures, but in the present context it is used to qualify applications that can prevent from the occurrence of interruptions, help users to resume from interrupted tasks, and/or ensure a minimum level of service for performing a task despite of the interruption [3].

Interruptions can also be very annoying when navigating Web sites that do not even require a connection because most Web browsers do not allow a natural navigation through content already stored in the local cache. Moreover, even if users are aware of the interruption, they are not able to decide what parts of the Web will be available for offline use.

Several studies have demonstrated negative effects of interruptions in users activity: resuming tasks after interruptions is difficult and can take a long time [6], interrupted tasks are perceived as harder than uninterrupted ones [7], interruptions cause more cognitive workload and they are quite often annoying and frustrating because they disrupt people from completing their work [8,7]. Interruptions can be particularly dreadful when navigating the Web because they often cause users to be disconnected from the applications, so that users should restart tasks from the beginning rather than simply resuming them.

2.1   Case Study

The University of Castilla-La Mancha has a Web site[1] where visitors can found useful information about the institution, related news and academic information among other content. For using this web, Internet connection is needed. But, if users are

---

[1] http://www.uclm.es

visiting the web and the connection to Internet is interrupted, they wouldn't be able of navigating visited web pages or those considered as important. They have to wait until the connection is restored.

Our proposal allows users to continue using the web according to predefined policies for dealing with interruptions. This process includes three steps. First, the structure and the behavior of the content must be described. Second, the content must be adapted when the interruption begins, following the behavior described in the previous step. At last, the content must be adapted when the interruption ends, providing the necessary mechanism for resuming previous work. This scenario allows students to continue working regardless of the connection status.

We have been working on tools for supporting the offline model. One approach is the use of a proxy[2] that: a) Allows developers and users to design the model; b) Manages interruptions and provides continuity of service when the interruption overcomes.

2.2   Objectives

Our aim is to develop a model for designing offline interaction when the connection is interrupted, providing means to: 1) help developers and users to make decisions about the content and the behaviour of the site when it is interrupted; 2) consume resources and use the web when it is interrupted; 3) recover from the interruption and resume the task normally.

The main goal is to provide a continuity of service despite of the interruption through a model for designing the offline interaction. In order to achieve this goal, the following issues have been identified: a) interruption management; b) incorporate features that support modern web applications (social, collaboration and awareness) c) design support tools to test and to evaluate the identified issues.

3   What Are Some Current Approaches to This Problem?

Disconnection is common in particular in mobile environments. For that Chang et al. [9] propose a standard browsing model that is aimed at supporting user work in disconnected mode by making the cache model transparent to both Web browsers and Web (proxy) servers. That tool contains a list of all HTML entries in the cache with a hyperlink to the corresponding contents stored locally, so it may be used for browsing local pages in offline scenarios. Other similar tools for supporting cache management are Web-Based Temwork [10] and BITSY [12]. However, all these tools don't allow tuning the Web application for working in offline mode.

Most browsers do not have mechanisms for managing Web sites in offline mode. Recently, Cannon and Wohlstadter [13] proposed a framework for offline storage that introduces automated persistence of data objects for JavaScript. Google Gears allows

---

[2]   Available proxy video at: http://www.youtube.com/watch?v=mglbzZwr7EU (Last access on May 15, 2013).

browsers with the ability to persist data for offline use. However, the management of persistent data in the browser is not straightforward due to the need of synchronization, management of throughput, latency and existence of non-standards browser.

The development of Web applications supporting offline work is complex [14]. Existing applications are harder to adapt with offline support, and usually implying writing alternate versions of code [15]. Tatsubori and Suzumura [16] propose a development method that speeds up the implementation of offline work in a Web application by deploying server functionalities on the local machine. However, replicating all data to the local server isn't practical for all applications. They overcome this by enhancing the local server with an adaptive pre-fetcher mechanism that keeps fetching useful data from the remote server. Benson et al. [17] propose the synchronization of relational database between the browser and the web server and a client-side template library. Whilst that work [17] can reduce the transfer between the client and the server it does not necessarily improve the navigation into local storage.

4   Why Is This Problem Worth Solving or Worth Solving Better?

There are several attempts to formalize cognitive models describing the impact of interruptions in the human behaviour [6]. The unpredictability of interruptions would favour the use of declarative models to describe what should be accomplished by the system (whatever it happens) rather than describe the steps required (i.e. control flow) to accomplish it. Notwithstanding, there are some situations where the interruption of tasks can be predicted (in particular when users decided to get interrupted), so that the systems should provide an alternative representation of the interrupted tasks.

Only a few works in the literature have addressed the description of interruptions in system specifications [3]. It is interesting to notice that despite the fact that model-based approaches [18] are prominent in the field of Web engineering, as far we could investigate there is no clear proposal for using Model-Driven Approaches for building Web sites resilient to interruptions.

Most of Web engineering methods such as UWE [8], WebML [19], WSDM [11], OOHDM [20] and SWC [21] are useful to describe the structure of Web applications that are aimed to be deployed on Web servers and run online. The occurrence of interruptions during the execution of the Web applications is not a concern of current MDA approaches that assume that interruptions should be treated by the browser alone. As a consequence, there is no construct in such models to describe an alternative navigation for the Web application when the connectivity is lost.

References

1. Fleck, J.: Blended learning and learning communities: opportunities and challenges. Journal of Management Development 31(4), 398–411 (2012)
2. Trafton, J.G., Monk, C.A.: Task Interruptions. Reviews of Human Factors and Ergonomics 3, 111–126 (2007)

3. Palanque, P., Winckler, M., Ladry, J.-F., ter Beek, M., Faconti, G., Massink, M.: A Formal Approach Supporting the Comparative Predictive Assessment of the Interruption-Tolerance of Interactive Systems. In: ACM EICS 2009, pp. 211–220. ACM Press (2009)
4. Czerwinski, M., Horvitz, E., Wilhite, S.: A diary study of task switching and interruptions. In: CHI 2004, pp. 175–182. ACM (2004)
5. ter Beek, M.H., Faconti, G.P., Massink, M., Palanque, P.A., Winckler, M.: Resilience of Interaction Techniques to Interrupts: A Formal Model-based Approach. In: Gross, T., Gulliksen, J., Kotzé, P., Oestreicher, L., Palanque, P., Prates, R.O., Winckler, M. (eds.) INTERACT 2009. LNCS, vol. 5726, pp. 494–509. Springer, Heidelberg (2009)
6. Trafton, J.G., Altmann, E.M., Brock, D.P., Mintz, F.E.: Preparing to resume an interrupted task: Effects of prospective goal encoding and retrospective rehearsal. International Journal of Human-Computer Studies 58(5), 583–603 (2003)
7. Mark, G., Gudith, D., Klocke, U.: The cost of interrupted work: more speed and stress. In: SIGCHI 2008, pp. 107–110. ACM (2008)
8. Koch, N., Knapp, A., Zhang, G., Baumeister, H.: Uml-Based Web Engineering - An Approach Based on Standards. In: Web Engineering, pp. 157–191 (2008)
9. Chang, H., Tait, C., Cohen, N., Shapiro, M., Mastrianni, S., Floyd, R., Housel, B., Lindquist, D.: Web browsing in a wireless environment: disconnected and asynchronous operation in ARTour Web Express. In: ACM/IEEE MobiCom 1997, pp. 260–269. ACM (1997)
10. Yang, Y.: Supporting Online Web-Based Teamwork in Offline Mobile Mode Too. In: WISE 2000, vol. 1. IEEE Computer Society, Washington, DC (2000)
11. De Troyer, O., Casteleyn, S., Plessers, P.: WSDM: Web Semantics Design Method. In: Web Engineering, pp. 303–351 (2008)
12. Mehta, N., Swart, G., Divilly, C., Motivala, A.: Mobile AJAX Applications: Going Far Without the Bars. In: 2nd IEEE Workshop on Hot Topics in Web Systems and Technologies (2008)
13. Cannon, B., Wohlstadter, E.: Automated object persistence for JavaScript. In: WWW 2010, pp. 191–200. ACM (2010)
14. Gutwin, C., Graham, N., Wolfe, C., Wong, N., de Alwis, B.: Gone but not forgotten: designing for disconnection in synchronous groupware. In: CSCW 2010, pp. 179–188. ACM (2010)
15. Kao, Y.-W., Lin, C., Yang, K., Yuan, S.-M.: A Web-based, Offline-able, and Personalized Runtime Environment for executing applications on mobile devices. Comput. Stand. Interfaces 34(1), 212–224 (2012)
16. Tatsubori, M., Suzumura, T.: HTML templates that fly: a template engine approach to automated offloading from server to client. In: WWW 2009, pp. 951–960. ACM (2009)
17. Benson, E., Marcus, A., Karger, D., Madden, S.: Sync kit: a persistent client-side database caching toolkit for data intensive websites. In: WWW 2010, pp. 121–130. ACM (2010)
18. Rossi, G., Pastor, O., Schwabe, D., Olsina, L. (eds.): Web Engineering: Modelling and Implementing Web Applications. Human-Computer Interaction Series. Springer (2008)
19. Ceri, S., Brambilla, M., Fraternali, P.: The History of WebML Lessons Learned from 10 Years of Model-Driven Development of Web Applications. In: Borgida, A.T., Chaudhri, V.K., Giorgini, P., Yu, E.S. (eds.) Conceptual Modeling: Foundations and Applications. LNCS, vol. 5600, pp. 273–292. Springer, Heidelberg (2009)
20. Rossi, G., Schwabe, D.: Modeling and Implementing Web Applications with Oohdm. In: Web Engineering, pp. 109–155 (2008)
21. Winckler, M., Palanque, P.: StateWebCharts: A Formal Description Technique Dedicated to Navigation Modelling of Web Applications. In: Jorge, J.A., Jardim Nunes, N., Falcão e Cunha, J. (eds.) DSV-IS 2003. LNCS, vol. 2844, pp. 61–76. Springer, Heidelberg (2003)

Toward Efficient Semantic Annotation: A Semantic Cloud Generation Scheme from Linked Data

Han-Gyu Ko[1] and In-Young Ko[1,2]

[1] Department of Computer Science
[2] Division of Web Science Technology,
Korea Advanced Institute of Science and Technology
291 Daehak-ro, Yuseong-gu, Daejeon, 305-701, Republic of Korea
{kohangyu,iko}@kaist.ac.kr

Abstract. As a bridge for evolution of the current Web toward Semantic Web, semantic annotation plays an important role to turn regular Web contents into meaningful ones. However, existing semantic annotation methods mostly use semantic terms in ontology created by domain experts. Therefore, they cannot cover the various subjects of contents, some of which frequently change. To deal with this problem by alternating ontology to Linked Data, we propose a semantic cloud generation scheme that finds and merges relevant terms from Linked Data for a given request. To reduce the complexity of handling a large amount of RDF data, we locate essential points at which to start searching for relevant concepts in Linked Data; we then iteratively analyze potential merges of different semantic data. In this paper, we describe the challenges of forming semantic clouds out of Linked Data and the approach of effectively generating semantic clouds by using the similarity link analysis method.

Keywords: Similarity link analysis, Semantic cloud generation, Linked Data, Semantic annotation, Semantic Web.

1   Introduction

Annotation on Web contents is a way of adding user-generated metadata, also known as *tags* to the contents by individual users. With the emergence of Web-based Social Network Services (SNS) and multi-media content sharing services such as YouTube, tags usually play an important role of efficiently finding appropriate contents from a large amount of content data [1]. However, merely allowing users to insert keyword-based tags may result in semantic ambiguity problems [2]. Users may experience difficulty of distinguishing between different semantics that can be represented by using the same keyword or phrase. For example, the word, 'apple' may be used in some tags to mean a company, Apple Inc. rather than a fruit. The semantic Web research community has developed semantic annotation approaches [1, 2] to overcome this problem.

Previous efforts for semantic annotation on Web contents have one essential problem. Most of them use semantic terms that are defined in an ontology created by

Q.Z. Sheng and J. Kjeldskov (Eds.): ICWE 2013 Workshops, LNCS 8295, pp. 315–319, 2013.

domain experts. Ontology, however, includes only a set of domain-specific terms and usually does not include new terms that reflect emerging trends and phenomena in the society. In addition, domain-specific ontologies do not cover various subjects of contents, some of which frequently change [3, 4]. This may restrict users' choice of adding semantic annotations to the social media and multi-media Web contents that include trendy issues and new topics. In order to tackle this limitation, we need a new knowledge source for semantic annotation.

There have been recent research efforts to use Linked Data to overcome the limitations of utilizing domain-specific ontologies. Linked Data is a large scale and evolvable Semantic Web data which contains more than 30 billion RDF triples in various datasets. It is driven by the idea of open access to structured data. Faviki [5] is a famous semantic annotation application. It uses Wikipedia concepts as common tags. When a user inputs a keyword, it recommends candidate tags that come from Wikipedia. Mirizzi et al. proposed an approach of generating semantic tag clouds from DBpedia [6]. Their approach finds relevant concepts by using Google Similarity Distance. However, both approaches depended on a single dataset such as DBpedia.

In this paper, we propose a semantic cloud generation scheme that searches through multiple Linked Data datasets based on a keyword given by a user and finds the essential concepts that are semantically relevant to the keyword. By using our approach, semantic annotation on Web contents can be done as follows. First, a user enters a keyword while accessing a Web content (e.g., watching a video content). Then, the user can see multiple groups of terms around the content. Since each group is made with coherent terms, the user can easily understand the semantics of the term group. We define a group of relevant terms as a *semantic cloud*.

In order to generate semantic clouds, the proposed scheme firstly locates essential points (we call them as *spotting points*) to start searching for relevant terms in Linked Data and then iteratively analyze potential merges of relevant semantic terms. For example, semantic clouds for the input keyword, 'apple' can be generated with a number of spotting points such as 'Apple Inc.' the IT company, 'Apple Records' the music company, and 'Apple' the fruit. The proposed scheme organizes the temporal graphs of terms that describe the same and relevant concepts by parsing semantic relations such as owl:samsAs, skos:broader, and skos:narrower which are defined as *similarity links* in this paper. Then, the proposed scheme chooses the terms that have higher centrality values than others as spotting points.

2   Challenges in Semantic Cloud Generation from Linked Data

In this section, we describe the issue of generating semantic clouds from Linked Data in an efficient way. In order to achieve this goal, we have identified challenges and requirements for semantic cloud generation as follows:

1) **Restrict the number of clouds:** To ensure the usability of semantic clouds in choosing the right semantics to annotate on a Web content, the number of clouds generated should be restricted. According to educational measurement research result, the number of options should be four at most to make users efficiently choose among the options [7].

2) **Maximize the semantic cohesiveness of terms within a cloud:** To allow users to intuitively recognize the meaning of a semantic cloud, it is essential to include only the semantically relevant and coherent terms in the cloud.

3) **Minimize the semantic ambiguity between clouds:** To make users easily recognize the different meanings embedded in different semantic clouds, we need to minimize the semantic ambiguity between the clouds.

In this paper, we focus on explaining how to efficiently retrieve and merge relevant concepts from Linked Data to meet the above requirements.

3   The Proposed Scheme for Semantic Cloud Generation

We developed a similarity link analysis method to meet the requirements in generating semantic clouds efficiently for semantic annotation. The process of generating semantic clouds from Linked Data is incremental and iterative. There are two steps in the semantic cloud generation process as shown in Figure 1. Firstly, spotting points for finding relevant concepts are located in Linked Data. This is done by finding the representative RDF nodes that cover the concepts that are related to an input keyword. The representative RDF nodes that have high centrality characteristic will be selected as spotting points. After locating the spotting points, the proposed scheme traverses the neighboring RDF nodes, which are connected via semantic similarity links. The visited RDF nodes are then merged with the spotting points to form semantic clouds.

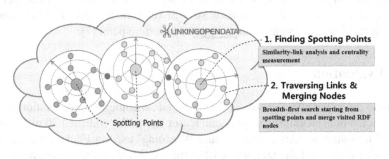

Fig. 1. Overall process of semantic cloud generation

3.1   Finding Spotting Points

If we can find a RDF node that is located in the center around many other nodes that are semantically relevant, we can efficiently reach to other relevant RDF nodes in a shortest distance. The process of finding the spotting points starts with querying Linked Data to obtain RDF triples. In order to find and group concepts that describe the same concept, we use the identity links such as `owl:sameAs` and `skos:exactMatch` relationships. We then find and merge semantically relevant concepts by using the similarity links such as `skos:broader` and `skos:narrower`. We use the similarity links along with the identity links in a complementary manner to group the relevant concepts retrieved from different datasets in Linked Data. The identity links are used to identify the same concepts across different datasets that use different ontologies. Then, the similarity links are used to find relevant concepts in a subsumption hierarchy in each dataset.

To select the spotting points, we measure the centrality of the concepts retrieved. The concepts that have the highest centrality value are selected as representative concepts. We use the betweenness centrality measure because it considers both the connectivity of a node and the efficiency (shortest paths) of reaching to other concepts. The betweenness centrality is calculated as follows:

$$C_B(v) = \sigma_{st}(v)/\sigma_{st} \tag{1}$$

where σ_{st} is the total number of shortest paths from node s to node t, $\sigma_{st}(v)$ is the number of shortest paths that pass through v. The betweenness centrality can be normalized by dividing its value by the number of node pairs that do not include v - $(n-1)(n-2)$ for directed graphs, and $(n-1)(n-2)/2$ for undirected graphs.

3.2   Traversing Links and Merging Relevant Concepts

After finding the spotting points for the input keyword, a semantic cloud is generated by traversing all the links connected to a spotting point. We use the breadth-first search algorithm for the traversal. The topological distance between a spotting point and other nodes can be used to measure the semantic relevance. We can limit the distance of traversing links from a spotting point to improve the performance of generating a sematic cloud. In our experiment, we limited the maximum distance as 2. Based on our investigation, more than 80% of relevant concepts can be found by traversing the concepts in the distance, 2 from a spotting point [7].

4   Evaluation

In order to prove the effectiveness of the proposed semantic cloud generation scheme, we conducted both an empirical study and a user study. We collected 30 most popular keyword tags such as 'Art', 'Travel', and 'Wedding' used in Flickr[1], and measured how much (in terms of the number of RDF triples) of the relevant concepts for each tag can be retrieved and grouped together as a semantic cloud. We found that in average, 19% of the relevant concepts can be merged together sucessfully. In the case of the keyword, 'Nature', 75% of the cencepts are merged. The concept reduction ratio is proportional to the ratio of having similarity links in the retrieved concepts.

In addition, we performed a user study to validate the practical efficiency of the proposed scheme. We collected photo images that correspond to the Flickr's popular tags that are used for the evaluation. We showed our participants each of images with a set of semantic clouds that were generated by using our approach. We then let the participants chose one of the semantic clouds that they thought the most relevant one for the image. If they could not find an appropriate cloud, they could ask the system

---

[1] www.flickr.com/photos/tags/

for a new set of semantic clouds. In the preliminary study, most of participants were able to find the appropriate semantic clouds for the images in few clicks.

5   Conclusion and Future Work

In this paper, we proposed a semantic cloud generation scheme that locates spotting points to start searching for relevant concepts in Linked Data and then incrementally analyze potential merges of different semantic data. The proposed scheme analyzes the similarity links between concepts and measures the betweenness centrality of each concept in order to find spotting points. Because similarity links are widely used in various datasets in Linked Data, it is possible to reduce the number of candidates that users need to consider for each annotation. In addition, because the proposed scheme incrementally traverses Linked Data to find relevant concepts starting from a spotting point, it is possible to improve the performance of the semantic cloud generation.

In our future research, we will carry out more intensive user studies to measure and prove the usability of the semantic cloud based annotation considering semantically ambiguous situations. We will use some semantically ambiguous keywords and check if the users can efficiently annotate Web contents with the semantic clouds generated based on the keywords.

Acknowledgments. This research was supported by the WCU (World Class University) program under the National Research Foundation of Korea and funded by the Ministry of Education, Science and Technology of Korea (Project No: R31-30007).

References

1. Uren, V., Cimiano, P., Iria, J., Handschuh, S., Vargas-Vera, M., Motta, E., Ciravegna, F.: Semantic annotation for knowledge management: Requirements and a survey of the state of the art. elsevier Journal of Web Semantics (2005)
2. Reeve, L., Han, H.: Survey of Semantic Annotation Platforms. In: ACM Symposium on Applied Computing (2005)
3. Popov, B., Kiryakov, A., Kirilov, A., Manov, D., Ognyanoff, D., Goranov, M.: KIM–Semantic Annotation Platform. In: Fensel, D., Sycara, K., Mylopoulos, J. (eds.) ISWC 2003. LNCS, vol. 2870, pp. 834–849. Springer, Heidelberg (2003)
4. Handschuh, S., Staab, S., Ciravegna, F.: S-CREAM – Semi-automatic CREAtion of Metadata. In: Gómez-Pérez, A., Benjamins, V.R. (eds.) EKAW 2002. LNCS (LNAI), vol. 2473, pp. 358–372. Springer, Heidelberg (2002)
5. Faviki, http://www.faviki.com (accessed May 8, 2013)
6. Mirizzi, R., Ragone, A., Di Noia, T., Di Sciascio, E.: Semantic tag cloud generation via DBpedia. In: Buccafurri, F., Semeraro, G. (eds.) EC-Web 2010. LNBIP, vol. 61, pp. 36–48. Springer, Heidelberg (2010)
7. Lord, F.M.: Optimal Number of Choices per Item – A Comparison of Four Approaches. Journal of Educational Measurement, 14(1), 33–38 (1997)

A Web-Based Approach
for Designing and Deploying
Flexible Learning Tools

Janosch Zbick

Department of Media Technology,
Centre of Learning and Knowledge Technologies(CeLeKT),
Linnaeus University, Sweden
janosch.zbick@lnu.se
http://www.celekt.info/

Abstract. This paper presents the current work in the development
of a web-based approach to offer an authoring-tool for the creation of
mobile applications with data collection purposes. The web-based solution additionally offers the possibility to visualize previously collected
data in the web-browser. An idea of a mobile web application is presented that uses a diversity of sensors of a mobile device for collecting
environmental data in the field. This paper describes how to integrate
such an approach in the context of the LETS GO [1] research project.
It also identifies and addresses current issues in end-user programming
and mobile cross-platform development.

Keywords: Web-based framework, Cross-platform development, End-
user programming, Authoring Tool.

1 Introduction

The rapid evolution of web and mobile technologies brings new opportunities
to developers and researchers in the process of creating novel mobile applications. Positioning technologies, high definition cameras and other sensors, as
well as continuous Internet access became standard features of modern mobile
devices. This leads to continuous growth of the market of mobile applications
that take include the functionalities of various sensors, so called mobile mashup
applications.

In spite of the multiple benefits that these technologies offer, a major challenge
for developers of mobile device applications arise due the huge fragmentation
of the market. The wide spread use of different devices and mobile operating
systems is an issue that mobile developers need to address. One example is lack
of a standardized way to access features and resources of mobile devices, e.g.
sensors differs from every operating system. This difference can be even found
among different versions of a same mobile operating systems and mobile devices.
Furthermore, programing languages used to access mobile sensors differ between

Q.Z. Sheng and J. Kjeldskov (Eds.): ICWE 2013 Workshops, LNCS 8295, pp. 320–324, 2013.

different mobile device platforms and models, forcing developers to spread their efforts between multiple languages in order to cover a high percentage of mobile devices in the market.

The emerging web technologies, including HTML5 and new JavaScript approaches, provide some of the requirements that can be used to address some of the challenges mentioned above [2].

Moreover, with the growing importance of web technologies in the area of mobile applications, it becomes crucial to give the end-user the possibility to create and deploy his own mobile application. A good example for this issue is the educational field. Mobile devices and applications can be effectively used in schools for supporting field trips to enhance the learning experience [3]. But one cannot assume that every person, specially teachers, that wants to create an application for mobile devices will have the technical and programming skills to compose scenarios and applications suiting his/her requirements. Thus, one area of concern developers and researchers are exploring, is how to give end-users the possibility to create his/her own mobile applications. A promising concept is to provide an authoring tool to design scenarios.

This leads to the main question that will guide this work is formulated as follows: How web technologies could facilitate a framework to support end-user programing to design and deploy flexible mobile learning applications across diverse devices and platforms?

2   Motivation and Related Work

Existing projects within the educational field but also in a variety of other fields, address the problem of end-user programming and also for mobile and cross-platform applications. For instance [4–7] discuss promising approaches for end-user programming and also mobile mashup development. Providing an authoring tool to enable end-users to design his/her own mobile application is the common approach. However, in the landscape of authoring tools for mobile learning applications, it is not an easy task to find projects like [4] that are addressing a cross-platform solution. The LEMONADE project [6] presents an interesting approach to introduce a way to visualize the data that is collected during the execution of a mobile application. Another interesting approach in the mobile learning domain with support of web-based applications its the nQuire project [8], but it lacks an authoring tool.

The previous projects present an initial overview of the possibilities to support the flow of mobile learning applications from designing to visualizing. However, there seems to be a need for cross platform solution to support the flow of designing mobile learning also concerning the visualization. As a result, I present a web-based approach that targets to close the gap described above. Recent developments in HTML5 and JavaScript allow to not only easily developing desktop web applications but also mobile web applications without much restrictions. HTML5 nowadays even offers access to internal resources from recent mobile devices, such as *iOS5* and *Android 4*.

Another benefit that comes with a web-based approach is the usage of Web services/APIs like GoogleMaps that can be integrated in mobile applications to generate mobile mashup applications. Those web services/API like Google Maps or Amazon Web Services usually providing a JavaScript interface. Therefore, a mobile web application based on HTML5 and JavaScript offers a good developing platform to these web services/APIs. HTML5 applications run on every device with a browser on it, so a developer doesn't need to take a certain OS in account to develop and deploy his application. With developing HTML5 applications also handle the requirements for different screen sizes and resolutions. This is why, the presented approach relies on HTML5, CSS3 and JavaScript for a cross-platform solution.

The ultimate goal of these efforts is the development of a web-based framework to allow end-users to design mobile learning activities and applications, make them automatically available on mobile devices, and offers visualization of the collected data either in a mobile or desktop browser. Furthermore, the mobile application is not limited to any device but runs on every device with a browser installed. Such a framework should be able to support the following aspects:

- **End-user programming.** An authoring tool for end-users to design his/her own mobile applications.
- **Mobile mashup application.** The mobile application can combine different web services or APIs to increase the opportunities how the application can be used.
- **Visualization.** The framework offers a tool that provides the visualization of the data that is generated by the mobile application, such as sensor data or user input.
- **Cross platform development.** All components of the framework are platform independent. This includes the authoring tool, the mobile application as well as the visualization tool.

3   An Authoring Tool to Create Forms for a Mobile Data Collection Application

The LETS GO (Learning Ecology with Technologies from Science for Global Outcomes) project [1] serves as a foundation of this initial approach to develop a web-based framework. The goal of the project, is to design challenging collaborative learning data collection activities by utilizing mobile and sensor technologies. However, in the current state the approach is lacking the possibility for end-users to design mobile applications for data collection activities, so the developer has to do the design with the requirements of the end-user. The data collection tasks within LETS GO are provided as XForm[1]. This XForm provides the data that is used for the mobile client to generate the mobile application. To access the XForm from the mobile client, a service provided by ODK (Open

---

[1] http://www.w3.org/MarkUp/Forms/

Data Kit)[2] is used. As of now, the XForm has to be created by a developer and end-users are not given any possibility to design their own XForms.

The first step towards the goal to support end-user programming is to introduce a prototype of an authoring tool for the LETS GO project. The mobile application of LETS GO consists of different input forms where it is possible to enter data that is collected either from observation or sensors. Therefore the authoring tool enables end-users to define certain input forms, e.g. sensor data, taking pictures and more as a web-based application. The end-user can add new screens and add forms into these screens. Afterwards, it is possible to define a sequence of appearance for the input forms created before. This is made possible by the canvas and drag and drop feature that HTML5 offers. Each screen has an anchor and the anchors can be connected. The created input forms are send as an XFrom to the ODK service and therefore available as an application for the mobile client.

4   Outlook

As a next step, the development of a web-based mobile application is scheduled. This enables not only the design of mobile learning tasks in a web-based manner but also the execution of these tasks. As of now, the input forms for the mobile application are saved as XForm. To be able to take full advantage of HTML5 combined with JavaScript, the forms will be stored as JSON objects. The last step to complete the support from designing to visualization is to develop a web-based visualization application.

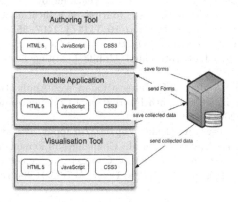

Fig. 1. Framework Architecture

The goal is to have three components, an authoring tool, a mobile application and a visualization application forming a framework. This framework enables an end-user to design the flow of a mobile application and store it. The mobile application loads the stored flow and is able to execute it. Actions that are performed with the mobile client are also stored, so it is possible to visualize

---
[2] http://opendatakit.org/

the data. Figure 1 shows the architecture of the framework. As described in the previous sections, the first step of this research is a prototype of an authoring tool to be integrated with the LETS GO project. To get more requirements detailed surveys and workshops with teachers is planned. In the future, this tool will be extended so it will not be limited to support just the LETS GO project but applications for a variety of use cases. As mentioned before, the forms will be transferred as JSON objects. In the same way the collected data will be transferred. Since the MongoDB[3] database stores data in as JSON-style documents, it will be used as a persistence technology. As a server technology, NodeJS[4] will be used.

References

1. Vogel, B.: An interactive web-based visualization tool: Design and development cycles. In: 2011 IEEE 35th Annual Computer Software and Applications Conference Workshops (COMPSACW), pp. 279–285 (2011)
2. Mikkonen, T., Taivalsaari, A.: Reports of the web's death are greatly exaggerated. Computer 44(5), 30–36 (2011)
3. Farmer, J., Knapp, D., Benton, G.M.: An elementary school environmental education field trip: Long-term effects on ecological and environmental knowledge and attitude development. The Journal of Environmental Education 38(3), 33–42 (2007)
4. Kaltofen, S., Milrad, M., Kurti, A.: A Cross-Platform Software System to Create and Deploy Mobile Mashups. In: Benatallah, B., Casati, F., Kappel, G., Rossi, G. (eds.) ICWE 2010. LNCS, vol. 6189, pp. 518–521. Springer, Heidelberg (2010)
5. De Jong, T., Van Joolingen, W.R., et al.: Learning by creating and exchanging objects: The SCY experience. British Journal of Educational Technology 41(6), 909–921 (2010), http://doi.wiley.com/10.1111/j.1467-8535.2010.01121.x
6. Giemza, A., Bollen, L., Seydel, P., Overhagen, A., Hoppe, H.U.: LEMONADE: A Flexible Authoring Tool for Integrated Mobile Learning Scenarios. In: WMUTE 2010, pp. 73–80 (2010)
7. Han, H., Tokuda, T.: A Method for Integration of Web Applications Based on Information Extraction. In: 2008 Eighth International Conference on Web Engineering, pp. 189–195 (July 2008),
   http://ieeexplore.ieee.org/lpdocs/epic03/wrapper.htm?arnumber=4577882
8. Jones, A., Scanlon, E., Gaved, M., et al.: Challenges in Personalisation: Supporting Mobile Science Inquiry Learning Across Contexts. apsce.net 8(1), 21–42 (2013),
   http://apsce.net/RPTEL/RPTEL2013MarIssue/RPTEL2013MarIssue-Article2_pp21-42.pdf

---

[3] http://www.mongodb.org/
[4] http://nodejs.org/

MockupDD: Facilitating Agile Support
for Model-Driven Web Engineering

José Matías Rivero[1,2] and Gustavo Rossi[1,2]

[1] LIFIA, Facultad de Informática, UNLP, La Plata, Argentina
{mrivero,gustavo}@lifia.info.unlp.edu.ar
[2] Conicet

Abstract. Model-Driven Web Engineering methodologies provide a more productive way of building Web Applications using high-level models and generating final implementations from them. However, they follow a waterfall-like development process, forcing to specify a different set of models sequentially to obtain a first runnable prototype of the Web Application. On the other hand, agile methodologies pursue an iterative process based on the delivery of application prototypes in short periods of time using manual coding, which results less productive and more error-prone in comparison to model-based approaches. In this work we propose a hybrid agile and Model-Driven approach called MockupDD that intends to blend the best of MDWE and agile development processes.

1 History

Model-Driven Web Engineering (MDWE) approaches like WebML [1], UWE [2] or OOHDM [3] have become mature solutions for developing Web Applications. These methodologies intend to apply Model-Driven Development (MDD) concepts to the Web Applications field, capturing high-level concepts relative to Web development (domain objects, pages, hyperlinks, rich interaction functionality, etc.) into models, letting developers automatically generate runnable applications from them. While standard MDWE processes improve productivity by describing Web Applications with such languages, they tend to leave User Interface (UI) aspects to the end of the development cycle [4]. The classical MDWE process starts building a content model describing the different types of objects that will be managed by the application and how they relate. Then, a hypertext model specifying the navigational structure of the Web Application and how the aforementioned objects will be shown and manipulated is defined. Finally, a presentation model is constructed detailing how the pages structured in the hypertext model should look in detail and refining interaction aspects.

On a different track, agile methodologies have shown a quick and massive adoption over the last years. These methodologies, instead of following a set of linear steps or high-level languages to define Web Applications, rely on direct coding to generate deliverable versions of the product being built to promote early and constant interaction with customers or end-users. The purpose of this strategy is to assert that the software being built complies with end-users requirements by constantly delivering

Q.Z. Sheng and J. Kjeldskov (Eds.): ICWE 2013 Workshops, LNCS 8295, pp. 325–329, 2013.

prototypes developed in short periods of time. Agile approaches argue that software specifications must emerge naturally, enhancing former prototypes along the development until the final application is obtained, and the same applies for good practices and patterns that help the developer teams day by day to build high-quality software products[1].

Both approaches show advantages and weak points. While MDD and agile approaches are usually seen as contradictory or incompatible, in this work, we propose to combine both in order to maximize their pros and reduce their disadvantages as much as possible. In order accomplish this task, we chose to use user interface prototypes (usually referred as *mockups*) as a starting requirements artifacts that end-users or customers can understand [5] and then introduce them as valuable model specifications in the process. Since user interface modeling and prototyping represents a very studied field (for instance, considering Canonical Abstract Prototypes [6] or UsiXML [7]) and also have been applied into agile processes [8], we argue that integrating them in a novel MDD process will provide a better requirements understanding and a more quick a less error-prone model-based development process.

2   Problem

While MDWE methodologies facilitate software specification portability, abstraction and productivity, they fail in providing *agile* interaction with customers because concrete software results are obtained too late, since they follow a waterfall-like modeling process with linearly structured steps. Modelers must define a set of models sequentially after reaching a final prototype of the application that can be shown to end-users or customers. Moreover, detailed requirements that cannot be fulfilled natively by the MDWE language concepts have to be coded manually (which leads to breaking the MDD abstraction and its inherent advantages) or force developers to extend the MDWE language and code generators, which implies additional time overheads to obtain a running prototype of the application as quick as possible.

On the other hand, agile methodologies are heavily based on implementation through direct coding. Thus, they have more freedom to code detailed business-related requirements ad-hoc and also they can adapt or *mock* they implementations more easily to speedily show running versions of the application to end-users or customers and assess that requirements have been correctly captured and implemented. However, the use of direct coding implies more proneness to human errors, forces developers to manually maintain an uniform coding style and also implies writing again and again repetitive and common functionalities (like, for instance, classical CRUD operations) that can be easily generated automatically or semi-automatically as in MDWE.

---

[1] Principles behind the Agile Manifesto –
  http://agilemanifesto.org/principles.html

3   Solution

We propose an hybrid model-based agile methodology – called Mockup-Driven Development (*MockupDD*) – aiming to extract the best of both approaches, i.e. a process driven by the active participation of users and customers, and a classical approach following the phases of analysis, design and implementation assisted with the use of models in all stages. Our approach starts by the requirement analysis defining a set of user interface mockups to agree upon the application's functionality. After being built with active end-user or customer participation, mockups are translated to an abstract User Interface model that can be directly derived to specific MDWE presentation models or technology-dependent UI prototypes [9].

After this stage, we propose to enrich mockups by a *tagging* process. In this step, mockups (now linked to presentation models) are enriched with navigation, data, data manipulation, business logic and interaction specs. Again, end-users or customers can actively participate in the most of the process (excluding technical specifications) since they understand the underlying concepts in the foundational models (mockups): widgets, pages, etc. This also facilitates a better traceability of the requirements being modeled, since they are associated to specs that were defined directly or with high participation and assessment of end-users or customers.

Following the MDD principles, MockupDD relies on artifacts generation from models – in this case, UI models expressed by mockups plus specs applied over them. Thus, it provides both code and models generation (for more popular MDWE approaches) as the final step of the process. In addition, after a tagging session, a functional prototypical version of the application can be run using a *demo sandbox* tooling provided by the methodology, without requiring any compilation or deployment. The application of the MockupDD approach within the well-known Scrum agile process is depicted in Fig. 1.

4   Current Approaches and Related Work

One of the key fields to which MockupDD is related to is UI modeling and prototyping. This is an extensively studied field. Currently, a lot of UI mocking tools has been defined like Balsamiq, Pencil, among dozens of many others including DENIM [10], in which several levels of UI sketching are provided in a *top-down* incremental way. Also, well-known UI modeling proposals like UsiXML exist [7], in companion of extensive tool support. While the former are oriented to build quick-and-dirty and disposable prototypes for requirements gathering purposes, the latter provide a modeling language and environment to formally define user interfaces and generate running implementation from them. However, MockupDD does not intend to provide *yet another* UI prototyping or modeling environment, but to use enriched mockups (that are good for requirements gathering and facilitate customer-developer interaction) as a foundation to *generate* models for existing MDWE and Model-Based User Interface (MBUI) approaches like UsiXML.

From the modeling point of view, user interfaces were used in numerous approaches as a basis for requirements or software specifications. For instance, Panach et al. propose gathering interaction requirements from UI sketches and then creating structural task models from them [11]. In [5] and [12], UI models are used to specify the structure and dynamics of the interface using formal or informal storyboard-oriented specifications. The Interaction Flow Modeling Langauge[2] (IFML) recently approved as a standard by the OMG, uses visual models (more technical-oriented than mockups) to assemble UI descriptions and specify detailed actions over them.

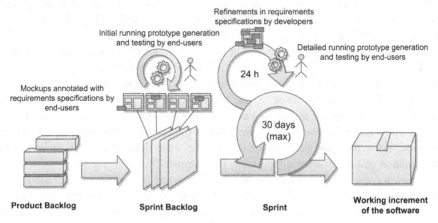

Fig. 1. MockupDD Scrum process adaptation

5   Research Methodology

We already built several tools to test the methodology. First, we implemented a Mockup Processing Engine [4] that is able to take mockups built with traditional mockup tools and abstract them into a common UI model to be further used in the modeling process. We also built a *tagging environment* for such processed mockups.

Using these tools, we already conducted a quantitative experiment in which we compared MockupDD performance vs. traditional modeling using WebML in terms of completion, speed and model quality. We are currently conducting a second experiment in which we are comparing detailed modeling using a refined MockupDD annotation set oriented to data models vs. data modeling using mainstream tools. As a result of the implementations and experiments, we expect to show that MockupDD is able to improve the modeling process both quantitative and qualitative in comparison to traditional existing modeling and agile *pure* code-based methods.

---

[2] IFML: The Interaction Flow Modeling Language - http://www.ifml.org/

6   Agenda and Further Work

After obtaining the final results of our experiments, we are aiming to improve Mock-upDD process to make it more complete and friendlier both for developers and end-users or customers. We are planning to extend the set of specifications that the methodology currently provides to cover other well-known Web Application fields like data validation, RIA behavior, etc.

Since MockupDD is in essence an MDD methodology, the problem of coping with detailed requirements is an important issue to tackle. Because it is founded on existing artifacts (User Interface mockups), we are planning to provide custom APIs to extend aspects modeled over the UI using direct coding in a non-intrusive fashion, considering also code reuse among different mockups and specifications.

References

1. Ceri, S., Fraternali, P., Bongio, A.: Web Modeling Language (WebML): a modeling language for designing Web sites. Computer Networks 33, 137–157 (2000)
2. Koch, N., Knapp, A., Zhang, G., Baumeister, H.: UML-Based Web Engineering. Springer, London (2008)
3. Rossi, G., Pastor, O., Schwabe, D., Olsina, L.: Modeling and Implementing Web Applications using OOHDM. In: Rossi, G., Pastor, O., Schwabe, D., Olsina, L. (eds.) Web Engineering: Modelling and Implementing Web Applications, pp. 109–155. Springer, London (2008)
4. Rivero, J.M., Rossi, G., Grigera, J., Luna, E.R., Navarro, A.: From interface mockups to web application models. In: Bouguettaya, A., Hauswirth, M., Liu, L. (eds.) WISE 2011. LNCS, vol. 6997, pp. 257–264. Springer, Heidelberg (2011)
5. Mukasa, K.S., Kaindl, H.: An Integration of Requirements and User Interface Specifications. In: 6th IEEE International Requirements Engineering Conference, pp. 327–328. IEEE Computer Society, Barcelona (2008)
6. Constantine, L.L.: Canonical Abstract Prototypes for Abstract Visual and Interaction Design. In: Jorge, J.A., Jardim Nunes, N., Falcão e Cunha, J. (eds.) DSV-IS 2003. LNCS, vol. 2844, pp. 1–15. Springer, Heidelberg (2003)
7. Limbourg, Q., Vanderdonckt, J., Michotte, B., Bouillon, L., López-Jaquero, V.: USIXML: A Language Supporting Multi-path Development of User Interfaces. In: Bastide, R., Palanque, P., Roth, J. (eds.) EHCI-DSVIS 2004. LNCS, vol. 3425, pp. 200–220. Springer, Heidelberg (2005)
8. Ferreira, J., Noble, J., Biddle, R.: Agile Development Iterations and UI Design. In: AGILE 2007 Conference, pp. 50–58. IEEE Computer Society, Washington, DC (2007)
9. Rivero, J.M., Rossi, G., Grigera, J., Burella, J., Luna, E.R., Gordillo, S.: From mockups to user interface models: An extensible model driven approach. In: Daniel, F., Facca, F.M. (eds.) ICWE 2010. LNCS, vol. 6385, pp. 13–24. Springer, Heidelberg (2010)
10. Lin, J., Newman, M.W., Hong, J.I., Landay, J.A.: DENIM: finding a tighter fit between tools and practice for Web site design, pp. 510–517 (2000)
11. Panach, J.I., España, S., Pederiva, I., Pastor, O.: Capturing Interaction Requirements in a Model Transformation Technology Based on MDA. J. UCS 14, 1480–1495 (2008)
12. Luna, E.R., Garrigós, I., Grigera, J., Winckler, M.: Capture and Evolution of Web Requirements Using WebSpec. In: Benatallah, B., Casati, F., Kappel, G., Rossi, G. (eds.) ICWE 2010. LNCS, vol. 6189, pp. 173–188. Springer, Heidelberg (2010)

Tag and Word Clouds as Means of Navigation Support in Social Systems

Martin Leginus and Peter Dolog

Department of Computer Science, Aalborg University,
Selma Lagerlofs Vej 300, 9220 Aalborg-East, Denmark
{mleginus,dolog}@cs.aau.dk
http://iwis.cs.aau.dk/

Abstract. Tag cloud is a visual interface that summarizes an underlying data by depicting the most frequent terms (also called as tags) from the dataset. Tags are linked to documents that contain given tags selection. A majority of tag clouds consists of the most frequent tags from a corpus that are alphabetically sorted. However, it has several drawbacks: frequent tags do not have to be relevant for all users, a vast number of terms are semantically similar hence a cloud contains many redundant depictions, an alphabetical sorting of tag cloud does not allow users to discover relations between terms. The objective of this PhD project is to propose, implement and evaluate novel tags selection methods for more relevant, diverse and novel tag clouds. Enhanced relevance of tag clouds should increase the likelihood that user will accomplish a given information retrieval task. Improved diversity and novelty of tag clouds should result into coverage of the entire spectrum of topics from folksonomy resources. Another objective is to expand a set of well-known synthetic metrics (i.e, Coverage, Overlap and Relevance) with new metrics that will capture diversity and novelty of tag clouds. Next ambition is to develop methods for tags clouds generation on top of social networks such as Twitter or Facebook. The objective is to propose words selection methods that will cover as many diverse subtopics from the underlying set of documents, tweets or statuses. The motivation is to minimize the user effort to skip redundant content.

1 The Scientific Content of the PhD Project

1.1 Background

Collaborative tagging has become an important and popular way of categorizing and retrieving various content within different Web 2.0 sites. Due to the simplicity and massive users engagement, tagging has been incorporated into the leading social web systems such as Facebook, Flickr, Delicious, Youtube, Mendeley, Connotea or Last.fm [16]. A user has possibility to classify and characterize a particular content item by annotating it with an arbitrary term – tag. Aggregated users's tagging activities with corresponding resources create a dataset that is commonly denoted as folksonomy. Folksonomy [16, 14] allows

Q.Z. Sheng and J. Kjeldskov (Eds.): ICWE 2013 Workshops, LNCS 8295, pp. 330–334, 2013.
© Springer International Publishing Switzerland 2013

a convenient retrieval and searching for the content according to a defined tag. Such folksonomy datasets can be visualized and summarized with a navigational interface called tag cloud. A tag cloud is a weighted list of terms - tags which are usually alphabetically sorted where more frequent tags have greater font size. Such visualization interface assists users to navigate through the web site content, discover new unexpected content (serendipitous discoveries) or follow the trends of the most popular and frequent topics of the web site. When no tags are available, words can be extracted from textual documents in order to generate a word cloud. For simplicity, in the rest of this document, we use tag clouds term to refer to word clouds as well.

In the following section, we present the state-of-the-art for this PhD project altogether with corresponding scientific challenges and problems.

Tag clouds usually depict a small subset from the most frequently used tags within the system. Such visual interfaces provide a rough overview about underlying data of the system. Hence, tag clouds are suitable for exploratory retrieval tasks (when user is not completely aware what he/she is looking for) and serve as a starting point for further more specific keyword-based search [1]. Tag clouds require less cognitive and physical workload as depicted tags facilitate an initial phase of the retrieval process [15]. In addition, users might discover unexpected content during a tag cloud exploration – such findings are as well classed as serendipitous [10].

Majority of tag clouds depict tags alphabetically sorted where the most frequent terms have greater font size. However, recent studies show that semantically aggregated tags enhance retrieval process [13, 8]. [8, 6] propose to group semantically related tags and depict them in a tag cloud near by with similar color. Such approach provides better orientation in the tag cloud as related tags can be easier identified by users. Such grouping of tags is usually achieved through a transformation of the underlying folksonomy graph into a co-occurrence graph [11]. We utilize a co-occurrence graph structure for estimating relevant tags for improved tag cloud generation and more detailed related work is presented in our second paper [9]. There are several studies that cluster tags into topics according to the tag pairs co-occurrences utilizing various similarity measures [2, 7, 17].

[18] introduces various synthetic metrics that measure a quality of tag clouds. The coverage, overlap, balance etc., are introduced. The advantage of these metrics is an ability to capture various aspects of a tag cloud without a need for an expensive user evaluation. On the other hand, these metrics do not capture important characteristics of tag clouds such as diversity or novelty of depicted tags and consequently diversity and novelty of their hyperlinked resources. Therefore, the outcome of this PhD project will be an extension of the existing synthetic metrics such that properties as diversity and novelty will be captured when measuring qualities of a tag cloud. Further, [18] proposes 4 tags selection algorithms for tag cloud generation. The first method selects the most popular tags within a system. The other two algorithms choose tags based on tf-idf (tags, documents). The last and most promising algorithm maximizes the coverage of selected tags

in the tag cloud. The proposed tag selection methods do not optimize a tag cloud structure towards relevance, novelty and diversity. Therefore, another objective of this PhD project will be a proposal of tag selection algorithms that will generate more relevant, novel and diverse tag clouds. It is important to mention, that proposed tag selection methods should not optimize only towards one particular tag cloud property. Instead, the methods should consider different tag cloud properties altogether during the generation process. The following paragraph presents related work about diversity and novelty from information retrieval perspective.

Diversity and Novelty. As there is no work about diversity and novelty for tag cloud generation, we present briefly related work from information retrieval perspective. [5] describes a brief history of diversity and novelty research. The initial idea claimed that a relevance of a document must be determined with respect to the documents appearing before it. [4] propose a marginal maximal relevance measure which attempts to maximize the relevance of the current document. At the same time, it strives for minimal similarity between the current document and previously selected documents. [19] introduces sub-topic retrieval methods which intuition is to include documents that cover many sub-topics early in the ranking and minimize the number of documents that redudantly cover the same subtopic. [5] proposes evaluation framework which distinguishes between novelty (minimisation of redudancy) and diversity (resolving of ambiguity).

Diversity and novelty are important aspects for developing information retrieval systems. Therefore, we plan to propose tag selection methods that will optimize tag cloud structure in terms of diversity and novelty. Moreover, we plan to propose a set of synthetic metrics that will appropriatelly capture diversity and novelty properties of tag clouds. These contributions will be based on the findings from the state-of-the-art of information retrieval diversity and novelty research studies.

Tag Clouds for Social Networks. [12] points out that microblog search needs a certain way of summarization. On the other hand trending topics presented at Twitter interface are characterized only by the single keyword or phrase. This results into more difficult understanding what a given topic is about. [12] proposes a system with tokenization module, where all unigrams, bigrams and trigrams are considered as possible sub-topics phrases for the final faceted search interface. Each phrase candidate is scored by the ratio of occurrences within query condition tweets and the entire tweets corpus. When candidate phrases are linking to the similar set of tweets, these topics are merged and represented by the more specific phrase. The final interface presents the top 40 sub-topic phrases related to the given query. This work is very similar to the proposed PhD objective, however, there are several drawbacks such as: it is difficult to quantify what is the real number of sub-topics and the effectiveness of the system was not evaluated by the users. It is important to know exact number of sub-topics to get a detailed understanding of the trending topic and to avoid reading redundant tweets, statuses or other resources. The problem with redudancy is even more evident within the trending topics which are available at Twitter interface. The reason is that thousands of users publish tweets (most of them are semantically similar) about the same event within a short time interval. Therefore, the objective of this PhD project is to propose sub-topics detection algorithms which will simplify exploration of trending topics on Twitter. Another goal will be to investigate a possibility to apply these sub-topics detection algorithms for enhanced tag cloud generation for Facebook, where users are overwhelmed with a large number of statuses.

Further, we briefly present related work about tag clouds used for social networks. [3] proposes a novel topic-based browsing interface called Eddi. The interface clusters user's feeds according to their topics. Each tweet is transformed into a search query which is passed to a search engine. The retrieved documents are used for derivation of the tweet topic. The tag cloud interface is utilized for the depiction of the most trending topics within user's tweets. The main limitation of this work is the complete dependence of topics derivation through the usage of external search engine. Moreover, the tag cloud interface does not depict relations between topics and sub-topics. Above presented work should be possible to extend with the outcome of this PhD project. In other words, it should be possible to integrate sub-topics detection algorithms for enhanced tag cloud generation within Eddi interface.

1.2 Project Objectives

The objectives of this PhD project are trying to address the above-mentioned drawbacks and challenges of the state-of-the-art of navigation algorithms for social systems. The main objectives are following:

- To propose and evaluate new tags and words selection algorithms for tag cloud generation. The aim is to enhance tag cloud's structure where only the most relevant, diverse and novel tags with corresponding documents should be presented. The proposed tags selection methods should compositely consider as many tag cloud properties as possible during the generation process. In other words, generation of more relevant tag clouds should not result into miserable diversity or novelty of the tag clouds and vice versa.
- To enhance the set of synthetic metrics for tag clouds generation such that these metrics will capture diversity and novelty of tag clouds.
- To propose methodologies for tag cloud generation on top of social networks. These methods should provide sub-topics detection algorithms and consequent words selection algorithms so that users will obtain an appropriate understanding of the underlying data from Twitter or Facebook.

References

1. Aras, H., Siegel, S., Malaka, R.: Semantic cloud: an enhanced browsing interface for exploring resources in folksonomy systems. In: Workshop on Visual Interfaces to the Social and Semantic Web (VISSW 2010), IUI 2010, Hong Kong, China, February 7 (2009)
2. Begelman, G., Keller, P., Smadja, F.: Automated tag clustering: Improving search and exploration in the tag space. In: Collaborative Web Tagging Workshop at WWW 2006, Edinburgh, Scotland, pp. 15–33. Citeseer (2006)

3. Bernstein, M.S., Suh, B., Hong, L., Chen, J., Kairam, S., Chi, E.H.: Eddi: interactive topic-based browsing of social status streams. In: Proceedings of the 23nd Annual ACM Symposium on User Interface Software and Technology, pp. 303–312. ACM (2010)

4. Carbonell, J., Goldstein, J.: The use of mmr, diversity-based reranking for reordering documents and producing summaries. In: Proceedings of the 21st Annual International ACM SIGIR Conference on Research and Development in Information Retrieval, SIGIR 1998, pp. 335–336. ACM, New York (1998)

5. Clarke, C.L., Kolla, M., Cormack, G.V., Vechtomova, O., Ashkan, A., Büttcher, S., MacKinnon, I.: Novelty and diversity in information retrieval evaluation. In: Proceedings of the 31st Annual International ACM SIGIR Conference on Research and Development in Information Retrieval, SIGIR 2008, pp. 659–666. ACM, New York (2008)

6. Durao, F., Dolog, P., Leginus, M., Lage, R.: SimSpectrum: A similarity based spectral clustering approach to generate a tag cloud. In: Harth, A., Koch, N. (eds.) ICWE 2011. LNCS, vol. 7059, pp. 145–154. Springer, Heidelberg (2012)

7. Grahl, M., Hotho, A., Stumme, G.: Conceptual clustering of social bookmarking sites. In: Proceedings of I-KNOW, vol. 7, pp. 5–7 (2007)

8. Hassan-Montero, Y., Herrero-Solana, V.: Improving tag-clouds as visual information retrieval interfaces. In: International Conference on Multidisciplinary Information Sciences and Technologies, pp. 25–28. Citeseer (2006)

9. Leginus, M., Dolog, P., Lage, R.: Graph based techniques for tag cloud generation. In: Proceedings of the 24th ACM Conference on Hypertext and Social Media. ACM (2013)

10. Mathes, A.: Folksonomies-cooperative classification and communication through shared metadata. Computer Mediated Communication 47(10) (2004)

11. Mika, P.: Ontologies are us: A unified model of social networks and semantics. In: Gil, Y., Motta, E., Benjamins, V.R., Musen, M.A. (eds.) ISWC 2005. LNCS, vol. 3729, pp. 522–536. Springer, Heidelberg (2005)

12. O'Connor, B., Krieger, M., Ahn, D.: Tweetmotif: Exploratory search and topic summarization for twitter. In: Proceedings of ICWSM, pp. 2–3 (2010)

13. Schrammel, J., Leitner, M., Tscheligi, M.: Semantically structured tag clouds: an empirical evaluation of clustered presentation approaches. In: Proceedings of the 27th International Conference on Human Factors in Computing Systems, pp. 2037–2040. ACM (2009)

14. Sinclair, J., Cardew-Hall, M.: The folksonomy tag cloud: when is it useful? J. Inf. Sci. 34, 15–29 (2008)

15. Sinclair, J., Cardew-Hall, M.: The folksonomy tag cloud: when is it useful? Journal of Information Science 34(1), 15–29 (2008)

16. Smith, G.: Tagging: people-powered metadata for the social web. New Rider Pr. (2008)

17. Specia, L., Motta, E.: Integrating folksonomies with the semantic web. In: Franconi, E., Kifer, M., May, W. (eds.) ESWC 2007. LNCS, vol. 4519, pp. 624–639. Springer, Heidelberg (2007)

18. Venetis, P., Koutrika, G., Garcia-Molina, H.: On the selection of tags for tag clouds. In: Proceedings of the Fourth ACM International Conference on Web Search and Data Mining, WSDM 2011, pp. 835–844. ACM Press, New York (2011)

19. Zhai, C.X., Cohen, W.W., Lafferty, J.: Beyond independent relevance: methods and evaluation metrics for subtopic retrieval. In: Proceedings of the 26th Annual International ACM SIGIR Conference on Research and Development in Informaion Retrieval, SIGIR 2003, pp. 10–17. ACM, New York (2003)

Was That Webpage Pleasant to Use? Predicting Usability Quantitatively from Interactions

Maximilian Speicher[1,2], Andreas Both[2], and Martin Gaedke[1,*]

[1]Chemnitz University of Technology, 09111 Chemnitz, Germany
{maximilian.speicher@s2013,martin.gaedke@informatik}.tu-chemnitz.de
[2]R&D, Unister GmbH, 04109 Leipzig, Germany
{maximilian.speicher,andreas.both}@unister.de

Abstract. Webpage usability is crucial for customer satisfaction and loyalty. Yet, evaluations of webpages are usually tedious or do not provide sufficient information. Thus, we aim at providing a novel layout-independent framework for automatically predicting a quantitative measure of usability from user interactions. A study has shown that it is necessary to take into account differences in user intention and structural features already for very similar webpages. We propose preprocessing steps in terms of structure-based clustering and determining user intention, which will make it possible to provide meaningful usability models that support satisfaction and loyalty.

Keywords: Classification, Interaction Tracking, Metrics, Usability.

1 Introduction

The usability of a webpage is a crucial factor for customer satisfaction and loyalty [9]. In today's IT industry, usability evaluations are commonly performed as lab studies, inspections by dedicated experts or split tests. While the first two options are costly and time-consuming, the latter is usually based on conversions (e.g., a completed checkout process) and cannot give insights into the actual behavior of the user [7]. Particularly, a higher conversion rate might even be *contradictory* to usability [7]. Yet, split tests are the most convenient and cost-effective way of evaluating an *online* webpage with real users. Thus, we aim at providing a novel quantitative measure for predicting usability based on user interactions. In this way, we can instantly measure the usability of a live webpage and split testing can be based on usability rather than conversions alone, among other things. This adds to customer satisfaction and loyalty.

Based on an instrument for measuring web interface usability [10], we have developed a webpage plug-in for tracking user interactions and asking for explicit usability ratings. Having obtained a set of training data from one or more webpages of the same type (e.g., news websites), it is possible to learn a statistical

---

* This work-in-progress is part of a PhD thesis carried out in cooperation with *Unister GmbH* and supervised by Prof. Dr.-Ing. Martin Gaedke and Dr. Andreas Both.

Q.Z. Sheng and J. Kjeldskov (Eds.): ICWE 2013 Workshops, LNCS 8295, pp. 335–339, 2013.

model which predicts usability quantitatively from implicit user behavior alone. Given similar websites and normalized interaction features (e.g., based on the amount of text content or number of media elements), we expected the usability measure to be *layout-independent* to a certain degree. Thus, our initial hypothesis was that *an according model should be able to predict usability, not only for webpages that delivered training data, but also for other pages of a similar kind.* In particular, this would enable internet companies that run several websites of the same type to launch a new website and instantly measure its usability based on training data obtained from the established ones. Additionally, comparison to competitors' websites would be more easily possible.

For generating a first training set, we have conducted a user study featuring four specifically prepared online news articles from different sources. Results suggest that—despite normalization of the tracked interaction features—user behavior varies considerably already for very similar webpages of the same type. *This means that the desired model needs additional preprocessing steps, i.e., clustering pages by structure and providing different models for different user intentions to provide a reliable measure for usability.*

2   User Study

We recruited a total of 81 non-unique participants (66 male) at an average age of 28.43 (σ=2.37) via Twitter, Facebook and internal mailing lists. Each participant had to read one out of four online news articles (published by CERN, CNN, Yahoo! News, Scientific American) about the Higgs boson[1] and was asked to answer a specific question. Once the user found the desired answer or was absolutely sure the article did not contain it, they had to indicate that they finished the task. Subsequently, they were presented a questionnaire for rating the usability of the online news article based on yes/no questions for the usability items *informativeness, understandability, confusion, distraction, readability, information density* and *accessibility* [10]. This means we determined an overall *usability value* between 0 and 7 points. It was possible to take part in the study multiple times with a different article each time.

Only two of the articles contained the necessary piece of information to answer the question (CERN, CNN). Moreover, two of the articles featured a rather short text (CERN, Yahoo! News: ~1 page) while the remaining two featured a longer text (CNN, Scientific American: ≥2 pages). Thus, the news articles constitute the four sets $ANSWER_{yes}$, $ANSWER_{no}$, $TEXT_{long}$ and $TEXT_{short}$.

User Interaction Tracking. We used a specifically developed jQuery plug-in to track participants' interactions during the study. That is, we recorded low-level mouse events and determined a number of features from these on the client side. The features were chosen based on existing research (e.g., [2,5]) as well

---

[1] Our aim was to choose a topic an average user would most probably not be familiar with. The complete set-up of the study can be found at
http://vsr.informatik.tu-chemnitz.de/demo/inuit.

as own experience with user interaction tracking (clicks, length of cursor trail and hovers, among others). Where appropriate, the features were determined separately for the whole page, the *area of interest* (AOI)[2], all media elements, all text elements and media/text elements in the AOI respectively.

The investigated news articles were slightly different concerning their structure (e.g., number of media elements or text length). Thus, the collected interaction features were normalized using certain features of the webpage to ensure comparability. For example, the page dwell time was normalized by the main article's word count (i.e., we assumed the dwell time to depend on the time needed for reading the article) and the total amount of scrolling was normalized by the height of the document.

3   Results

Let IF be the set of interaction features { "clicks", "hovers", ...}, UI be the set of usability items { "informativeness", "understandability", ...}, and $X(A)$ be the random variable X for the set of webpages A. Then,

$$\mathcal{NC}(A) \stackrel{\text{def}}{=} \{(if, ui) \in IF \times UI \mid corr\big(if(A), ui(A)\big) \geq 0.3 \tag{1}$$
$$\wedge \, \%RSD\big(if(A)\big) < 100 \, \wedge \, \%RSD\big(ui(A)\big) < 100\}$$

is the set of noteworthy correlations for the set of webpages A.[3] We have computed $\mathcal{NC}(A)$ for five sets, i.e., the set containing all four articles ALL as well as $ANSWER_{yes}$, $ANSWER_{no}$, $TEXT_{long}$ and $TEXT_{short}$. Based on our initial hypothesis and the fact that all interaction features were normalized we expected large commonalities among all sets of webpages in this respect. However, out of 46 noteworthy correlations that were identified only five occured for more than one set. In fact, the largest set of common noteworthy correlations was $\mathcal{NC}(ALL) \cap \mathcal{NC}(TEXT_{short})$ with a size of only three. This result indicates that already for very similar webpages of the same kind, patterns of user interaction vary considerably.

Furthermore, patterns of user behavior vary, not only due to structural features of a webpage ($TEXT_{long}$ vs. $TEXT_{short}$), but also due to differences in users' intentions. These differences were "simulated" by providing only two articles containing the answer to the posed question. While users who can answer the question should act like a *fact finder* [3], users who cannot should behave more like an *information gatherer* [3]. This assumption is underpinned by the fact that $ANSWER_{yes}$ and $ANSWER_{no}$ have no common noteworthy correlation.

The complete list of noteworthy correlations per set of webpages can be found at http://vsr.informatik.tu-chemnitz.de/demo/inuit.

---

[2] The AOI, i.e., the main article text was annotated manually for each news article. Confer [2] for a different, more automatic approach.

[3] The thresholds of 0.3 for correlations and 100% for relative standard deviations (%RSD) were chosen after qualitative inspection of the data and are rather generous.

4   Implications for Future Work

The above results indicate that despite similarity in type and content, there are only very few common patterns of interaction across webpages. This rejects our initial hypothesis that it should be possible to predict a webpage's usability based on training data from different webpages of the same type (e.g., news websites). Instead, our results suggest that users' interactions on a webpage depend, not only on its *usability*, but also on *lower-level structure* and *user intention*. Thus, a framework for layout-independent prediction of usability must include two additional preprocessing steps. First, we need to cluster webpages according to their structure to minimize variations of user behavior in this respect. A different experiment (that we will not discuss in detail here) has shown that users indeed behave very similarly on similarly structured pages. Hence, based on the structure s of a page and the collected user interactions b, we can infer the user intention i [3] using an appropriate classifier I_s: $i = I_s(b)$.

Once we know both the structure of the webpage and the user's intention, it should be possible to predict the webpage's usability u with an according classifier $U_{s,i}$: $u = U_{s,i}(b)$.

To summarize, the hypothesis we derive from the above is as follows: *Within a cluster of webpages, we can provide a common model to predict a quantitative measure of usability for a given user intention (e.g.,* fact finder *or* information gatherer*)*. Investigating this hypothesis and providing an according layout-independent framework is currently our main direction of future work.

5   Related Work

Our research is related to a variety of existing work in the fields of automatic usability evaluation, page clustering and prediction of user tasks. In [6], Nebeling describes usability metrics for large screens that are of a rather static nature and do not depend on user interactions. He also proposes an automatic approach for detecting potentially usability-critical components of webpages on touch devices. However, no quantitative measure for usability is provided. In [5], the authors aim at measuring user experience based on mouse tracking. Yet, their work is focused on the effect of advertisements/images on user attention. Again, no quantitative measure is provided.

In terms of page clustering, [4] describe an approach that is already based on user interactions. However, for clustering based on structure, it could also be possible to use existing approaches for page segmentation (e.g., [8]). We intend to build on these starting points to realize the structure-based clustering of webpages.

Regarding the prediction of user tasks, [3] presents an approach distinguishing between three kinds of user intentions based on the analysis of client logs. This approach can reach "accuracy values of up to 95% of correctly identified user tasks" [3]. As a more specific use case, [1] engage mouse movements to determine searcher intention on web search results pages. We intend to build on these starting points for determining user intention.

6 Conclusion

This work-in-progress paves the path to automatically predicting the usability of a webpage based on user interactions rather than questionnaires or tedious evaluations. Our intended approach bears numerous advantages concerning the evaluation and comparison of webpages and helps to ensure visitor satisfaction and loyalty. An initial study has shown that type-similarity of webpages and normalization of interaction features are not sufficient for providing a common and layout-independent usability model. Thus, we aim at providing a framework that involves additional necessary preprocessing steps, i.e., a) structure-based clustering of webpages and b) determining user intention. Moreover, we want to reinvestigate normalization of interaction features since our current approach might not be optimal yet. Grouping certain features of interaction (e.g., using an exploratory factor analysis) for finding stronger correlations with usability items might be an additional way of optimizing our desired model for usability prediction.

Acknowledgments. We would like to thank our industry partner *Unister GmbH*. This work has been supported by the ESF and the Free State of Saxony.

References

1. Guo, Q., Agichtein, E.: Exploring Mouse Movements for Inferring Query Intent. In: Proc. SIGIR (Posters), pp. 707–708. ACM, Singapore (2008)
2. Guo, Q., Agichtein, E.: Beyond Dwell Time: Estimating Document Relevance from Cursor Movements and other Post-click Searcher Behavior. In: Proc. WWW, pp. 569–578. ACM, Lyon (2012)
3. Gutschmidt, A.: The Prediction of Web User Tasks by Analyzing Client Logs. IADIS Int. J. on WWW/Internet 7(1), 79–93 (2008)
4. Leiva, L.A., Vidal, E.: Assessing Users' Interactions for Clustering Web Documents: A Pragmatic Approach. In: Proc. HT (Posters), pp. 277–278. ACM, Toronto (2010)
5. Navalpakkam, V., Churchill, E.F.: Mouse Tracking: Measuring and Predicting Users' Experience of Web-based Content. In: Proc. CHI, pp. 2963–2972. ACM, Austin (2012)
6. Nebeling, M.: Lightweight Informed Adaptation: Methods and Tools for Responsive Design and Development of Very Flexible, Highly Adaptive Web Interfaces. PhD thesis, ETH Zurich (2012)
7. Nielsen, J.: Putting A/B Testing in Its Place, http://www.nngroup.com/articles/putting-ab-testing-in-its-place/
8. Sano, H., Swezey, R.M.E., Shiramatsu, S., Ozono, T., Shintani, T.: A Web Page Segmentation Method by using Headlines to Web Contents as Separators and its Evaluations. IJCSNS 13(1), 1–6 (2013)
9. Sauro, J.: Does Better Usability Increase Customer Loyalty? http://www.measuringusability.com/usability-loyalty.php
10. Speicher, M., Both, A., Gaedke, M.: Towards Metric-based Usability Evaluation of Online Web Interfaces. In: Mensch & Computer Workshopband, pp. 277–281. Oldenbourg, Munich (2013)

A Modelling Based Notation for the Automated Extraction and Analysis of Social Networking Data

Samantha J. Dixon, Mark Dixon, Edward Halpin, and Colin Pattinson

Leeds Metropolitan University, Leeds, UK
{s.j.dixon,m.dixon,e.halpin,c.pattinson}@leedsmet.ac.uk

Abstract. There is a growing need for, often non-technical, organisations to analyse valuable information stored within often separate social networking systems
(SNSs). Open architectures provide programmatic access to most SNSs permitting
the creation of applications which may leverage information, for example statistics regarding the impact of marketing campaigns or new product or service announcements. This type of information is necessary for the development of sound
evidence based social media strategies. Software products are available which
provide this type of information, though for organisations to be able to tailor these
to their specific needs, solutions are often very expensive. One solution would be
for organisations to have the facility to build their own systems. This paper describes a research programme that will investigate developing, amending or extending a modelling notation, capable of being used by non-technical people for
the development of systems to extract and analyse social networking data.

Keywords: Social network, domain specific notation, modelling notation, model driven development.

1 Background

The availability and usage levels of social networks have increased vastly over the
last 10 years [1]. Research undertaken on behalf of Meeting Professionals
International (MPI) [2], has shown that there is a growing need for non-technical
organisations to gain access to and analyse the valuable information stored within the
numerous SNSs. Many social networks provide programmatic access to their systems
allowing the building of third party applications. Most major social networks such as
Facebook, Twitter and LinkedIn provide specific application programming interfaces
(APIs) [3] which allow automatic extraction and analysis of site usage data. These
open architectures provide the opportunity for the development of systems which
leverage available information, for example commercial organisations can be provided with useful statistics regarding the impact of marketing campaigns or new
product and service announcements.

2 The Research Problem

Products are already appearing which provide exactly the type of information described above [4], though for organisations to have the flexibility with regard to the

Q.Z. Sheng and J. Kjeldskov (Eds.): ICWE 2013 Workshops, LNCS 8295, pp. 340–344, 2013.
© Springer International Publishing Switzerland 2013

type of information that is retrieved solutions are often extremely expensive. A major obstacle for many 'would be' developers is that the published APIs of the more popular sites are perceived to be not very well designed or user friendly [5]. This combined with the speed of technological development and the growing number of available social networking APIs has forced organisations down one of three routes:

1. Organisations get little or no social networking analytical information.
2. Organisations choose a low cost solution, though these are often limited and inflexible.
3. Organisations opt for a high cost social media solution.

Currently many organisations have either limited or no social media strategies in place [6]. If organisations had the facilities to build their own social networking analytical solutions then social media strategies could be devised based on their own sound historical data.

2.1   Aims and Objectives of the Proposed Research

The primary aim of the proposed research programme is to develop, extend or amend a modelling notation, specifically for use by non-technical people[1], for the development of custom applications to extract and analyse cross platform social network data. The key objectives are to:

1. Provide an abstract mechanism of accessing a diverse set of social network information, with limited regard for the technical requirements of the underlying APIs.
2. Identify and examine useful metrics which are commonly required for typical social network analysis scenarios.
3. Provide pre-defined services which would allow such common metrics to be applied to extracted data in real-time.
4. Develop a modelling notation, which adheres to current software standards, that combines both graphical and textual elements[2]. Reasons for using a combination of the two include:

   (a) When used at an abstract level graphical notations are easier to understand and faster to grasp [7], this is important as users may be non-technical and not using the notation on a regular basis. Graphical notations are typically less concerned with *how* a particular element will perform its operation and more with *what* it shall do [8].
   (b) As the notation will be ultimately used to produce a working system the addition of textual annotations will add clarity where needed, especially to rule out ambiguities.

---

[1]   Non-technical people are defined as those within an organisation who are not software developers but have the ability to understand modelling concepts.

[2]   After the requirements analysis stage the notation may change from being graphical and textual.

3   Suggested Approach to the Problem

In defining a modelling language work will need to be undertaken to identify which of the currently available modelling techniques would provide a starting point for the development of a model based approach. Procedural and data oriented systems are traditionally modelled using data-flow diagrams (DFDs) and entity relation models (ERDs) whereas object oriented systems are predominantly modelled using the Unified Modelling Language (UML). It is likely however that the proposed research would be better supported by techniques designed specifically for Service Oriented Architectures (SOAs), such as the Business Process Modelling Notation (BPMN) since this provides an approach to modelling systems via orchestration of other available services. This would inevitability lead to an examination of other related technologies such as the Business Process Execution Language (BPEL) and the Web-Services Description Language (WSDL). When obtaining requirements suitable metrics to be supported by the modelling technique would need to be identified. Initial research has identified several appropriate measurements [9-11]. The existing modelling techniques would need to be analysed and extended in a manner which would allow automated extraction of social networking data. This would then need to be coupled with the application of appropriate metrics on that data. Previous academic studies that have addressed a similar problem include ones which explore the use of WebML [12] for model driven development of SNSs. These papers, though relevant to this research, are more concerned with the development of social network platforms such as Facebook or Twitter, rather than the development of systems to extract and analyse the information from within these platforms.

4   Justification of Research

This work will contribute to existing knowledge by providing a validated modelling technique that will allow non-technical staff to develop custom applications to analyse cross platform social network data. This will not only provide organisations with the ability to measure their usage of social networking sites, e.g. event organisers and advertisers could view the impact of their campaigns, but it will also provide a framework in which new metrics could be validated, e.g. does Klout [13] tell us anything useful? These models will provide the abstract layer in a multi-layered architecture and will sit above a physical mapping layer where the elements of the notation are mapped to the various underlying APIs.

5   Research Methodology

The research programme will consist of three main steps. The first will be to determine user requirements using interviews and surveys. The second will be to define a modelling language and the third will be to evaluate that language. Given the technical nature of the suggested research a scientific method is most appropriate in which a mixture of qualitative and quantitative primary data collection will be used. Potential users of the proposed notation from a variety of industries will be selected for in-depth, semi-structured and structured interviews, questionnaires and surveys. Targeted organisations will either be actively using or considering using social networks. Qualitative in-depth and semi-structured interviews shall be used together; with the in-depth interviews helping to form questions for the structured interviews, questionnaires and surveys as well as adding to the overall pool of data to be analysed. The main purpose of data collection will be to:

- Find out why social networks are used for business.
- Investigate how end users normally work with social networks.
- Identify a detailed list of requirements for a social network/media data extraction and analysis system.

An interview schedule will be produced which will be updated as new requirements are identified.

Literature reviews will be carried out to determine a suitable modelling technique to be either extended or amended in order to allow support for the extraction and analysis of social network information, including the application of metrics. Secondary research will also be performed to understand how to formally define models; this will include an examination of the Meta-Object Facility (MOF) [14].

For validation purposes an organisation shall be identified and a case study carried out to apply the proposed modelling notation, this will provide a basis for some repeatable experiments. Staff will be selected to use the notation for modelling specific scenarios. The resulting models will be analysed against the original requirements of the organisation, this will include assessing the ease of modelling for the end users.

6   Future Work

Following the successful completion of the research programme future extensions may include:

- Use of the notation to devise a metrics validation framework.
- The development of a complete CASE tool to support the notation directly.

There will also be a number of smaller improvements that could be made in the short-term, for example, a richer set of pre-defined functions available for use within the notation.

References

1. Boyd, D.M., Ellison, N.B.: Social Network Sites: Definition, History, and Scholarship. Journal of Computer-Mediated Communication 13(1), 210–230 (2007), http://onlinelibrary.wiley.com/doi/10.1111/j.1083-6101.2007.00393.x/full

2. MPI, MPI Home (2013), http://www.mpiweb.org/Home (accessed March 11, 2013)
3. Hawker, M.D.: Developer's Guide to Social Programming: Building Social Context Using Facebook, Google Friend Connect, and the Twitter API. Addison-Wesley (2010)
4. The Brick Factory, ImpactWatch, Impact Watch: monitoring made simple, The Brick Factory (2012), http://www.impactwatch.com/ (accessed June 25, 2012)
5. Perez, S.: Facebook Wins "Worst API", Techcrunch (2011), http://techcrunch.com/2011/08/11/facebook-wins-worst-api-in-developer-survey/ (accessed June 25, 2012)
6. Grant, M.: 76% of Companies Do Not Have a Social Media Policy. Social Business News (2012), http://www.socialbusinessnews.com/76-of-companies-do-not-have-a-social-media-policy/ (accessed January 25, 2013)
7. Petre, M.: Why looking isn't always seeing. Communications of the ACM 38(6), 33–44 (1995), http://rtsys.informatik.uni-kiel.de/teaching/ws03-04/s-synth/papers/p33-petre.pdf (accessed January 28, 2013)
8. Groenniger, H., et al.: Text-based Modeling. In: Proceedings of the 4th International Workshop on Software Language Engineering, Nashville, TN, USA, Johannes-Gutenberg-Universitat Mainz, p. 2 (October 2007), http://www.se-rwth.de/~rumpe/publications20042008/Groenniger_et_al_ATEM_07.pdf (accessed January 28, 2013)
9. Chapron, P., Sibertin-Blanc, C., Adreit, F.: Analysis of Power Networks among the Actors of a Social Organisation. In: Kazakov, D., Tsoulas, G. (eds.) AISB 2011 Social Networks and Multiagent Systems, April 4-7, pp. 2–7. The Society for the Study of Artificial Intelligence and the Simulation of Behaviour, York (2011)
10. Chun, H., Kwak, H., Eom, Y., Moon, S., Jeong, H.: Comparison of online social relations in volume vs interaction: a case study of cyworld. In: Papagiannaki, K., Zhang, Z. (eds.) Proceedings of the 8th ACM SIGCOMM Conference on Internet Measurement, October 20-22, pp. 57–70. ACM New York (2008)
11. Golbeck, J., Hendler, J.: Inferring binary trust relationships in Web-based social networks. ACM Transactions on Internet Technology (TOIT) 6(4), 497–529 (2006)
12. Brambilla, M., Mauri, A.: Model-Driven Development of Social Network Enabled Applications with WebML and Social Primitives. In: Grossniklaus, M., Wimmer, M. (eds.) ICWE 2012 Workshops. LNCS, vol. 7703, pp. 41–55. Springer, Heidelberg (2012)
13. Klout, Inc. The KLOUT Score (2008), http://klout.com/corp/kscore (accessed 26, 2012)
14. Object Management Group, OMG's MetaObject Facility (MOF) Home Page (2012), http://www.omg.org/mof/ (accessed February 12, 2013)

Understanding Eye Tracking Data
for Re-engineering Web Pages

Sukru Eraslan[1,2], Yeliz Yeşilada[1], and Simon Harper[2]

[1] Middle East Technical University, Northern Cyprus Campus, Guzelyurt, Mersin 10, Turkey
{seraslan,yyeliz}@metu.edu.tr
[2] University of Manchester, School of Computer Science, United Kingdom
sukru.eraslan@postgrad.manchester.ac.uk,
simon.harper@manchester.ac.uk

Abstract. Existing re-engineering, namely transcoding, techniques improved disabled and mobile Web users experience by making Web pages more accessible in constrained environments such as on small screen devices and in audio presentation. However, none of these techniques use eye tracking data to transcode Web pages based on understanding and predicting users experience. The overarching goal is to improve the user experience in such constrained environments by using a novel application of eye tracking technology. Thus, this PhD research project aims to propose an algorithm to identify common scanpaths, which are eye movement sequences, and relating those scanpaths to elements of Web pages. It can then be used to transcode Web pages, for instance, unnecessary information can be removed. It is obvious that both visually disabled and mobile users would benefit from such development.

Keywords: eye tracking, scanpaths, commonality, transcoding, re-engineering.

1   What Is the Setting and History Behind This Project?

The Web can be accessed by different devices with different requirements and constraints. For example, many people access the Web using their small screen devices while they are mobile and visually disabled people typically access the Web using screen readers. Since Web pages are mainly designed for visual interaction, it is difficult to access them in alternative forms [1]. To address this problem web page transcoding has been proposed. Although existing transcoding techniques improve disabled and mobile Web users experience on the Web [2,3], none of these techniques use eye tracking data to transcode Web pages based on understanding and predicting users' experience.

2   What Is the Problem to Be Addressed?

When people access Web pages with their small screen devices, they can experience many difficulties. For example, they may need to scroll a lot which can be annoying and it can be costly to download complex and long pages. Likewise, Web experience can be challenging for visually disabled users. As screen readers follow the source code

Q.Z. Sheng and J. Kjeldskov (Eds.): ICWE 2013 Workshops, LNCS 8295, pp. 345–349, 2013.

of Web pages, visually disabled people have to listen unnecessary clutter to get to the main content. These show that Web pages cannot be accessed properly on small screen devices and in audio presentation. The overarching goal is to improve the user experience in such constrained environments by using a novel application of eye tracking technology. Eye tracking has widely been used to investigate cognitive processes for over 30 years [4], but it is relatively new area in the Web use [5,6]. While reading, the eyes make quick movements which are called saccades [7]. Between the saccades, the eyes make fixations where they become relatively stationary [7]. Scanpaths are sequences of fixations and saccades on visual stimulus [7]. The **objective** is to use eye tracking data to generate an algorithm for identifying common scanpaths and relating those scanpaths to elements of Web pages, such that Web pages can be transcoded to improve the user experience. Hence, the following **research questions** helps to achieve the objective: (1) How can we identify the salient visual elements of Web pages based on aggregated scanpaths? (2) How can we transcode Web pages by using these salient elements of Web pages? (3) How can we quantify efficacy of newly transcoded web pages with regard to mobile and visually disabled users?

3   What Are Some Current Approaches to This Problem?

Our literature review has two parts: transcoding and scanpath analysis techniques. Transcoding is a technique used to re-engineer web pages to make them more accessible. Different methods have been used to transcode web pages such as adding a skip link, ranking or reordering or removing irrelevant content [3]. It is observable that they improved disabled and mobile Web user's experience. These methods tended to focus underlying source code of Web pages for visual rendering but they did not concentrate on understanding and predicting users' experience.

Scanpaths on Web pages have been analysed using different methods and algorithms. Most of them use string representations of scanpaths. String representations are created using the sequence of Areas of Interests (AoIs) that gets fixation [8]. Web page AoIs can be generated in different ways such as using grid-layout [8], the source code of Web pages [9] or the fixations' distribution over Web pages [10].

Levenshtein Distance (String-Edit) algorithm has been widely used to analyse scanpaths [5,8]. This algorithm calculates the dissimilarity between scanpaths by transforming the string representation of one scanpath into another one's string representation using a minimum number of operations which are insertion, deletion and substitution. For instance, the dissimilarity between ABCD and ABCE is calculated as 1 (one) by String-Edit algorithm because the transformation can be done by only substituting D with E. The dissimilarities can be used to categorize scanpaths [11]. Also, it can used to investigate differences between the behaviors of people on Web pages [5]. However, this algorithm has considerable weaknesses. Firstly, the substitution costs between all pairs of AoIs may not be the same because their size and distances between AoIs may be different. Substitution cost matrix can be used to store the substitution costs for all pairs of AoIs and then this matrix can be used while calculating the dissimilarity [8]. Needleman and Wunsch algorithm which uses a substitution cost matrix to calculate the similarity between two strings was also used for scanpath analysis [12]. Secondly, String-Edit algorithm does not consider duration metrics, such as fixation duration. However, these metrics can be interpreted in different ways. For example, longer fixations can be interpreted as the difficulty for extracting information [7]. ScanMatch method [13] considers fixation duration by defining a particular time duration to cause repetitions of the AoI names in the string representation of the scanpath. For example, if the fixation duration is 200ms in AoI A and the particular duration is 100ms, A is duplicated.

These methods and algorithms have been applied to scanpaths in pair-wise manner but this project aims to find common patterns in a group of scanpaths. One of the techniques used is Transition Matrix which is created using all the scanpaths [11]. In this matrix each cell has the row and column probabilities. Row probabilities allow identifying the next AoI of the particular AoI and column probabilities allow identifying the previous AoI of the particular AoI. When the transition matrix is tried to be used to identify a common scanpath, some significant problems arise: What is the start and end point of the common scanpath? and Which probabilities should be considered?

To address these problems, some other methods can be considered. Shortest Common Subsequence [14] has been mentioned in literature to determine a common scanpath for more than two people but this method has significant weaknesses. For instance, it produces ABDFE as a common scanpath for scanpaths ABE, ADE and AFE. The common scanpath is longer than all of the three scanpaths and it is not supported by the individual scanpaths, for instance, ABE does not include D which is included by the common scanpath.

Some methods, such as T-Pattern [6] and eyePatterns's Discover Patterns [11], try to detect sub-patterns in eye tracking scanpaths. eyePatterns's Discover Patterns [11] have no tolerance to extra items. For instance, ABC can be found as a sub-pattern for ABC and ABCD but it cannot be found for ABC and ABXCD because of X. This shows its reductionist approach. eyePatterns [11] also has a method to locally align only two sequences to detect sub-patterns. Furthermore, eSeeTrack tool [15] shows the sequence in a time line which allows to see fixation durations. It also considers frequency, so it is able to show which AoIs come after a particular AoI with highlighting the probabilities.

Using multiple sequence alignment was proposed to identify a common scanpath but it was not validated [16]. Also, Dotplots-based algorithm which constructs a hierarchal structure by finding a common scanpath of two sequences with Dotplots algorithm was proposed [17]. The scanpaths are leafs and the common scanpath is the root of the hierarchal structure. In order to eliminate the reductionist approach of the Dotplots algorithm, some statistical methods have been applied.

4   Why Is This Problem Worth Solving or Worth Solving Better?

Eye tracking may allow us to drive Web page transcoding by providing a better understand a users' experience and enable the predicting of future interactions. Firstly, it should be understood how sighted users read Web pages on desktop screens. Web pages can then be transcoded to improve the user experience. We assert that both visually disabled and mobile users would benefit from such development. Most mobile operators are also interested in transforming Web pages before they are served to end user [1], so the results would be beneficial for mobile operators. Moreover, this project will provide

---

[1] http://www.w3.org/TR/ct-guidelines/

benefits for designers, engineers, and practitioners working on Web accessibility and the mobile Web. Since no current approaches consider eye tracking scanpaths, our work will be practical contribution to Human Computer Interaction and Web Science fields.

5   What Is the Research Methodology to Be Used?

The programme is split into three work packages (WP). WP1 is related to literature review and testing of the current approaches. Literature Review is essential to understand the existing work in the field. The strengths and weaknesses of these current approaches will be investigated by testing them in the scope of WP1. Eye tracking data will be major material for testing. Existing eye tracking datasets will initially be used [18].

WP2 is the scanpath analysis algorithm development and validation. WP2 consists of two tasks. First task is associated to developing the algorithm. The algorithm will be iteratively developed and tested. Thus, these will be done in parallel. Eye tracking data will be major material for this task, too. Some datasets will be used for the development purpose only and others will be used for the testing purpose to prevent the results being biased. We will start with String-Edit algorithm which has been commonly used in scanpath analysis. Second task is related to experimenting and testing this algorithm. The algorithm will be validated to see whether or not it successfully identifies scanpaths in terms of visual elements. To have different eye tracking dataset for the validation purpose an eye tracking study will be conducted. Thus, this WP concentrates on the first research question.

WP3 focuses on how Web pages can be transcoded by using these salient elements of Web pages and how we can quantify efficacy of newly transcoded web pages with regard to mobile and visually disabled users. Current transcoding techniques will be investigated to see how they can be used with eye tracking data to transcode web pages based on understanding and predicting users experience. Hence, this WP is related to the second and third research questions.

6   What Is the Agenda Ahead?

As this is a three-year PhD project, the work packages (WP) are distributed over thirty-six months as shown in Fig. 1 where dark gray shows main tasks and light gray shows background tasks. WP1 (Literature Review and Testing of Current Approaches) will be continued until the end of this project to see whether or not relevant works have been done. WP2 (Algorithm Development and Validation) will be started after eight months. The algorithm will be developed by considering the strengths and weaknesses of the

Work Packages (WP)		Months 1–36
WP1		
WP2	Task 1	
	Task 2	
WP3		

Fig. 1. Agenda

current approaches (Task 1) while testing the current approaches. Algorithm Validation stage (Task 2) will be started before the completion of algorithm because some weaknesses can be recognised at this stage. Eight months are allocated for WP3 which is related to transcoding because this project's supervisors have significant knowledge about transcoding [3,2]. This project has started in September 2012 and therefore we are currently working on WP1 and about the start to WP2.

References

1. Harper, S., Yesilada, Y.: Web accessibility and guidelines. In: Web Accessibility: A Foundation for Research, 1st edn. Human-Computer Interaction Series, ch. 6, pp. 61–78. Springer, London (2008)
2. Yesilada, Y., Stevens, R., Harper, S., Goble, C.: Evaluating dante: Semantic transcoding for visually disabled users. ACM Trans. Comput.-Hum. Interact. 14(3), 14 (2007)
3. Asakawa, C., Takagi, H.: Transcoding. In: Harper, S., Yesilada, Y. (eds.) Web Accessibility: A Foundation for Research. Human-Computer Interaction Series, pp. 231–260. Springer (2008)
4. Rayner, K.: Eye movements in reading and information processing: 20 years of research. Psychological Bulletin 124, 372–422 (1998)
5. Josephson, S., Holmes, M.E.: Visual attention to repeated internet images: testing the scanpath theory on the world wide web. In: ETRA 2002, pp. 43–49. ACM, NY (2002)
6. Mast, M., Burmeister, M.: Exposing repetitive scanning in eye movement sequences with t-pattern detection. In: IADIS IHCI 2011, Rome, Italy, pp. 137–145 (2011)
7. Poole, A., Ball, L.J.: Eye tracking in human-computer interaction and usability research: Current status and future. In: Ghaoui, C. (ed.) Prospects. Encyclopedia of Human-Computer Interaction. Idea Group, Inc., Pennsylvania (2005)
8. Takeuchi, H., Habuchi, Y.: A quantitative method for analyzing scan path data obtained by eye tracker. In: CIDM 2007, March 1-April 5, pp. 283–286 (2007)
9. Akpinar, E., Yesilada, Y.: Vision based page segmentation: Extended and improved algorithm. Technical report, Middle East Technical University Northern Cyprus Campus (2012)
10. Santella, A., DeCarlo, D.: Robust clustering of eye movement recordings for quantification of visual interest. In: ETRA 2004, pp. 27–34. ACM, New York (2004)
11. West, J.M., Haake, A.R., Rozanski, E.P., Karn, K.S.: Eyepatterns: software for identifying patterns and similarities across fixation sequences. In: ETRA 2006, pp. 149–154. ACM, NY (2006)
12. Day, R.F.: Examining the validity of the needleman&wunsch algorithm in identifying decision strategy with eye-movement data. Decision Support Systems 49(4), 396–403 (2010)
13. Cristino, F., Mathot, S., Theeuwes, J., Gilchrist, I.D.: Scanmatch: a novel method for comparing fixation sequences. Behav. Res. Methods 42(3), 692–700 (2010)
14. Räihä, K.-J.: Some applications of string algorithms in human-computer interaction. In: Elomaa, T., Mannila, H., Orponen, P. (eds.) Ukkonen Festschrift 2010. LNCS, vol. 6060, pp. 196–209. Springer, Heidelberg (2010)
15. Tsang, H.Y., Tory, M., Swindells, C.: eseetrack: Visualizing sequential fixation patterns. IEEE Transactions on Visualization and Computer Graphics 16(6), 953–962 (2010)
16. Hembrooke, H., Feusner, M., Gay, G.: Averaging scan patterns and what they can tell us. In: ETRA 2006, p. 41. ACM, New York (2006)
17. Goldberg, J.H., Helfman, J.I.: Scanpath clustering and aggregation. In: ETRA 2010, pp. 227–234. ACM, NY (2010)
18. Brown, A., Jay, C., Harper, S.: Tailored presentation of dynamic web content for audio browsers. International Journal of Human-Computer Studies 70(3), 179–196 (2012)

Author Index